THE CIVILIZATION OF THE AMERICAN INDIAN SERIES

The
POTAWATOMIS

The POTAWATOMIS
Keepers of the Fire
by R. David Edmunds

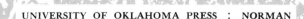

UNIVERSITY OF OKLAHOMA PRESS : NORMAN

Library of Congress Cataloging in Publication Data

Edmunds, Russell David, 1939–
   The Potawatomis, keepers of the fire.
   (The Civilization of the American Indian series)
   1. Potawatomi Indians—History. I. Title.
II. Series.
E99.P8E35   970'.004'97   78–5628
ISBN 0–8061–1478–9

The Potawatomis: Keepers of the Fire is Volume 145 in The Civilization of the American Indian Series.

12-11-78

This volume is dedicated to my parents, Russell and Eunice Weerts Edmunds. They have worked hard to provide me with many opportunities denied to them by the Great Depression.

Preface

As a boy, growing up in central Illinois, I often wondered about the Indian people who once had pitched their lodges amidst the prairies bordering the Illinois River valley. Although the library in my small home town held many books about the five southern tribes or the plains Indians, it contained few volumes on the tribesmen of the Old Northwest. I knew that the Illinois Valley had been held by many tribes, each being forced south and west by successive waves of northern invaders. When the French entered the Illinois country, the region was occupied by the Illinois Confederacy, but they were a declining people, and by the middle of the eighteenth century the remnants of the Peorias, Kaskaskias, and other Illinois tribesmen had fled to the American Bottom, opposite St. Louis. In central Illinois the confederacy was replaced by northern Indians anxious to claim the prairies as their own. First came the Kickapoos, fierce warriors whom the French encouraged to settle in the Vermilion and Wabash valleys. The Kickapoos expanded into the Sangamon River country, but they, too, were pressed by more recent arrivals from the north. During the last half of the eighteenth century, Potawatomi hunters descended the Kankakee and Fox valleys, establishing villages and eventually claiming control over most of northern Illinois. The Potawatomis remained in the region until the 1830's, when white pressure forced them across the Mississippi.

When I entered the graduate program at the University of Oklahoma I was encouraged to pursue my interest in Indians by Professors Donald J. Berthrong, Arrell M. Gibson, and Savoie Lottinville. Professor Berthrong suggested that I concentrate my investigation upon the Potawatomis, but warned me that they were a numerous people, dispersed over several states. Since any comprehensive history of the Potawatomis before their removal would necessitate research in widely scattered manuscript collections and archives, few historians had written about the tribe.

As I began my research into Potawatomi history, I soon learned to appreciate the problems involved in collecting materials on the tribe, yet certain patterns slowly appeared which attracted my interest. By far the most prominent of these patterns was that of Potawatomi ties to New France. During the colonial period the Potawatomis emerged as the most faithful of all of France's red allies. Indeed, the close Potawatomi-French relationship continued well after the official French withdrawal from the Midwest, playing a major role in tribal acculturation patterns in the nineteenth century.

I also encountered Potawatomi leaders, often forgotten, who had made important contributions to both Potawatomi and American history. Onanghisse exerted great efforts in behalf of La Salle's ill-fated schemes to monopolize the western fur trade. During the American Revolution, Siggenauk consistently supported the colonists against the Crown, neutralizing British influence in Wisconsin and Illinois. In the years preceding the War of 1812, Main Poc joined with Tecumseh and the Shawnee Prophet to organize the red confederacy, and many American officials considered the old chief to be the staunchest opponent of American control of the Northwest. After the War of 1812, mixed-blood leaders such as Billy Caldwell and Alexander Robinson dominated Indian affairs at Chicago.

The Potawatomi mixed-bloods are of particular interest since they led the tribe throughout the removal period. A product of two (and sometimes three) cultures, many of the mixed-bloods subscribed more to the value systems of the Creole French traders than to either Potawatomi or American ideals. They served as mediators between the red and white communities, often protecting Potawatomi interests, but also amassing personal fortunes in their negotiations with the federal government. Frontier opportunists, the mixed-bloods offer an interesting study in acculturation.

In the following pages I have attempted to examine the subjects mentioned above. Although I am not an anthropologist, I have tried to include such cultural materials as are pertinent to my discussion. Yet this volume remains a study of Potawatomi-white relations, relying more on history than anthropology. If there are errors in either fact or interpretation, they are my own.

Many people assisted me in completing this project. Although he no longer was associated with the University of Oklahoma, Donald J. Berthrong shared his Potawatomi materials with me and graciously agreed to read my dissertation, which later was incorporated into this volume. Arrell M. Gibson also read the dissertation, supplying valuable advice regarding Potawatomi contacts with the Kickapoos and Chickasaws. Other chapters of this book were read by Francis Paul Prucha, Martin Zanger, and Donald Worcester, all of whom made helpful suggestions regarding style and content. James Clifton provided information on Potawatomi kinship and nomenclature.

In collecting materials for this history, I received invaluable assistance from many people. Special recognition is extended to Jack Haley, Alice Timmons, and Glen Jordan of the Western History Collections at the University of Oklahoma; to James Kellar and Cheryl Munson of the Great Lakes–Ohio Valley Indian Archives; to John Aubrey of the Edward E. Ayer Collection at the Newberry Library; to Robert Kvasnicka of the National Archives; and to Ellen Whitney of the Illinois State Historical Society, who provided me with copies of her Black Hawk War chronology. I also wish to thank Arlene Kleeb and John Dan of the William L. Clements Library; Alice C. Dalligan, Mildred Hilton, Gloria Birkenmeir, and Mrs. Noel Van Garden of the Burton Collection at the Detroit Public Library; Leona T. Alig and Tom Rumer of the Indiana Historical Society Library; Frances Macdonald and Mrs. Floyd Hopper of the Indiana State Library; John M. Harris and Cable Ball of the Tippecanoe County Historical Association; James Sullivan of the Northern Indiana Historical Society; Peter Lombardo of the University of Notre Dame Archives; Mrs. Trevor Staulbaum of the Historical Society of Porter County, Indiana; Paul Spence of the Illinois State Historical Society; Orvetta Robinson of the Illinois State Museum; Wayne C. Temple of the Illinois State Archives; Julia Cracraft, Joseph Zywicki, Mary Frances Rhymer, and Archie Motley of the Chicago Historical Society; Mrs. E. A. Stadler and Mrs. John Dotzman of the Missouri Historical Society; Charles A. Isetts of the Ohio Historical Society; George Talbot and Melodie Rue of the State Historical Society of Wisconsin; Joseph Gambone and Eugene Decker of the Kansas State Historical Society; Donald G. Humphrey of the Stark Museum of Art; and Geraldine Fickel of the Mills County Historical Society, Glenwood, Iowa.

I also wish to express my appreciation to Miss Kelly Patterson and the staff of the interlibrary loan service at the University of Wyoming and to Miss Deborah Mikulich, who typed the manuscript for this volume.

Finally, I gratefully acknowledge the generous financial assistance provided by the Ford Foundation and by the Center for the History of the American Indian at the Newberry Library. Without their support, this volume would have been impossible.

R. David Edmunds

Fort Worth, Texas

Contents

Preface		*page* ix
1.	Forging the French Alliance	3
2.	The Fox Wars	24
3.	In Defense of a Dying Empire	39
4.	Partisans of Pontiac	75
5.	Serving Two Fathers	96
6.	The Red Confederacy	116
7.	The Prophet's Disciples	153
8.	"Our Most Cruel and Inveterate Enemies"	178
9.	"The Ploughshare is Driven Through Our Tents"	215
10.	Removal	240
	Epilogue	273
	Notes	277
	Bibliography	331
	Index	347

Illustrations

Fishing by torchlight   *Following page* 58
Bark-covered Algonquian summer house
Coe-coosh, or The Hog
D'Mouche-kee-kee-awh
Indian burial ground
Robert Cavalier, Sieur de La Salle
The Marquis de Montcalm
Clark's conference with the Indians at Cahokia
Clark's march against Vincennes
St. Clair's defeat
The Battle of Fallen Timbers
Braddock's defeat
Signing of the Treaty of Greenville
Shabbona (Burly Shoulders)
Canoku (Fat Woman)
The Battle of Tippecanoe

Alexander Robinson (Chechepinquay,
    or The Squinter)   *following page* 136
Ninian Edwards, governor of Illinois
Waubansee (He Causes Paleness)

Metea (Sulker)
Abel C. Pepper
Isaac McCoy, founder of Carey Mission
Topinbee (He Who Sits Quietly)
Alexander Wolcott
William Marshall
The Treaty of Prairie du Chien
Chicago in 1820
Ashkum (More and More)
Kee-wau-nay (Prairie Chicken)
Iowa
Alexis Coquillard
G. W. Ewing

No-taw-kah (Rattlesnake)   *following page* 206
Keewaunay Council
Me-no-quet
Sun-a-get (Hard Times)
Senator John Tipton
Pach-e-po (Pashpoho)
Leopold Pokagon

Maps

The French West   *Page* 33
The Pontiac Uprising   82
The Northwest, 1770–1810   103
The Northwest in the War of 1812   180
Major Potawatomi Land Cessions   245

The
POTAWATOMIS

1. Forging the French Alliance

During the summer of 1615, a small party of Frenchmen left the Saint Lawrence Valley and paddled their canoes up the broad Ottawa River toward the west. After battling the current for over three hundred miles, they reached the portage to Lake Nipissing and then guided their bark vessels down the French River to the Georgian Bay region of Lake Huron. Led by Samuel de Champlain, the Frenchmen spent the winter of 1615–16 among the Huron Indians whose villages were scattered inland from the southern shore of Georgian Bay. Champlain was curious about the neighboring tribes, and the Hurons informed him that the Neutrals, a tribe living along the northern shore of Lake Ontario, currently were at war with the Asistaguerouons, a term the Hurons applied indiscriminately to the Algonquian-speaking peoples inhabiting the lower peninsula of Michigan. Among these Algonquian tribes were a people whom the Chippewas of the Sault Sainte Marie called "people of the place of the fire," or Potawatomink. Although Champlain did not visit these western tribesmen, his report contains the first European account of the Potawatomis.[1]

Champlain's sketchy narrative is indicative of the early history of the Potawatomi people. Potawatomi tradition states that the Ottawas, Chippewas, and Potawatomis originally were one tribe, part of the great wave of Algonquian-speaking peoples who entered the Great Lakes region from the north and east. Chippewa legends suggest that the three tribes separated at the Straits of Mackinac no later than the sixteenth century, the Ottawas remaining at the strait, the Chippewas migrating to the north and west, and the Potawatomis moving down the eastern shore of Lake Michigan. Since the Potawatomis continued to keep the council fire of the originally united tribes, they received their name as "Keepers of the Fire," or Fire Nation.[2]

More recent investigation suggests that the Potawatomis separated from the Ottawas and Chippewas at an earlier date. Linguists agree that the Potawatomi language is closely related to Chippewa, but they point out certain significant differences and argue that the two tribes divided before they reached the upper Great Lakes. Archaeologists indicate that the prehistoric economic and settlement patterns of the Potawatomis resemble "prairie" cultures more than do the early Ottawa and Chippewa patterns and suggest that the forefathers of the Potawatomis were the people of the Dumaw Creek culture in west-central Michigan. The Dumaw Creek culture flourished on a sandy plain along the Pentwater River shortly after A.D. 1600, its people subsisting on a mixed economy based on hunting, gathering, and horticulture. Living in semipermanent settlements of dome-shaped wigwams, the Dumaw Creek people grew corn and pumpkins, fished in nearby streams, and hunted neighboring regions for elk, deer, beaver, and bison. In the winter the villagers split into smaller bands which scoured the region for food. Both men and women took part in these hunting parties, establishing small temporary camps as bases for their hunting activities. The Dumaw Creek people wore clothing made of skins and adorned themselves with objects acquired through intertribal trade. Tubular copper beads were obtained from the Lake Superior region and were used as hair ornaments, while marine shells from the Gulf of Mexico were used for a variety of purposes. The Dumaw Creek area is contiguous to the region in which the Potawatomis were living when they were first mentioned by Champlain.[3]

If the Dumaw Creek people were the Potawatomis, their lives were disrupted shortly after Champlain's visit to Lake Huron. The Neutrals obtained firearms from the Iroquois and launched a series of attacks against the tribes in Michigan. To escape the onslaught, the Potawatomis fled north to the upper peninsula, then scattered westward along the northern shores of Lake Michigan. There they encountered a Siouan-speaking people, probably the Winnebagos, who drove them back to the north, and in 1642 the Jesuits found them living with the Chippewas in the Sault Sainte Marie region.[4]

The Potawatomi flight was only part of a much larger tribal dispersion that occurred during this period. Well armed by Dutch traders in the Hudson Valley, the Iroquois surged north and west from their homelands in upper New York, cutting the French trade routes between Montreal and the western Great Lakes. The Iroquois then extended the war to New France's allies, and by the late 1640's Seneca and Mohawk war parties had completely decimated the Hurons and had forced the Hurons' kinsmen, the Petuns or Tobaccos, to flee the Bruce Peninsula and seek sanctuary in the west. Meanwhile, the Neutrals continued their attacks on the Algonquian peoples of southern Michigan, pushing such tribes as the Sacs, Foxes, Kickapoos, and Mascoutens west into Wisconsin. But the victory celebrations of the Neutrals were short-lived, for they also fell prey to the Five Nations. Between 1650 and 1653 the Iroquois overran the Neutrals, destroying them as a tribal entity, although many Neutral captives were spared and later adopted into Iroquois villages.[5]

As the Iroquois spread their conquest to the west, a major tribal realignment appeared on the western shores of Lake Michigan. The Winnebagos, who once had dominated the region, suffered a series of disasters. Although they successfully repulsed the first advance of the Potawatomis, they lost several hundred warriors when a flotilla of canoes capsized in a storm on Lake Michigan. This loss was coupled by a plague that swept through the tribe and further decreased their population, and finally, they treacherously murdered a party of Illinois who were visiting in the Winnebago villages. The Illinois Confederacy repaid their treachery with a war of extermination, and the once proud Winnebagos were no longer able to defend their homeland. Therefore, as the Algonquian tribes fled from Michigan, many were able to seek refuge in the Green Bay area and in southern Wisconsin.[6]

The Potawatomis were among these refugees. With the decline of the Winnebagos, the Potawatomis successfully established themselves on the islands at the mouth of Green Bay and on the neighboring mainland. Joined by refugee Petuns and Ottawas, the Potawatomis erected a fortified village on the western shores of Green Bay, and by 1652 this village, known as Mechingan, was the most important Indian settlement in Wisconsin.[7]

This concentration of large numbers of Indians in Wisconsin soon attracted the interest of New France. During the middle 1650's, two French traders, Pierre-Espirit Radisson and Medart Chouart de Groseillers, journeyed to Green Bay and spent several months in a Potawatomi village. The Indians were impressed with the Frenchmen's trade goods, and after Radisson and Groseillers left Wisconsin, the Potawatomis journeyed to Chequamegon Bay on Lake

Superior, where the Ottawas had established villages and had assumed the role of middlemen between the western tribes and the French. Anxious to maintain a monopoly over the western fur trade, the Ottawas exaggerated the danger of Iroquois attacks on the trade routes to Montreal and discouraged the Potawatomis and other tribes from visiting the French settlements. Lured by the trade goods, during the 1660's Potawatomis from Green Bay regularly visited the Ottawa village, sometimes remaining several months. Father Claude Allouez, a Jesuit missionary among the Ottawas, described the Potawatomis as "warlike," but commented that they were more friendly to the French than any of the other tribes he had encountered. He estimated that they could muster three hundred warriors.[8]

But the Potawatomis soon became dissatisfied with the Ottawa trade monopoly, and in the spring of 1668 a large party of warriors left Green Bay and voyaged to Montreal, intending to acquire firsthand knowledge of French merchandise. Upon their arrival in the French village, the warriors were overawed by the accommodations of the white men. Jean Talon, governor of New France, met with the Potawatomis and provided them with such delicacies as white bread, wine, prunes, and raisins. After listening to Talon talk of political ties between the two peoples, the warriors traded their fur for French muskets and large quantities of other trade goods. Bidding the governor farewell, the Potawatomis promised to return to Montreal during the following summer. In August, 1668, they left Montreal for Wisconsin.[9]

Ironically, while the Potawatomi trading party enjoyed the accommodations of Montreal, their villages at Green Bay were visited by other Frenchmen. During the early summer of 1668, Nicolas Perrot and Toussaint Baudry, two traders from Lake Superior, arrived at Green Bay, where the remaining Potawatomi villagers treated them with almost religious adoration. Potawatomi warriors lavished gifts upon the Frenchmen, carrying Perrot and Baudry aloft on their shoulders, while the Potawatomi women and children seemed awestruck, refusing even to approach the bearded strangers. Perrot was impressed with the Potawatomis and described them as affable people, intelligent and with good physical appearances. He also depicted them as the dominant tribe of the Green Bay region, stating that they arbitrated intertribal disputes among their neighbors.[10]

Perrot remained at Green Bay throughout the summer of 1668,

trading among the nearby villages and strengthening his friendship with the Indians. He was present when the trading party returned from Montreal firing their newly acquired trade muskets and frightening the villagers, who first thought them to be an Iroquois war party. The returning warriors were surprised to learn that a Frenchman was at Green Bay, but they welcomed Perrot, again parading him through their village and holding a feast in his honor.[11]

The voyage to Montreal proved informative to the Potawatomi canoemen. Not only did they establish political ties with New France, but they also realized the vast economic opportunities to be gained through the fur trade. Since the warriors brought back a large quantity of trade goods to Green Bay, they hoped to supplant the Ottawas as middlemen to the other tribes of Wisconsin. After feasting Perrot, the Potawatomis sent runners to the Illinois, Miamis, Sacs, Foxes, Mascoutens, and Kickapoos, informing them that French merchandise was available in the Potawatomi villages and inviting them to come and trade.[12]

The lure of trade goods at Green Bay enticed many of the Wisconsin tribes to move their villages closer to the Potawatomis. In the fall of 1668 the Foxes established a new town on the Wolf River about thirty-five miles west of Green Bay. In the following summer, villages of Miamis, Mascoutens, Kickapoos, and Illinois also assembled in the region. To the Potawatomis' dismay, the growing assemblage of Indians soon attracted large numbers of French traders who flocked to the region, anxious to tap the new source of fur. Although the Potawatomis tried to keep the Frenchmen from visiting their new neighbors, they were unsuccessful, and by early 1669 Potawatomi plans for a trade monopoly had been abandoned.[13]

Yet the warriors still turned a handsome profit on the merchandise they brought back during the summer of 1668, and in the following year they made another voyage to Montreal. But this trip was less advantageous, since they did not leave until late summer and much of the more desirable trade merchandise already had been purchased by Indians from the Lake Nipissing region. Moreover, the great quantity of fur brought to Montreal in 1669 glutted the market, causing a rise in the price of available goods. French officials tried to mend the situation, meeting with the Potawatomi traders and providing them with gifts, but the warriors remained unhappy over the high prices and returned to Green Bay dissatisfied.[14]

During the following autumn, the Potawatomi-French dispute

over the price of trade goods was somewhat ameliorated by the arrival of Jesuit missionaries at Green Bay. As the trading party returned home, the warriors passed through Sault Sainte Marie, where they were joined by Father Allouez, who accompanied the Indians back to their villages. The Potawatomis evidently hoped that Allouez would send the French traders away from the region, but the Jesuit was more interested in spreading the gospel. Upon his arrival, Allouez chose a site near a large Potawatomi village and erected a church, founding the mission of Saint Francis Xavier. Allouez was surprised at the large Indian population in eastern Wisconsin and spent the next several months visiting Indian villages in the Green Bay region. During the summer of 1670, Allouez decided that additional priests were needed, and he journeyed back to Sault Sainte Marie, where he persuaded Father Claude Dablon to join him among the Potawatomis. The two Jesuits returned to Green Bay during the fall of 1670.[15]

Upon his arrival, Allouez found that the friction over trade prices had increased. During the priest's absence, Perrot had returned to Montreal, and the other French traders had quarreled with the Potawatomis over the prices charged for muskets and powder. In the summer of 1670 the Potawatomi trading fleet again had visited Montreal, but the Indians remained unhappy over the high cost of merchandise on the Saint Lawrence. After returning to Green Bay, the Potawatomis attempted to recoup their losses by demanding excessive prices for their furs from traders who were active in Wisconsin. Allouez attempted to mediate the dispute, but he reported to his superiors that French prestige in Wisconsin was declining.[16]

Anxious to restore the Crown's influence, officials in Montreal made plans for a show of force in the west. Since Perrot had many friends at Green Bay, he was instructed to assemble the western tribes at Sault Sainte Marie so they might witness an official ceremony claiming the entire Great Lakes region for France. Perrot spent the winter of 1670–71 on Lake Huron, dispatching messengers to the western tribes and inviting them to come to the Sault during the following summer. But to his dismay, only the Winnebagos accepted. The Potawatomis still resented the French traders, and many of the other Wisconsin tribes were angry that the French were trading with the Sioux, a tribe who recently had raided their villages.[17]

Relying upon personal diplomacy, Perrot journeyed to Green Bay, where he finally convinced Potawatomi leaders to accompany him to Sault Sainte Marie. Perrot and the Potawatomis, escorted by delegations of Sacs, Winnebagos, and Menominees, arrived at the Sault early in June. The ceremony took place on June 14, 1671. French officials were led by François Daumont, sieur de Saint Lusson, who had traveled to the west specifically to preside over the affair. The French gave presents to the Indians, who then acknowledged the authority of the French king and promised to remain in perpetual alliance with him. With much pomp and ceremony, Saint Lusson turned over three spadefuls of soil and claimed the vast interior of North America for France. He then attached the royal coat of arms to a cedar cross while the Potawatomis and other tribesmen inscribed the signs of their various clans upon a French proclamation. When the festivities ended, the Potawatomis promised to carry news of the French proclamation to the other tribes in Wisconsin.[18]

The ceremony of 1671 evidently impressed the Potawatomis, for when they returned to Green Bay, relations with New France improved. Meanwhile, the Jesuits expanded their efforts to the tribes along the Fox River, also strengthening French influence in Wisconsin. In 1671 Dablon was replaced by Father Louis André, who earlier had worked among the tribes of Lake Huron. André concentrated his efforts among the Potawatomis and other tribes near Green Bay while Allouez ministered to the Indians of the Fox River valley. In June, 1673, Father Louis Marquette also passed through the Green Bay region on his voyage to the Mississippi, and upon his return he spent the winter of 1673–74 among the Potawatomi villages near Saint Francis Xavier.[19]

Although the Jesuits converted a growing number of Indians, they did encounter some opposition. In September, 1672, Allouez erected a large wooden cross near the Potawatomi village at the foot of Green Bay. Later in the fall the cross was destroyed by a war party of young Potawatomis who were leaving to attack the Sioux. To the Jesuits' horror, the warriors burned the cross, believing its destruction would increase their "medicine." But the campaign against the Sioux was disastrous, and the war party was forced to retreat in humiliation. The Jesuits then seized upon the Potawatomi defeat to warn the warriors that they were being punished for destroying the Christian symbol. Several warriors apologized for their actions and brought gifts to the Jesuits for atonement. After this incident the Jesuits met with increased success. Before 1672 the priests had baptized fewer than forty Indians, but by 1676 Andre reported that there were more than four hundred converts in the Green Bay region.[20]

Many of these Christian Potawatomis became involved in Robert Cavelier de La Salle's attempt to gain control over the fur trade of New France. During the summer of 1679, La Salle sent agents into Wisconsin to collect the fur from the Potawatomis and other tribes. Since La Salle's traders offered good prices, the Potawatomis willingly cooperated, and the agents collected the pelts from Potawatomi villages scattered throughout the Green Bay country.[21]

While his traders purchased fur from the Indians in Wisconsin, La Salle constructed the first sailing vessel to appear on the Great Lakes. Built at Cayuga Creek, above Niagara Falls, the *Griffon* was designed to sail to Green Bay and carry all of the western furs back to the Niagara portage. In early September, 1679, the *Griffon* arrived at Washington Island, where La Salle's agents had stockpiled the furs in the Potawatomi village. The Potawatomis on the island were led by Onanghisse (Shimmering Light), who earlier had visited Montreal and was anxious to cooperate with the Frenchmen. Onanghisse and his people welcomed La Salle and entertained the French in the Potawatomi village during the four days needed to load the ship and prepare it for the return voyage to the east. On September 18, 1679, the *Griffon* set sail for Niagara.[22]

Shortly after the *Griffon*'s departure, La Salle and a small party of his followers also left Onanghisse's village and voyaged down the western shore of Lake Michigan. Onanghisse had presented the French leader with a calumet, and La Salle used the pipe to gain access to several Potawatomi villages that dotted the shoreline. Warriors in these villages were less receptive to the Frenchmen than the Potawatomis at Green Bay had been, but upon seeing Onanghisse's pipe, they provided La Salle's party with food, enabling the Frenchmen to continue their journey on to the mouth of the Saint Joseph River, in southwestern Michigan.[23]

La Salle's visit had a lasting impact upon Onanghisse. The chief continually attempted to assist La Salle's agents in establishing a trade monopoly in the Green Bay region, periodically seizing the goods of other French traders who operated in the Potawatomi villages. Onanghisse also encouraged the Miamis and Illinois to cooperate with La Salle, but the chief was strongly opposed by the Jesuits, who distrusted the French adventurer and his influence among the Potawatomis.[24]

La Salle's grand plan for a western trade monopoly ended in disaster. The *Griffon* sank in the autumn storms that plague northern

Lake Michigan, carrying her full cargo of furs to the bottom. La Salle's financial losses were compounded by political opposition in the French government, and he was forced to return to France to seek additional support for his ventures. In the west, his plans were upset by the Iroquois.

As the Potawatomis and other Algonquian-speaking peoples had fled from Michigan and Indiana, Iroquois war parties continually had ranged further west in search of trade and plunder. In the early 1650's, shortly after the Potawatomis established Mechingan on the shores of Green Bay, the Potawatomis and their allies were besieged in the village by a large Iroquois war party. The Wisconsin Indians were well protected behind strong log pallisades, and the Iroquois eventually gave up the siege and retreated back to New York, but the warfare continued, and in 1670 the Senecas again raided into Wisconsin, taking thirty-five Potawatomi captives and disrupting the fur trade along the Fox River.[25]

Angered over the loss of their kinsmen, the Potawatomis and their allies struck back, sending their warriors into Michigan, where they attacked Iroquois traders or hunting parties. Encouraged by their success, the Potawatomis boasted of their exploits, and La Salle warned:

> It is not to be wondered that the Iroquois speak of waging war against our allies inasmuch as they receive affronts from them each year. I have seen, among the Potawatomi and Miami at Michilli-mackinac, the spoils and scalps of numerous Iroquois whom the Indians from this region had treacherously killed while hunting last spring and earlier; which is not unknown to the Iroquois, our allies having the improvidence of celebrating this feast in their presence while they were trading with them, as I have seen Potawatomi at Michillimackinac who, dancing with the calumet, boasted of their treachery, holding up the scalps at arms length in the sight of three Mohawks who were there to trade.[26]

For several years the Iroquois did not retaliate, but in 1680 they invaded the west, anxious to avenge themselves and disrupt French trade. Their heaviest blows fell upon the hapless Illinois Confederacy. During August and September, Iroquois war parties swept through the Illinois Valley, devastating Illinois villages and forcing Henri de Tonty, La Salle's lieutenant at Fort Crevecoeur, to seek refuge among the Potawatomis at Green Bay. A similar attack occurred in 1681, and in the following year a Jesuit priest among the

Onondagas informed Governor Frontenac of New France that the Iroquois were planning to carry the war to the Potawatomis. Although that raid never materialized, during 1683 the Iroquois besieged Mackinac, and in March, 1684, they struck again at the Illinois Confederacy.[27]

Reeling from the Iroquois attacks, the French attempted to forge the western tribes into an anti-Iroquois alliance which would provide warriors to protect French trade routes and drive the Five Nations back across Ohio. The Potawatomis willingly joined in the coalition, and in 1686, when a large Seneca war party attacked a Miami village near Chicago, the Potawatomis rallied the Foxes and Mascoutens to the Miami defense. The combined Algonquian force pursued and overtook the Senecas, killing many of their warriors and freeing several Miami captives.[28]

Yet the French were anxious to carry the conflict to the Iroquois homeland, and in 1687, Jacques Brisay, Marquis Denonville, planned a major expedition against the Senecas and Mohawks. Denonville sent Perrot to Green Bay to solicit the assistance of the western tribesmen, and the Potawatomis, Menominees, and Winnebagos gladly accepted the opportunity to strike at their enemy. Their enthusiasm spread to nearby tribes, and in the spring of 1687 a vast army of western warriors assembled to aid the French. The Kickapoos, Foxes, Miamis, and Mascoutens set out overland to join the French expedition at Niagara, while Perrot led the Potawatomis, Menominees, and Winnebagos, who were to travel by canoe through the Great Lakes to reach the rendezvous.[29]

On July 4, 1687, the Potawatomis and the other western Indians joined with a French force from Montreal at Irondequoit Bay, on the southern shore of Lake Ontario. Unfortunately for the French and their allies, an Iroquois warrior who had been captured by the Hurons escaped and spread the alarm to the Seneca villages. As the French force advanced inland, they found the first Seneca village deserted, but as they approached the abandoned settlement, they were attacked by approximately five hundred Senecas who lay in ambush along the flanks of the French column. Although the French and their allies at first recoiled under the Seneca attack, they soon rallied and forced the Senecas to retreat. The Potawatomis and other western Indians urged Denonville to pursue the fleeing Iroquois, but the French governor was content with the victory. After destroying the village and the surrounding cornfields, the expedition withdrew. Yet Denonville's victory was not decisive. The

Senecas lost about 80 men while the French and their allies suffered 110 killed. But the victory strengthened the Potawatomi-French alliance and turned the direction of future Seneca attacks toward the Saint Lawrence and away from the western Great Lakes.[30]

Two years later, the Senecas retaliated. In August, 1689, a large force of Iroquois surprised French settlements at Lachine, killing more than two hundred Canadians, and then raided into the very outskirts of Montreal. Shortly after the raids, a large delegation of western tribesmen arrived at Montreal on a trading expedition. The western Indians quickly perceived the seriousness of the French defeat, and upon their return to Lake Michigan, the Foxes and Ottawas sent messages to the Iroquois suggesting an alliance. Although the Potawatomis were not involved in this intrigue, they watched in dismay as the tide of anti-French sentiment seemed to swell around them. The Mascoutens also were angry with the French for selling arms to the Sioux, who repeatedly attacked Fox and Mascouten villages. If the Ottawas, Foxes, and Mascoutens left the French alliance, full-scale warfare would break out in the west and would certainly involve the Potawatomis.[31]

Fortunately for both the Potawatomis and the French, in the fall of 1689, Frontenac returned from France and once again resumed control over French fortunes in North America. The aging governor acted quickly to regain the initiative against the Iroquois and to reforge the western alliance. Michilimackinac was strengthened, and Frontenac dispatched Perrot to Wisconsin, where he traveled among the Foxes and Mascoutens, convincing them to remain within the French confederacy.[32]

Perrot also met with the Potawatomis at Green Bay, thanking them for their loyalty and urging them to join in renewed attacks upon the Iroquois. The Potawatomis responded to Perrot's pleas, and during the next five years they joined with several other western tribes to carry the war to the Five Nations. Hundreds of Senecas were killed, and that tribe was forced to abandon outlying villages and retreat toward the east. By 1694 the Iroquois had suffered such losses that they sent a delegation to Frontenac asking for peace. The French governor distrusted the Iroquois and dismissed their emissaries, but in 1695 he welcomed a large number of western tribesmen who arrived at Montreal in August. The Indians were led by Onanghisse, who again pledged his loyalty to New France and assured Frontenac that Potawatomis from his village would champion the French cause among all the tribes in Wisconsin.[33]

Yet Onanghisse's loyalty soon was tested by conditions over which neither he nor Frontenac had any control. In May, 1696, Louis XIV issued a royal ordinance forbidding all citizens of New France to carry goods into the west and revoking all licenses for the fur trade. The new policy resulted from the large quantity of furs which had been brought to Montreal during the past three years and which had glutted the market. This policy also reflected the rising influence of the Jesuits at the French court. The Jesuits opposed the fur trade since they believed French traders corrupted the Indians and in turn were led astray by the carefree life of the interior. Although the Potawatomis still could bring their furs to Montreal to trade, they and their neighbors no longer would be able to purchase French goods from traders in the west. Yet by the 1690's, all the tribes in Wisconsin were dependent upon such traders for goods which once had been luxuries but now were deemed necessities. Most tribesmen no longer preferred to make the long journey to Montreal, and Frontenac wisely procrastinated for two years before completely enforcing the king's decision. But in 1698 all traders were forbidden to carry their goods into the west, and the diminished supply of merchandise was sorely missed by the Indians. Once again, the winds of discontent arose over the western Great Lakes.[34]

The Iroquois took advantage of the dissatisfaction and offered both trade goods and alliances to the western tribes. Part of the Miamis, Hurons, and Ottawas accepted the Iroquois offer, but the Potawatomis remained loyal to New France. Inspired by Antoine de la Mothe Cadillac, the French commander at Michilimackinac, in 1696 the Potawatomis and their allies attacked an Iroquois party that had made friends with the Hurons. The Iroquois attempted to flee but were overtaken by the Potawatomis, and in the ensuing battle the French allied tribesmen killed thirty Iroquois and captured thirty-two prisoners. Anxious to keep the Iroquois reeling, Cadillac encouraged the western Indians to continue their attacks, and in 1697 the Potawatomis and their allies killed or captured more than one hundred Senecas. By the following summer the Iroquois trade and diplomatic offensive into the west had ended.[35]

Yet all was not well for the French. By 1697 the western tribes were suffering from a growing shortage of trade goods, and in August more than three hundred Potawatomis, Ottawas, Sacs, and Hurons accompanied Cadillac and Onanghisse to Montreal, where they complained to the French governor. Onanghisse informed Frontenac that the Potawatomis and other western tribesmen had become accustomed to acquiring trade goods from French traders who journeyed to their villages and that they no longer wished to bring their furs to Montreal. He reminded the governor of the Potawatomis' past fidelity and warned Frontenac that if French trade goods were not available in the west, Potawatomi ties with the French might be broken.[36]

Onanghisse's speech had a chilling effect on the French governor. Frontenac realized that if the Potawatomi alliance was broken, most of the other western tribes probably would transfer their allegiance to the English. In replying to Onanghisse and to the speeches of other Indians, the governor tried to regain the tribesmen's confidence. He thanked the Potawatomis for their support against the Iroquois and assured them that goods again would be sent to the western Great Lakes. Although the Potawatomis and other Indians evidently were satisfied with Frontenac's explanation, and shortly returned to Wisconsin, the French remained worried over their declining position in the west.[37]

French worries were well founded. The temporary decline of French influence in the west was evidenced by Potawatomi tribal movements in the 1690's. Although the French wished to keep the Potawatomis concentrated in the Green Bay region, Potawatomi villages spread south along the western shores of Lake Michigan. Since the Potawatomis no longer feared Iroquois war parties, they moved back toward the sites of their ancestral villages in Michigan. In 1695, Cadillac reported that a group of Potawatomis had moved to the Saint Joseph River in Michigan, and by 1698 other French officials indicated that Potawatomis were living at villages near the present sites of Manitowoc and Milwaukee, Wisconsin. This migration continued into the eighteenth century and eventually resulted in the dispersal of the majority of the Potawatomis from Green Bay.[38]

By the end of the seventeenth century, the Potawatomis were well known to the French on the Saint Lawrence. From the accounts of early French travelers and from the investigations of later writers, a picture of Potawatomi life during this early period emerges which indicates the Potawatomis were well adapted to their wilderness environment.

Potawatomi life followed the rhythm of the seasons. During the summer the Indians formed large villages, usually along streams or rivers, where Potawatomi women planted small fields of beans, peas, squashes, pumpkins, melons, and tobacco. They also raised an abundance of corn, which was traded to the French or to more northern tribes such as the Ottawas or Chippewas. Crops from their fields were supplemented by a variety of products which the Indians gleaned from the nearby lakes and forests. Wild rice was harvested, when it was available, as were many types of nuts, roots, and berries. In the spring the Potawatomies collected maple sugar, which they used extensively as a condiment. Surplus vegetable foods were stored in clay pots, baskets, or skin bags until they were needed.[39]

The lakes and streams of the Green Bay region abounded with aquatic life, and during the spring and summer the Potawatomis relied heavily upon fish as a major source of protein. Fishing from dugouts and birchbark canoes, the Indians used nets, weirs, harpoons, and hooks and lines to catch a variety of species common to Wisconsin. Most important were such "rough" fish as suckers, catfish, and buffalo, but "sport" fish, including sturgeon, pickerel, and panfish, also were taken. In the neighboring forests and prairies Potawatomi hunters killed deer, elk, bear, bison, and a variety of smaller game. Fish and game not consumed immediately were dried and smoked for use during the winter.[40]

Although most summer activity took place outdoors, the Potawatomis constructed summer houses of rectangular shape, with high arched roofs. A framework of poles was covered with elm or cedar bark and often surrounded by an extended roof which covered an open-sided cooking area adjacent to the structure. Inside these dwellings the Potawatomis kept such items of everyday life as extra clothing, storage vessels, and cooking utensils. Potawatomi women made baskets and bags from cedar or linden bark, while other containers were manufactured from birch, elm, and hickory bark and from animal skins. Before French contact, Potawatomi women used wooden or mussel-shell spoons and ladles, but by the end of the seventeenth century such trade items as iron kettles and metal utensils were in common use by the tribe.[41]

In the winter the Potawatomis lived in the domed wigwams common to most of the tribes of the Old Northwest. Potawatomi wigwams were constructed of saplings set in the ground and joined at top with basswood or skin strips. They were covered with either elm bark or mats woven from cattails. Oval in shape, the wigwams were smaller and more tightly constructed than the summer houses. Inside the wigwam was a central hearth whose smoke escaped through an opening in the roof. Near the sides of the dwelling were skins or simple sleeping platforms serving as beds. At the back of the wig-wam, opposite the door, was a small storage area.[42]

During the winter the Potawatomis dispersed into smaller family-related villages or hunting camps and scattered throughout their territory. Although the Indians continued to catch a few fish through the ice, in the cold months they depended more heavily upon hunting, tracking animals, especially deer, through the snow. They also relied upon food stored from the summer and upon mi-gratory waterfowl which had been killed and preserved during the autumn. Winter was a time of hardship, with food sometimes be-coming scarce, but it also was a time when tribal stories and tradi-tions were shared among the members crowded around the family hearth.[43]

Many of the animals killed by the Potawatomis for food also fur-nished skins for clothing. Deerskin was fashioned into shirts, breech-clouts, leggings, and moccasins for men, and into loose dresses and moccasins for women. The buckskin breechclouts of the men were almost four feet long, passing between the legs and held in place by a belt around the waist. The ends of the breechclout, often decor-ated with porcupine quills or glass beads, hung down to the knees in both front and back. Men's leggings were constructed from a single piece of buckskin folded lengthwise and sewn together along the outside of the leg. They were flared toward the bottom, and the outer edges also were fringed or embellished with quills or beads. Women's dresses consisted of two deerskins sewn together at the shoulders and on both sides, reaching just below the knee. Sleeve-less, the dresses were belted at the waist and were worn with leggings which were attached at the knees and extended to the ankle. All members of the tribe wore soft deerskin moccasins, and in the winter both sexes kept warm in robes made from bearskins or bison hides. The pelts of smaller animals were used for pouches and ornamenta-tion. As the Potawatomis gained greater access to French trade goods, they began to replace their traditional deerskin costumes with shirts and leggings of brightly colored cloth, but some skin clothing continued well into the nineteenth century.[44]

The Potawatomis took great pride in their personal appearance, elaborately ornamenting their hair and bodies. Men usually wore their hair long except in war, when warriors shaved their heads, leaving only a scalp lock and often adding a roach of deer or porcu-pine hair adorned with an eagle feather. Women wore their hair in a single braid which hung down their back. Both sexes used silver jewelry such as bracelets and earrings, and Potawatomi women especially were fond of silver brooches, which they fastened to their dresses. When on the warpath, Potawatomi men adorned themselves in red and black paint, and both men and women painted their faces and bodies on ceremonial occasions.[45]

Potawatomi marriages sometimes were polygynous, with warriors marrying two or more sisters. Tribal custom encouraged cross-cousin marriage, and residence usually was matrilocal. Often wigwams contained extended families as several generations joined together to form a single economic unit, and formal regulations governed most relationships within family life. A warrior was expected to avoid his mother-in-law and to treat his sisters with respect, thus minimizing the chance of both conflict and incest. He also was obligated to develop a close relationship with his sister's son, helping the boy to achieve those skills that would serve him as a warrior. In turn, the warrior's daughters could expect similar assistance from their aunts.[46]

The Potawatomis traced their descent through patrilineal relationships and were organized into an extensive system of exogamous clans and phratries. During the seventeenth century the clans performed several important functions, both religious and social. In this early period many Potawatomi clans evidently held medicine bundles which were used to protect and further the interests of clan members. Although this role eventually declined, the clans continued to regulate the marriage choice of members and to provide kinship ties among the scattered Potawatomi villages. In addition, the clans "owned" certain names, which they bestowed upon members during naming ceremonies.[47]

Almost all aspects of daily life were governed by formal sexual divisions in which men and women followed different patterns of behavior. Men hunted, fished, trapped, traded, and made war. Women planted crops, cooked meals, prepared clothing, and cared for the children. Potawatomi youngsters were raised in accordance with this division, and their childhood play prepared them for their roles as adults. Fastened to a cradle board shortly after birth, a Potawatomi infant was diapered with sphagnum moss and blanketed in soft rabbit skins inside a buckskin wrapper. A piece of the baby's umbilical cord was sewn into a deerskin pouch and attached to the cradle board as a "protector" against evil. The child remained in the cradle board for about one year, or until it outgrew the confines of the buckskin wrapper. Within a few years Potawatomi boys learned to fish and to hunt small game with bows and arrows. Girls helped their mothers in household chores. Both sexes also associated with other family members and were taught to venerate their grandparents and other elders who could give them valuable advice or training. All Potawatomi children were expected to be able to withstand hunger, cold, and physical pain without complaining, and during the winter boys were encouraged to bathe in the icy waters of a neighboring lake or river so that their endurance might be strengthened.[48]

Potawatomi children entered adulthood shortly after puberty. The onset of menstruation signaled the end of Potawatomi girlhood, and the young woman sequestered·herself in a menstrual hut, where she fasted and received instructions from other female family members. The women informed the girl that during her monthly periods she must be careful not to come into contact with other members of her family so that they would not be harmed. She was forbidden to prepare food or clothing for family members and was even advised not to cross the path of warriors for fear she might bring them some ill fortune. For the rest of her adult life, until she reached her menopause, she would be expected to isolate herself in the menstrual hut during her monthly period.[49]

Potawatomi boys entered manhood through a vision quest which took place shortly after the onset of puberty. Upon receiving instructions from male relatives, the young Potawatomi entered the forest alone, fasting and praying for several days or until his guardian spirit appeared in a vision and gave him his personal "medicine." If no vision occurred, the process was repeated throughout the summer until the desired results were obtained. During the seventeenth and eighteenth centuries a warrior's personal medicine was quite important, and the vision experience enabled him to acquire a medicine bundle, sacred articles usually associated with an animal that would assist and protect him during the rest of his life.[50]

At death, the Potawatomi was dressed in his or her finest clothing, and the body was surrounded with the deceased's most valued possessions. A fallen warrior was encircled with his musket, tobacco, knife, silver ornaments, and food for his trip to the spirit land. Dead Potawatomi women were surrounded with favorite household utensils or jewelry. After a funeral ritual, the body was wrapped in a blanket and placed in a tree or buried in a four-foot grave. If the dead Potawatomi was interred, his relatives usually constructed a small "grave house" over the burial place and sometimes added a "grave stick" or marker to the grave.[51]

The Potawatomis believed that departed souls traveled to the west, beyond the sunset, and were assisted on their journey by Chibiabos, a mythological figure who guided them to heaven. Wiske, an older brother of Chibiabos, served as the Potawatomi cultural hero, and their traditions state that he gave the tribe tobacco, corn, and other useful products. To the Indians the universe was full of both good and bad spirits, and the Potawatomis took pains to propitiate such *manidogs* and keep them happy. Among the most feared of the evil powers was Kegangizi, a malevolent water monster, usually described as "the Great Fish with horns," who often was invoked by shamans for evil purposes.[52]

A continual concern over shamans and their ability to practice sorcery permeated traditional Potawatomi society. Although tribe members relied upon shamans to cure many of their ailments, they also feared the medicine men and believed that much illness and misfortune resulted from their sorcery. Two types of shamans practiced their arts upon members of the tribal community. A *chasgied* used herbal medicines, but he also cured his patients through divination, entering a special lodge where he talked with the spirits, who informed him of the illness and the methods needed to affect a cure. Mastering ventriloquism, jugglery, and other sleight-of-hand skills, within the confines of the lodge the *chasgied* often spoke in several voices and caused the lodge to shake or tremble. He attempted to draw the illness from his patient, often sucking on the invalid and then producing an object which was blamed for the malady. In contrast, a *wabeno* was believed to be more powerful, but also more malevolent. He also relied upon sleight-of-hand techniques, but his medicine usually was of a preventive nature, designed to protect his followers and shield them from misfortune. Most Potawatomis believed that *wabenos* could control the weather and handle hot coals with impunity and had the power to transform themselves into animals or balls of fire.[53]

Both *chasgieds* and *wabenos* claimed power from their medicine bundles and were powerful figures within tribal society. Since most misfortune was attributed to their influence, individual Potawatomis lived in dread of the shamans' disfavor. For protection, tribal members often allied themselves with one of the shamans, hoping to share in his medicine and shield themselves from the intrigues of other medicine men. In turn, shamans vied among themselves for influence, using their skills against each other and their respective followers. While some of the medicine men and their cohorts enjoyed such contests, other Potawatomis were constantly defending themselves against shamans, and the widespread belief in sorcery created considerable suspicion and some paranoia among many members of the tribe.[54]

Yet Potawatomi life had a lighter side, for many early French accounts mention the tribesmen's fondness for practical jokes and ribald humor. Describing the Potawatomis as a stocky, muscular people, more darkly complexioned than their neighbors, the French also added that the tribesmen were "affable" and "cordial" to strangers. Allouez considered them to be the most polite and best-mannered tribe in Wisconsin, and Canadian traders found Potawatomi women "modest" and unwilling to prostitute themselves as did many women from other tribes in the Green Bay region.[55]

The Potawatomis enjoyed a wide variety of organized social activities, holding dances and games on many occasions. Usually the activities had religious significance, such as the rites of the Midewin, a tribal curing society, but most were festive occasions attracting many participants. Especially fond of games, the Potawatomis prided themselves on their skill at lacrosse. Sometimes the warriors played against each other, but they also challenged neighboring tribes, including the Sacs and Ottawas. Intertribal contests encouraged heavy betting, and competition was fierce, but when the match ended participants and spectators often feasted and danced into the night. In addition to lacrosse, the Potawatomis also played the moccasin and hand games, both guessing contests, and gambled with bone dice.[56]

The Potawatomi political system was characterized by a decentralized structure. Different villages often were comprised of clans or clan segments and were led by village chiefs supported by a council of warriors. Chiefs held no formal authority, and their power depended upon their personal influence within the village. Other individuals, including shamans, served as war chiefs, and their influence depended upon their personal following among the warriors of their village or the tribe. Intervillage relationships based upon cultural or kinship ties and similarities of interest forged the different villages of Potawatomis into a loose coalition. During periods of stress or warfare, prominent individuals often assumed a position of leadership over several villages, but like that of the village chiefs, their authority was based on the consent of their followers. Therefore, Potawatomi chiefs such as Onanghisse could act as tribal representatives in conferences with the French, but their command was limited by personal influence and the willingness of other Potawatomis to subscribe to their viewpoints.[57]

After half a century of French contact, the Potawatomis' world was changing. Formerly a tribal people interacting within the framework of a relatively stable sociopolitical equilibrium, Potawatomi society was bound together through ties of family and kinship. Personal and group behavior patterns were governed by an extensive series of customs and mores well known to all tribe members and shared, to some extent, by other Algonquian-speaking peoples in the Old Northwest. Until disrupted by Neutral and Iroquois expansion, their forefathers had lived in Michigan for generations, interacting with other tribes but centering their efforts upon providing for the physical and spiritual subsistence of their families.

At first the flight to Wisconsin brought only minor changes. Settling in a new homeland, the Potawatomis allied themselves with other Indians, but their life style continued to mirror the old ways. Economic patterns still followed subsistence models as Potawatomi hunters and fishermen provided meat for their families while Potawatomi women harvested and dried their small crops of corn, beans, and pumpkins. Skins from the forests offered protection from the cold, and age-old rituals both propitiated and offered protection against the many *manidogs* that inhabited the sky, lakes, and forests. Shamans still worked their magic, both for good and evil, and many tribesmen lived in terror of their sorvery, but others allied themselves with the medicine men or relied upon personal medicine for defense against the shamans' activities. Life still followed the rhythm of the seasons, and the old Potawatomi world remained intact.

But the French entrance into the western Great Lakes irrevocably altered the Potawatomi universe. Unlike the other tribes of Michigan and Wisconsin, the pale-skinned strangers possessed a technology that would enable them to exert a growing influence over the Indian peoples at Green Bay. The political and economic equilibrium shattered as the Wisconsin tribes sought ties with the French which would assist them in gaining hegemony over the other Indians. More skillful than some of his competitors, Onanghisse forged an alliance with New France that later Potawatomi leaders would cultivate and strengthen, but the lure of French technology was a double-edged sword, both enriching and destroying traditional Potawatomi culture.

This dichotomy of French influence was most apparent in the changing Potawatomi economic structure. Before the French arrival, the Potawatomis had been a self-sufficient people, growing their own crops or gathering whatever else they needed from the surrounding streams and forests. Enticed by the fur trade, the tribesmen readily trapped beaver and other fur-bearers, trading their pelts to the French for such luxuries as clothing, metal utensils, guns, and gunpowder. Undoubtedly the French products made most Potawatomi lives easier and more comfortable, but as the years progressed and the former luxuries became necessities, the tribesmen began to lose their self-sufficiency.

The entrance of the Jesuits into Wisconsin also brought change to Potawatomi society. Of course most tribesmen still worshiped the *manidogs* and feared sorcery, but the new black-robed shamans also won some adherents, and although their medicine bundles were strange, their influence increased. Most Potawatomis could easily fit the Jesuits' description of a heavenly father into their pantheon of sky spirits and did not view Christianity and their traditional beliefs as mutually exclusive. The kinship systems and family structure remained strong, but the Jesuits' protests against polygyny caused changes in some Potawatomi families.

Patterns of Potawatomi warfare also were undergoing change. Formerly most Potawatomi warriors had limited their fighting to small skirmishes designed to either win personal honors or to avenge the death of a kinsmen. But the Neutral and Iroquois invasions of the Potawatomi homeland had evoked a tribal response, and spurred on by the French, Potawatomi warriors readily had enlisted in Denonville's and Frontenac's campaigns against the Senecas. Such large-scale warfare would have been alien to the Potawatomis before they reached Wisconsin, but as their ties with the French increased, Potawatomi warriors faithfully assisted their ally in the successful expeditions against the Iroquois.

Yet Onanghisse and his tribesmen were not destined to live in peace. As the Iroquois threat diminished and the Potawatomis moved back toward their old villages in Michigan, the declining power of New France would bring unforeseen problems. Once again, Potawatomi warriors would be asked to rally to Onontio's banner.[58]

2. The Fox Wars

The beginning years of the eighteenth century found the Potawatomis surrounded by change and uncertainty. For more than five decades they had opposed the Iroquois, and during the fifteen years before 1700, Potawatomi warriors had formed the vanguard in the pro-French alliance which had carried the conflict into the Seneca homeland. But Frontenac died in 1698, and his successor, Louis Hector Count de Callieres, received orders to make peace with the Five Nations. Since England and France were at peace in Europe, the French court was anxious to terminate the fighting between her allies and the Iroquois in the New World.

In the spring of 1701, after a series of preliminary negotiations with the Iroquois, Callieres sent messengers to the western tribes inviting them to meet with the Iroquois at Montreal. Augustin le Gardeur de Repentigny de Courtemanche journeyed to Lake Michigan, where he found large numbers of Potawatomis settled with the Miamis and other Indians on the Saint Joseph River. The Potawatomis were unaware of the plans for peace, and to Courtemanche's dismay he learned that a Potawatomi war party recently had left the Saint Joseph Valley to raid against the Senecas. Fearing that any attack upon the Iroquois would sabotage the proposed peace negotiations, Courtemanche persuaded the Miamis to intercept the Potawatomi raiders and bring them back to their villages. After the Indians on the Saint Joseph agreed to attend the conference at Montreal, Courtemanche traveled on to Green Bay, where he found villages of Potawatomis, Sacs, Foxes, Winnebagos, Menominees, and Kickapoos. These Indians also agreed to go to Montreal, and in July, Courtemanche returned to Michilimackinac, where he prepared to accompany the western Indians on their voyage to the Saint Lawrence.[1]

Many Potawatomis were included in the large party of western tribesmen who arrived in Montreal on July 21, 1701. Led by Onanghisse and Winamac (Catfish), a chief from the villages along the Saint Joseph, the Potawatomis brought all of their Iroquois prisoners, whom they planned to exchange for Potawatomis held by the Iroquois. Although problems emerged over the exchange, the French negotiated between the two sides and facilitated the return of the prisoners. Both the Potawatomis and the Iroquois then agreed to conclude the treaty.[2]

Callieres conducted the treaty ceremony with a Gallic splendor designed to impress the Indians. The ceremony was held on a plain near Montreal on which a large canopy of branches had been erected. Under this canopy sat Callieres and other French officials, flanked on both sides by lines of French troops who extended forward from the canopy onto the plain. In the area in front of the canopy, Callieres assembled approximately one thousand Indians: eight hundred western tribesmen and two hundred Iroquois. The governor addressed the throng, admonishing both the western Indians and the Iroquois to live in peace and to treat each other as brothers. Distributing belts of wampum to the Indians, Callieres asked both sides not to seek revenge against each other, but to submit intertribal grievances to the French. Onanghisse spoke for the Potawatomis, assuring Callieres of his people's loyalty. He also presented the former Iroquois captives with a calumet, symbolizing Potawatomi friendship. After completing the negotiations, the Potawatomis returned to the West.[3]

Although the peace treaty of 1701 often was violated, the agreement did end the period of large-scale raiding between the western tribesmen and the Iroquois. The treaty also encouraged the further migration of the Potawatomis from Wisconsin. With the Iroquois threat eliminated, the Miamis moved from western Michigan to new villages near Detroit and along the Wabash-Maumee waterway. In turn, large numbers of Potawatomis left the Green Bay region and joined their kinsmen in the Saint Joseph Valley, where they clustered around a mission established by the Jesuits during the 1690's.[4]

But unfortunately for the Potawatomis, the new peace in the west did not last. With the Iroquois menace gone, the cohesion that had kept the western tribes together also disintegrated. No longer facing invasion by a powerful enemy, the western peoples squabbled among themselves. Petty jealousies and minor incidents sparked intertribal conflict, and the Potawatomis soon became involved.

The French were partly to blame. They continued to limit the amount of trade goods entering the west, causing a perennial shortage of necessities. Moreover, French officials attempted to resettle the Miamis, Ottawas, and Hurons at Detroit, where they hoped the Indians would prove an effective barrier to any future Iroquois incursions into the region. But the plan failed. The Miamis and Ottawas quarreled, and in 1706 the Miamis murdered several Ottawas. Honoring the treaty of 1701, the Ottawas sought satisfaction through the French rather than initiating a vendetta against the murderers. But when the French failed to punish the Miamis, the Ottawas threatened to take matters into their own hands.[5]

Fearing an Ottawa attack, the Miamis decided to make a preemptive strike of their own. They enlisted the aid of the Hurons, the Kickapoos, and a small party of Iroquois trading at Detroit and planned to assault the Ottawa village while many Ottawa warriors were absent on a raid against the Sioux. Learning of the intrigue, the Potawatomis warned the Ottawa warriors, who returned to their village before the Miamis could act. In anger, the Ottawas then attacked the Miamis, and in the ensuing melee a priest and several French soldiers accidently were killed.[6]

After the battle, the Ottawas withdrew to Michilimackinac, and the Potawatomis were left alone to face the Miamis and their friends. Fearing that the Miamis and Hurons would seek revenge, the Potawatomis refused to visit Detroit and asked the French to build a fort near their villages on the Saint Joseph River. They also sought alliances with the Sacs and Ottawas as a defense against the Detroit tribes.[7]

Although the French attempted to settle the dispute, their efforts at mediation were interrupted by events on the Saint Lawrence. In 1702, France again had declared war against England, and the conflict dragged on through the first decade of the eighteenth century. Most of the fighting took place along the New England frontier, but in 1711, Governor Vaudreuil of New France received reports that a great English fleet had left New England and was en route to capture Quebec. Fearing that the invasion might succeed, the governor dispatched messengers to French commanders in the west, instructing them to send large numbers of western tribesmen to Montreal. Vaudreuil hoped that such a force of western Indians would at least insure Iroquois neutrality if the English fleet reached the Saint Lawrence.[8]

The Potawatomis willingly accepted Vaudreuil's invitation.

They believed the Iroquois had instigated the recent Miami-Ottawa dispute, and in 1710, Potawatomi warriors had sought revenge for the alleged treachery by seizing two Iroquois hunters and cutting their ears off. One year later, when the French sought allies against their old enemy, the Potawatomis were anxious to volunteer.[9]

Large numbers of Potawatomis and other warriors arrived in Montreal during the summer of 1711, but neither the English nor the Iroquois threat materialized. The English fleet was wrecked by a storm near the mouth of the Saint Lawrence, and the Iroquois remained in their villages south of Lake Ontario. Although the French no longer needed the assistance of the western warriors, Vaudreuil welcomed the opportunity to meet with the Indians and urged them to stop their intertribal bickering. Reminding the western tribesmen that their conflicts disrupted the fur trade, the governor warned the warriors that continued fighting would bring French retribution. The Indians assured Vaudreuil that they would keep the peace, and after receiving French presents, they returned to their homes.[10]

Although Vaudreuil was anxious to mediate the dispute between the Ottawas and the Miamis, his speech was primarily directed at the Foxes. Throughout the first decade of the eighteenth century the Foxes had disrupted the fur trade in Wisconsin. A quarrelsome people, they had collected few furs and were perennially short of trade goods. The Potawatomis and other western tribesmen considered the Foxes to be barbarians and disliked trading with them, since the Foxes often seized trade goods without paying for the merchandise. Moreover, the Foxes and their Mascouten allies continually warred against the Sioux and resented the French commerce with their enemies. Fox war parties scoured the Mississippi, waylaying French merchants and confiscating their supplies of muskets and powder. Other Fox warriors ranged throughout Wisconsin, intercepting French and Potawatomi voyageurs and exacting a growing tribute from the hapless traders. Since many of these merchants were unlicensed, at first French officials took no measures to stop the banditry. In turn, the Foxes believed themselves immune from French power and expanded their depredations into Illinois.[11]

During 1710, in an effort to restore peace in the west, Cadillac invited the Foxes and their Mascouten allies to settle near Detroit. The French commander believed that the Foxes would be "tamed" through a closer association with the French and hoped the Fox removal from Wisconsin would separate them from the Sioux, reducing intertribal warfare in the upper Mississippi Valley. Although several villages of Foxes and Mascoutens accepted Cadillac's invitation, the French plan proved disastrous, for the troublemakers of Wisconsin soon played a similar role at Detroit.[12]

But Cadillac did not reap the whirlwind he had sown. In 1711 he was appointed governor of Louisiana and was replaced at Detroit by Charles Regnault, Sieur Dubuisson. Unlike Cadillac, Dubuisson had no desire to "civilize" the Foxes and resented their resettlement in Michigan. Moreover, the Foxes assumed that their migration was supported by the French, and they immediately claimed the Detroit region as their own. In turn, the Foxes' arrogant lawlessness fostered such resentment among the Potawatomis, Ottawas, Miamis, and Hurons that these tribes forgot their former bickering in a growing enmity toward the newcomers.

The tribal powder keg exploded in 1712. During the previous year a band of Mascoutens allied with the Foxes established a village in the midst of Potawatomi hunting lands on the upper Saint Joseph River. The Potawatomis resented this intrusion, and their anger increased when the Illinois Confederacy informed them that the Foxes, Mascoutens, and Kickapoos planned to attack the French post at Detroit and then flee east to the Iroquois. Deciding to expose the conspiracy, the Potawatomis joined with Ottawas from the Grand River and launched an attack on the Mascouten village, killing fifty of their enemy.[13]

Unaware of the Potawatomi-Ottawa raid, other Mascoutens and Foxes had assembled at Detroit and were awaiting the Kickapoos before assaulting the French garrison. When the Foxes and their allies learned of the attack on the Mascouten village, they angrily burned several Ottawa wigwams within sight of the fort, alarming Dubuisson, who sent messengers to nearby Ottawa and Huron villages. Foiled in their subterfuge, the Foxes then besieged the French fort, erecting a rude pallisade of their own within range of the French walls. Dubuisson's position was desperate, since his garrison was under strength and the Fox and Mascouten besiegers numbered in the hundreds. Yet the Ottawas and Hurons sought additional help from other tribes, and in mid-May, 1712, the French fort was relieved by a large force of western tribesmen led by the Potawatomi war chief Mackisabe (Eagle).[14]

The arrival of the Potawatomis and their allies turned the tide of battle in favor of the French. The Foxes and Mascoutens, who formerly had surrounded the French fortress, now found themselves besieged in their own stronghold. Yet they defended themselves valiantly, and after several days of hard fighting the Potawatomis and their allies were unable to capture the Fox fortress. But the Foxes were not prepared for a prolonged siege and eventually exhausted their supply of food and water. Facing defeat, the Foxes asked for a truce, but the Potawatomis and their allies refused. Speaking for the assembled warriors, Mackisabe and other chiefs scoffed at the Fox request, rebuking them for their treachery and warning them not to expect any quarter. The siege continued for twenty days, and since the Foxes were unable to bury their dead, sickness slowly spread throughout the Fox stronghold. Finally, during a midnight thunderstorm, the Fox chief Pemoussa led his people through the French and Potawatomi lines.[15]

But the Foxes and Mascoutens did not escape. When Mackisabe and Dubuisson found that their enemies had fled, they immediately made plans to follow them. Pemoussa expected pursuit, and the Foxes and Mascoutens laid an ambush, but they were no match for the well-armed French and Potawatomis. Although about one hundred Fox warriors escaped and sought refuge among the Senecas, the remainder of the Foxes and Mascoutens were overwhelmed and taken prisoner. Mackisabe spared only the women and children. The captured Fox and Mascouten warriors were either killed or bound for future torture.[16]

Yet Mackisabe's victory was short-lived. Many Foxes and Mascoutens had been killed, but other members of their tribes were incensed over the slaughter and were anxious to avenge the deaths of their kinsmen. Fearing Fox vengeance, both Mackisabe and Winimac journeyed to Montreal, warning French officials that the conflict was not over and asking for assistance against their mutual enemies. Vaudreuil assured the Potawatomi leaders that the Fox threat had diminished, but when Mackisabe and Winamac returned to the west they learned that Fox, Mascouten, and Kickapoo warriors were infesting the trade routes, killing French travelers and their allied tribesmen indiscriminately. The fur trade was in shambles, as the western Indians hesitated to leave their villages for fear of meeting Fox war parties in the forest.[17]

Fearing that their towns in the lower Saint Joseph Valley were exposed to Fox and Mascouten raids, most of the Potawatomis in western Michigan abandoned their homes and followed Winamac to Detroit, where they established a village near the Hurons on the north bank of the Detroit River. During the next five years other Potawatomis joined with Winamac's people, and by 1718 the Potawatomis were the most populous tribe at Detroit, mustering about 180 warriors while the Ottawas and Hurons could raise only 100 warriors apiece. Other Potawatomis from the Saint Joseph returned to the old villages in Wisconsin, although a few may have scattered along the Illinois River valley.[18]

Secure in the new villages, Potawatomi warriors readily enlisted in French campaigns to crush the Foxes and their allies. In November, 1715, a war party of Potawatomis and other tribesmen killed more than one hundred Kickapoos and Mascoutens in a battle in southern Wisconsin, and during the following year, Potawatomi warriors participated in Louis de la Porte de Louivigny's successful campaign against a Fox fortress near Little Butte des Morts Lake. Leaving Montreal on May 1, 1716, Louivigny and 255 Frenchmen picked up additional forces at Detroit and Michilimackinac and arrived at Green Bay during the middle of the summer. Louivigny seemed assured of success. As he approached the Fox fortress, the French commander led an army of over eight hundred men. Moreover, his troops carried several mortars and cannon that had been ferried all the way from Montreal. But the Foxes were ready. They had fortified their village with a moat and a strong pallisade of pointed oak logs, and within the walls five hundred Fox and Mascouten warriors were determined to sell their lives dearly. Louvigny attacked the fortress using the best methods of European warfare. While their cannon and mortars bombarded the pallisade, the French dug trenches which gradually approached the walls. Yet the Foxes defended themselves with such determination that the French and their allies made little progress. After three days of fighting, the Foxes asked for a truce. On the following day Louivigny met with the Foxes, and the battle ended.[19]

The Potawatomis were appalled at the leniency of the French terms. The French asked the Foxes to cease their raids, encourage the Kickapoos and Mascoutens to make peace, give up all prisoners, and pay the cost of the expedition against their village. When the Foxes agreed, Louivigny returned to Montreal, where he and Vaudreuil congratulated themselves that the Fox wars were over. But the Potawatomis were less certain. They knew the Foxes still were angry over their losses at Detroit, and they feared that the Foxes were only biding their time, waiting for a new opportunity to strike at the French and their allies.[20]

The truce achieved through Louivigny's campaign brought the Potawatomi-French alliance a temporary respite from the Foxes.

The armistice also enabled the French to meet a growing threat from British traders. By 1714, French officials realized that their attempts to keep French traders away from the west had ended in failure. Dozens of *coureurs de bois* were trading illegally with the Indians, and this unlicensed traffic brought little income into the coffers of New France. But even the large numbers of unlicensed traders could not supply the Indians' great demand for trade goods. Fearing that British merchants might penetrate into the region, the French decided to officially reopen the west. Between 1714 and 1717, licenses again were issued to French traders, and French military forces reoccupied several strategic positions in the Great Lakes region.[21]

This change in French policy did not come too soon. Anxious to expand their market, Iroquois and British traders contacted the Miamis in the Maumee Valley, offering them rewards if they would carry British trade goods to Detroit. The Miamis accepted the offer and met with the Potawatomis, Ottawas, and Hurons, promoting trade with the British and urging the French-allied Indians to establish closer ties with the Iroquois. Unfortunately for the French, the Miami efforts were unwittingly aided by Jacques Sabrevois, the French commander at Detroit. Appointed to the post in 1714, Sabrevois was a haughty man who treated the Potawatomis and other Indians with disdain. He also tried to monopolize the fur trade at Detroit, causing a rise in the prices of merchandise sold to the Indians.[22]

Although the Potawatomis at first resisted the Iroquois trade offensive, by 1717 Miami cajolery achieved some success, and part of the Detroit Potawatomis and Ottawas accepted an invitation to journey to Albany to trade their furs for British muskets. In May, 1717, seventeen canoes manned by Potawatomis and Ottawas left Detroit for New York.[23]

As the trading caravan glided over the waters of Lake Ontario, they encountered a French party led by Alphonse de Tonty, who was journeying to Detroit to relieve Sabrevois of his command. Tonty was astonished to find the Potawatomis en route to Albany and immediately distributed French goods to the warriors, promising them that the price of merchandise would be lowered in their homeland. Convinced of Tonty's sincerity, part of the Potawatomis and Ottawas returned with the new commander to Michigan, but others, accompanied by part of Tonty's party, journeyed on to Montreal to lay their grievances before Vaudreuil.[24]

Before reaching Montreal, one canoe of these Indians deserted the party for Albany, but the others continued on and met with the French governor. Speaking for the Potawatomis, Otchik, a village chief from Detroit, informed Vaudreuil that his people had been persuaded to go to Albany only through their dislike of Sabrevois. He asked the governor to lower the price of trade goods and to send more brandy into the west. Vaudreuil was conciliatory in his reply. He assured the Potawatomis that the price of merchandise would be reduced and provided them with brandy to take back to their lodges. The governor accepted Otchik's explanation of the Albany journey, but he admonished the Indians to bring all future complaints to Montreal instead of seeking solace from the British. Satisfied with the conference, the Indians returned to Michigan.[25]

Vaudreuil realized that the Potawatomis were the key to good Indian relations in the west, and he was anxious to strengthen his ties with the tribe. Since Winimac earlier had asked the French to build a fort in the lower Saint Joseph Valley, the governor decided to honor the Potawatomi request. In 1718 Fort Saint Joseph was erected on the Saint Joseph River at the site of modern Niles, Michigan. Designed to protect the Saint Joseph–Kankakee portage, the post also attracted Potawatomis back into the region, drawing tribesmen from both Detroit and Wisconsin.[26]

The post also attracted a number of French traders, who settled among the Potawatomi villages, marrying Potawatomi women and intensifying the Potawatomi-French relationship. Meanwhile, at Detroit, Tonty lowered the price of French trade goods and regained the confidence of the Indians. Anxious to cooperate with the new commander, Potawatomi village chiefs helped Tonty mediate a minor dispute between the Miamis and the Ottawas.[27]

With conditions improving in the west, the French hoped that the construction of Fort Saint Joseph would usher in a decade of peace and prosperity. But French optimism was not shared by the Potawatomis. Unlike Vaudreuil, Winimac and other Potawatomi chiefs continued to distrust the Foxes. Although the Foxes had been subdued since the truce in 1716, their power was not broken, and both the Potawatomis and French had failed to integrate the Foxes into the French alliance. In 1719, Winimac had accompanied a delegation of Fox chiefs to Montreal, where they assured Vaudreuil of their fidelity, but the Fox promises were worthless, and the tribe continued to cause problems in the west.[28]

Wary of a direct confrontation with the French or Potawatomis,

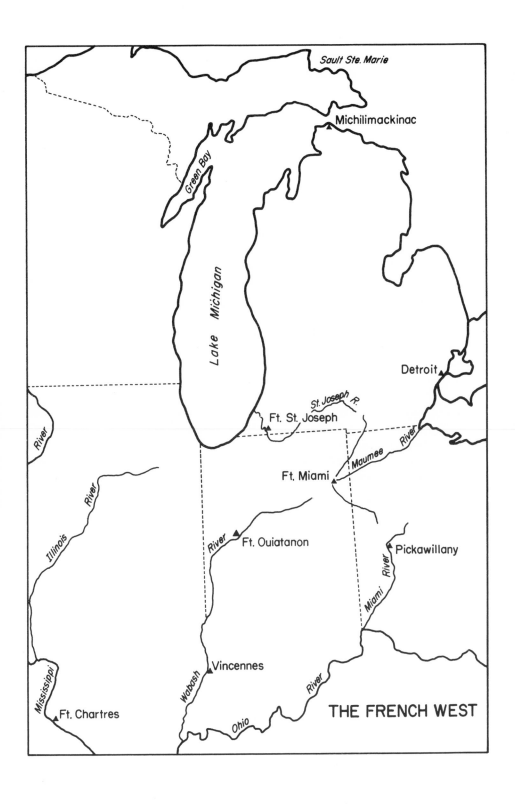

Sault Ste. Marie

Michilimackinac

Green Bay

Lake Michigan

Detroit

St. Joseph R.

Ft. St. Joseph

Maumee River

Ft. Miami

River

Illinois River

River

Ft. Ouiatanon

Pickawillany

Miami River

Mississippi River

Wabash River

Vincennes

Ohio River

Ft. Chartres

THE FRENCH WEST

the Foxes focused their aggression upon the Illinois Confederacy. Claiming that the Illinois continued to hold Fox prisoners, small parties of Fox, Mascouten, and Kickapoo warriors raided into the Illinois Valley, periodically attacking Illinois villages. At first Vaudreuil ignored the warfare, for in 1718, officials in France removed the Illinois country from Canada and annexed the region to Louisiana. Vaudreuil opposed the annexation and temporarily refused to restrain the Foxes, since the Illinois Confederacy no longer was under his jurisdiction. But the policy proved a failure, for the Foxes were encouraged by the French inactivity and the warfare soon spilled over to the Potawatomis.[29]

In 1720, while returning from central Illinois, Fox warriors indiscriminately attacked a Potawatomi hunting camp near Chicago, capturing two Potawatomis. One of the prisoners was the son of Winimac. Although the Kickapoos and Mascoutens freed the two captives, the Potawatomis were incensed. During the same year, the Foxes also killed a Miami who was visiting in a Sac village and murdered a French trader who was living among the Kickapoos. These actions so frightened the Mascoutens that they informed the French commander at Fort Saint Joseph that they wished to leave the Foxes and settle near the Potawatomis.[30]

Angered by the Fox attacks, the Potawatomis asked Tonty for permission to retaliate. They assured the French commander that they would join with several other tribes and crush the Foxes if the French would only give their approval. Tonty hoped the Foxes would cease their raiding and denied the Potawatomi request, but the attacks continued, and by 1722 the western fur trade was in shambles.[31]

Aware that the Potawatomis were enlisting other tribes against them, the Foxes threatened retribution. In 1722, at a council with French officials, the Fox chief Oushala declared that the Potawatomis were his "most cruel enemies" but that he had not attacked them since they were under French protection. Yet he warned the Potawatomis that "they owed their lives to Onontio," and if they continued to plot against his people, the Foxes would "devour them." But Oushala's boasts masked a growing fear that the Potawatomis and their allies might strike back at his tribe. To counter such a threat, the Foxes made new friends, sharing the plunder from their raids with several bands of Sacs and Winnebagos. They also made peace with the Sioux, enabling them to retreat to the west if confronted by the Potawatomi-French alliance and ending their fear of being caught between two powerful enemies.[32]

Secure in their new diplomacy, the Foxes cast caution aside and launched a full-scale war against the Illinois. They refused all French attempts to mediate a peace, and raiding in the upper Illinois Valley reached such proportions that French posts at Cahokia and on the Saint Joseph were forced to communicate via the Wabash. Conditions in the west grew worse, and the Potawatomis were bewildered at French reluctance to put an end to the chaos.[33]

Finally, in 1728, the French had enough. French officials detached the Sacs and Winnebagos from the Fox coalition and concluded a treaty with the Sioux, shutting off a Fox retreat to the west. During the same year, a Jesuit priest, Michel Guignas, was captured by the Kickapoos and Mascoutens. Guignas was held prisoner for five months, but during that time he was able to convince his captors to desert the Foxes and rejoin the Potawatomi-French alliance.[34]

With the Foxes isolated in Wisconsin, the French at last prepared to move against them. Vaudreuil had died in 1725, but his successor, Charles de la Boische Beauharnois, made plans for a war of extermination. In 1728 he sent an expedition to Green Bay which returned without striking the enemy, but the failure only inspired Beauharnois toward greater efforts. During the following summer he assembled delegations of Potawatomis, Ottawas, Chippewas, Sacs, Hurons, and Miamis at Montreal and exhorted them to destroy the Foxes. The Potawatomis needed little encouragement. They returned to the west in the late summer of 1729, and the great war against the Foxes was initiated.[35]

The first blow was delivered within a few months. A large party of Chippewas, Ottawas, and Winnebagos attacked a Fox village in Wisconsin, killing thirty Fox warriors and seventy women and children. The Foxes now realized that their friends had deserted them and they were surrounded by enemies. Faced with destruction, the Foxes attempted to make peace with the French, but their overtures were refused. Decades of Fox duplicity had reaped its harvest.[36]

Rebuffed in their attempts to regain French friendship and isolated from their former friends, the majority of the Foxes decided to forsake their homeland and seek sanctuary among the Iroquois. First, however, they struck at the Winnebagos, their recent allies, who aided the Ottawas and Chippewas in the attack on the Fox village. When the attack failed, the Foxes deserted their villages in Wisconsin and fled across the prairies of northern Illinois toward refuge in New York.[37]

But the Fox flight did not go unnoticed. Encumbered by their families, the Fox warriors were forced to stop and hunt to provide food for their women and children. During July, 1730, they crossed the upper Illinois River, where they encountered their bitter enemies, the Illinois. The Illinois sent messengers to the French posts on the Mississippi River and also alerted a mixed party of Potawatomis, Kickapoos, and Mascoutens who were hunting nearby. The Illinois warriors then attacked the Foxes, hoping to hold them until help arrived.[38]

The Illinois tactics were successful. The hunting party of Potawatomis, Kickapoos, and Mascoutens was led by the Potawatomi chief Madouche, who immediately brought his men to the site of the Fox-Illinois battle. The Foxes did not expect the hunting party, and Madouche's warriors completely surprised their enemy, cutting off escape to the east. Entrapped on the prairie, the Foxes fought desperately and forced the Illinois to retreat, but the Potawatomis, Kickapoos, and Mascoutens maintained their position, and the fugitives could not escape. Seeking what natural advantage the terrain could afford, the Foxes took refuge in a small grove of trees. Madouche's warriors surrounded the grove, digging holes in the ground to provide cover from the Fox fire.[39]

The Potawatomis soon were buttressed by the arrival of large numbers of allies. Jean Saint Ange, the French commander at Fort Chartres on the Mississippi, arrived on August 17, accompanied by a force of five hundred French and Illinois. Two days later, Nicolas Coulon, Sieur de Villiers, accompanied by three hundred French, Potawatomis, Sacs, Kickapoos, Mascoutens, and Miamis, arrived from the Saint Joseph. His arrival was followed by the appearance of the Weas and Piankashaws from the Wabash, and on September 1, Nicolas Joseph des Noyelles, Sieur de Fleurimont, entered the camp followed by ten French soldiers and two hundred Miamis. The combined strength of the French force numbered nearly fourteen hundred men.[40]

Knowing that they had little chance against such overwhelming odds, the Foxes asked the French for leniency, but De Villiers refused. Many of the Indians however, took pity on the Foxes and asked the French to spare them. The Sacs sent a present of food to their enemies and smuggled several Fox children away from the grove. Yet the Potawatomis counseled no quarter, and the French were determined to crush the Foxes as a military power in the west. Although the French-allied Indians refused to storm the Fox position, they kept up the siege, and the Foxes slowly exhausted their supply of food and water.[41]

The siege lasted for twenty-three days. On the evening of September 8, 1730, a violent rainstorm swept across the prairie, providing cover for a Fox retreat. Enshrouded in darkness, the Foxes crept through the French lines and fled to the east, but the crying of the hungry Fox children alerted the French, and a straggler informed the allies of the refugees' route.[42]

De Villiers and Madouche took up the pursuit at daybreak. During the morning of September 9, the Potawatomis and their allies caught sight of the wearied Foxes struggling eastward across the prairie. The Foxes anticipated their pursuers and assembled their warriors in the rear of the fleeing women and children, but they were no match for the French and their allies. Hopelessly outnumbered by the better-fed and better-supplied French Indians, the Foxes were overwhelmed. The Potawatomis and their allies killed between two hundred and three hundred warriors, besides countless women and children. Only about sixty Fox warriors escaped.[43]

The massacre of the Foxes during September, 1730, marked a turning point in Potawatomi-Fox relations. The Saint Joseph Potawatomis had been committed to the French offensive, but the complete devastation of the Foxes seemed to have given them second thoughts about the war of extermination. With Fox military power crushed, the Potawatomis now argued for leniency for the Fox survivors. Later in the fall the Potawatomis provided Fox refugees with sufficient corn for the winter, and they refused to prosecute the war against the few Fox villages remaining in Wisconsin. During the autumn of 1732 the Potawatomis at Detroit, who had not participated in the slaughter of the Foxes on the prairie, joined with the Ottawas and Hurons in attacking a small fortified Fox village in northern Illinois. Yet the attack was half-hearted, for no siege was attempted and the raiders left after the Foxes promised to surrender to the French some time in the future.[44]

After these raids, many of the Foxes settled among the Sacs at Green Bay, who refused to surrender the refugees to the French. When French officials attempted to seize the fugitives, both the Sacs and the Foxes fled to the Wapsipinicon River in Iowa, marking the beginning of the permanent union between those two tribes. Meanwhile, the Saint Joseph Potawatomis continued to plead for mercy for the Fox refugees, and in 1735, when the French sent an expedition against the Sacs and Foxes in Iowa, the Saint Joseph warriors refused to join. The expedition did contain a few Potawatomis from Detroit, but they deserted before the French arrived in Iowa, and the French campaign returned to Illinois without achieving any success.[45]

With the failure of the expedition, the Potawatomis increased their efforts to bring peace between the Foxes and the French. In 1736 the Saint Joseph Potawatomis welcomed Sacs from Iowa into their villages, and during the following year, Winimac led an intertribal delegation to Montreal to plead the Sac and Fox cause. Accompanied by Ottawas, Winnebagos, and Menominees, the Potawatomis asked Beauharnois to stop the war against the Foxes and spare the lives of the Fox prisoners still held captive by the French. Since the Foxes no longer threatened the fur trade, and since he wished to retain the good will of his western allies, Beauharnois agreed. He informed the Potawatomis that he would meet with a delegation of Fox chiefs if they would come to Montreal. During the summer of 1737 the remaining Fox leaders visited the French governor, and Beauharnois welcomed them back within the French alliance.[46]

The conclusion of the Fox Wars brought a tenuous peace to the west. The Potawatomi-French alliance had been strengthened as the Potawatomis had led the other tribes in the campaign against the Foxes. Moreover, marriages between French traders and Potawatomi women produced growing families of mixed-blood children who also cemented the bonds between the two peoples. The fur trade was restored, and beaver pelts again flowed down the western waterways toward Montreal. Yet all was not well. British traders remained envious of the French fur monopoly and were poised at the Appalachians, seeking opportunities to penetrate the west. Potawatomi villagers from Green Bay to Detroit were anxious for peace and prosperity, but once again they would serve Onontio in a futile attempt to stop the westward expansion of British influence.

3. In Defense of a Dying Empire

During the third decade of the eighteenth century, while the Potawatomi-French alliance concentrated their efforts upon defeating the Foxes, British traders from the Carolinas skirted the southern flanks of the Appalachian Mountains and penetrated the broad forests stretching westward toward the Mississippi. Eager to tap the fur trade of the interior, the British merchants sought markets for their wares among the Muskhogean-speaking peoples of the Old Southwest. Although many warriors from the Creek Confederacy traded with the merchants, the British were anxious to spread their influence to tribes farther west. Crossing modern Alabama and Mississippi, the traders contacted villages of Choctaws and Chickasaws, hoping those tribesmen could be enticed into the British trade network.

Although most of the Choctaws refused to cooperate with the merchants, the Chickasaws proved to be an ideal target for the British trade offensive. During the 1720's, Chickasaw and Natchez warriors had risen against Louisiana, attacking French commerce on the Mississippi and killing French traders. In 1729 a French expedition crushed the Natchez, but refugees from the Natchez villages were adopted by the Chickasaws, and Chickasaw warriors continued the campaign against Louisiana. Expanding their raids, the Chickasaws struck along the lower Ohio River, disrupting communications between Illinois and French posts on the Wabash. Meanwhile, Chickasaw villagers in northern Mississippi and western Tennessee welcomed British traders, bartering their fur for muskets and powder to be used in the war against new France.[1]

Angered by the Chickasaw depredations, the French encouraged their Indian allies to strike back. Throughout the early 1730's, Potawatomi war parties crossed the Ohio, but they achieved little success. Although the Potawatomis took a few scalps, Chickasaw raiding increased, and French commerce on the Mississippi was paralyzed.[2] In 1736 the French sent two expeditions against the Chickasaw villages, but the Indians defeated both parties, capturing several French officers, whom they first tortured, then burned at the stake. Elated over their victories, the Chickasaws secured additional arms from the British and carried the war north of the Ohio, striking at Piankashaw villages along the Wabash. For the French and Potawatomis, it seemed as if the Fox Wars had begun anew, but with a more dangerous and better-supplied adversary.[3]

Unwilling to admit defeat, the French organized another campaign against the Chickasaw villages. During the autumn of 1739, Potawatomis and other warriors joined a force of French soldiers who floated down the Mississippi to Fort Assumption, at the Chickasaw Bluffs, near modern Memphis, Tennessee. The French expedition comprised troops from both Louisiana and Canada and was led by Governor Bienville of Louisiana, who hoped that a major French victory would restore French prestige and finally divorce the Chickasaws from their ties with the British traders. Bienville planned well. Large stores of supplies, including cannon, mortars, and mines, were assembled at Fort Assumption for use against the fortified Chickasaw towns, and by October, 1739, nearly thirty-six hundred men were camped near Fort Assumption awaiting Bienville's orders to march against their enemy.[4]

But the orders were never delivered. Before Bienville could organize his forces, western Tennessee was drenched by a series of storms which flooded the region, making overland travel impossible. Bienville kept his men at Fort Assumption, but after several days of incessant rainfall, it became apparent that he could not move his heavy ordnance. Attempting to salvage some success from the costly campaign, Bienville sent Pierre Joseph Celoron with a force of six hundred soldiers and northern Indians into the Chickasaw country. The governor hoped that this demonstration of French strength would convince the Chickasaws to negotiate a peace. Many Potawatomis accompanied Celoron, and although the expedition failed to intimidate the Chickasaws, the French did meet in council with their enemies. Potawatomi emissaries carried the French invitation to the Chickasaw towns, where they left a letter containing the offer of negotiation attached to the log gates of an Indian stronghold. Accepting the French offer, the Chickasaws met with Bienville at Fort Assumption, but the conference produced few results. Chickasaw promises to remain at peace were never honored, since Bienville's failure only confirmed the Chickasaw opinion that they could raid the French with impunity.[5] The Chickasaw-British alliance continued, and although a few Potawatomi war parties still crossed the Ohio, after 1740 their numbers declined.[6]

British traders also were active in the Old Northwest. In 1740, officials in Canada decided to lease the western trading posts to the highest bidder, hoping that the change in economic policy would increase the revenue of New France. But the new system proved disastrous for French traders were forced to sell their goods at a high price to recover the cost of the lease. Taking advantage of the French mistake, British merchants moved into eastern Ohio, again offering the Indians trade goods at prices much lower than those of the French. During King George's War (1742–48), the British navy blockaded the Saint Lawrence, compounding French economic problems and assisting the British trade offensive. Unable to match the British in economics, French officials relied upon their military power. The French threatened to punish those tribes who traded with British merchants, and they relied upon the Potawatomis to drive the British traders back across the Appalachians.[7]

The British penetration of Ohio was facilitated by an intertribal quarrel at Detroit. In the spring of 1738 the Hurons made a unilateral peace with the Chickasaws and Cherokees, warning the Potawatomis, Ottawas, and Chippewas to no longer support French campaigns against the southern tribes. Taken aback by the Huron ultimatum, the Three Fires denounced the Hurons, accusing them of planning to attack the French and then seek refuge in the south. To thwart the Huron diplomacy, the Potawatomis, Ottawas, and Chippewas sent a mixed war party across the Ohio to attack the southern tribesmen. But as they journeyed south, the war party was passed by two groups of Hurons, who warned the southern Indians, for the war party was ambushed and only three of seventeen warriors escaped death or capture. One of the three, an Ottawa, returned to Detroit, where he reported that the Hurons had assisted the southern Indians in the ambush. Angered by the treachery, the Ottawas threatened the Hurons with war.[8]

Fearing that the Potawatomis and Chippewas would join with the Ottawas, most of the Hurons fled Detroit and took refuge in Ohio. Huron leaders asked the French for permission to move their villages to Montreal, but French Indians along the Saint Lawrence opposed the move, and the French urged the Hurons to return to Michigan. Meanwhile, the British and the Iroquois learned of the dissension and invited the Hurons to settled among the Senecas. Afraid that the villages in Ohio would attract British trade, the French belatedly granted the Huron request to settle on the Saint Lawrence, but by 1741 few of the Hurons were interested. Although part of the Hurons eventually returned to Detroit, others, led by Chief Orontony, or Nicolas, established permanent villages near Sandusky, where they welcomed British traders.[9]

Foremost among the British visitors at Sandusky was George Croghan, a British trader and Indian agent. Croghan erected several storehouses on Lake Erie and supplied Nicolas' people with British merchandise. In turn, Nicolas attempted to bring other Indians to the British traders, and in 1747 he enlisted the aid of the Hurons in Michigan in a conspiracy against the French garrison at Detroit. According to Nicolas' plan, the Detroit Hurons were to enter the French fort and spend the night, but during the early morning hours they would massacre the sleeping French and then burn the stockade.[10]

Fortunately for the French, the plot failed. Before the proposed attack the Hurons prematurely killed a Frenchman near Detroit, arousing French suspicion. A Huron woman then disclosed the conspiracy to a priest, who warned Baron de Longueuil, the French commander at Detroit. Longueuil spread the alarm, rallying his soldiers and bringing French citizens into the stockade.[11]

The extent of the Huron conspiracy remains unclear, but other tribes certainly were involved. Nicolas' promises of British trade goods persuaded scattered bands of Ottawas and Chippewas to destroy French property at Detroit and to murder a few French traders near Michilimackinac. The Miamis also succumbed to Nicolas' intrigue and attacked Fort Miamis, the French post at the headwaters of the Maumee, where they seized French merchandise and set several buildings afire.[12]

Unlike the other tribes, the Potawatomis did not participate in the conspiracy. During the 1740's, their ties with New France had increased as Potawatomi chiefs journeyed to Montreal, where they were lavishly rewarded for their assistance against the Chickasaws.[13] In the summer of 1747, the year of the Huron conspiracy, many Potawatomi warriors from both the Saint Joseph and Detroit were absent from their villages, supporting the French in King George's War. Potawatomi warriors raided on the New England frontier, attacking British settlements near Albany and along the Connecticut River. Other war parties left Fort Saint Frederick (Crown Point), near Lake Champlain, and struck the British at Saratoga, taking several scalps and collecting information about British troop movements in the region. When the Potawatomis in New England learned of the Huron uprising, they informed French military officers that they considered the revolt to be a personal affront and asked permission to return to Michigan to assist Longueuil in protecting their families.[14]

At Detroit, the Huron revolt caught the Potawatomis by surprise. Aware of the strong Potawatomi-French alliance, Nicolas carefully had concealed his plans from the Potawatomi tribesmen living near the French fort. Although their kinsmen on the Saint Joseph suspected that pro-British Indians were active among nearby tribes, the Detroit Potawatomis watched in amazement as a suspicious Longueuil ordered French citizens into the fort in preparation against an Indian attack. Since many of their warriors were absent in the east, the Potawatomis hesitated to come to Longueuil's assistance. They offered to mediate between the two sides, but when their efforts failed, they sent messengers to Montreal asking French officials to send reinforcements.[15]

In the autumn of 1747, when additional French troops arrived in Detroit, the Huron conspiracy collapsed. The hostile Ottawas and Chippewas sued for peace, surrendering those tribesmen responsible for the death of the French traders. Nicolas and the Sandusky Hurons fled to the Cuyahoga and Muskingum valleys in eastern Ohio, and the hostile Miamis sought sanctuary in a new village, Pickawillany, near the juncture of the Miami River and Loramie's Creek.[16] Although Longueuil at first suspected the Detroit Potawatomis of complicity in the revolt, a subsequent French investigation exonerated them. French officials in Illinois reported that of all the western tribes, the Potawatomis "were the only nation to be relied upon," and the new governor of New France, Michel Rolland Barin, Comte de la Galissonniere, wrote to Paris that the Potawatomis were involved in the events only through "their offers of service and protestations of loyalty."[17]

The Huron conspiracy convinced La Galissonniere that the French lease system had failed. Indian discontent over high prices continued to permeate the west, and in 1748 even the Saint Joseph Potawatomis asked that no more lessees be sent to the trading post on their river. During the same year, in an effort to increase the

supply of trade goods, the French governor abolished the lease system and returned to the earlier practice of selling licenses to any
trader wishing to go west. Yet this change did not solve the French
problem, for inexpensive British goods continued to flood Ohio.
and although the Huron conspiracy had been thwarted, the new
Miami village at Pickawillany soon replaced Sandusky as a center of
British influence.[18]

Led by the Piankashaw chief, La Demoiselle, the Miamis at Pickawillany were anxious to continue the British trade. La Demoiselle
had been nicknamed "Old Briton" because of his previous affinity
for British intrigue, and the old chief lived up to his reputation.
Soon after moving to Pickawillany, La Demoiselle contacted the
Iroquois, requesting a formal alliance with the British colonies. The
Iroquois relayed his message to officials in Pennsylvania, and during July, 1748, Miamis from Pickawillany journeyed to Lancaster,
where they signed a treaty with the British. Governor James Hamilton of Pennsylvania was delighted with the treaty, optimistically
predicting that the agreement not only would extend British trade,
but also would weaken French control over the Ohio and Mississippi
valleys. Hamilton's predictions proved true. British traders flocked
to the Miami village, and British influence again expanded westward toward the heart of New France.[19]

Alarmed by the renewed British threat at Pickawillany, the Potawatomis and French worked to minimize Old Briton's influence.
When the Piankashaw chief attempted to lure other tribes into
Ohio, the Potawatomis refused his invitations and used their influence to keep their neighbors within the French alliance. Although Old Briton's messengers tried to persuade a village of
Miamis on the Tippecanoe River to resettle near Pickawillany, the
Saint Joseph Potawatomis convinced Le Gris, the chief of the Miami
village, to remain in Indiana. They also invited Le Gris and his
followers to settle along the Saint Joseph River, hoping to remove
them from Old Briton's temptations.[20]

Meanwhile, the French attempted to counter the British economic offensive with military power. La Galissonniere gambled
that a display of French strength would frighten British traders
from Ohio and induce the rebellious Miamis to return to their
former villages. During the spring of 1749, the governor dispatched
a party of Canadians and pro-French Indians under the command of
Pierre Joseph Celoron to descend the Ohio and reassert French
control over the region. Celoron's force journeyed down the Ohio,

burying metal plates which claimed the region for France. Ascending the Miami River, Celoron arrived at Pickawillany in September, 1749. Although he forced British traders to leave the village, the French officer could not convince Old Briton to return to Indiana. Since the Miami warriors outnumbered the French, Celoron was forced to return to Detroit empty-handed.[21]

Celoron's failure to bring the Miamis back from Ohio weakened the French position in the west. Convinced that he was immune to French and Potawatomi retribution, Old Briton increased his attempts to bring other tribes to Pickawillany. Old Briton's messengers ranged as far west as Illinois, distributing British trade goods and advocating political alliances. During the spring of 1750, he achieved some success. In May, Charles de Raymond, the French commander at Fort Miamis on the Maumee, reported that 250 Weas and Piankashaws had left the Wabash to join the Miamis in Ohio. Meanwhile, George Croghan and other British traders moved into the Miami village, erecting a fortified trading post and warehouse.[22]

The Potawatomis remained aloof from Old Briton's intrigues. Although a few Potawatomi warriors traded with the pro-British Indians, the majority refused offers of British political alliances and continually assured Celoron of their loyalty to New France. When Raymond complained that they had accepted British trade goods, the Saint Joseph Potawatomis sent a delegation of warriors to Fort Miamis, presenting the French commander with six belts of wampum as a pledge of their fidelity. Other warriors from the Saint Joseph voyaged to Montreal, where they met with the Marquis de Jonquiere, the new governor of New France, and promised to assist him against Old Briton. The governor believed the Potawatomis were sincere, but he warned them to stop all trade with the British.[23]

At Detroit, Celoron was anxious to atone for the failure of his expedition and repeatedly sent loyal Potawatomis and Ottawas to Pickawillany, asking Old Briton and the Miamis to return to the Maumee. When the old Piankashaw refused, Louis Coulon de Villiers, the new commander of Fort Miamis, also journeyed to the Miami village, but he received a similar response. Although De Villiers was accompanied by Potawatomis and pro-French Miamis, Old Briton informed the officer that the Indians at Pickawillany were supported by the British, Iroquois, Shawnees, Delawares, and several other tribes and no longer feared the Potawatomi-French alliance. In defiance, the Piankashaw chief boasted that he had no father other than the British and that the French were all knaves and traitors. Humiliated, De Villiers and his Potawatomi escort returned to Fort Miamis.[24]

Old Briton's denunciation of New France and her allies prompted French officials into action. During the winter of 1750–51, French officials at Montreal planned a new expedition against the hostile Miami village. A force of French soldiers and Indians were dispatched from Canada and were ordered to rendezvous with Celoron and loyal Indians at Detroit. The combined party then planned to march upon Pickawillany, capture all British traders, and force the Miamis to return to the Maumee.[25]

But the plan failed. At Detroit the Potawatomis knew that Pickawillany contained nearly four hundred warriors, in addition to a growing number of British traders. At first they agreed to support the French expedition, believing that Jonquiere had dispatched a large force of French and Indians from Montreal. However, when the French party reached Detroit, it consisted of one French officer and fifty Nipissing and Algonkian warriors. Dismayed over the small size of the French force, the Potawatomis and Ottawas refused to join in the venture. They complained that the French raiding party was much too small and that the French had promised to send a larger detachment of soldiers. Assuring Celoron that they still remained loyal to New France, the Potawatomis pledged to support a similar compaign during the following spring if the French could assemble a more sizable expedition.[26]

Ironically, although Celoron capitulated to the Potawatomi defection, the expedition achieved some short-term success. Marie François Picote, Sieur de Bellestre, the French officer from Montreal, continued on to Pickawillany with only seventeen warriors but found the Miami town practically deserted. Almost all of the Miami warriors were absent on their autumn hunt, and the small raiding party swept through Pickawillany unopposed. Although most of the Miami women and children took shelter in the British stockade, Bellestre's warriors took two Miami scalps and captured several British traders.[27]

Yet Bellestre's raid only angered the Miamis and made them more contemptuous of the French. In January, 1752, Old Briton retaliated by ceremoniously killing three captured French soldiers and cutting the ears off another before sending him to Canada as a warning to the governor. The Piankashaw chief again sent warriors to the western tribes, and this time even the Potawatomis lent a sympathetic ear to his proposals. Although they refused to leave the

French, the Saint Joseph Potawatomis informed Old Briton that they would not support any expedition against his village. Meanwhile, a smallpox epidemic swept through the Potawatomi and Ottawa villages near Detroit. The epidemic killed about eighty Indians, but the social disruption brought by the illness caused many Potawatomi warriors to lose interest in the campaign against Pickawillany.[28]

Faced with a deteriorating alliance, the French reevaluated their policy toward the Miami village. If the Potawatomis would not support the war against Old Briton, the French had little chance of success. Moreover, French officials believed that another abortive expedition against Pickawillany might alienate the Potawatomis and drive them into the arms of the British. Therefore, during the early months of 1752, French policy makers decided to stop their campaign against the hostile Miamis.[29]

Yet the new policy never was implemented. At Michilimackinac, Charles Langlade, a mixed-blood trader and French Indian agent, spent the spring organizing a party of Ottawas and Chippewas for another attack on Pickawillany. Unaware of the change in French plans, he gathered more than two hundred warriors from northern Michigan, and in June the raiding party passed through Detroit, where Langlade recruited other Ottawas and several Pottawatomis. The raiding party struck Pickawillany on June 21, 1752, completely surprising the hapless Miamis. Langlade's warriors swept down on the village so suddenly that they captured many of the Miami women in their cornfields. Most of the Miami warriors were absent hunting, but those in the village took refuge with a few British traders in the British stockade. After several hours of fighting, Langlade persuaded the British and Miamis to surrender, promising that he would spare their lives. Yet the promise was broken. Old Briton had taken refuge in the fort, and when he emerged, Langlade's warriors killed the old Piankashaw and then devoured part of his body. One of the British traders suffered a similar fate,, and most of the other British traders were forced to accompany Langlade back to Detroit.[30]

Langlade's raid destroyed Pickawillany and forced most of the Miamis to return to the Maumee. British traders retreated toward Pennsylvania, and New France regained control of the Ohio Valley. The impact of Langlade's victory was not lost on the Potawatomis. A few warriors from Detroit had accompanied the mixed-blood to Pickawillany, and when they returned to their villages, they were flushed with victory and loudly proclaimed the French success. Although the Saint Joseph tribesmen did not support the expedition, they did assist the French in resettling part of the Miamis along the Wabash. If the Potawatomi-French alliance had been shaken by Pickawillany, Langlade's raid restored Potawatomi faith in French military power and convinced the tribe to continue in their close relationship with New France.[31]

The Saint Joseph Potawatomis had been reluctant to support the French against Pickawillany because they were embroiled in a dispute with the Illinois Confederacy. During the late 1740's, Potawatomis from the Saint Joseph established a new village on the Chicago River, where they were joined by a few kinsmen from the west coast of Lake Michigan. This migration into northeastern Illinois resulted from several causes. As the population along the Saint Joseph increased, internal dissension within the villages motivated groups of Potawatomis to leave Michigan and seek new homes near Chicago. The region once had been claimed by the Illinois Confederacy, but the Illinois tribesmen were a declining people, wasted by disease and decimated by intertribal warfare. By the middle of the eighteenth century the Illinois had withdrawn from the Illinois River valley, concentrating their villages near French posts on the Mississippi. In turn, French officials in Illinois encouraged the Potawatomis to move into their district, envisioning the tribe as a faithful ally and a source of stability in the region.[32]

But the stability never materialized. The Wisconsin tribes continually harassed the Illinois Confederacy and the Potawatomis soon became involved. In 1750 a party of Saint Joseph Potawatomis returning from French posts on the Mississippi passed through a village of Peorias, where a quarrel arose, resulting in the death of a Potawatomi warrior. The dead man, La Grue (The Crane), had been a notorious trouble-maker and had started the dispute in the Peoria village, but the Peorias were afraid the Potawatomis would retaliate. The French attempted to mediate the controversy, and the Peorias sent gifts to La Grue's relatives, attempting to "cover" his death, but the dead Potawatomi's kinsmen remained dissatisfied and anxious for revenge.[33]

In the spring of 1751 a mixed party of Potawatomis, Menominees, Mascoutens, and Chippewas descended the Illinois River, planning to attack the Peorias, but the Illinois tribesmen learned of their intentions and surprised the invaders, capturing three Potawatomis and a Mascouten. Anxious to placate the Potawatomis, the Peorias released their prisoners, telling them:

> Why do you disturb the earth for a fool who has been killed? What is your reason for coming to such extremes? Some of our people who were married in your villages have been killed there and we have never taken up arms to revenge ourselves. Moreover, if you attack us we will revenge ourselves; the earth will be disturbed and the roads will be closed through your fault.[34]

Although the Saint Joseph Potawatomis were satisfied with the Illinois' plea, the war was taken up by their kinsmen at Chicago. During the summer of 1752 they joined with a few Potawatomis from Wisconsin and with large numbers of Sacs, Foxes, Winnebagos, Chippewas, Menominees, and Sioux to attack Cahokia and Michigamea villages along the Illinois River. The raiders were eminently successful. They killed or captured more than seventy of the hapless Illinois, burned twelve of their lodges, and scattered the bones of the dead over the ground. Five days later the Chippewas struck a Peoria village on Lake Peoria, and the panic-stricken Illinois fled to the French settlements in southern Illinois, where they sought sanctuary and attempted to form a defensive alliance with the Osages.[35]

Although French officials attempted to stop the outbreak of Indian warfare in Illinois, they were more concerned with events in western Pennsylvania. By 1754, France and Britain again were on the brink of war, and the Marquis Duquesne, newly appointed governor of New France, was anxious to take advantage of Langlade's raid and regain the initiative in the Ohio Valley. Since war was imminent, Duquense ordered a fortress to be erected at the forks of the Ohio. During the summer of 1754, French forces built Fort Duquesne and then defeated the British at Fort Necessity, assuring French control of western Pennsylvania.

Fort Duquesne posed a serious threat to the security of British colonists in Pennsylvania and Virginia. No longer would the Ohio River serve as an avenue for British penetration of the west. By 1755 the broad western river was in French possession, and Fort Duquesne loomed as a staging point from which French-allied Indians could be sent against the British frontiers. Earlier colonial attempts to dislodge the French had failed, so in 1755 Great Britain sent two regiments of British regulars to aid the colonial forces in pushing the French back from the forks area. Led by General Edward Braddock, these regulars were to join with colonial troops and seize Fort Duquesne and then assist Governor William Shirley of Massachusetts in attacking the French at Fort Niagara.[36]

French officials in Canada knew of the British plans and were determined to defend Fort Duquesne. Since the French could not muster enough troops to match Braddock's forces, they relied upon their red allies. During the spring of 1755, messengers were sent to the west, and in the early summer large numbers of western tribesmen arrived at the forks of the Ohio. Potawatomi villages at Detroit, the Saint Joseph, and Chicago contributed many warriors to the Indian army.[37]

As the French greeted their red allies, Braddock and more than fourteen hundred British and colonial troops approached Fort Duquesne from the southeast. The British general knew that the French were aware of his intentions, and he expected to be attacked while crossing the Monongahela River near the mouth of Turtle Creek, about eight miles southeast of the French fort. But as the British column forded the river, they met no opposition, and by the afternoon of July 9, Braddock's forces completed the crossing and marched toward a clearing a few miles ahead, where they planned to spend the night before attacking Fort Duquesne.[38]

Braddock's approach did not go unnoticed. French scouts had followed his progress through southern Pennsylvania, and on July 8, Claude Pierre Pecaudy, Sieur de Contrecoeur, the French commander at Duquesne, assembled the western tribesmen and admonished them to attack Braddock as he crossed the Monongahela. Although the other Indians agreed to the proposal, the Detroit Potawatomis refused. The reason for their refusal is unknown, but the Potawatomis assured Contrecoeur that they gladly would attack Braddock on July 9. The Potawatomi hesitancy spread to the other Indians, and the French postponed the attack until the following day. Therefore, on the morning of July 9, 1755, the Potawatomis and approximately six hundred other warriors joined a force of 290 French regulars and militia led by Captain Daniel de Beaujeu. At about 8:00 A.M. the Potawatomis and their allies left Fort Duquesne to meet the British.[39]

Ironically, the Potawatomi procrastination proved to the French advantage. Braddock had expected to be attacked while crossing the river, and as his column neared their proposed campsite during the afternoon of July 9, the British troops proceeded carelessly, believing that the French and Indians preferred to meet them behind the bastions of Fort Duquesne. Before reaching their campsite, the British army was forced to follow the trail as it passed between a small rounded hill and a ravine. Although Braddock dispatched skirmishers to protect his flanks, he did not occupy the hill, which loomed to the right of the British column. Just after the advance guard of Braddock's forces passed the hill, they encountered the French and Indians, who rushed forward to meet them.[40]

A skirmish occurred, after which Braddock's advance guard fell back upon the main body of British troops, who continued to slowly advance forward. Unfortunately for the British, the forest pathway was too narrow to allow them to maneuver, and when the advance guard retreated into the foremost ranks of the main body of troops, the soldiers became confused and bewildered. To add to the pandemonium, the rear echelons of Braddock's force continued to move forward, piling men and wagons together in the narrow pathway.[41]

The Potawatomis and their allies quickly took advantage of the situation and spread their forces throughout the underbrush bordering both sides of the trail. The Indians also gained command of the hill, and hidden behind the dense foliage, they poured a deadly fire on the panic-stricken British. The battle lasted about three hours. The British soldiers, unfamiliar with forest warfare, huddled together in the open pathway and were cut down by assailants they could not see. Braddock was mortally wounded, and of the eighty-six British officers in his command, sixty-three were killed or wounded. Finally, the British survivors broke and ran, eventually reaching Braddock's supply column fifty miles to the rear. Of the fourteen hundred troops who had followed Braddock across the Monogahela, more than one thousand were either killed or wounded. The Potawatomis and their allies suffered only about sixty casualties.[42]

Following their victory in Pennsylvania, the Potawatomis returned to their homes in the west. There they were greeted like conquering heroes, as grateful French officials praised their deeds and lavished gifts upon them. Encouraged by their success, many warriors from Detroit returned east to scourge the frontiers of Virginia, Maryland, and Pennsylvania. By October, 1755, French officials at Detroit reported that Potawatomis from that post had killed or captured more than 120 British settlers.[43]

Braddock's defeat and the Potawatomi successes along the British frontier reflected French fortunes during the opening year of the

Seven Years' War. During the summer of 1756, French officials in Illinois finally concluded a peace between the Illinois Confederacy and their antagonists, including the Potawatomis from Chicago and Wisconsin. In August the Marquis de Montcalm captured Oswego, giving New France control of Lake Ontario, and French prestige among all the western tribes appreciated. No longer could British traders at Oswego advocate British alliances to the western Indians. No longer would French traders be forced to compete with less expensive British goods. By September, 1756, the French commanded both the Ohio River and the Great Lakes trade routes, and they made plans to carry the war to the British.[44]

French attentions focused upon New England. Lakes Champlain and George stretched as a natural highway between Montreal and Albany, and the French were anxious to gain control of the waterway so that they might carry the war into the Hudson Valley. During 1756, French engineers began the construction of Fort Carillon at Ticonderoga, and by late summer the French hoped to use the new post as a base for raids against the British. To provide raiders for the new post, the French solicited the aid of their red allies. Messengers were sent to the western lakes, inviting the Indians to participate in an autumn campaign of raids into New York and to serve as scouts against British posts such as Fort William Henry.[45]

The Potawatomis responded eagerly to the French request. During late August, 1756, a large flotilla of Potawatomis and Ottawas descended the Saint Lawrence to Montreal. Since the French had proposed a late autumn campaign, many of the Potawatomis brought their families to Montreal to live with the French while the warriors raided against the British. The Potawatomis were greeted by the Marquis de Vaudreuil, who had been appointed governor of New France during 1755. Vaudreuil assured the warriors that the French would provide for their women and children, and he exhorted the tribesmen to strike the British. Pleased by Vaudreuil's speech, the Potawatomis responded by chanting their war songs, telling the governor, "Father, we are famished: give us fresh meat; we wish to eat the English; dispatch us quickly."[46]

Late in September the warriors arrived at Fort Carillon, where they met in council with French officers and other Indians. Slow and deliberate in their speeches, the Potawatomi warriors impressed the French officers, who considered them to be more reliable than the Indians from the lower Saint Lawrence Valley. The Potawatomis agreed to descend Lake George, planning either to ambush British parties on the road leading to Fort William Henry or to disperse into small war parties and raid into New England.[47]

During October, 1756, Potawatomi war parties penetrated the British frontier as far south as the Albany region, where they attacked a British supply train en route to Fort Edward, taking several scalps and one prisoner. After the prisoner was carried to Fort Carillon and delivered to French officers, most of the Potawatomis returned to Montreal, where some spent the winter with their families while others voyaged back to their villages in the west.[48]

The Potawatomis who returned to Michigan spent the winter of 1756–57 recruiting additional warriors for the campaign in New York. Many of the Detroit Potawatomis preferred to raid against Virginia, but in the spring of 1757, large numbers of Saint Joseph tribesmen accompanied other Indians to Fort Carillon. The Potawatomis then proceeded on to the portage between Lake Champlain and Lake George, where they joined with nearly two thousand other Indians in preparation for an attack on Fort William Henry. The vast assemblage of Indians were bored by the inactivity of camp life and continually demanded food and other provisions from French officers. Although many of the Indians began to slaughter and eat French oxen, the Potawatomis refused to join in the feast, and Louis Antoine de Bougainville, an aide-de-camp to Montcalm, again praised the Potawatomis for their loyalty, calling them "the wisest and most obedient of all the Indians."[49]

On July 23, 1757, the routine of camp life was disrupted when French scouts reported a fleet of British barges proceeding up Lake George toward the portage. The barges contained a force of New Jersey militia who had been sent from Fort William Henry to reconnoiter the French position. The Potawatomis, Ottawas, Chippewas, and Menominees prepared an ambush, and at daybreak on July 24, as the barges rounded a point on the lakeshore, the underbrush exploded with musket fire. The attack claimed many casualties and caused the uninjured British to seek safety in more open water, but as the barges frantically pulled away from shore, the Potawatomis pursued them in canoes that had been hidden in the underbrush. Many of the heavy barges were overtaken by the Indians, and the militia panicked. As the Potawatomis and their allies seized control of the barges, some of the British offered no resistance, but other soldiers attempted to escape by jumping into the lake and swimming towards shore. The swimmers were in desperate straits. The Indians in the canoes speared them like sturgeon, and most of those who avoided such a fate either drowned or were captured when they reached shore.[50]

Yet those militiamen who died in the water were fortunate compared to some of the captives. The Indians found a quantity of rum in one of the barges, and after consuming it, they began to torture several of the prisoners. The Ottawas led in the slaughter and eventually killed, cooked, and devoured some of the prisoners. The Potawatomis' role in such distasteful activity is unknown, but since they had led the attack upon the barges, they probably participated in the aftermath.[51]

On August 1, 1757, Montcalm and his army set sail in bateaux for the southern end of Lake George. Accompanying the French force were eighty-eight Potawatomis: seventy from the Saint Joseph and eighteen from Detroit. The Potawatomi warriors were led by Millouisillyny, Ouakousy (Fox), Nanaquiba (Water Moccasin), Oybischagme, and Ninivois. The French and Indian expedition landed near Fort William Henry, and Montcalm dug trenches to position his artillery. Meanwhile, the Potawatomis and other Indians encircled the British fortress to cut off any reinforcements.[52]

The siege lasted seven days. While the French cannons bombarded the fort, the Indians attacked several outbuildings and repulsed a British sortie. Colonel George Munro, the British commander, was determined to withstand the attack, but Montcalm's forces captured a British dispatch informing Munro that he could expect no reinforcements, and Montcalm relayed the message to Munro with a demand that he surrender. At first the British officer refused, but smallpox erupted within the British garrison, and Munro bowed to the inevitable. On the morning of August 9, 1757, he surrendered Fort William Henry.[53]

The French surrender terms were generous. The British gave up their artillery, but were allowed to keep their side arms and personal possessions. Although the French confiscated all ammunition, they agreed to escort the British troops to Fort Edward if the British promised not to serve against the French for eighteen months following their capitulation. But French generosity toward the captives was not shared by the Potawatomis and other Indians. Many of the Potawatomis had journeyed over one thousand miles to fight against their enemy, and they were anxious for the spoils of victory. Although Montcalm pleaded with them to honor his surrender terms, his pleas were ignored. As soon as the British garrison evacuated the fort, the warriors stormed into the structure, pillaging property left behind and killing all the smallpox patients too ill to follow the garrison. The Indians then followed the British back to the French camp, where they roamed among the terrified prisoners, seizing the captives' possessions and threatening them with death. Although the French guards could not stop the warriors, Montcalm eventually restored order, and two chiefs from each tribe promised the French general that they would accompany the British to Fort Edward in an attempt to guarantee the captives' safety.[54]

But the promises were broken. On the morning of August 10, the British assembled before dawn in their anxiety to start for the safety of Fort Edward. Montcalm had entrusted the prisoners to the questionable care of Canadian forces, and before the regular troops who were to form the escort could arrive, the Indians once again entered the encampment. Seventeen British soldiers who were too wounded or ill to make the journey to Fort Edward still were in their beds. The Indians dragged them from their shelters and killed them before the eyes of the other captives. The warriors again pillaged the camp, and when the escort of regulars arrived, the soldiers seemed powerless to stop them. The French formed the British into a column and started down the road toward Fort Edward, but a party of Abnakis fell upon a group of New Hampshire militia at the rear of the procession and began to methodically kill them. The Abnaki attack spread panic throughout the entire British column, and many of the prisoners bolted for the woods in a desperate bid for freedom. But the Potawatomis and other tribesmen pursued the hapless refugees, cutting them down in the forest. Before Montcalm finally restored order, more than two hundred British prisoners had been killed and another two hundred had been carried away as captives by the Indians.[55]

The Potawatomis and other Indians left for Montreal on the day after the massacre, but the British had their revenge. Many of the prisoners killed by the Potawatomis had been infected with smallpox, and the warriors carried the disease back to the west. During the spring and summer of 1758, the disease raged among the tribes of Michigan, reaching epidemic proportions in the villages along the Saint Joseph. Although such chiefs as Ninivois and Nanaquiba survived, many other Potawatomi leaders who had supported the French perished.[56]

The epidemic disrupted the western tribes, and their frustration was fanned by a renewed shortage of trade goods. In July, 1758, British forces captured Louisbourg, tightening the naval blockade at the mouth of the Saint Lawrence, and in August, Lieutenant Colonel John Bradstreet destroyed Fort Frontenac, the French supply center on Lake Ontario. The fall of Fort Frontenac not only cut off provisions from the Potawatomis, but also isolated Fort Duquesne, forcing the French to abandon the post at the forks of the Ohio.

Wracked by disease and discouraged by the French defeats, few Potawatomis journeyed east during the summer of 1758. Although a small war party from Detroit raided into Pennsylvania, most of the warriors remained in their villages, recuperating from smallpox and hunting for their families. Powder was in short supply, and the Potawatomis were hard pressed to provide adequate food for their women and children. But in the fall they harvested a good corn crop, and their spirits improved. Although the French military situation continued to deteriorate, Potawatomi warriors spent the winter of 1758–59 making plans to again assist Onontio.[57]

During June, 1759, a war party left Detroit for western Pennsylvania, where they attacked a supply train and inflicted about forty casualties on the British. Meanwhile, other Potawatomis accompanied Ottawas and Chippewas to Fort Niagara, where Captain Francis Pouchot was attempting to defend the post against a force of British and Iroquois led by General John Prideaux. In late June the Potawatomis served Pouchot as scouts, reporting upon Prideaux's advance and carrying requests for additional reinforcements to French posts at Venango and Presque Isle. Although the Iroquois made a concerted effort to detach the western tribesmen from the French, the Potawatomis refused, stating that their fathers always had been the foremost friends of the French and that they would not break the alliance.[58]

In mid-July, after Prideaux's army surrounded Fort Niagara, many Potawatomis slipped away to guide a French relief force dispatched from Presque Isle and Venango. Although Prideaux was killed when an artillery shell prematurely exploded, William Johnson led the British army against the relief column, soundly defeating the Potawatomis and their allies. Most of the French officers were either killed or taken prisoner, but the Indians escaped, retreating along the shores of Lake Erie. On July 25, 1759, Johnson captured Fort Niagara, isolating French posts in the west.[59]

Johnson's victory at Niagara and the British capture of Quebec in September had a profound effect on the Potawatomis. For two years they had suffered from an acute shortage of trade goods, and the British victories caused them to reassess their alliance. During the summer of 1759, many of the western tribes deserted the French, and in August, George Croghan met with warriors from eight tribes at Pittsburgh. Although the Potawatomis still were allied to Onontio, many warriors from the villages near Detroit believed the French had lost the conflict, and when Croghan opened the conference, eight Potawatomis, led by Opewas, were in attendance. Neither Opewas nor his companions spoke formally at the council, but they watched closely as tribe after tribe made peace with the British. When the conference ended, the Potawatomis returned to Detroit, but during the winter of 1759–60 they sent messengers to the British in Pennsylvania, asking that British traders be sent to their villages.[60]

The French opposed the Potawatomi defection, but they were powerless to stop it. Although French officers at Detroit spread rumors of the impending arrival of massive French armies, they no longer could supply the Indians with trade goods, and the Potawatomis desperately needed powder. Warriors from Detroit continued to meet with the British in Pittsburgh, asking for British traders and receiving British gifts. Croghan assured the Potawatomis that the British soon would occupy the Great Lakes to "protect and lay open a free and uninterrupted Trade for You and for all Nations," and in August, 1760, Wabanum (White Dog) and four other Potawatomi warriors attended a multitribal council in Pittsburgh, where they informed Croghan they would welcome the British to Michigan.[61]

In November, 1760, a British expedition commanded by Major Rogers occupied Detroit. The neighboring Potawatomis, Ottawas, and Hurons welcomed the British, and on December 3 the British officers met with the Indians to discuss the new state of affairs in the west. Croghan had accompanied the British force, and he assured the Potawatomis that British traders would operate at Detroit as long as the Indians remained peaceful. He asked them to give up any remaining British prisoners and then introduced Captain Donald Campbell as the new commander of the fort. Campbell also asked the Indians to remain at peace and requested that they supply his garrison with meat, offering to pay in powder and lead.[62]

The Indians gave their reply in early December. On December 4, Achonenave of the Hurons spoke for all three tribes, assuring the British that the Indians had given up all prisoners except those who refused to return. On the following day, Ninivois, who had led the

Potawatomis at Fort William Henry, opened the conference by asking the British to increase the supply of low-priced trade goods at Detroit. He agreed to treat all the white inhabitants of Detroit as his "brothers" and requested that a large Indian council be held during the following spring so that a formal peace could be made by all the western tribes.[63]

The conference ended on December 5, and the British settled down at Detroit as the first step in their occupation of the western Great Lakes. For the first time in almost a century, part of the Potawatomis were nominally allied with white men other than Onontio. The Detroit Potawatomis realized that French military power in North America had been broken. They also were aware that Onontio no longer could supply them with the trade goods they so desperately needed. Anxious to sample the beneficence of their new British father, the Potawatomis at Detroit willingly made friends with Campbell and his garrison. They hoped that British trade would restore the prosperity of their homeland.

Yet the Saint Joseph Potawatomis remained relatively untouched by the new British presence in the west. The onrushing winter kept Rogers from occupying the Lake Michigan posts, and although the French garrison abandoned Fort Saint Joseph and fled to Illinois, no British garrison replaced them. Moreover, many *coureurs de bois* had settled among the Saint Joseph tribesmen, and the French traders continued to exert an anti-British influence. Unlike their kinsmen at Detroit, the Saint Joseph Potawatomis had not visited Croghan in Pennsylvania, and when the British occupied Detroit, the Saint Joseph chiefs sent no delegates to meet them. All the Potawatomis were desperately short of trade goods and ammunition, but the villages along the Saint Joseph and at Chicago remained more closely tied to the French and less willing to desert Onontio for a new father.

Fishing by Torchlight, by Paul Kane. Kane's painting of Indians spearing fish on the Fox River in Wisconsin illustrates a fishing technique widely used by the Potawatomis and neighboring tribes. *Courtesy Royal Ontario Museum.*

The bark-covered Algonquian summer house was a traditional type of dwelling used by the Potawatomis and other tribes in the Old Northwest. *Courtesy National Archives*

Coe-coosh, or The Hog, by Paul Kane. The clothing and hair of this warrior from Wisconsin reflect styles common among the more northern Potawatomis. *Courtesy Stark Museum of Art, Orange, Texas*

D'Mouche-kee-kee-awh, by George Winter. This wealthy Potawatomi woman is proudly displaying the silver earrings and brooches so popular among members of her tribe. *Courtesy Tippecanoe County Historical Society*

Indian Burial Ground, by George Winter. The miniature grave house in Winter's painting was commonly used by the Potawatomis in their burials. *Courtesy Tippecanoe County Historical Society*

Robert Cavalier, Sieur de La Salle, won many friends among the Potawatomis at Green Bay. *Courtesy Illinois State Historical Library*

During the French and Indian War the Marquis de Montcalm led many
Potawatomi warriors in campaigns against Fort William Henry. *Courtesy Public Archives of Canada*

Col. George Rogers Clark's Conference with the Indians at Cahokia, 1778, by Ezra Winter. During the summer and fall of 1778 Clark met with Siggenauk and other Potawatomis to enlist their aid against the British. *Courtesy Fine Arts Commission, National Archives*

Clark's March against Vincennes Across the Wabash River, Through Wilderness and Flood, by Ezra Winter. The winter march across Illinois enabled Clark to surprise British forces at Vincennes and to capture Lieutenant Governor Henry Hamilton, British commander in the Old Northwest. *Courtesy Fine Arts Commission, National Archives*

St. Clair's Defeat, by C. W. Jeffery. The 1791 victory by the northwestern tribes over St. Clair was the most disastrous defeat ever suffered by American military forces at the hands of Indians. *Courtesy Ohio His torical Society*

The Battle of Fallen Timbers, by W. W. Clarke. Anthony Wayne's victory on the Maumee in August, 1794, temporarily crushed the military power of the northwestern tribes. *Courtesy Ohio Historical Society*

Braddock's Defeat, by E. Deming. Ironically, Potawatomi hesitancy to attack Braddock on July 8, 1755, contributed to the successful ambush of the British by the French and their allies on the following day. *Courtesy State Historical Society of Wisconsin*

The Signing of the Treaty of Greenville, by H. C. Christy. In Christy's painting Anthony Wayne is standing just to the right of the treaty table. William Clark and William Henry Harrison can be seen over his left shoulder. William Wells, dressed in buckskin, stands at the left of the table interpreting the speech of Little Turtle. Keesass, a Potawatomi chief from the Wabash, is signing the treaty. *Courtesy Ohio Historical Society*

Shabbona (Burly Shoulders), an Ottawa, married a Potawatomi woman and rose to prominence among his wife's people. An active opponent of the Americans during the War of 1812, in the postwar period Shabbona urged the Potawatomis to cooperate with their white neighbors. *Courtesy Illinois State Museum*

Canoku (Fat Woman), wife of Shabbona, survived the War of 1812 and the removal period. She drowned in Mazon Creek, near Morris, Illinois, on November 30, 1864. *Courtesy Chicago Historical Society*

Battle of Tippecanoe, from a painting by Chappel. Many Potawatomis supported the Shawnee Prophet's ill-fated attack on William Henry Harrison's army in November, 1811. *Courtesy Indiana Historical Society*

4. Partisans
of Pontiac

The Potawatomi speeches to British officials at Detroit during the fall of 1761 reflected the key to British occupation of the Northwest. The Indians were desperately short of trade goods. Although the French had been hard pressed to supply the western tribes with goods during the past two years, they had shared available lead and powder with the Indians, and the Potawatomis expected similar generosity from the British. Moreover, the French maintained a camaraderie with the Potawatomis and treated them as equals. They lavished gifts upon tribal leaders, entertaining them as honored guests worthy of great respect and deference. The Potawatomis expected similar treatment from the British; indeed, they expected the British to be even more generous with presents, for in the past the British always had tempted them with more durable and less expensive trade goods.

Yet the British soon fell short of Potawatomi expectations. There were few trade goods at Detroit, and the approaching winter kept British traders from reaching the isolated post. Powder was in short supply, and the British even refused to issue rum to the Indians, afraid that the fiery liquid might make the tribesmen unmanageable. To add insult to injury, General Jeffrey Amherst, the British military commander in America, ordered that presents to Indians should be limited and encouraged his officers to economize in entertaining Indian guests. Unfamiliar with frontier politics, Amherst considered the presentation of gifts to be a wasteful expense and hoped to force the tribesmen to become self-sufficient through the fur trade. Although such experienced agents as William Johnson and George Croghan warned against this policy, the general persisted, and British hospitality declined.[1]

Fortunately for the British, Detroit was isolated from the east, and Campbell acted independently of Amherst's directive. Fearing the "fatal consequences" of Amherst's policy, Campbell continued to parcel out his limited supply of trade goods and powder to the Potawatomis and neighboring tribes. In December, 1760, Campbell wrote to Henry Bouquet, a fellow officer: "The Indians here are in great distress for want of ammunition. I have had two of the Tribes that depend upon Michilimakinac that came at a great distance—they were absolutely starving, as their whole subsistence depends upon it. I was obliged to give them what I could spare."[2]

Campbell's disobedience served the British well. By 1761 the Senecas already were disenchanted with British supremacy in the west and fomented a conspiracy among the tribes of Ohio and Detroit. During the spring, they sent war belts to the Delawares and Shawnees, proposing attacks on Fort Pitt, Presque Isle, Venango, and Niagara. They also sent messengers to the Potawatomis, Hurons, Ottawas, and Chippewas, encouraging them to attack the British at Detroit.[3]

The Seneca overtures to the Potawatomis fell upon deaf ears. The Potawatomis and other Detroit tribes were grateful for Campbell's limited generosity, and when the Seneca messengers invited them to meet with Seneca chiefs at Sandusky, the Detroit tribes refused. They informed the messengers that they had no intention of traveling to Lake Erie, but if the Seneca chiefs would come to Detroit, they would meet with them in the Huron village. The Senecas were anxious for the cooperation of the Potawatomis and their allies, and during the first week of July, a delegation of Seneca chiefs arrived in Detroit. On July 3, 1761, two Seneca chiefs, Teaatoriance and Gayachiouton, met with the Detroit tribes and urged them to attack the British. After listening to the Senecas' appeal, the Detroit tribes informed the chiefs that they would give a formal reply on the following day.[4]

To the Senecas' astonishment, on the following morning the Potawatomis and their neighbors notified the visiting chiefs that they wished to deliver their answer at the British fort in the presence of Campbell. When the British and Indians had assembled, the bewildered Senecas were forced to admit their conspiracy to Campbell, who warned them that their plans could lead only to "ruin and destruction." The Detroit tribes concluded the council by formally rejecting the Seneca conspiracy. The Potawatomis and their neighbors warned the Senecas not to attack the British, or the Detroit tribes would "interpose to put a stop to your proceedings." Humiliated, the Senecas meekly promised to keep the peace.[5]

The refusal of the Detroit tribes caused the Seneca conspiracy to collapse. Campbell's actions during the previous winter had convinced the Potawatomis that the British intended to supply them with the provisions necessary for daily life, and the Indians assumed that the shortage in trade goods would be remedied as soon as the British occupied the west in force. To the Detroit tribes, the Seneca conspiracy was premature; they still believed that British traders would flock to their villages, and British trade goods would fill their lodges.

At first, their assumptions seemed correct. In the fall of 1760, when the British first had occupied Detroit, Ninivois had asked that a multitribal council be held to formalize the peace in the west. By the summer of 1761 the British also were anxious for such a meeting. In August, Croghan arrived at Detroit, where he informed the Potawatomis and other tribes that William Johnson and Major Henry Gladwin soon would arrive with a large force of soldiers. Gladwin would assume command at Detroit, and the troops would complete the British occupation of western posts at Michilimackinac, Green Bay, and Saint Joseph. As a reward for their loyalty against the Senecas, Croghan gave each of the tribes a keg of rum. The Indian agent hoped the rum would make them more receptive to Johnson, for he knew that Johnson carried news that would antagonize the tribesmen.[6]

Johnson arrived at Detroit in September, and like Croghan, he distributed rum and gifts to the Potawatomis. Although he thanked the Detroit tribes for their fidelity, Johnson made no mention of ammunition or trade goods, two subjects which were the key to Indian relations in the west. Johnson's reticence was understandable. En route to Detroit, he had received orders from Amherst to further limit presents and ammunition to the tribesmen. Johnson was aware of the Indians' dependence upon such merchandise and was afraid to tell them the truth. Although he met with the Potawatomis and their neighbors for several days, Johnson did not mention Amherst's new policy.[7]

While Johnson was meeting with the Potawatomis at Detroit, Captain Henry Balfour led a force of 120 men towards Michilimackinac to occupy the post for the British. Balfour reached the island on September 28 and staffed the fort with 29 men before leaving for Wisconsin. He arrived at Green Bay early in October. Balfour left 18 men at the post on Green Bay and then proceeded down the shore of Lake Michigan to the Saint Joseph River. The old French fort and mission on the Saint Joseph occupied land on the east bank of the river, within modern Niles Township, Berrien County, Michigan. At Fort Saint Joseph, Balfour assigned a garrison of 15 men under the command of Ensign Francis Schlosser. In November, 1761, Balfour and the remainder of his party returned overland to Detroit.[8]

Ensign Schlosser faced a difficult task at Fort Saint Joseph. Although they agreed to the British occupation of the fort, the Saint Joseph Potawatomis did not welcome British traders into their villages. French officials in Illinois still considered the Saint Joseph warriors to be "the most faithful to our interests of all the Indians," and many Saint Joseph Potawatomis resented the British presence in their homeland. Moreover, the French mixed-blood traders among the Saint Joseph villages were eager to supply the Potawatomis through French merchants in Illinois. Led by Louis Chevalier, a French trader married to a Potawatomi woman, the French community on the Saint Joseph was afraid to openly oppose the British, but many disliked the British garrison and spread rumors that the French king would send a new army into the west. Chevalier played a waiting game, maintaining his ties with the Potawatomis but taking measures to ingratiate himself with the British. Meanwhile, Schlosser failed in his attempts to enforce British trading regulations, and French influence remained strong.[9]

If the Detroit Potawatomis believed that Johnson's generosity at the council in September, 1761, was indicative of future British policy, they were mistaken. During January, 1762, Amherst issued another order further limiting presents to the tribes and ordering his western officers to suppress the rum trade. Commanders in the west ignored the orders as best they could, including the costs of Indian presents in the requisitions for their garrisons. At Detroit, Campbell continued to sparingly share trade goods and ammunition with the Potawatomis,, but he complained to Bouquet:

> The General says the Crown is to be noe longer at the expense of maintaining the Indians, that they may very well live by their hunting, and desires to keep them scarce of powder. I should be glad to know what to doe in that respect. I am certain if the Indians in this country had the least hint that we intended to prevent them from the use of Ammunition it would be impossible to keep them quiet. I dare not trust even the Interpreters with the secret.[10]

Yet Campbell's attempt to keep Amherst's policy a secret failed. During the spring of 1762, the Potawatomis continued to suffer from a shortage of trade goods, and British attempts to stop the rum trade only aggravated the problem. In the following summer the Saint Joseph Potawatomis learned just how frugal the British had become. On August 7, 1762, Thomas Hutchins, a British Indian agent, arrived at the Potawatomi villages in western Michigan. Earlier in the summer Hutchins had been dispatched by Croghan to journey among the tribes of Lakes Huron and Michigan to sample Indian opinion of British policy. When Hutchins reached the Saint Joseph, he met with the Potawatomis but failed to distribute the customary rum and presents. Offended by what they considered to be a serious breach of etiquette, the Potawatomis asked Hutchins why he had no presents "to keep their women and children from the cold." In reply, Hutchins expounded upon the benefits of British Indian policy, but he noticed that his audience expressed "great uneasiness," and on the following day he wisely left the Potawatomi villages.[11]

Although the summer of 1762 passed quietly, the Potawatomis at Detroit began to doubt the wisdom of their new allegiance to the British. They now realized that even though Onontio often could not supply them with adequate provisions, his commanders in the west had been willing to share what was available. In contrast, the British, who always had tempted them with large quantities of ammunition and rum, refused to share any of their vast wealth with the Indians. War belts circulated among the Miamis, Shawnees, and Delawares, and during August, two Frenchmen from Illinois met with the Detroit Potawatomis and other tribes in the Ottawa village on the Detroit River. Although the details of this meeting remain unknown, it did not bode well for the British.[12]

Other events emerged which also moved the Potawatomis towards war. In the upper Ohio Valley a prophet, who preached a nativistic doctrine and predicted that war with the whites would purge the tribes of all their problems, appeared among the Delaware. The Senecas again were seething over white advancement onto their hunting grounds, and at Detroit, Pontiac, who possessed the ability to channel red resentment toward meaningful goals, emerged as an important leader among the Ottawas. Rumors of a spreading conspiracy filtered from the Old Northwest during the fall of 1762, and although British Indian agents were concerned, they were not alarmed. In Pennsylvania, George Croghan believed the tribes to be too disunited to pose a serious threat, but he underestimated the resentment of the Indians. He also underestimated Pontiac. The Ottawa chieftain spent the winter of 1762–63 agitating the Detroit tribes against the British.[13]

By the spring of 1763, Pontiac's endeavors produced results. On April 27 the Potawatomis, the Ottawas, and part of the Hurons met with the Ottawa leader on the Ecorse River about ten miles southwest of the British fortress. Pontiac informed his audience that he had received war belts from the French king, who wanted the tribesmen to attack the British. Pontiac also reminded the Potawatomis and others of the hardships they had suffered at the hands of the British and expounded upon the visions of the Delaware Prophet.[14]

The council was a success. The Detroit Potawatomis and those Hurons led by Takay eagerly joined in the Ottawa's conspiracy. The Potawatomis near Detroit numbered about 150 warriors and were led by Ninivois, who admired the Ottawa chief and was willing to follow his leadership. On May 5 the Potawatomis again met with Pontiac and finalized their plans for an attack on the British fort. The meeting took place in the Potawatomi village, and the women and children were sent away to insure security. Pontiac informed the Potawatomis and other Indians that he had sent belts to the Chippewas at Saginaw and to other villages of Ottawas in northern Michigan. The Indians decided that on May 7, Pontiac and sixty Ottawa warriors would enter the fort and ask to meet with the British officers. The Indians planned to carry knives under their blankets, and they also plotted to hide sawed-off muskets under the blankets of some women who would accompany them. At a prearranged signal, the Ottawas intended to attack the garrison and seize control of the fort. Meanwhile, the Potawatomis and Hurons would establish ambushes downstream from Detroit to prevent any reinforcements from reaching the fort from Lake Erie.[15]

The plot failed. Major Henry Galdwin learned of the Indian plans from an informer. On May 7, when Pontiac entered the fort, he found the garrison under arms and ready for any emergency. Realizing that their plot was discovered, the disgruntled Ottawas left the post without striking a blow. On the following day, to reinforce an illusion of normality, the Potawatomis and other Indians staged a lacrosse game. Yet when Pontiac attempted to meet with Gladwin and assure him that the Indians wished the British no harm, Gladwin refused to admit the chief into the fort. Finally, on

May 9 Pontiac abandoned the subterfuge and launched a general attack on Fort Detroit and on British settlers in the region.[16]

Since Ninivois had concentrated his warriors downstream from Detroit, the Potawatomis did not take part in the initial attacks on the British. On May 10, however, Potawatomi warriors scattered through the forest west of Fort Detroit intercepted two messengers arriving from Fort Saint Joseph. They delivered their prisoners to the Ottawas, who confiscated the dispatches and then killed the messengers. The Potawatomis also stationed a party of warriors close to the fort to keep the British under surveillance and prevent them from visiting nearby French houses and securing provisions.[17]

On May 12 Pontiac launched another general attack on Fort Detroit. The Potawatomis, assisted by the Hurons, assaulted the south side of the pallisade, while the Ottawas attacked the north. Yet the venture produced few results. The British defenders kept the Indians away from the walls, and although a desultory fire was kept up by both sides throughout the day, neither the British nor the Indians suffered any casualties. The Indians also fired on two British sloops that were moored opposite the fort in the Detroit River, but they were unable to inflict much damage.[18]

Failing to capture Fort Detroit through subterfuge or assault, Pontiac decided upon siege. On May 18 he met in council with the Potawatomis and other tribes, dispatching messengers to Fort de Chartres, the French post in Illinois, to ask for French officers to conduct the lengthy operation. The messengers were also instructed to inform the Miamis of the attack on Detroit and to urge them to assault British posts at Fort Miamis and at Ouiatanon.[19]

While Ninivois' warriors were besieging Fort Detroit, their kinsmen on the Saint Joseph planned a similar attack on the British post in western Michigan. Shortly after the first assault on Gladwin's garrison, Ninivois sent messengers to the Saint Joseph Potawatomis asking them to take up the hatchet against the British. The messengers also carried the details of Pontiac's initial plot, and the Ottawa's plans were used by Washee (Swan), a war chief among the Saint Joseph villages.[20]

On the morning of May 25, 1763, the Saint Joseph Potawatomis informed Schlosser that several of their relatives from Detroit had arrived and wished to pay their respects to the British commander. Flattered, Schlosser agreed to welcome the visitors, but before the

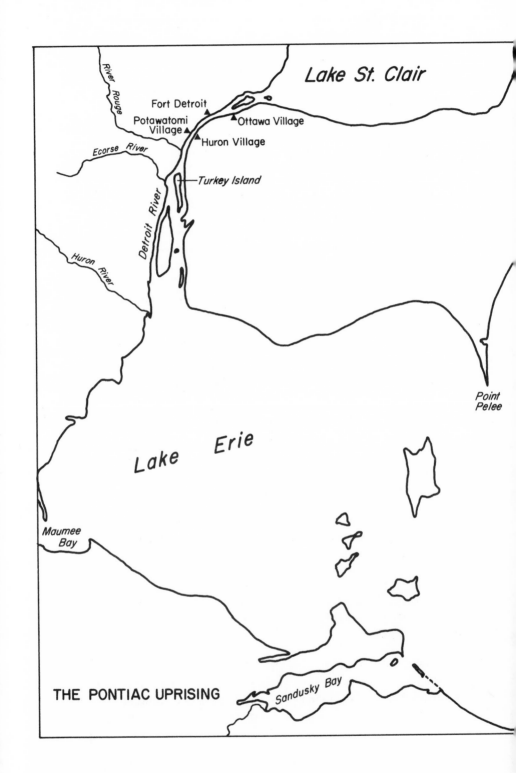

River Rouge

Fort Detroit

Potawatomi Village

Ottawa Village

Huron Village

Ecorse River

Turkey Island

Detroit River

Huron River

Lake St. Clair

Point Pelee

Lake Erie

Maumee Bay

THE PONTIAC UPRISING

Sandusky Bay

Potawatomis returned, a trader rushed into Schlosser's quarters, warning the commander that the Potawatomis had plotted against the British and that he was in danger. Schlosser rushed to the barracks to warn the garrison, but when he reached his destination, he found the barracks full of Potawatomi warriors, who were talking with the soldiers. Since the Potawatomis frequently entered the fort to trade or carry on other business, the soldiers were not suspicious and had welcomed the Indians into their quarters. Although the Potawatomis seemed friendly, Schlosser ordered his sergeant to call the men to arms and then hurried back to meet the delegation of Detroit warriors. When he returned to his quarters, he found the Potawatomis already had arrived, but before he could question them about the purpose of their visit, screams rang out from the barracks. Schlosser attempted to defend himself, but he was easily captured by the Potawatomi warriors.[21]

The Potawatomi attack was a complete success. Within two minutes of the initial assault in the barracks, Washee's warriors swarmed through the fort, killing ten soldiers and capturing three others. The Potawatomis then seized all ammunition and trade goods stored in the fort by the garrison or British traders. Two such traders who were operating in the area also were the target of the Potawatomi attack, but they were saved from death by Chevalier, who hid them in his house. After the attack, the Potawatomis carried Schlosser and the other prisoners to their village, where plans were made to take the captives to Detroit.[22]

Fort Saint Joseph was not the only target of the expanding Indian rebellion. On May 16 Fort Sandusky had fallen to a force of Ottawas and Hurons, and on May 27 the Miamis captured Fort Miami, on the headwaters of the Maumee River. During June the revolt spread to other tribes. After Fort Ouiatanon was taken on June 1 by a mixed party of Miamis, Kickapoos, and Mascoutens, the British post at Michilimackinac fell one day later. At Michilimackinac the Chippewas and Sacs gained entrance to the post during a lacrosse game and easily overcame the garrison. The fall of Michilimackinac caused the British to evacuate Fort Edward Augustus at Green Bay, so that by the end of June there were no British posts west of Detroit.[23]

The uprising also spread to the east. The Delawares and Shawnees besieged Fort Pitt, while the Senecas swept through western Pennsylvania. During the middle of June a Seneca war party completely overran Fort Venango and then turned north to strike at Fort Le

Boeuf. Although part of the garrison at Le Boeuf escaped, the Indians burned the fort to the ground. The Senecas then attacked Presque Isle. Aided by a force of Indians from Detroit, which included some Potawatomis, the Senecas opened fire upon the British fort on June 20. On the next day the fort surrendered, and the British inside were taken prisoner and divided among the tribes which contributed warriors to the attack.[24]

While the tide of red rebellion surged through the west, Ninivois' warriors at Detroit continued to aid Pontiac in the siege of the British garrison. During the last week of May, Potawatomi warriors fired upon a British construction party in an unsuccessful effort to keep the British from building a portable bastion to protect soldiers as they traveled between the fort and the river. They also joined with other warriors in a futile attempt to capture one of the British sloops in the Detroit River. Yet Potawatomi failures at Detroit soon were counterbalanced by a spectacular success on the shores of Lake Erie. On May 13 Lieutenant Abraham Cuyler and ninety-seven men left Fort Niagara to convoy a fleet of ten provision-laden bateaux to Detroit. The Indians learned that the British were expecting the bateaux, and late in May a large war party of Potawatomis and Hurons journeyed eastward along Lake Erie, hoping to intercept them. On May 28, 1763, the Potawatomis spied Cuyler's fleet as it approached Point Pelee, a forested finger of land stretching into Lake Erie about twenty-five miles east of the mouth of the Detroit River.[25]

Cuyler was unaware that fighting had erupted at Detroit, and late in the evening he ordered his men to beach their bateaux on the sandy shore along the west side of the point. While many of the soldiers were preparing their camp, a man and a boy from Cuyler's command walked along the beach in search of firewood. As they wandered away from their companions, the boy was seized by Indians, but the man escaped and ran back toward the bateaux, shouting a warning. Unknown to the British, the Potawatomis and Hurons had followed the fleet along the shore and now lay in ambush among the trees about 150 feet from the water. Realizing that they had been discovered, the Indians swarmed from the tree line and rushed down on the camp. The British attempted to form a line of defense, but the Potawatomis and Hurons were in their midst before they could maneuver. Surprised by the attack, and confused in the darkness, the soldiers broke and ran for the bateaux, which they tried to launch to safety on Lake Erie.[26]

Most of the British failed to reach the boats. Of the ninety-seven men in Cuyler's command, fifty-seven were either killed or captured. The survivors crossed Lake Erie to Sandusky, where they found the British fort had been burned, then journeyed on to Presque Isle. The Potawatomis captured eight bateaux, several prisoners, and a large supply of provisions. They placed the prisoners and provisions in the captured bateaux and rowed the vessels back to Detroit, where they gave part of the prisoners and contraband to the Ottawas.[27]

A few days after the warriors returned from Lake Erie, a party of Saint Joseph Potawatomis arrived at Detroit, bringing Schlosser and six other prisoners. The Saint Joseph Potawatomis learned that two warriors from their villages, Big Ears and Nokaming (Burrowing Wolf), had been captured by the British. The events surrounding the capture are unknown, but Ninivois informed Washee that Gladwin held two Potawatomis prisoner in the British fortress. Concerned over the safety of their imprisoned kinsmen, the Saint Joseph Potawatomis secured the assistance of Antoine Gamelin, a French trader from Detroit, and attempted to obtain the release of the two prisoners. On June 10 Gamelin and a delegation of Saint Joseph warriors approached Fort Detroit, proposing to trade Schlosser for Big Ears and Nokaming.[28]

Gladwin refused their proposal. He demanded that the Saint Joseph Potawatomis give up all seven prisoners in exchange for the two captured warriors. The Saint Joseph warriors returned to the Potawatomi village on the Detroit River, but on the following day they came back to the fort and again tried to bargain with Gladwin. The British commander wisely permitted the Potawatomis to speak with the captives, who pleaded with their kinsmen to secure their release. Touched by the plight of the prisoners, the Potawatomis begged Gladwin to release them, stating that the Saint Joseph villages held no animosity toward the British and had been forced into the rebellion by pressure from Pontiac. Gladwin scoffed at the Potawatomi statement, asking them if they were slaves to Pontiac and had no wills of their own. He also warned the Potawatomis that the rebellion eventually would fail and bring disaster to all those who opposed the British crown.[29]

Unable to obtain the release of their kinsmen, the Saint Joseph

Potawatomis returned to Ninivois' village on the Detroit River, where they soon became involved in a dispute with Pontiac. The quarrel resulted from several causes. The Saint Joseph warriors had been so singularly successful in their capture of Fort Saint Joseph that they were disappointed in Pontiac's lack of success at Detroit. Although Ninivois acquiesced in the Ottawa's leadership, Washee was jealous of Pontiac and considered him to be high-handed. On June 11, Washee's jealousy was aggravated when a French trader, Jacques Lacelle, arrived from Montreal with two canoes full of trade goods. As the Frenchman approached Detroit, he was stopped by a party of Saint Joseph Potawatomis, who demanded that Lacelle give them two kegs of wine. Lacelle grudgingly complied, but when Pontiac heard of the incident, he ordered the trader to bring the rest of his goods to the Ottawa village, where Pontiac would "protect" them from the Potawatomis. But after the merchandise had been transported, the Ottawa chief seized the remaining five kegs of wine and distributed them to his Ottawa tribesmen. A drunken brawl resulted, in which several British prisoners were killed and their bodies thrown into the Detroit River. Pontiac's actions and the resulting slaughter of the British prisoners angered the Potawatomis. Since Gladwin still held Big Ears and Nokaming captive, Washee feared that the British would seek revenge against his kinsmen.[30]

Four days later, on June 15, Washee made another bid to secure one of the Potawatomis' release. During the morning, he brought Schlosser and two other prisoners to the fort and offered to trade them for Big Ears. Although Nokaming was disliked by many of his fellow tribesmen, who considered him to be shiftless and unreliable, Big Ears was highly respected and had many relatives among the Saint Joseph villages. When Nokaming learned of the proposal, he confirmed the Potawatomi assessment. Before the exchange could be made, Nokaming met privately with Gladwin and informed him that Big Ears was a prominent leader whom the Potawatomis greatly admired. If he were released, the Potawatomis would be far less anxious to trade other prisoners for a warrior so many of them disliked. Therefore, after Gladwin obtained the three British prisoners, he released Nokaming instead of Big Ears. Disappointed in the exchange, Washee was forced to accept the wily Nokaming and then returned to the Potawatomi village.[31]

Frustrated in their attempts to obtain Big Ears, the Potawatomis returned to Pontiac's more militant position against the British. Undoubtedly their decision was influenced by news of the Chippewa victory at Michilimackinac, but they also were enticed to join with the Ottawas in an attack on what appeared to be an easy target. On June 21 the Indians at Detroit learned that the sloop *Michigan* was returning from Niagara and soon would enter the Detroit River. Pontiac mustered the Indians at Detroit and instructed them to build log bastions on Turkey Island, from which they could ambush the sloop as it passed up the river. The *Michigan* entered the river late in the afternoon on June 23, and by 6:00 P.M. it had ascended as far as the island. While passing the island however, the wind fell, and the sloop was forced to drop anchor. The Indians were jubilant. They had held their fire and now believed that the British aboard the ship were unaware of their presence. After dark the Indians paddled their canoes toward the vessel, hoping to take her by surprise, but confident that their superior numbers would give them a victory under any situation.[32]

They were mistaken. Unknown to the warriors, the sloop carried a reinforcement of fifty-five soldiers, who were hidden below deck. A lookout aboard ship spotted the oncoming canoes, and the soldiers silently filed on deck, where they remained hidden behind the gunwales. The first indication the approaching Potawatomis had that their assault was discovered was the crash of a wooden mallet striking the deck. The next clue was the last thing that many of the warriors ever saw. The hammer blow was the signal for a volley of musket and cannon fire which swept through the approaching canoes, killing fourteen Indians and wounding many others. Bewildered by their discovery, the Potawatomis frantically turned their canoes about and paddled for the refuge of Turkey Island. There they fired upon the sloop from the safety of the log barricades, but they failed to inflict much damage. On the following morning the wind remained calm, and the sloop was forced to weigh anchor and drop back into Lake Erie.[33]

The disastrous attack on the *Michigan* had a sobering effect on the Potawatomis' desire to continue the siege at Detroit. On June 30 the sloop finally sailed up the river and deposited both the reinforcements and the supplies at the British fortress. The Union Jack still flew over Fort Detroit, and Gladwin remained determined not to surrender. As the Potawatomis watched the troops go ashore, many warriors held serious doubts about the future of the rebellion. Meanwhile, French citizens of Detroit, who earlier had provided the Indians with both moral support and ammunition, now moved toward strict neutrality, claiming that the former French governor had instructed them to lay down their arms and accept the British.[34]

Wavering in their relationship with Pontiac, some of the Potawatomis decided to make a separate peace. During the first week of July, warriors from both the Detroit and Saint Joseph villages sent delegations to meet with Gladwin and inquire about ending the war. The Potawatomis stated that they had grown weary of the conflict and offered to return all prisoners and go home to their villages if the commander would release Big Ears. Envisioning an opportunity to split his enemies, Gladwin chided the Potawatomis for their futile attack against the sloop, but he promised to exchange prisoners and recommend amnesty if they would withdraw from the rebellion.[35]

On July 12, 1763, the Potawatomis returned to the fort with three prisoners, whom they proposed to exchange for Big Ears. Gladwin refused, since he knew there were additional captives in the Potawatomi village. Later in the day the Potawatomis reappeared with seven additional prisoners, including two British traders, Hugh Crawford and Chapman Abraham. They turned the captives over to Gladwin and he was about to release Big Ears when Abraham informed the commander that the Potawatomis still held other prisoners in their village. Gladwin then refused to give up his Potawatomi captive. Enraged by the refusal, the Potawatomis momentarily threatened Gladwin's life, but since they were under the guns of the fort, they reconsidered and angrily stalked back to their village.[36]

Gladwin's refusal to release Big Ears precipitated the last outburst of Potawatomi hostility at Detroit. The warriors spent the following day brooding in their village, and on the evening of July 13, a party of Potawatomis crept up to the fort under the cover of darkness and fired upon the sentinels. One soldier was mortally wounded and died the next day. Still angry, two weeks later the Potawatomis joined with Pontiac to oppose another party of British reinforcements.[37]

On July 6, 1763, Captain James Dalyell left Niagara with a force of 260 men. Crowded into twenty-two bateaux, Dalyell's party sailed along the southern shore of Lake Erie, where they burned the Huron village at Sandusky Bay, and then turned north toward the mouth of the Detroit River. Fortunately for Dalyell, a dense fog shrouded the Detroit region, and when he entered the river on the night of July 29, his movements were hidden from the Indians.

During the early morning hours of Friday, July 30, the British flotilla crept silently upstream, and their progress went unnoticed until they passed opposite the Potawatomi and Huron villages. There they were discovered, and while sleepy Potawatomis and Hurons hurried from their lodges to fire from the river bank, the British surged forward toward the safety of the fort. Finally, at dawn, the fog lifted, and Dalyell's force emerged out of the mist to land at their destination. The British suffered fifteen wounded, but Fort Detroit was measurably strengthened.[38]

Dalyell's arrival convinced the Potawatomis that Pontiac's rebellion had failed. Although the Ottawas, the Chippewas, and part of the Hurons kept up the siege, the Potawatomis withdrew from active warfare. They did not support Pontiac's victory over the British at the Battle of the Bloody Bridge, and during August the Detroit Potawatomis sent food and information about Pontiac's activities to the garrison. Since the Potawatomis refused to intercept any British vessels ascending the Detroit River, Pontiac was forced to move the Ottawa village to a new location near the mouth of the River Rouge in a futile attempt to guard the southern approach to the fort.[39]

In mid-August, Washee led most of the Saint Joseph Potawatomis back to their villages in western Michigan. One month later they returned to Detroit in another attempt to obtain Big Ears, but Gladwin refused to negotiate, and the hapless Potawatomi remained a prisoner. The British finally released him in November, 1763, after the rebellion was over.[40]

Meanwhile, the siege at Detroit dragged on. Although the Potawatomis no longer supported the rebellion, Pontiac still held the allegiance of other tribes. Yet the Ottawa chief's influence diminished as summer turned to fall and the Indians began to prepare for winter. During September, most of the Hurons withdrew from the uprising and made peace with the British. In mid-September the Chippewas also abandoned Pontiac and returned to their village at Saginaw. Even part of the Ottawas lost faith in the siege and approached the British, seeking a peaceful solution to the hostilities. Although Pontiac tried to continue the blockade, on October 29 he received the news that sounded the death knell of his rebellion. A message arrived from the French in Illinois informing the Indians that Britain and France had signed the Treaty of Paris. The French commander at Fort Chartres instructed all the tribes to "lay down their arms" and to "cease spilling the blood of your Brethern the

English." The siege had failed. During the first week in November, Pontiac and his Ottawa followers abandoned Detroit for the Maumee River in Ohio.[41]

In late October, 1763, the Detroit Potawatomis left their village on the Detroit River and established scattered hunting camps throughout southeastern Michigan. Part of the Saint Joseph Potawatomis also dispersed for the winter, but some of their resettlement was of a more permanent tenure. They earlier had erected villages in the Chicago region, but by 1763, Potawatomis from the Saint Joseph and Chicago joined with Sacs and Ottawas to form a new village near the mouth of the Milwaukee River, in southeastern Wisconsin. Other Saint Joseph Potawatomis continued to expand their occupancy down the Illinois River Valley, and in the winter of 1763–64 they established a new village a few miles below Lake Peoria.[42]

Although the Saint Joseph Potawatomis also learned of the Treaty of Paris, they received the message with indifference. Fort Saint Joseph remained deserted, and the nearby Potawatomi villages seemed immune from British military power. As soon as Big Ears returned from Detroit, many of the young warriors forgot their promises of peace and made plans to renew the war against the British. They were encouraged by several French traders and by a party of Delawares who arrived in their villages in November. The Delawares brought war belts and informed the Potawatomis that the Ohio tribes planned to renew the war in the spring. The Chippewas at Michilimackinac also urged the Potawatomis to again take up the hatchet, and young warriors listened eagerly. Nanaquiba, Washee, and Machiouquisse (Little Bad Man), a chief from Detroit, all counseled for peace, but their advice was ignored.[43]

The winter snow of 1763–64 kept the Saint Joseph warriors in their lodges, but it did not cool the desire of the young men to reopen the warfare. In March, 1764, a war party from the Saint Joseph swept through the Detroit region, killing livestock and stealing property. Ninivois' people refused to assist the raiders, and Gladwin dispatched a force of soldiers who overtook the Saint Joseph warriors in the forest. A skirmish took place, but neither side suffered casualties, and the Potawatomis slipped away after night fell.[44]

Encouraged by their success, the Saint Joseph warriors returned to Detroit on several occasions during the spring and summer of 1764. They failed to inflict any casualties upon the British garrison.

but they continued to kill livestock and captured several prisoners. Two Potawatomi warriors also were taken by Gladwin, who held them as hostages until the captured British were released.[45]

The Detroit Potawatomis opposed the raids and refused to take part in them. They feared that the British would retaliate against their people, and they did not reoccupy the old village on the Detroit River. In an effort to illustrate their desire for peace, they collected British prisoners held captive by other tribes and turned them over to Gladwin. The British commander reported favorably on their behavior, but Ninivois' people still remained fearful that they would be punished for supporting Pontiac, and in July, 1764, they declined an invitation to journey to Niagara and attend a British-sponsored Indian conference.[46]

Meanwhile, during the summer of 1764, the British launched two punitive expeditions against the tribes of Ohio. Colonel Henry Bouquet marched from Fort Pitt to strike Delaware and Shawnee villages along the Ohio River, while Colonel John Bradstreet sailed along the southern shore of Lake Erie for Detroit. Bradstreet was ordered to attack any Shawnees or Delawares he might encounter, but at Presque Isle he met in council with delegates from both tribes and arbitrarily signed a peace agreement with the Indians. The colonel then sailed to Detroit, where he sent messages to the Potawatomis, Ottawas, Chippewas, and Hurons, asking them to meet with him in September.[47]

Bradstreet hoped that Pontiac would attend the conference, but on September 5, 1764, when the Indians assembled, the Ottawa chief was absent. Also absent were Ninivois and Washee, the Potawatomi chiefs who had led their tribesmen against the British. Although both chiefs wished to make peace with Bradstreet, they still feared British punishment. Instead, the Potawatomis were represented by Nanaquiba and Kiouqua (Returning Bear). Wasson, a Chippewa chief from Saginaw, spoke for all the Indians and promised that the tribesmen would return all their prisoners. After the Indians swore allegiance to the British king, Bradstreet naïvely declared that peace had been restored in the west.[48]

Bradstreet's declaration was overly optimistic. En route to Detroit, he had dispatched Captain Thomas Morris down the Maumee-Wabash waterway to Illinois. Morris was ordered to make peace with all the tribes he encountered and to secure the assistance of French officers at Fort Chartres in pacifying the tribes in Illinois. Morris traveled no farther than the Miami village near modern

Fort Wayne before angry Miamis and Kickapoos forced him to flee to Michigan. Although he passed through friendly Potawatomi villages as he fled to Detroit, Morris reported that a party of hostile Shawnees and Delawares had preceeded him down the Wabash, urging the Wabash Indians to renew the war against Great Britain. The Delawares and Shawnees also visited the Saint Joseph Potawatomis, who received them warmly. Many of the younger warriors opposed Nanaquiba's conference with Bradstreet, and while the chief swore allegiance to King George at Detroit, his kinsmen danced the war dance on the Saint Joseph.[49]

During October and November, 1764, Colonel Henry Bouquet led a force of British regulars against the Shawnee and Delaware villages in Ohio, preventing the Indians from launching their planned attacks against the British. Unaware that the Shawnee and Delaware offensive had miscarried, some of the Saint Joseph warriors honored their promises to the two tribes and again struck at Detroit. Late in November they ambushed and killed two British soldiers near the River Rouge, slipping away before the garrison could retaliate.[50]

Anxious to convince the British that their people had no part in the affair, the Detroit Potawatomis hurried to the fort and informed the officers that the attack had been made by a few young warriors and did not reflect the wishes of the tribe. Machiouquisse volunteered to go to the Saint Joseph and bring back the young warriors responsible for the deaths if Colonel John Campbell, the new commander at Detroit, would treat the warriors mercifully. Late in January, 1765, Machiouquisse and a small delegation of Saint Joseph tribesmen returned to the British fortress. Machiouquisse could not convince the young warriors responsible for the killings to come to Detroit, but the Saint Joseph delegation contained Onanghisse and Peshibon, two minor chiefs, who assured Campbell that their people were opposed to the killings. The chiefs asserted that the attack had been perpetrated by irresponsible young warriors whom they would surrender later in the spring. They also promised to return certain British prisoners recently captured by other members of their villages. Campbell accepted their explanation upon condition that they leave two of their party behind as hostages. The Saint Joseph leaders protested, but eventually they surrendered two of their number before leaving for their villages.[51]

While the Saint Joseph Potawatomis were attempting to come to terms with the British, Pontiac was active in Illinois. After fleeing Detroit in the autumn of 1763, the Ottawa leader had established a temporary village on the Maumee River and then proceeded on to Illinois, where he attempted to form a new alliance against the British. During the winter of 1765, Pontiac sent war belts to the remnants of the Illinois Confederacy and to the Osages and Quapaws across the river in Spanish Louisiana. The Ottawa chief received encouragement from French creoles in Illinois, who also supplied the Indians with ammunition. Aware of Pontiac's activities, British officials realized they had to occupy Illinois if they wished to bring order to the west. In April, 1765, Lieutenant John Ross was dispatched from a British post at Mobile to Fort Chartres. Ross was ordered to meet with the French commander still in charge at Chartres and to make plans for a British occupation. Yet Ross encountered such hostility among the Indians in Illinois that he returned to the Gulf of Mexico without accomplishing his mission.[52]

Meanwhile, at Pittsburgh, George Croghan made plans to descend the Ohio River and meet with the Illinois tribes during May. Croghan's departure was delayed, so he sent Lieutenant Alexander Fraser and a small party of soldiers on ahead to Illinois to collect the Indians for the conference. Fraser arrived at Fort Chartres on April 17 and immediately found himself in danger. Pontiac tried to seize the British officer, but Louis Saint Ange, the French commander at the post, put Fraser under his personal protection. Yet two of Fraser's men were captured by Illinois warriors loyal to Pontiac, and the lieutenant was forced to ransom them by providing the Indians with a banquet of a roasted bullock and 130 pots of French brandy. Finally, however, Fraser and Saint Ange convinced Pontiac that British occupation of the Illinois country was inevitable, and the Ottawa chief agreed to meet with Croghan in council.[53]

On April 28 the growing peace in Illinois was shattered by the arrival of a war party of Saint Joseph Potawatomis. The Saint Joseph warriors had learned that Fraser was in Illinois, and they hoped to capture the officer and exchange him for the two hostages held by Campbell at Detroit. Fraser escaped the warriors by hiding in the French fort, but the Potawatomis seized several of the British soldiers and made plans to carry them to the Saint Joseph. Fortunately for the British, Pontiac intervened, informing the Potawatomis that Croghan soon would arrive and demanding that the soldiers be released. Outnumbered by the Ottawa's followers, the Potawatomis gave up the soldiers and apologized to Fraser. They also agreed to meet with Croghan.[54]

Yet Croghan never arrived at Fort Chartres. On his way down the Ohio he was captured by a party of Kickapoos and Mascoutens near the mouth of the Wabash River. The Indians carried Croghan up the Wabash to Vincennes and then on to their village near Ouiatanon. When Pontiac learned of Croghan's fate, he journeyed to the Wabash and secured the trader's release. Croghan then proposed to move the Indian conference from Fort Chartres to Detroit. Pontiac agreed and accompanied the British trader to Michigan.[55]

In September, 1765, Croghan met with many tribes at Detroit. The Saint Joseph Potawatomis did not attend the conference, but many of their kinsmen from the Detroit region were present. The Detroit Potawatomis promised to remain at peace, but they warned the British against any attempts to seize their homeland. They also agreed to attend a large multitribal conference in New York during the following year.[56]

Although the Saint Joseph Potawatomis failed to attend the initial conference at Detroit, a delegation of their chiefs and warriors arrived to meet with Croghan on September 25. They still failed to give up the warriors responsible for the raid on Detroit, but they did release two British prisoners, and the British reciprocated by freeing the Potawatomi hostages. The Saint Joseph leaders apologized for the actions of their young men and assured Croghan that they continued to counsel their warriors against attacking the British. They pleaded that since their French father had been overthrown, they had been "wandering in the dark like blind people," but they now planned to partake of the British "light." Croghan replied that their past conduct had been far from satisfactory and that the British had doubted their allegiance, but he now was convinced they were sincere. Yet he warned them to control their young warriors or face certain punishment. After accepting gifts of clothing, powder, vermillion, and rum, the Saint Joseph Potawatomis returned to their villages.[57]

During the following summer, Ninivois, Machiouquisse, and other Detroit Potawatomis accompanied Pontiac to Oswego to meet with William Johnson. After the usual ceremonies and series of speeches, the Detroit Potawatomis signed a treaty of peace and alliance with the British. Pontiac's rebellion was over, and the Ottawa chief kept the peace with the British. The Detroit Potawatomis did the same. Yet Nanaquiba, Washee, and the chiefs from the Saint Joseph did not attend the conference in New York. By the summer of 1766, their young men again had raided near Detroit, and they no longer were welcome at the British council. To many young warriors along the Saint Joseph, the menace of British military power was no more than an idle threat. Fort Saint Joseph remained unoccupied, and the British still cowered behind their walls at Detroit. French and Spanish traders from Louisiana visited the Potawatomi villages, and ammunition was plentiful. Moreover, although the great Pontiac had failed to conquer Detroit, the Saint Joseph tribesmen had easily captured the western fort. If Ninivois and Machiouquisse preferred to serve the British, that was their choice. But many of the western Potawatomis remained loyal to Onontio. The Potawatomi-British feud would continue.[58]

5. Serving Two Fathers

In the decade following Pontiac's rebellion, the Saint Joseph Potawatomis continued their dispersal to the south and west. The old
village near Fort Saint Joseph declined, although Petit Coeur de
Cerf, a small village a few miles upstream, remained in existence,
and Terre Coupe, a village at the Saint Joseph–Kankakee portage,
grew in population. Other Potawatomis left the Saint Joseph River
to establish new towns in Illinois. By 1768, Potawatomis were
securely settled in the Kankakee Valley, with villages near the site
of modern Kankakee and at the juncture of the Kankakee and Des
Plaines rivers. Although the British continued to refer to all of these
Indians as "Saint Joseph Potawatomis," many no longer lived in
the Saint Joseph Valley.[1]

As the Potawatomis scattered over a larger area, their clashes with
the British increased. Traditional village chiefs such as Nanaquiba
never had exercised much control over the young warriors, but as
many Potawatomis moved west into Illinois, they turned to new
leaders and refused to honor the earlier pledges of friendship to the
British. Moreover, the new Potawatomi villages in Illinois were
easily accessible to French and Spanish traders operating from
Louisiana. After the British occupation of Fort Chartres, many of
the former French citizens simply moved across the Mississippi to
Spanish territory, where they continued to carry on an intensive
trade with the Indians. Since the Potawatomi villages in northern
Illinois were far removed from British merchants, the creole
traders maintained a monopoly over the Indian trade. Unfortunately for the British, many of the French and Spanish traders used
all their influence to oppose closer Potawatomi-British ties. They
also endeavored to exclude all British traders from the Potawatomi
villages. Croghan and other British agents tried to counteract the

creole influence, but their efforts generally were unsuccessful.[2]

The western Potawatomi-British feud continued. In February, 1766, while Pontiac, Ninivois, and the British made plans for the peace conference in New York, Potawatomis from northern Illinois attacked two British soldiers cutting firewood near the mouth of the River Rouge. One soldier was killed instantly, and the other was taken captive and carried a few miles to the west before he also was slain. Campbell ordered a detachment of soldiers after the Potawatomis, but the Indians escaped. A few weeks later, in retaliation, a force of British soldiers ambushed another party of Potawatomis who were traveling to Detroit. Several Indians were injured, and the British took two warriors prisoner.[3]

Campbell was incensed over the outbreak of hostilities and suggested to Gage that an expedition be formed to attack the villages along the Saint Joseph and "put to death all Indians of Said Nation they may meet whether men, women, or Children." Before Gage could reply, Pontiac interceded for the captured Potawatomis, informing Campbell that they were not from the village that had sent the raiders to Detroit and asking that they be released. Campbell refused, so the Potawatomis in northern Illinois seized a British settler near Fort Chartres, and the old impasse over prisoner exchange began anew. Finally, in the fall of 1766, after the peace treaty in New York, both sides released their prisoners, but the Potawatomi-British quarrel continued.[4]

Violence flared again in the spring of 1767. During May a Potawatomi war party from the old village near Fort Saint Joseph crossed the Ohio to raid the Chickasaws. But near modern Memphis, Tennessee, they found an easier prey, intercepting a party of British traders en route to the Chickasaw villages. The Potawatomis killed three white men and took four prisoners. Two of the captives escaped, but the other two were carried back to the Saint Joseph, where Nanaquiba ransomed them and brought them to Detroit. In August a mixed delegation of Saint Joseph and Detroit chiefs met with Campbell and apologized for the raid, but the chiefs disclaimed any responsibility for the deaths, stating that they had warned their young men against attacking the British "with as good Advice as was Capable of before they went away." Although the old chiefs were telling the truth, their explanation did not satisfy the British.[5]

Anxious to end the warfare, British officials instructed George Croghan to travel to Michigan and assemble the Detroit Potawatomis. Croghan hoped to use his influence to urge the Detroit warriors to keep their western kinsmen at peace. The Indian agent met with the Potawatomis in November, 1767, but achieved little success. The Detroit Potawatomis admitted that the western tribesmen were anti-British, but claimed they had no control over them. Ironically, as if to emphasize the point, while Croghan was in council at Detroit, Potawatomi warriors on the Kankakee killed a British trader who dared to venture to their village. After tomahawking the merchant and plundering his goods, the assailants journeyed to the Saint Joseph, where they bragged that they "would not Suffer an English Man to come near their Place."[6]

The Potawatomi boast was not an idle threat. In the five years following Croghan's abortive conference at Detroit, warriors from northern Illinois and the Saint Joseph continued to prey upon any British trader unfortunate enough to encounter them. In 1768, Potawatomis from the Kankakee killed two other British traders, and warriors from the Saint Joseph captured a British soldier and his wife near Fort Chartres.[7] In 1771 they took another scalp in southern Illinois, and the following year two more British traders were killed in northern Indiana. By 1773 the British fur trade still was excluded from the lower Lake Michigan area, and General Thomas Gage complained to William Johnson: "Scarce a year passes that the Pouteatamies are not guilty of killing Some of the Traders and of course plundering their Effects, which it becomes absolutely Necessary to put a Stop to. . . ."[8]

During April, 1773, Johnson enlisted the aid of the Iroquois in a final attempt to bring peace. The British Indian agent persuaded the Senecas to send a message to the Saint Joseph and Illinois tribesmen, asking them to stop their attacks against the British and warning them that future incidents would bring Iroquois retaliation. The western Potawatomis received the Seneca message and sent one of their own in reply. Although the substance of the Potawatomi message is unknown, the Potawatomis evidently agreed to comply with the Seneca wishes, for attacks against British traders decreased. Yet other factors also turned the Potawatomi attention away from the British. In the early 1770's, tribesmen in Illinois became embroiled in a dispute with the Osages, and by 1772, Spanish officials in Louisiana complained that they were hard pressed to keep the two tribes from going to war.[9]

While the western Potawatomis continued to plague the British, their kinsmen near Detroit remained at peace. During the early

1770's the old village at Detroit remained unoccupied, as Ninivois' and Machiouquisse's people also spread their villages to the south and west. By 1774 the Detroit tribesmen had erected new towns near modern Ann Arbor on the Huron River west of Detroit, on the Salt Fork of the River Raisin, and on the Grand River near modern Eaton Rapids in south central Michigan. They also contributed a few occupants to an intertribal village on the Kalamazoo River in the vicinity of modern Battle Creek, but that village was populated primarily by Ottawas.[10]

The Potawatomi response to the outbreak of the American Revolution reflected the political divisions that had emerged within the tribe. In 1776, Potawatomis at Saint Joseph and to the west were reluctant to commit themselves to either side. They held no allegiance to the Crown and watched in detached amusement as their former enemies, the British, divided into two armed camps and prepared to fight. The western tribesmen continued to trade with the creoles, and although many of the latter favored the colonists over Great Britain, the Potawatomis in Illinois and Wisconsin bided their time, waiting to see which group of Englishmen would gain the upper hand.

In contrast, the Detroit Potawatomis rallied to the British cause. During the years since Pontiac's rebellion, the old Detroit chiefs such as Ninivois and Machiouquisse had developed personal ties with the British Indian Department. Moreover, although the British had failed to reoccupy Fort Saint Joseph, Detroit remained a center of British strength in the west. Political realists, the eastern Potawatomis knew that their villages were vulnerable to British military power. When the war erupted, they were more than willing to aid the Crown.

On August 29, 1776, the Detroit Potawatomis, Hurons, Ottawas, and Chippewas met with Lieutenant Governor Henry Hamilton at Detroit. Although Hamilton was reticent to send the warriors against the unprotected American frontier, he did inform the Indians that the Crown expected their assistance. To dramatize British strength and minimize American influence, Hamilton seized a peace belt sent to the Potawatomis by some pro-American Delawares and destroyed the emblem in the presence of the assembled warriors. After the conference, Hamilton dispatched a mixed force of Potawatomis, Chippewas, Ottawas, and Hurons aboard the schooner *Gage* to join the Iroquois in New York. Most of the Potawatomis disembarked at Oswego, where they left the other tribes, and then raided through the Pittsburgh region in October.[11]

Later in the fall the Potawatomis returned to their villages in eastern Michigan, where they spent the winter of 1776–77 in relative peace and prosperity. Anxious to maintain the loyalty of the Indians, the British discarded their old policy of thrift and distributed food and other provisions in a manner reminiscent of the French. Yet British generosity was not without its costs. During the winter, Hamilton received orders to abandon the earlier policy of restraint and to launch a full-scale Indian war against American settlements along the Ohio. The Indian raids were part of a major British offensive planned for the summer of 1777 and were designed to distract the Americans while British Generals John Burgoyne and Barry St. Leger invaded New York.[12]

In June, 1777, the eastern Potawatomis and nearly nine hundred other warriors again met with Hamilton at Detroit. The lieutenant governor presented the Indians with a war belt from the Iroquois and admonished them to strike the Americans. He warned the tribesmen that the Americans considered all Indians to be enemies and would attack them if they had the chance. Yet contrary to American opinion, Hamilton urged the warriors not to "dip their hands in the blood" of women and children, but to concentrate their attacks upon men, as befitted their status as warriors. The speeches were interspersed with feasts and the presentation of gifts, and the conference generally was a success. When it ended, Hamilton reported to his superiors that more than one thousand Indians would soon descend upon the Ohio Valley.[13]

Although the British invasion of New York faltered, the Indian raids along the Ohio were a success. In late June a Potawatomi war party passed through Detroit, where Hamilton supplied them with ammunition. The Potawatomis then struck south towards the Ohio, where they fell upon isolated settlements in Kentucky. The Potawatomi war party was followed by many others, and by autumn, 1777, Kentucky was paralyzed. American settlers were forced to seek shelter behind stockades at Boonesborough, Harrodsburg, and Saint Asaph's while the Indians roamed through the countryside. The warfare kept the settlers from their farms, and during the winter of 1777–78 white Kentuckians suffered a severe food shortage. Meanwhile, the Potawatomis and other warriors returned to Detroit laden with prisoners and American property.[14]

Since the Indian warfare threatened to drive them back across the Appalachians, white settlers in Kentucky appealed to Virginia for relief. The Kentuckians believed that the cure for their dilemma lay in the conquest of Illinois. An American Illinois would provide a base for expeditions against Detroit and hostile Indian villages. Virginia was sympathetic to their plea, and during the winter, Governor Patrick Henry authorized George Rogers Clark to raise a small army of volunteers for an invasion of the Illinois country.[15]

In June, 1778, Clark's force of 175 men left Kentucky, traveling down the Ohio to the Fort Massac region of southern Illinois. There they beached their boats and proceeded overland to the British post at Kaskaskia, which capitulated on June 5. Clark's men then occupied Cahokia and several small villages in the American Bottom, where they informed the creole citizens of the newly concluded alliance between France and the United States. In July, Clark dispatched Captain Leonard Helm and 30 men to Vincennes, and the Wabash post also surrendered peacefully.[16]

The American occupation of Illinois had a significant impact upon the neighboring Indians. Tribes from Illinois and Wisconsin who earlier had professed allegiance to Great Britain now rallied to the Americans. During the summer and fall of 1778, Clark met with many Indians at Cahokia, where he relied upon "harsh language to supply the want of men, well knowing that it was a mistaken notion in many that soft speeches were best for Indians." Attending the meetings were Potawatomis from Illinois and Wisconsin led by Siggenauk (Blackbird), also called Le Tourneau, a chief from the village at Milwaukee.[17]

The western Potawatomis admitted that a handful of their warriors had journeyed east to fight with Burgoyne in New York, but they reminded the American leader that the vast majority of their people had remained neutral and had refused British overtures. Clark warned the Indians against aiding the British, stating that the "Long Knives" soon would be victorious and then would fall upon the Crown's red allies, since American soldiers "would get rusty without they get somebody to fight." Awed by Clark's brashness, the Potawatomis assured the American that they would remain at peace.[18]

Clark was especially impressed with Siggenauk, the chief from Milwaukee. Of mixed Potawatomi-Ottawa descent, Siggenauk dominated the Potawatomi villages in northern Illinois and southeastern Wisconsin. Closely tied to the French and Spanish in Louisiana, the chief had been instrumental in keeping many of the

Potawatomis out of the war. Since 1777, Colonel Arent De Peyster, the British commander at Mackinac, had tried to bribe Siggenauk with presents, but the chief refused the trade goods and remained aloof from British control. Upon his arrival at Cahokia, Siggenauk informed Clark that he wanted no elaborate ceremonies but was more interested in a frank discussion of the war between the British and Americans. The chief stated that he was well acquainted with the British position in the conflict and that he welcomed an opportunity to hear the American point of view. Siggenauk and Clark spent several hours in Clark's quarters, where the frontiersman explained the American cause and answered "a great number of questions very pertinent." Clark described the chief as a "polite gentleman" who spoke "as much in the European manner as possible." When the conference ended, Clark presented Siggenauk with two pack horses laden with gifts, and the chief returned to Milwaukee.[19]

Clark's occupation of Illinois also had a profound impact upon Hamilton. The lieutenant governor realized that the new American offensive threatened British control over the western tribes, and he was anxious to regain the initiative. The Detroit Potawatomis and several neighboring tribes remained loyal to the British, but Hamilton feared that the Americans would ascend the Wabash, winning control of the tribes of Indiana and threatening the British post at Detroit. To counter the American success, during August, 1778, Hamilton met with the Detroit Potawatomis, Ottawas, and Chippewas, convincing them to join him in an effort to recapture Vincennes.[20]

Hamilton also sought the assistance of the Saint Joseph Potawatomis. Earlier in the summer, five Saint Joseph Potawatomis closely tied to Nanaquiba had visited Hamilton at Detroit and had promised to aid the British against the Americans. Although the lieutenant governor realized that many other Saint Joseph Potawatomis remained devoted to the French, he was anxious to win their loyalty and to include them in his expedition down the Wabash. Both Hamilton and De Peyster believed that Chevalier was the key to the Saint Joseph villages. Hamilton distrusted the trader, but De Peyster was convinced that Chevalier was loyal to the Crown, and he urged Hamilton to work through the Frenchman to spread British influence among the Potawatomis. Late in August, Hamilton wrote to Chevalier, asking him to rally Nanaquiba's people and to join the expedition at the Miami villages on the Wabash River.[21]

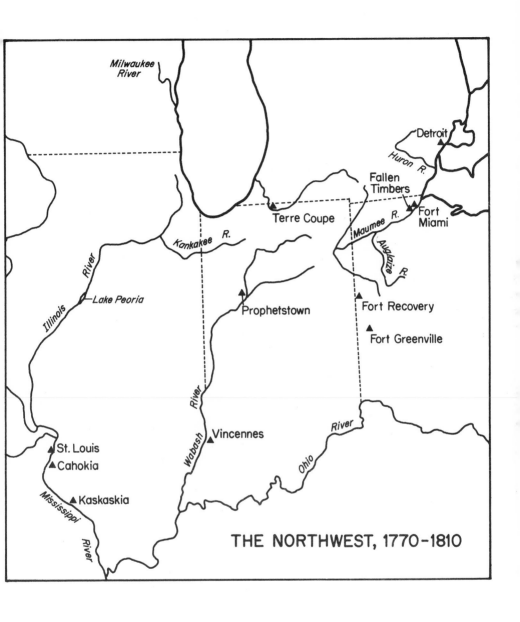

THE NORTHWEST, 1770–1810

At Mackinac, De Peyster also made plans to support the attack on Vincennes. In October he dispatched Charles Langlade to raise the Ottawas and Chippewas, and he sent Charles Gautier, Langlade's nephew, to help Chevalier organize the Potawatomis. Yet De Peyster's plans failed. The Ottawas and Chippewas already had dispersed for their winter hunt, and most were unwilling to accompany Langlade. Gautier encountered similar problems. When he arrived on the Saint Joseph, the handful of Potawatomis still in residence there informed Gautier that Chevalier and the few warriors he could muster already had left for the Wabash.[22]

Meanwhile, on October 7, 1778, Hamilton and about 240 men left Detroit for Vincennes via the Maumee-Wabash waterway. Only fifteen Potawatomis, led by Ashkibee and Windigo (Man Eater), accompanied them. Like their kinsmen on the Saint Joseph, the Detroit Potawatomis did not relish a winter campaign and also had scattered to their hunting camps. Hamilton's party journeyed to the forks of the Maumee, where Chevalier and fifteen Saint Joseph Potawatomis joined the expedition. The Saint Joseph warriors were led by Nanaquiba, but the old chief was so senile that in preparing to meet Hamilton, he bedecked himself with a French medal given to him after the fall of Fort William Henry. Hamilton replaced the medal with a British medallion and congratulated the old Potawatomi for his efforts at such an advanced age. The expedition then proceeded down the Wabash, where it was joined by other Indians, including a few more Potawatomis from a new village on the headwaters of the Tippecanoe. On December 17, Hamilton and his allies arrived at Vincennes, where Captain Leonard Helm, the American commander, surrendered both the fort and the village.[23]

On the trip down the Wabash, part of the Saint Joseph Potawatomis left Hamilton and traveled to Cahokia to spy on the Americans. On December 18 they returned to Vincennes, informing the British officer that there were thirty soldiers at Cahokia but that discipline was lax and the Americans were unaware of Hamilton's expedition. Windigo, Ashkibee, and the Detroit Potawatomis also ventured into Illinois, where they captured one prisoner but gathered little information. In January, Nanaquiba and the Saint Joseph warriors returned to their villages, but the Detroit Potawatomis left Vincennes to raid along the Ohio.[24]

Before the Potawatomis departed, Hamilton met with their chiefs and reminded them that he intended to attack the Americans in the spring. The Detroit warriors agreed to return to Vincennes and accompany Hamilton across Illinois, while Nanaquiba promised to rally the Saint Joseph Potawatomis and descend the Illinois River, falling upon rebel settlements in the American Bottom. Yet Hamilton's plans never materialized. During February, 1779, Clark led a force of Americans across the flooded timberlands of southern Illinois, and on February 23 he surprised Hamilton at Vincennes. Many of Hamilton's Indian allies deserted, and on February 24 the lieutenant governor surrendered, again giving the Americans control of the lower Wabash Valley.[25]

Since Ashkibee's and Windigo's warriors still were raiding along the Ohio, there were no Potawatomis at Vincennes to witness Hamilton's capture and the British defeat. Nevertheless, the Potawatomis recognized the significance of the events on the Wabash. Although the Detroit Potawatomis remained loyal to the Crown, their western kinsmen scrambled to accommodate themselves to the renewed American presence in Indiana. British influence along the Saint Joseph dwindled as Potawatomi warriors seized British trade goods and the village chiefs, including Nanaquiba, accepted letters of American friendship.[26] Potawatomis from the upper Illinois journeyed to Cahokia, while the chiefs from the village on the Tippecanoe met with Clark at Vincennes, assuring the American that they, too, desired peace with the Long Knives. On the Saint Joseph, Chevalier absolved himself of any blame in the British decline, but he complained bitterly to British officials that the Potawatomis were:

> very inconsistent in its [their] friendships, but never in its [their] hatred, wavering in their good resolutions even on the point of abandoning them. Timid in danger, proud and haughty when they believe themselves in safety, credulous to the last degree, easily led away by great promises and frightened by threats. These are the two means the Rebels use to corrupt part of this nation.
>
> It does not seem to me, however, impossible to keep this nation in dependence, if they were united under the same chief, but divided as it is into six villages distant fifteen or twenty miles from each other it is very difficult to impose this yoke. Each village has its own chief who disposes his young men according to his private ideas, too attentive to the poisoned speeches of certain traitors who sacrifice honor and duty to sordid interest. . . .[27]

At Mackinac, De Peyster believed that the Americans were planning a major offensive against British posts in Michigan. He feared that American forces would march up the Illinois Valley, rendezvous with friendly Potawatomis at Saint Joseph, and then strike overland for Detroit. British informants reported that American agents were purchasing horses from the Potawatomis near Chicago and that Siggenauk's people were constructing a fleet of boats to launch an attack against Mackinac. In the early summer Maurice Godfroy Linctot, a French trader, led a small party of Americans to Lake Peoria, where they met with friendly Indians. Although Clark had ordered Linctot just to make a show of strength in the region and then march to the Wabash, De Peyster believed Linctot's party was the initial step in the American invasion.[28]

De Peyster was convinced that the Potawatomi villages near the tip of Lake Michigan held the key to British defense. If the Potawatomis helped the Americans, other tribes also would join the rebels, and Michigan would be lost. But if the Crown could turn the Potawatomis against the Americans, a rebel expedition would be forced to march hundreds of miles through hostile territory, and the Americans might easily be turned back. Hoping to regain the initiative, De Peyster sent Langlade down the western shore of Lake Michigan to gather any Indians he could enlist. De Peyster also dispatched Lieutenant Thomas Bennet to the Ottawas and Saint Joseph Potawatomis. The officers were instructed to rendezvous near Chicago and then attack Linctot at Peoria.[29]

Bennet collected a party of Ottawas in northern Michigan, but when he arrived on the Saint Joseph, he was unsure of his reception. Although he invited the Potawatomis to a council, the British officer fortified his camp in case the Indians proved hostile. On July 28, 1779, the Potawatomis met with Bennet and seemed willing to support his expedition. Pleased, Bennet dispatched a scouting party toward Peoria before settling down to check his equipment and await Langlade.[30]

Bennet's decision to send the Indians toward Peoria was a mistake. Although the Saint Joseph Potawatomis seemed willing to support the British, they preferred to consult with other villages before making an actual commitment. As the scouting party descended the Kankakee, they encountered other Potawatomis, who opposed the British attack. The party then returned to their villages where the Saint Joseph chiefs decided to withdraw from the expedition. The Potawatomis met with Bennet and informed him of their decision. Speaking for the assembled tribesmen, the war chief Le Petit Bled (The Little Corn) told the officer that the Potawatomis preferred the peace pipe to the tomahawk and feared that he had come "to disturb the peace that reigns in our lands." The chief informed Bennet that his people had no intention of joining either side but would remain as "spectators" of the war.[31]

Bennet was surprised by Le Petit Bled's speech, and although he tried to persuade the Potawatomis to reconsider, they refused. The Potawatomi sentiments then spread to the Ottawas, who also began to desert the camp, and by August 9, Bennet's following had shrunk to fewer than twenty Indians. Langlade's arrival did not alleviate the situation. The former French agent had been opposed by Sigge- nauk and could enlist only sixty Chippewas. When the latter learned of the Potawatomi and Ottawa defection, they agreed to attack Linctot only if Bennet continually supplied them with rum. Bennet refused, and the expedition collapsed. He returned to Mackinac late in August.[32]

Angered over the failure of the campaign, De Peyster struck back at Siggenauk. He blamed the chief not only for Langlade's poor showing, but also for the opposition encountered by the scouting party. In October, 1779, De Peyster ordered military personnel aboard the sloop *Felicity* to sail to Milwaukee and seize the Pota- watomi chief. When the ship reached the mouth of the Milwaukee River, the British officers were afraid to go ashore. They attempted to bribe other Indians to capture Siggenauk and bring him to the vessel, but their plot failed. Although several of the Milwaukee Indians accepted British merchandise, they made no effort to kidnap the chief, and the *Felicity* was forced to sail back to Mackinac with- out him.[33]

The autumn of 1779 marked the zenith of American influence among the western Potawatomis. The British had fled to Mackinac, Siggenauk remained at Milwaukee, and Clark seemed destined to invade Detroit. Yet the American suzerainty did not last. Linctot left Peoria and traveled to Ouiatanon, where he planned to join with an American expedition ascending the Wabash. But when Linctot reached his destination, the American soldiers failed to ap- pear. Short of finances, Clark abandoned his plans to take Detroit and was forced to retrench his position in southern Illinois. Mean- while, Le Petit Bled led a party of Saint Joseph Potawatomis to Kaskaskia, hoping to receive a reward for their refusal to support Bennet. Although the Americans thanked the Potawatomis, they had few gifts for the warriors, and Le Petit Bled returned to his village much dissatisfied.[34]

During the winter of 1779–80 the British slowly began to regain the ascendancy. Since Spain had declared war against Britain in 1779, British officials planned a campaign against St. Louis. The British hoped to assemble a large force of Indians at Prairie du Chien, descend the Mississippi, and attack St. Louis and American posts in southern Illinois. To support the raid on St. Louis, the British planned to dispatch war parties led by Langlade down the Illinois River valley. They also made provisions to send a large force of troops and Indians against Clark at the falls of the Ohio.[35]

The Potawatomis figured prominently in British plans. Since the warriors from Detroit had proven themselves consistently faithful, British officials at Detroit asked them to journey to the tribes of Wisconsin and Iowa, enlisting the western Indians in the British campaign. Potawatomi messengers ventured as far west as the Des Moines River, informing the Sacs and Foxes of the British plans. En route to the Mississippi, the Detroit Potawatomis passed through the villages of their kinsmen near Lake Michigan, where they encountered a mixed reception. Although the Potawatomis in northern Illinois and southern Wisconsin remained noncommittal, many of the Saint Joseph villagers expressed an interest in joining the Crown. Le Petit Bled still smoldered over the alleged snub at Kaskaskia, and many of the warriors believed the American position had weakened. In March, 1780, Chevalier reported, "I do not know by what prodigy, Sir, the Poutawatamies have suddenly come out from a Sloth or rather a lethargy, that three years of want have not been able to cure, they have risen ashamed of a sleep from which the voice of their Father and mine could not awaken them."[36]

In the spring of 1780, Emanuel Hesse assembled a contingent of British traders and Indians at Prairie du Chien. In May the British army sailed down the Mississippi, arriving at St. Louis. There they found the Spanish well prepared, and after an initial assault against the Spanish defenses the Indians foraged through the adjoining countryside. Achieving little success, the British and Indians retreated in two parties, one returning up the Mississippi while the other crossed Illinois towards Chicago.[37]

Although a handful of Potawatomis accompanied Hesse to St. Louis, the vast majority of the tribe took no part in the attack. A small party of warriors from Chicago followed Langlade down the Illinois River, hoping to share in any spoils from a British victory. But when Langlade met the retreating British forces in central Illinois, the Potawatomis joined the retreat and accompanied the British back to Chicago. There the British boarded two vessels which took them to Mackinac.[38]

Other Potawatomis opposed the British campaign. Warriors from northern Illinois informed French creoles of Hesse's plans, and most Potawatomis from Illinois and Wisconsin refused to accompany either Hesse or Langlade. Although they could not stop the British from marching through their homeland, warriors loyal to Siggenauk joined with a force of Americans who pursued the British up the Illinois Valley in a futile attempt to cut them off before they could reach the vessels on Lake Michigan.[39]

At Terre Coupe the most recent British recruit, Le Petit Bled, also failed to support the attack upon St. Louis. Although he was anxious to avenge himself on the Americans, the chief turned his attentions against Vincennes instead of Spanish Louisiana. During March he convinced a large number of Saint Joseph warriors to follow him down the Wabash in an ill-fated venture against Vincennes. On the way to their objective the Potawatomis met a French trader, who learned of their plans and informed them that a French army of four thousand men recently had joined the garrison at the post. Such a tale was enough to convince most of the Saint Joseph warriors to return to their villages, but Le Petit Bled and a small group of diehards continued on to Vincennes, where they found that the fort contained only thirty American volunteers. Angry over the trickery, Le Petit Bled threatened the Americans with death, but they only scoffed at the chief and forced him to leave the settlement.[40]

Humiliated, Le Petit Bled journeyed to Detroit, where he met with De Peyster and apologized for the debacle on the Wabash. De Peyster furnished the Potawatomis with guns and powder and hired Dagneaux Du Quindre, a friend of Chevalier, to lead the Saint Joseph Potawatomis on a new expedition against Vincennes. The Indians assured De Peyster that they would storm the fort and then raid along the Ohio River.[41]

If Le Petit Bled's raid ended in humiliation, Du Quindre's expedition ended in disaster. Unknown to the Potawatomis, the Americans evacuated the post during the late spring, but as the warriors proceeded down the Wabash, they were ambushed by the Piankashaws. The Piankashaws recently had lost a chief to the Ottawas, and in revenge they mistakenly fired on the Potawatomi war party, killing four warriors and wounding several more. Most of the Potawatomis returned to Michigan, where they sent messengers to the Ottawas and Chippewas, unsuccessfully seeking assistance for future attacks against the Wabash tribe.[42]

Ironically, although the British-sponsored military attacks upon

St. Louis and Vincennes had failed, British influence among the Saint Joseph Potawatomis increased. Hesse's presence at Prairie du Chien and the campaign against St. Louis kept French and Spanish traders from visiting the Saint Joseph villages. Although the Potawatomis in Wisconsin and Illinois still traded with the creoles, the Saint Joseph villages were cut off from their major source of trade goods. At Detroit, De Peyster realized the significance of the disruption. During the spring he had cemented his ties with Le Petit Bled, and he used the growing friendship to increase his economic penetration of the Potawatomi villages. Since the Potawatomis were short of goods, De Peyster sent a party of British traders to occupy old Fort Saint Joseph and to trade with the Indians. The traders also were instructed to order all French residents, even Chevalier, out of the Saint Joseph villages. Therefore, by the fall of 1780 the Saint Joseph Potawatomis were dependent upon the British for the necessities of life.[43]

Most of the Saint Joseph Potawatomis viewed the British traders as a mixed blessing. Although some of the Indians still preferred the French, a growing number of warriors, including Le Petit Bled, now favored the British. Yet all of the Saint Joseph people needed the trade goods, and they were willing to accept anyone who made such merchandise available.

Creole traders in Louisiana were less willing to accept the new British competition. For half a century they had supplied the Saint Joseph villages, and the creoles had no intention of losing their market without a fight. Moreover, many French and Spanish traders believed that the Saint Joseph Potawatomis still were loyal to the French and would reject the British if they had a chance. In the fall of 1780 a party of fifteen creoles and one American, led by Jean Baptiste Hamelin, left Cahokia for the Saint Joseph villages. Combining political and economic motives, they planned to seize British trade goods and drive the British traders from the Saint Joseph.

Hamelin's party arrived at Fort Saint Joseph in November. Almost all the Potawatomis had left their villages, scattering through the forests for their autumn hunt. The raiders overran the fort, seizing fifty bales of British trade goods and capturing several British traders. Hoping to carry the prisoners and captured merchandise back to Cahokia, Hamelin's party set out towards Chicago. Meanwhile, Du Quindre, whom De Peyster had assigned as an agent among the Saint Joseph Potawatomis, learned of the attack and searched through the forest, gathering Le Petit Bled and his warriors. The Potawatomis pursued the creoles, overtaking them near the southern tip of Lake Michigan. Du Quindre demanded that the raiders surrender, but Hamelin refused, believing that the Saint Joseph warriors would not attack Frenchmen. He was mistaken. Le Petit Bled's warriors opened fire, killing four creoles and wounding two others. The other raiders tried to flee, but the Potawatomis captured seven of them, including the lone American, Thomas Brady, who was turned over to De Peyster at Detroit.[44]

The defeat of Hamelin's raiders had important repercussions in the Old Northwest. Not only did it indicate that many Saint Joseph Potawatomis were clearly in the British service, but it also angered Siggenauk, who reported the event to the Spanish in Louisiana. Siggenauk warned the Spanish that British influence was increasing and that the Saint Joseph villages might be used as a staging area for new attacks on St. Louis. The chief asked the Spanish to launch an expedition against the British traders on the Saint Joseph and promised to support the venture with friendly Potawatomis from Milwaukee and the Upper Illinois. Since another creole expedition led by Augustin Mottin de La Balme also had been defeated by the Miamis in Indiana, and Spanish prestige seemed to be declining, Francisco Cruzat, the Spanish commander at St. Louis, agreed to the proposal. He hoped that a successful campaign would drive the British from western Michigan and keep Siggenauk allied to the Spanish and American cause.[45]

On January 2, 1781, a force of sixty-five Spanish soldiers, commanded by Captain Eugene Poure, left St. Louis and ascended the Illinois River. Along the way they were joined by Siggenauk and Naakewoin (Wind Striker), another chief from Milwaukee, who led a force of sixty Potawatomis, Ottawas, and Chippewas. Ice at Lake Peoria forced the Spanish and Indians to leave the river and trek across the frozen prairie. The invaders arrived near Fort Saint Joseph on the evening of February 11, 1781. After setting up camp, Poure dispatched a Potawatomi warrior, La Gesse (The Quail), to inform the Saint Joseph tribesmen of their arrival and to warn them not to interfere. La Gesse found few of his kinsmen in their villages, and although they posed no threat to the Spanish, Poure offered them half the trade goods to be captured from the British. The Potawatomis accepted, and Poure and Siggenauk spent the night making preparations to attack the British traders living in the fort.[46]

Early in the morning of February 12, 1781, the Spanish and Indians crossed the frozen Saint Joseph River and completely surprised the British traders. Two of the British tried to flee, but they were cut down by Siggenauk's warriors. The remaining eight traders offered no resistance and were made prisoners. Poure then divided the British trade goods among the Indians and burned any British supplies not wanted by the Potawatomis. After claiming the region for Spain, Poure occupied the post for twenty-four hours, and then the Spanish and Indians retreated toward St. Louis.[47]

The Saint Joseph Potawatomis made no attempt to oppose Poure and Siggenauk. Le Petit Bled had been willing to fire upon Hamelin's party of fifteen traders, but he had no intention of attacking a force of 120 heavily armed Spanish and Indians. Yet the Saint Joseph villagers knew the British would suspect them of complicity in the raid, so in March they sent a delegation of chiefs to Detroit. The Potawatomis reminded De Peyster that they had rallied to overtake Hamelin, but they claimed all their warriors were absent when Siggenauk and the Spanish captured Fort Saint Joseph. Although the Potawatomis failed to mention that they had shared in the plundered merchandise, they asked the British to send other traders to their villages.[48]

After the Spanish raid on Fort Saint Joseph, the Potawatomis focused their attention on the east. Since most American troops had been withdrawn from Illinois, the British no longer feared an invasion from that region, and they concentrated their red allies against rebel forces in Kentucky and Ohio. The shift in theaters took most of the Illinois and Wisconsin Potawatomis out of the war. Siggenauk had been willing to support the Spanish and Americans in opposing the expansion of British influence west of Lake Michigan, but he refused to assist the Long Knives in their defense of Kentucky. In contrast, the Saint Joseph villages sent large numbers of warriors east, strengthening their ties with De Peyster and joining with the Detroit Potawatomis to fight against the Americans in Ohio.

In 1780, while most of their kinsmen were embroiled in events to the west, a few Detroit Potawatomis had followed Captain Henry Bird in his raid into Kentucky. During the following summer they joined with kinsmen from the Saint Joseph to infest the Ohio, ambushing American settlers and stealing horses. Although the winter of 1781–82 passed quietly, in the spring the Potawatomis learned that a force of American militia had butchered ninety peaceful Delawares at Gnadenhutten, in eastern Ohio. On May 15, 1782, they met with De Peyster, who informed them that the Americans were planning an invasion of the Delaware towns along the Sandusky River. Angry over the Gnadenhutten massacre, the Detroit Potawatomis promised De Peyster that they would send warriors to assist the Delawares against the Long Knives.[49]

While the Potawatomis were meeting with De Peyster at Detroit, an American expedition of four hundred militia, commanded by Colonel William Crawford, left the Mingo Bottom near Steubenville, Ohio, and proceeded toward the villages on the Sandusky. The Ohio tribes monitored the American advance and sent messengers to Detroit asking the British for assistance. The Detroit Potawatomis and other nearby tribes rushed warriors to the Sandusky, while De Peyster dispatched messengers to the Saint Joseph villages, asking their warriors to assemble at Detroit so they could be supplied and sent to fight the Americans.[50]

Although the Saint Joseph Potawatomis arrived too late to take part in the action, on June 4, 1782, the Detroit Potawatomis joined with large numbers of Delawares, Wyandots, and Mingos to attack the Americans as they neared the Indian towns on the Sandusky River. The battle raged for two days, but on the evening of June 5 Crawford and his men attempted to retreat. Confused in the darkness, many of the Americans became separated from their comrades and wandered aimlessly in the woods. At daybreak the Potawatomis and their allies set out in pursuit of their enemies, capturing several soldiers, including Crawford. Most of the captives were killed immediately, but Crawford was taken to the Delaware village near modern Crawford, Ohio, and slowly tortured to death. Crawford's defeat was a lopsided victory for the Indians. Although the tribesmen lost five warriors, they killed more than seventy Americans.[51]

Excited by the victory over Crawford, the Potawatomis launched new raids against the American frontier. During July, 1782, warriors from the Saint Joseph lurked along the Ohio, hoping to ambush American shipping. Although they encountered no white settlers, they did capture a runaway slave, whom they turned over to the British. Meanwhile, other warriors from the Saint Joseph and Detroit met with Alexander McKee and William Caldwell to plan an attack against Wheeling, in what is now West Virginia. The assault upon Wheeling was abandoned, but in August, Potawatomi warriors followed Caldwell and McKee into Kentucky, where they besieged Bryan's Station in modern Fayette County. Although the British and Indians ambushed a relief party approaching the fort from Lexington, they could not gain entrance to the station, and on

August 17 they withdrew, slowly retreating toward the Licking River.[52]

The raiders expected to be followed, and they made no attempt to hide their trail. Shortly after the Potawatomis and their allies left Bryan's Station, the defenders welcomed reinforcements from other settlements who were anxious to pursue the attackers. One hundred eighty-two Kentuckians, led by Daniel Boone, Stephen Trigg, and John Todd, set out after the Indians, and on August 19, 1782, they caught their enemies on the Licking River near the Lower Blue Licks. The British and Indians watched the Kentuckians cross the Licking, and as the Americans stumbled up the river bank they were greeted with a volley of musket fire. The Kentuckians fled back into the river, but the Potawatomis and other Indians surged from their hiding places and overwhelmed the frontiersmen in the water. In the ensuing melee, 70 Kentuckians died. The British and Indians suffered only eleven killed and fourteen wounded.[53]

The Battle of the Blue Licks was the last major Potawatomi action of the Revolutionary War. Although a few war parties raided along the Ohio during the fall and winter, they accomplished little, and most returned to their villages empty-handed. Meanwhile, after the American victory at Yorktown, the British and Americans moved towards peace. A preliminary treaty was signed on November 30, 1782, but news of the event did not reach Detroit until the following April. When De Peyster learned of the treaty, he called the Detroit Potawatomis, Ottawas, Chippewas, and Hurons to Detroit and advised them that the war was ending. He also asked them to cease all hostilities toward the Americans. The Detroit warriors notified their kinsmen to the west, and during the summer of 1783 the Potawatomi villages remained at peace.[54]

While De Peyster was meeting with the Indians at Detroit, Congress dispatched Ephriam Douglass, a former Indian trader, to visit the northwestern tribes and present the American version of the treaty. Douglass was instructed to inform the Indians that the British had relinquished their claims to the territory east of the Mississippi and that the lands now belonged to the United States. When Douglass reached Sandusky, most of the Indians refused to meet with him, so he journeyed on to Detroit. De Peyster would not allow the American agent to meet separately with the Indians, or to discuss any British land cessions, but the British officer did assemble the tribes, and in Douglass' presence he admonished the Indians to remain friendly toward the United States. On July 7, 1783, Douglass left Detroit for Niagara, where he met with the Iroquois, and he then returned to the east.[55]

De Peyster's refusal to allow the American agent to meet with the Indians was indicative of British policy at the end of the war. Uncertain that the new United States would last, the British were determined to maintain their ties with the tribesmen and to continue their occupation of military posts north of the Ohio. During August, 1783, Alexander McKee also met with the Potawatomis and other tribes at Sandusky Bay, assuring the Indians that the British remained their friend. McKee promised the tribesmen that the British-American treaty was not meant "to deprive you of an extent of country, of which the right of Soil belongs to, and is in yourselves as Sole Proprietors. . . ." He also informed the Indians that "the King still considers your happiness by his protection and encouragement of your usual intercourse with Trade."[56]

To the Potawatomis and other tribesmen at Sandusky, McKee's promises only reinforced their assessment of the Indian position at the end of the Revolution. From the Indian point of view, they had won the war in the west. The Detroit and Saint Joseph Potawatomis had helped defend the area north of the Ohio, and they had inflicted property damage and loss of life in Kentucky. Since the Indians never had given the French or the British title to their lands in the Northwest, the tribesmen believed they still owned the region and that American claims to the area were groundless. Yet the war had brought some significant change to the Potawatomi villages. The Saint Joseph warriors, the former defenders of Onontio, now joined with the Detroit Potawatomis in supporting the British Crown. Even though the Long Knives had allied themselves with the French, the Saint Joseph warriors distrusted the Americans, and in the next decade both the Saint Joseph and Detroit Potawatomis would oppose American attempts to occupy Ohio. But the western villages, the Potawatomis from Illinois and Wisconsin, remained suspicious of the Sauganash[57] and kept their ties with the French and Spanish in Louisiana. The tribal division that emerged after Pontiac's rebellion had changed, but it also would continue.

6. The Red Confederacy

The six years following the Treaty of Paris were a period of frustration for the Indians of the Old Northwest. Although the Shawnees, Wyandots, and Delawares continued to claim the lands just north of the Ohio, they were hard pressed to maintain their position against the rapidly expanding United States. In October, 1783, American officials announced that Indian claims to Ohio had been forfeited because the tribes had supported the British, but that the United States would allow the Ohio tribes to occupy small reservations within their former homeland, since the Americans were "disposed to be kind" to their "red children." Meanwhile, the new American government made plans to negotiate separately with the individual tribes and to secure their acquiescence in American occupation of southern Ohio.[1]

The American position was opposed by the eastern Potawatomis and by other tribes in the Old Northwest. Encouraged by the British, the Indians hoped to unite in resisting American expansion and to meet the Long Knives as a confederacy instead of separate tribes. But Indian unity emerged slowly, and in 1784, at the Second Treaty of Fort Stanwix, the Iroquois relinquished all claims to lands west of Pennsylvania and New York. Three months later, in January, 1785, several bands of Delawares, Wyandots, Chippewas, and Ottawas were pressured into ceding all their lands north of the Ohio except for a reservation west of the Miami River. Encouraged by their success, American officials next invited the Potawatomis, Kickapoos, Shawnees, Miamis, Weas, and Piankashaws to assemble at Fort Finney and to renounce their claims to lands in Ohio. But this time the American plans failed. Although the few Shawnees who attended the conference were coerced into signing away their lands east of the Miami, the Potawatomis and other tribes rejected the American invitation.[2]

Angered over the recent treaties, Potawatomis from eastern Michigan and the Saint Joseph met with the British and other tribes at Detroit. The Indians repudiated the land cessions and reaffirmed their intentions to unite against the Americans. Since the British still occupied Detroit and feared American ambitions toward Canada, British Indian agents attended the conference and supported the conception of a red confederacy. Yet the British followed a precarious policy. Although they were anxious to retain the loyalty of the western tribes and promised to supply the Indians with ammunition, British officials did not wish to become involved in another war with the United States. Therefore, the Crown encouraged the tribes to stand fast against white expansion north of the Ohio but attempted to restrain the Indians from taking the offensive against the Americans.[3]

The Potawatomis and their allies ignored the British restrictions. During 1785, Shawnee warriors crossed the Ohio to raid against Kentucky, and in the following year Potawatomi warriors from the Saint Joseph joined with the Miamis to kill several Americans in southern Illinois. In retaliation, during October, 1786, Benjamin Logan led five hundred Kentuckians into Ohio, where they burned seven Shawnee villages and destroyed innumerable corn fields. For all practical purposes, the Ohio Valley was again at war.[4]

After Logan's invasion of Ohio, the Shawnees fled north to the Maumee River, where they met with other Indians. In November, 1786, the Potawatomis, Shawnees, and many other tribesmen assembled at the Huron village on the Detroit River and drafted a letter to Congress renouncing the recent treaties and demanding that the United States negotiate with the confederacy instead of individual tribes. The Indians informed Congress that they were willing to discuss the cession of some lands north of the Ohio, but they warned the government to keep settlers and surveyors south of the river until any cessions were finalized.[5]

The United States reacted cautiously to the Indians' message. Government officials were uncertain of Indian strength and considered several policies as a possible response to the Indian position. The new American government was not anxious to renegotiate for the lands north of the Ohio, but it was less anxious to become involved in an expensive Indian war. Secretary of War Henry Knox reported to Congress, "In the present embarrassed state of public affairs and entire deficiency of funds an indian war of any considerable extent and duration would most exceedingly distress the United States—The great distance by land which the stores and supplies must be transported would render the expenses intolerable. . . ." Therefore, in the fall of 1787, Congress authorized Arthur St. Clair, the governor of the Northwest Territories, to assemble the Indians for the purpose of negotiating a peaceful solution to the land problem.[6]

Although St. Clair sent messages to the Potawatomis and other tribes inviting them to meet with him in the spring, the Indians failed to appear. Upon receiving St. Clair's message, the tribesmen again met in council to decide upon a unified policy in negotiating with the Americans. But the conference soon disintegrated into a series of intertribal quarrels over what position the confederacy should take. The Delawares and Wyandots, tribes whose lands lay adjacent to the Ohio River, were reluctant to cede any of their territory, but they also were afraid of American military power and refused to take the initiative in opposing the United States. In contrast, the Potawatomis, Ottawas, and Chippewas lived far north of the river and were willing to compromise to avoid war with the Americans. The Potawatomis urged the confederacy to cede the area east of the Muskingum River in return for an American guarantee of other lands in Ohio. Brant and the Mohawks supported this position, since American settlement already was pouring into the region. In contrast, the Potawatomi argument was adamantly opposed by the Kickapoos, Miamis, and Shawnees. These tribes were located in the Maumee and Wabash valleys and saw any compromise in eastern Ohio as a dangerous precedent which might ultimately threaten their homelands.[7]

During December, 1788, St. Clair eventually convinced segments of seven tribes to assemble with American officials at Fort Harmar. With Indian unity disintegrating, the resulting treaties, signed in January, 1789, had little meaning for either the tribesmen or the United States. Only four of the tribes had any legitimate claims to the lands in question. Two separate treaties were signed by the Indians and the Americans. On January 9, 1789, the Senecas reaffirmed the land cessions made at the Treaty of Fort Stanwix, and later in the day representatives from the Potawatomis, Sacs, Chippewas, Ottawas, Delawares, and Wyandots affixed their signatures to a document accepting the terms of earlier treaties at Forts Stanwix, Mc-

Intosh, and Finney. Although the Potawatomis played only a minor role in the treaty proceedings, they had no valid claims to any of the ceded lands. A small party of Detroit Potawatomis led by Windigo had been lured to Fort Harmar through promises of American presents. They hoped that the Long Knives would make major concessions, but when the Americans remained firm, the Indians realized that the new treaty would be no better than the earlier ones. Disgruntled, the Potawatomis and the other tribesmen signed the treaty document. They knew that the agreement would be repudiated by most of the Indians in the Old Northwest.[8]

St. Clair optimistically reported that the Treaty of Fort Harmar was a success and that it had broken the Indian confederacy. He was wrong. Instead of causing further dissension among the tribes, the treaty convinced the Indians of the futility of negotiating with the government. At Fort Harmar the United States had refused to compromise and had exploited intertribal jealousies to its own advantage. Angry over their failure to gain any concessions, the Potawatomis and other tribes now moved toward the militant position of the Miamis, Shawnees, and Kickapoos. By the summer of 1789, British agents at Detroit reported that the northwestern tribes again were unanimously opposed to white settlement north of the Ohio and had sent warriors to attack American outposts in Kentucky.[9]

Since 1786 the Shawnees, Kickapoos, and Miamis had continued to wage war along the Ohio, and during 1789, Potawatomi warriors again joined in the raids. In March a war party led by Le Grand Couete (The Big Tail) struck at northern Kentucky but was overtaken by a force of Kentucky militia and suffered one killed and four wounded. The attacks continued through the summer, and during the fall, warriors from northern Indiana and southern Michigan plundered several American traders, threatening their lives if they resisted the robberies.[10]

At first American officials blamed the resurgence of hostilities upon the Kickapoos and Miamis, and during the spring of 1790, American Indian agents initiated a last effort to make peace with the two tribes. In March and April, 1790, government messengers were sent up the Wabash to Kickapoo and Miami villages, asking the Indians to remain at peace and inviting them to meet with the Long Knives. Yet the mission failed. The warriors threatened the lives of the messengers and rejected the American proposals.[11] Meanwhile, Indian attacks along the Ohio increased as the Potawatomis and other warriors ambushed boats and swept through isolated settlements on both sides of the river. In May, government spies reported that many Potawatomis were raiding in Kentucky, and by early summer, American travel upon the lower Ohio had become almost impossible.[12]

Frustrated in his attempts at negotiation, St. Clair decided upon a military expedition against the hostile tribes. During the summer of 1790 the governor planned a two-pronged campaign against the Indians along the Wabash and Maumee valleys. General Josiah Harmar was to march on the Miami and Shawnee towns on the Maumee, while Major John Francis Hamtramck was ordered to leave Vincennes and invade the Kickapoo and Wea towns along the Wabash. By late September, both expeditions had assembled and were waiting to march.[13]

Meanwhile, the Potawatomis and their allies made plans of their own. After reports of American preparations reached Indian villages in northern Indiana, Potawatomis from eastern Michigan and the Saint Joseph journeyed to the Miami town at the headwaters of the Maumee, where they promised to assist the Shawnees and Miamis in repelling any American invasion of their homeland. Confident that they could defeat the Long Knives, the Indians boasted that if Harmar dared to approach the Shawnee and Miami villages, Indian women would chase him away with switches.[14]

On September 30, 1790, Harmar and a force of 320 regulars and 1,133 Kentucky militia marched north from Fort Washington toward the Indian towns along the Maumee. In a final attempt to split the confederacy, St. Clair sent messages to the Potawatomis, Ottawas, and Chippewas assuring them that Harmar's expedition would not strike their villages and urging them to keep their warriors at home. Yet St. Clair's efforts were ignored, for as Harmar's expedition straggled north through Ohio, Potawatomi warriors hurried toward the Miami towns on the upper Wabash. Meanwhile, the Indians along the Maumee abandoned their villages and moved their women and children to temporary camps along the Elkhart River.[15]

By the middle of October, Harmar's expedition reached the Maumee Valley, where he burned several Indian villages and destroyed a quantity of Indian corn. On October 18, a force of 300 militia and regulars was dispatched to scout through the adjoining country in an attempt to find the Indians. Harmar ordered the scouting party to spend as long as three days on their mission, but they retreated to the main camp in the evening after killing two

Indians. Displeased with their return, on the following morning Colonel John Hardin led a mixed force of 180 militia and 30 regulars on a similar mission. The militia were reluctant to follow Hardin, and by the time his party had traveled two miles from camp, many militiamen had deserted.[16]

Indian scouts had watched as the Americans advanced along the Maumee, and when Hardin's party left camp on October 19, his march was reported to a large war party of Potawatomis and Shawnees. About ten miles northwest of the American camp, the war party took cover in the forest adjacent to Hardin's path. As the Americans approached, the warriors fired from ambush, surprising the regulars and panicking the militia. Most of the militia took to their heels, but the regulars stood their ground and returned the Indians' fire. Yet the Potawatomis and Shawnees were well protected by the underbrush, and their marksmanship took a heavy toll upon the Americans. When the regulars and those militiamen who supported them finally retreated, only nine survived. The attacking party of Potawatomis and Shawnees was composed of approximately one hundred warriors. American casualties in the action numbered about the same.[17]

Two days later, in a subsequent battle, a war party of Shawnees, Miamis, Ottawas, and Delawares inflicted similar casualties on another force of regulars and militia commanded by Major John P. Wyllys. Although his subordinates urged him to continue the campaign against the Indians, Harmar refused. With one-fourth of his regulars dead and the militia unreliable, the American commander was afraid to risk any further encounters with the tribesmen. On October 22 he retreated back toward Fort Washington.[18]

The Potawatomis did not take part in the second battle, but they did make a substantial contribution to the failure of the American expedition. Of the 183 Americans killed during Harmar's sojourn on the Maumee, more than half fell in the Potawatomi-Shawnee ambush of Hardin's force on October 19. The Potawatomis also shared in the plunder. As the Americans retreated, they discarded much of their equipment, and the Indians captured many of their pack horses.[19]

While Harmar was marching to the Maumee, Major John Hamtramck led a force of 330 Americans up the Wabash against the Weas and Kickapoos. Although Hamtramck did not meet with a disaster similar to Harmar's, he achieved little success. Plagued by illness and lack of supplies, the Americans destroyed several Indian villages near the mouth of the Vermilion and then returned to Vincennes. Hamtramck's decision to retreat was fortunate for the Americans. Awaiting them further up the Wabash was a large number of Kickapoos, Weas, and Potawatomis from the Tippecanoe. When the Americans failed to appear, some of the tribesmen attempted to catch Hamtramck's column as it returned to Vincennes. Although a war party intercepted the Americans, the Indians did not attack. Among Hamtramck's followers were several creoles who had been forced to guide the Americans, and the warriors did not wish to endanger them.[20]

The Indians were elated with their victory over Harmar's expedition and were more determined than ever to oppose American settlement north of the Ohio. Flushed with success, the Potawatomis and their allies launched a rare winter campaign against white settlers along the Miami River. During January, 1791, three hundred Potawatomis, Delawares, Shawnees, and Miamis attacked Dunlap's Station, about eighteen miles north of modern Cincinnati. Although the Indians were repulsed, several Americans were killed, and a captured surveyor, Abner Hunt, was slowly burned to death within sight of the station. Later in the month the warfare spread to Illinois, where Potawatomis from Chicago killed a French trader friendly to the Americans, and during the spring other warriors again raided along the Ohio Valley.[21] In March, Potawatomis from eastern Michigan joined a party of Ottawas and Chippewas, intending to attack American shipping on the Ohio. They encountered a large force of American bateaux but failed to fire upon the boats since they feared the Americans were too well armed. During early April, however, the war party killed and scalped two settlers whom they surprised near the mouth of the Licking River. In May, other warriors swept through southern Illinois, and by June, 1791, land speculators in Ohio loudly complained that their business had been destroyed, since "Indians kill people so frequently that none dare stir into the woods to view the country...."[22]

Reeling from the onslaught, the Kentuckians struck back. During the summer of 1791, Brigadier General Charles Scott and Lieutenant Colonel James Wilkinson led expeditions against the Wea and Kickapoo towns on the central Wabash. Although the American forays crushed the Weas and forced them to make peace, the Potawatomis, the Kickapoos, and other tribes remained undaunted.[23]

With the Indians in the ascendancy, British officials attempted to mediate between the two sides, hoping to end the warfare along the

Ohio. Not only did the fighting disrupt the fur trade, but the British also feared that the growing conflict might spread to their posts in the Northwest, involving the Crown in a confrontation with the Americans. In July the Potawatomis and other tribes met with Alexander McKee on the Maumee, where the British Indian agent offered his services in restoring peace with the United States. During August a delegation of Potawatomis joined with other Indians and traveled to Quebec, where they received a similar offer from Lord Dorchester, the governor of Canada. The warriors informed the governor that although they might relinquish territory east of the Muskingum, they would not give up any lands in central Ohio.[24]

Yet before any significant peace negotiations could be initiated, the United States launched another military expedition against the tribes along the Maumee and upper Wabash. Disgraced over Harmar's defeat, in March, 1791, Congress appropriated over $300,000 to finance another campaign against the northwestern Indians. During the summer, American officials raised additional troops and made preparations to construct a series of forts stretching from Cincinnati north to the Maumee Valley. When another American diplomatic offensive failed during the spring of 1791, the plans for the military expeditions were put into operation.[25]

The American plans were poorly executed. The Potawatomis and other tribes knew of the American preparations, and during September they assembled large numbers of warriors along the Maumee. Meanwhile, on September 17 Governor Arthur St. Clair and an army of approximately twenty-three hundred men left Fort Washington and proceeded up the Miami Valley. St. Clair's army consisted of two small regiments of regular infantry and large numbers of six-month volunteers and militia. The volunteers and militia were poorly trained, and the entire expedition suffered from inadequate and shoddy provisions. In an outstanding display of poor judgment, St. Clair allowed about two hundred women, mostly prostitutes and camp followers, to join the expedition. Some of the women were accompanied by their children.[26]

Traveling at a snail's pace, the American army reached the headwaters of the Wabash in late November. En route, the expedition had been plagued by continual rain, and more than nine hundred of the militia had deserted. St. Clair's personal health was indicative of the American situation; the old governor suffered so severely from gout that he had to be carried in a litter. On the evening of November 3, 1791, St. Clair's army made a bedraggled camp on the

East Fork of the upper Wabash near modern Fort Recovery, Ohio.[27]

Aware of St. Clair's progress, on October 28, 1791, the Potawatomis and their allies left the camps along the Maumee and moved south to meet the Americans. Indian morale was high. Their medicine had been good against Harmar, and it would be even better against St. Clair. The war party numbered more than one thousand warriors, including Potawatomis from eastern Michigan and the Saint Joseph. All of the tribesmen had been well supplied by British traders, and they were anxious to strike the Long Knives.[28]

After nightfall on November 3 the Potawatomis and their allies surrounded the American encampment. Although an American patrol encountered some of the warriors, the officer in charge failed to notify St. Clair of his discovery. Still, the governor expected an attack, and an hour before sunrise St. Clair mustered his sleepy men from their blankets. From the shelter of the woods the Potawatomis watched as the troops assembled and then were dismissed thirty minutes later when American officers concluded that no attack was imminent.[29]

The Americans were mistaken. As the militia units returned to their camp across the river, the war cry sounded and the underbrush exploded with musket fire. Panic-stricken, the militia fell back on the regulars and six-month volunteers, who attempted to form ranks to meet the Indians. Although an initial Indian assault was repulsed, the Potawatomis and other warriors fired from behind the dense cover, taking a terrible toll on the soldiers. The Americans answered with artillery, but most of their cannon were aimed too high, and the shells and grapeshot passed harmlessly above the heads of the tribesmen. The battle raged throughout the early morning, but by 9:30 the American position was untenable. Indian marksmen had killed or wounded hundreds of American soldiers, and the remaining troops huddled together in the middle of the encampment, seeking shelter from enemy fire. Finally St. Clair and his followers broke through Indian ranks on the southern perimeter and fled south toward safety. In their panic the Americans abandoned their wounded comrades and most of their equipment to the Indians. By noon the battle was over.[30]

St. Clair's defeat was the greatest Indian victory over an American military force in all of American history. The United States suffered 647 men killed and hundreds wounded. The number of women and children killed is unknown. The Potawatomis and their allies lost about 150 warriors.[31]

Discouraged in their attempts to subdue the Indians with military force, the Americans again resorted to diplomacy. In the spring of 1792, American officials sent two agents disguised as traders to villages near Detroit in an attempt to ascertain Indian sentiments and to influence the Indians toward a negotiated peace. Messengers also were dispatched directly to the Potawatomis and to other tribes, informing the tribesmen that although they had defeated two American armies, their victories were only temporary. Secretary of War Knox warned the Potawatomis that if they failed to negotiate a settlement, the United States would move against them with "destructive consequences." Yet the American efforts produced few results. The two agents disguised as traders were captured by the British, and the other messengers were killed by the Wyandots and Miamis before they could reach the other tribes. Although the Potawatomis learned of Knox's message, they ignored the warning, and during the summer the usual war parties again raided along the Ohio.[32]

Since their diplomatic efforts in Ohio and Indiana had failed, American officials turned their attention to the west, hoping to isolate the hostiles from other Indians. Scott's and Wilkinson's raids during the summer of 1791 had intimidated the Weas and Piankashaws into suing for peace, and the Americans hoped that any treaty with those members of the Miami Confederacy could be enlarged to include the western Potawatomis. Government agents had some grounds for optimism. In the early 1790's Potawatomis from the Kankakee had established new villages on the Illinois River near the northern shores of Lake Peoria. Since their villages remained far to the west, the Illinois River Potawatomis were isolated from British influence and were not threatened by American expansion. Led by La Gesse, who had aided Siggenauk in the attack on Fort Saint Joseph, the Illinois River villagers remained tied to traders from Spanish Louisiana and had not fought in the war against the Americans. During the spring, Hamtramck inquired if La Gesse would meet with government officials, and in June, 1792, the Potawatomi chief replied that he wished to remain friends with the Long Knives and would participate in any peace treaty negotiated on the Wabash.[33]

Encouraged by La Gesse's reply, during September, 1792, American officials met with nine western tribes at Vincennes. La Gesse and ten other warriors represented the Potawatomis, while Brigadier General Rufus Putnam spoke for the United States. Most of the tribes in attendance were from Illinois or the lower Wabash Valley and were not closely tied to the hostiles. Putnam assured them that the government wanted peace and that the "great Chief General Washington" desired to "establish a good and lasting Friendship between all his Brothers and the United States." After accepting American presents, La Gesse, Gomo or Masemo (Resting Fish), and Waweachsetoh signed a "Treaty of Peace and Friendship" with the Americans. After the treaty, La Gesse and Gomo joined with a delegation of other tribesmen who journeyed to Philadelphia to see Washington.[34]

The Treaty of Vincennes was more an exercise in wishful thinking than a realistic step toward peace. Most of the Indians attending the proceedings already were friendly toward the United States, and the treaty only confirmed their policies. Moreover, the hostile tribes were not impressed by the negotiations, and the Potawatomis on the Saint Joseph denounced their kinsmen from Peoria for signing the document. Ironically, since the agreement did not guarantee the exclusive rights of the American government over Indian lands in the region, the Senate refused to ratify it.[35]

In the west, however, the Vincennes treaty was deemed a success, and government agents renewed their attempts to negotiate with the red confederacy. Since the Indians had killed white messengers, American officials hired Iroquois and Stockbridge spokesmen to carry their peace offers to the hostile tribesmen. In the fall of 1792 the Potawatomis and other Indians assembled on the Maumee, where they received the Iroquois messengers. Although they treated the Iroquois respectfully, the Potawatomis and their allies were not receptive to the American pleas. Flushed with their victories over Harmar and St. Clair, the tribesmen informed the messengers that they no longer would relinquish claims to the region east of the Muskingum but now demanded that all land north of the Ohio be abandoned by the United States. Finally, however, the confederacy agreed to meet with the Americans at Sandusky in the spring if the government promised to destroy its forts in Ohio.[36]

During November the Iroquois relayed the information back to the Americans, but overemphasized the confederacy's desire for peace. Anxious to negotiate, Secretary of War Henry Knox informed the Indians that the United States "embraces your proposal and will send Commissioners, to meet you at the time and place appointed." But the winter of 1792–93 held little to confirm the Americans' optimism. In November a war party of Potawatomis,

Shawnees, Delawares, and Miamis attacked a camp of mounted infantry near Fort St. Clair, stealing the American horse herd and killing five soldiers. Meanwhile, American spies reported that the Saint Joseph Potawatomis remained anti-American and that they threatened the lives of La Gesse and Gomo for signing the treaty at Vincennes. The villages along the Saint Joseph held more than thirty American prisoners, and the Saint Joseph tribesmen continued to bedeck their families with American military uniforms captured at St. Clair's defeat.[37]

Undaunted, the United States appointed three commissioners: Benjamin Lincoln, Timothy Pickering, and Beverly Randolph, to meet with the Indians during the summer of 1793. The commissioners were instructed that the government would relinquish the lands ceded at the Treaty of Fort Harmar, except for those areas purchased by private citizens, and such military forts as supposedly were given up by the British in the Treaty of Paris. The United States also was willing to evacuate most of its other military posts north of the Ohio and agreed to pay the red confederacy fifty thousand dollars in goods and an annuity of ten thousand dollars.[38]

The Potawatomis and their allies also prepared for the negotiations. During June, 1793, the confederacy met with Joseph Brant and the Iroquois at the rapids of the Maumee. The Indians asked the British at Detroit to supply them with copies of all treaties, maps, and records involving Indian affairs in the Northwest. They also requested that Lieutenant Governor John Simcoe allow British agents to participate in the negotiations. Finally, the confederacy decided to send delegates to meet the American commissioners, who had proceeded no farther than western New York, and to escort them to Detroit.[39]

In early July the Potawatomis and other delegates journeyed to Niagara, where they met with the American commissioners. The officials assured the Indians that the United States wanted peace and that Anthony Wayne was recruiting an army on the Ohio only to protect the tribesmen from illegal raids by frontiersmen, but the commissioners also warned that "concessions must be made by both sides." After listening to the American peace terms, the Potawatomis and other warriors escorted the Americans across Lake Erie to Matthew Elliott's farm near the mouth of the Detroit River. The commissioners agreed to remain at Elliott's residence while the Indians returned to the Maumee to discuss the American proposals with the assembled tribes.[40]

On the Maumee, the old disagreement over the cession of lands east of the Muskingum again emerged. Although the Potawatomis, Ottawas, and Chippewas were willing to relinquish the region, they reluctantly agreed to Shawnee demands that the Ohio River serve as the boundary between the Indians and the Americans. The Iroquois, however, refused to support the confederacy's position, and when the tribesmen sent a message to the commissioners demanding that the United States give up claims to eastern Ohio, Brant and his followers refused to sign the document.[41]

The confederacy's demands also were rejected by the commissioners. Lincoln, Pickering, and Randolph argued that American settlement already was well established in eastern Ohio and that the lands ceded at Fort Harmar were not negotiable. They countered the Indian proposal with an offer of additional payments and annuities and promised to recognize all other Indian land north of the Ohio River. The confederacy then suggested that the government take the money offered to the Indians and divide it among the settlers in southern and eastern Ohio, for

> we are persuaded that they would most readily accept it, in lieu of the Lands you sold them. If you add also the great sums you must expend in raising and paying armies, with a view to force us to yield you our country you will certainly have more than sufficient for the purposes of repaying these settlers for all their labor and their improvements.

The American commissioners answered that since the tribesmen were unwilling to make any compromises north of the Ohio, the negotiations were at an end. On August 17, 1793, the Americans left Elliott's farm and returned to the east.[42]

The breakdown in diplomacy did not surprise Major General Anthony Wayne, who had spent the past year rebuilding the American army. After investigating Harmar's and St. Clair's defeats, Wayne drilled his recruits mercilessly, making careful preparations for a new expedition. In September, 1793, he received news that the negotiations had failed, but he decided to wait until the following summer before launching a campaign against the Indians. Meanwhile, during the fall of 1793, Wayne erected two new American forts in western Ohio: Fort Greenville, about twenty miles west of Piqua, and Fort Recovery, at the site of St. Clair's defeat.[43]

Since the Indians knew that the Americans were planning another expedition, Wayne's activities were closely monitored by the

Potawatomis and other warriors. Yet many Potawatomis seemed uncertain in their support of the confederacy's defense of Ohio. The Saint Joseph and Tippecanoe villages had been most anxious to negotiate a compromise over the lands east of the Muskingum, and during the fall of 1794 they enlisted in a last futile attempt by the Ottawas, Chippewas, and Iroquois to reach an agreement with the Americans. In contrast, the Potawatomis from the Huron River valley near Detroit continued to support the militant Shawnees. In November, 1793, they received false reports that Wayne was planning an immediate invasion along the Maumee, and they rushed warriors to the defense of Indian towns in northern Ohio. When the invasion failed to occur, the Huron River Potawatomis returned to their villages, but they remained faithful to the Shawnee position of no compromise.[44]

Meanwhile, the British did their best to hold the red confederacy together. In February, 1794, Lord Dorchester met with Indian leaders in Quebec and rashly implied that the tribesmen could expect the full support of the British government. As proof of their commitment, during April the British began construction of a new post, Fort Miami, on the lower Maumee near modern Toledo. When news of the British actions reached the Potawatomis on the Tippecanoe and the Saint Joseph, they abandoned their overtures to the United States and rejoined the militants.[45]

While the Royal engineers were constructing Fort Miami, Wayne made careful preparations for a summer campaign against the Indian villages along the Auglaize and Maumee rivers in northwestern Ohio. During the spring the Americans reinforced Fort Recovery, and Wayne stockpiled supplies at his advance posts to provide support for the upcoming expedition. The increase in American activity triggered a similar response on the part of the Potawatomis. In May, warriors in Michigan and Indiana left their villages to join a large assemblage of other tribesmen awaiting Wayne near the juncture of the Auglaize and Maumee rivers. By the middle of June the warriors became impatient, and one June 20 more than one thousand warriors left their camps and started south, expecting to meet the Americans near Fort Recovery.[46]

Nine days later the Indian army arrived at the American fort. Although Wayne's expedition still remained at Fort Greenville, several supply trains of pack horses constantly plied the trail between the two posts, and the Indians learned that a supply column was scheduled to leave Fort Recovery during the following morning.

On the night of June 29 the Potawatomis and their allies surrounded the post, and when the Americans attempted to leave on the following morning, the warriors swarmed from their hiding places and overwhelmed their enemy. The attack took place at about seven o'clock, and in the initial assault the Indians killed fifteen Americans and captured approximately three hundred horses. Exhilarated by their success, the Potawatomis, Ottawas, and Chippewas launched a general attack on the American post. The Three Fires attempted to storm the palisades, but the other Indians failed to support their action and the Potawatomis and their friends were beaten back with heavy losses. The Indians then took cover in the surrounding forest and kept up a continuous fire upon the garrison for the remainder of the day. During the evening, however, most of the Potawatomis retired toward the Maumee.[47]

The attack on Fort Recovery was a minor skirmish to the Americans, yet it had a great impact upon the Indians. Although the Indians lost only about twenty killed, they suffered many wounded. More importantly, the Potawatomis, Ottawas, and Chippewas, tribes that had led the assault on the fort, sustained a high percentage of the casualties. The Huron River Potawatomis were bitter over their losses, and as the war party returned to the Auglaize, they accused the Delawares and Shawnees of cowardice in failing to support their attack on the palisade. Although several of the Saint Joseph warriors remained in northern Ohio, the Ottawas, Chippewas, and Huron River Potawatomis, about one-third of the Indian army, withdrew from the Auglaize and returned to their villages.[48]

With the Indian army weakened, Wayne took the offensive. On July 28, 1794, the general led a force of thirty-five hundred men north toward the Maumee Valley. Potawatomi scouts reported on his progress, and the Indians along the Maumee sent messengers to all the tribes in the confederacy urging them to reassemble their warriors for the defense of northern Ohio. By August 8 the American army reached the Indian towns on the Auglaize and found them deserted. The tribesmen had abandoned the towns to concentrate their forces near Roche de Bout, on the lower Maumee, where they awaited reinforcements. Wayne remained near the mouth of the Auglaize for a week. While his men pillaged the surrounding countryside and destroyed Indian villages, construction crews erected a new American post, Fort Defiance. On August 13 Wayne sent a message to the confederacy asking them to send delegates "to settle the preliminaries for a lasting peace." The Indians made no reply, and on August 15 the Americans left Fort Defiance and marched down the Maumee Valley toward the Indian stronghold.[49]

At Roche de Bout the red confederacy desperately played for time. Although they numbered nearly thirteen hundred warriors, including many Potawatomis from the Saint Joseph, the Indians still awaited the arrival of the Ottawas, Chippewas, and Huron River Potawatomis. These tribesmen remained angry over the failure of the Shawnees and Delawares to support their assault on Fort Recovery, and they were slow in responding to the confederacy's plea. On August 17, as Wayne's army drew closer, the Indians on the Maumee sent an evasive reply to Wayne's message, asking the Americans to halt their advance and wait for ten days, after which the confederacy would send a formal answer to Wayne's request for negotiations. Yet the Potawatomis realized a battle was imminent, and on August 18 they joined other warriors in a defensive position among a grove of storm-felled trees on the north bank of the Maumee below Roche de Bout.[50]

Since Wayne was less than ten miles away, the Potawatomis and their allies expected the Americans to attack on the following morning. They were mistaken. On August 18 the American commander had stopped to begin construction on a new post, Fort Deposit, where his army rested two days before again moving forward on the morning of August 20. Meanwhile, when the Americans failed to appear on August 19, many of the warriors returned to Fort Miami for food and other provisions. During the night of August 19 thunderstorms swept through the lower Maumee Valley, and other Indians left the tangle of fallen trees to seek sanctuary in their camp near the British fort. Therefore, on the morning of August 20, fewer than four hundred Indians and a few British traders remained at Fallen Timbers.[51]

The battle began at mid-morning. Wayne's army did not leave camp until eight o'clock, and after marching about five miles a party of mounted volunteers was ambushed as they approached the Indian position. The volunteers turned and fled back toward Wayne's regulars, who momentarily were thrown into confusion. Yet Wayne's legion was a different army from the ill-disciplined rabble that had followed Harmar and St. Clair, and the Indians failed to take advantage of the situation. Wayne rallied his forces, and the regulars held. The Americans slowly advanced, and the Potawatomis and their allies fell back into defensive positions among the trees. As the Americans approached the Indian lines, the warriors fired at them from behind the cover of their natural barricade and then sent a party away from the river in an attempt to outflank the left end of the American line. Yet Wayne anticipated their moves, sending his cavalry in wide sweeps around the Indian position so that his mounted volunteers and dragoons successfully gained the rear of the Indian defenses. Wayne then ordered his legions to fix their bayonets and charge the Indian center. The American maneuvers were too much for the Potawatomis. As Wayne's infantry stormed over the trunks of the fallen trees, the Indians broke and fled for the safety of Fort Miami.[52]

But the safety of the fort was denied them. As the fleeing Potawatomis approached Fort Miami, the British commander, Major William Campbell, closed the gates and refused them sanctuary. The Crown was willing to furnish arms and encouragement to the confederacy, but it was not willing to risk a confrontation with the United States. The surprised Indians then continued their flight down the Maumee, where they congregated near Lake Erie.[53]

Wayne remained on the lower Maumee for two days, exchanging notes with Campbell and destroying Indian villages and cornfields. He then marched back to Fort Defiance. Both sides had suffered similar casualties. The United States lost forty-four killed and eighty-nine wounded. Indian casualties were harder to ascertain. Wayne estimated Indian losses to be at least double those of his army, while McKee stated that the confederacy had suffered only nineteen killed. Actual Indian casualties probably lie somewhere between these two extremes and may have reached fifty warriors. Yet Fallen Timbers was a greater American victory than the figures would indicate. The failure of the British to give sanctuary to the fleeing warriors demoralized the Indians, and Wayne's army destroyed the vast amounts of property and extensive stockpiles of food the tribesmen had stored along the Maumee.[54]

The extent of Potawatomi participation in the battle remains unclear. Prisoners captured by the Americans reported that Potawatomi warriors fought behind the barricade of fallen trees, but the captives did not mention how many Potawatomis were present. Approximately fifty Saint Joseph warriors had remained on the Maumee after the attack on Fort Recovery, and they later were joined by about twenty-five other Potawatomis from their villages. Since the Potawatomis from eastern Michigan did not arrive in time to oppose Wayne, and the villages on the Kankakee and near Chicago suffered from a smallpox epidemic during the summer of 1794, the seventy-five Saint Joseph warriors were probably the only Potawatomis to fight Wayne at Fallen Timbers.[55]

After the battle on the Maumee, the confederacy was shattered. Fort Defiance remained at the mouth of the Auglaize, and in October the Americans built Fort Wayne near the Miami village at the headwaters of the Maumee. In September Wayne sent messages to the Potawatomis and other tribes, again promising peace if the Indians would surrender their white prisoners and negotiate with the Americans. He reminded them that the British had refused them entry into Fort Miami and had "neither the power nor inclination to protect you."[56]

Wayne's message was well received. Although the British supplied the tribes with food during the fall of 1794, and British dignitaries journeyed to the west to renew their pledges of friendship, the Potawatomis and their allies could not forget the closed gates at Fort Miami. In October, Simcoe, Elliott, and McKee met with the Potawatomis and other tribes at Brownstown, near the mouth of the Detroit River. The Indians listened politely to the British speeches, but they remained bitter. Speaking for the assembled tribesmen, a Wyandot chief answered the British by stating that he had listened to British promises before, but that the Indians "were low spirited by waiting so long and we are nearly at the end of our expectations."[57]

Later in the fall the Potawatomis began to make peace with the Americans. During November, Five Medals, a chief from the Elkhart River, led a delegation of warriors to Fort Wayne, where they made arrangements to confer with Wayne at Fort Greenville. In January, 1795, Five Medals and his warriors met with Wayne and agreed to a formal armistice with the Americans. The Potawatomis also promised to return to Greenville during the following June to sign a permanent peace treaty with the United States. Wayne treated the Potawatomis cordially, presenting them with gifts of clothing and trade goods, and the tribesmen returned to their villages favorably impressed with the Americans.[58]

Two months later Windigo led the Huron River Potawatomis on a similar mission. During March, 1795, they also met with Wayne, signing an armistice and promising to attend the upcoming peace conference. Windigo was accompanied by Cashkoa (Fast Walker), another war chief, and by Okia (Bay), a village chief from eastern Michigan. Speaking for his people, Okia assured the Americans that he was pleased with the armistice and that the Potawatomis were "determined to bury the hatchet so deep that it will never again be found."[59]

To the west, Potawatomis from the Tippecanoe also sought peace with the Long Knives. In February, Keesass (Sun) journeyed to Vincennes, where he met with Major Thomas Pasteur and pledged his good intentions. Two months later the Potawatomis gave up several American prisoners, and in May, Keesass moved his village to the Wabash River a few miles below the mouth of the Tippecanoe so that his people could be near American traders. Unfortunately, many of Keesass' warriors were more intransigent than their chief. The warriors continually attempted to exact tribute from Americans passing up and down the Wabash, and the new village soon became notorious as a center for stolen American horses.[60]

Ironically, while the pro-British Potawatomis in Michigan and Indiana moved toward an accommodation with the Americans, their western kinsmen threatened to disrupt the treaty negotiations at Greenville. Although most of the Potawatomis in Illinois and Wisconsin had remained at peace with the Long Knives, during January, 1795, a few young warriors from Siggenauk's village touched off a conflict in southern Illinois. Full of frontier whiskey, they attacked an isolated farm near Belleville, killing five people and taking two prisoners. One of the prisoners escaped, but the Potawatomis carried the other back to Milwaukee. Although Siggenauk ransomed the captive and later returned her to St. Louis, white settlers were incensed over the murders and attacked a party of friendly Potawatomis from Lake Peoria, killing six men and two women. Meanwhile, two of the Potawatomis responsible for the raid were captured by the Illinois Confederacy, who turned their prisoners over to the Americans at Kaskaskia. Officials at Kaskaskia ordered the two Potawatomis transported to Cahokia, but while en route the Indians were seized by a mob near Belleville and murdered.[61]

Angry that the Americans had killed eight of their kinsmen, Potawatomis from Lake Peoria joined with Kickapoos and retaliated by raiding southern Illinois. During the spring they attacked several farms and ambushed an American convoy on the Ohio, killing eighteen persons and plundering their possessions. In response, American settlers in southern Illinois clamored for troops and urged Wayne to build a new fort at Lake Peoria.[62]

At Greenville, Anthony Wayne feared that the outbreak of fighting in Illinois would sabotage the treaty negotiations to be held during the following summer. Both Wayne and Governor St. Clair realized that both the Potawatomis and the settlers shared in the blame for the bloodshed, and while they took measures to punish the guilty Indians, they also endeavored to keep the whites from attacking the Potawatomis. Messages were sent to officials in Illinois demanding that those responsible for the murder of the Potawatomi prisoners be punished, and St. Clair issued proclamations forbidding all American citizens to enter into the Potawatomi homeland or to kill, injure, or insult any member of the tribe.[63]

Yet Wayne's fears for the treaty proceedings were premature. Since the Potawatomi villages were politically autonomous, the skirmishes taking place in Illinois had little impact upon those tribesmen from Indiana and Michigan. Of the 240 Potawatomis attending the treaty proceedings, most came from villages along the Saint Joseph, Tippecanoe, Elkhart, and Huron rivers. But Siggenauk also wanted peace and led delegations of warriors from Illinois and Wisconsin. Most of the Potawatomis arrived in Ohio during the first week of July.[64]

The official treaty negotiations began on July 15, 1795. During the negotiations Okia spoke for the tribesmen on the Huron River, Kessass represented the villages on the Tippecanoe and the Wabash, and the elderly Le Petit Bled served as spokesman for the Potawatomis along the Saint Joseph. In conjunction with the Ottawas and Chippewas, the Potawatomis vigorously pushed their claim to the ceded lands in Ohio and were happy when Wayne agreed to award each of the three tribes an annuity of one thousand dollars. The confederacy agreed to relinquish all claims to lands in southern and central Ohio, and the Potawatomis consented to cede small sections of land at Lake Peoria, at the mouth of the Chicago River, and near Detroit. The Potawatomis also agreed to allow American travelers access to the Illinois River and to the Chicago portage. On August 3, 1795, twenty-three Potawatomis attached their signatures to the Treaty of Greenville.[65]

Although the Potawatomis had few legitimate claims to the lands ceded by the Indians at the Treaty of Greenville, they agreed to the cession and shared in the payments. The treaty only formalized a new set of conditions that had existed since the Indian defeat at Fallen Timbers. Potawatomi warriors from Michigan and Indiana had supported the red confederacy, but the confederacy had been beaten. Moreover, the British again had proven unreliable. Although they had supplied the tribesmen with powder and promises, they had failed to support the warriors fleeing Wayne's army. In the years to come, as the Americans moved closer to the Potawatomi homelands, tribal leaders again would disagree over what policy to follow. Ironically, the Potawatomis near Lake Michigan, warriors traditionally more friendly to the United States, would now turn to the British for assistance and would seek strength in the mysticism of a Shawnee holy man. In contrast, the eastern Potawatomis, who had been friends with the Redcoats since Pontiac's rebellion, now sought an accommodation with the United States. As American soldiers occupied Detroit and Fort Wayne, chiefs such as Okia and Five Medals realized that the Long Knives were in the ascendancy. Wayne's legions had proven that the Americans could be a formidable enemy, and many Potawatomis could not forget the closed gates at Fort Miami.

Alexander Robinson (Chechepinquay, or The Squinter), a mixed-blood, consistently befriended white settlers and rose to prominence among the Potawatomis during the removal period. He died at Chicago in 1872. *Courtesy Chicago Historical Society*

Governor Ninian Edwards of Illinois led an expedition which attacked the Potawatomi villages near Peoria in October, 1812. *Courtesy Illinois State Historical Library*

Although Waubansee (He Causes Paleness) led an attack on Harrison's supply vessels as they ascended the Wabash before the Battle of Tippecanoe, in 1812 he intervened in the Fort Dearborn Massacre to protect some of the white prisoners. He later signed the 1833 Treaty of Chicago. From McKenney-Hall. *Courtesy Western History Collections, University of Oklahoma Library*

Metea (Sulker), a chief from northeastern Indiana, was wounded opposing Harrison's relief of Fort Wayne. In 1821 Metea, an eloquent orator, denounced Potawatomi land cessions at the Treaty of Chicago. From McKenney-Hall. *Courtesy Western History Collections, University of Oklahoma Library*

Stern-countenanced Abel C. Pepper, closely associated with the Potawa-
tomis throughout the removal period, negotiated for vast tracts of
Potawatomi lands in northern Indiana. He presided over the question-
able 1836 annuity payments and adamantly opposed attempts by the
Indians to remain in their homeland. *Courtesy Indiana Historical
Society Library*

Isaac McCoy, founder of Carey Mission among the Saint Joseph Potawatomis, later was involved in the selection of Potawatomi lands in the
trans-Mississippi west. *Courtesy Kansas State Historical Society, Topeka*

Topinbee (He Who Sits Quietly), a leading chief of the Saint Joseph Potawatomis, supported McCoy's efforts at Carey Mission. *Courtesy Northern Indiana Historical Society*

While serving as Indian agent among the Potawatomis at Chicago, Alexander Wolcott assisted in the questionable negotiations surrounding the 1821 treaty. *Courtesy Chicago Historical Society*

William Marshall served as Indian agent at Logansport from 1832 to 1835, befriending Quiquito's people when they fled into Indiana after the Black Hawk War. *Courtesy Indiana Historical Society Library*

View of the Great Treaty Held at Prairie du Chien, September, 1825, by J. O. Lewis. Although Senachewine and other Peoria Potawatomis refused to attend the treaty proceedings at Prairie du Chien, their lands in northern Illinois were ceded by other Potawatomis from Chicago and Wisconsin. *Courtesy Western History Collections, University of Oklahoma Library.*

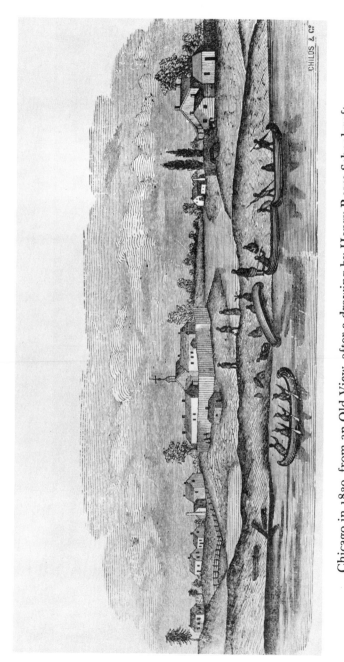

Chicago in 1820, from an Old View, after a drawing by Henry Rowe Schoolcraft.
Courtesy Chicago Historical Society

Ashkum (More and More), by George Winter. A chief from the Eel River, Ashkum refused government overtures to buy his reservation. In 1836 government officials purchased Ashkum's land from other Potawatomis. *Courtesy Tippecanoe County Historical Association*

Kee-wau-nay (Prairie Chicken), by George Winter. A Wabash Potawa-tomi, in 1836 Keewaunay conspired with Iowa, Pashpoho, and others to sell Ashkum's and Menominee's reservations. *Courtesy Tippecanoe County Historical Association*

Iowa, by George Winter. A leading spokesman for one faction of the Wabash Potawatomis, Iowa sold other tribesmen's reservations and was threatened with death. He accepted government bribes to urge removal upon his people. *Courtesy Tippecanoe County Historical Society*

Alexis Coquillard, a trader from the South Bend region, held considerable influence among the Saint Joseph Potawatomis. In 1851 he conducted the final government removal of Potawatomis from the Old
Northwest. *Courtesy Northern Indiana Historical Society*

Many Potawatomis in Indiana were heavily indebted to G. W. Ewing's trading company, and the trader's excessive claims at the 1836 Potawatomi claims payment sparked violent protests from other frontier merchants. *Courtesy Indiana Historical Society Library*

7. The Prophet's Disciples

The decade and one-half following the Treaty of Greenville witnessed the further dispersal of Potawatomi villages. By 1795, Potawatomis were spread from the Huron River in Michigan to the central Illinois Valley. Potawatomi fishermen near Milwaukee speared fish from Lake Michigan, while their kinsmen on the Tippecanoe hunted deer among the thickets along the Wabash. They were a populous people, for their warriors in northern Illinois and southeastern Wisconsin had intermarried with the Ottawas and Chippewas, and their villages had escaped the ravages of border warfare during the 1790's. But the geographic diffusion of the tribe continued to foster political autonomy among the different towns. After 1795, Potawatomis from the Illinois River rarely met with their kinsmen from Detroit, and although they all faced problems common to other Indians in the Old Northwest, they often sought different solutions.

One problem facing the tribesmen in eastern Indiana and Michigan was the renewed American presence north of the Ohio. In October, 1795, Anthony Wayne built Fort Wayne at the headwaters of the Maumee, and during the following summer American troops occupied Detroit. But the American influence diminished further west. Among the villages scattered along the Tippecanoe and across the prairie to the Illinois, Potawatomi warriors realized that the Americans now were the dominant power in the region, yet they were not intimidated by American forts and garrisons. Unlike the Potawatomis near Fort Wayne and Detroit, the western tribesmen were isolated from American military power and continued to act independently of American policy.

This independence was buttressed by Spanish officials in Louisiana. The western Potawatomis still traded with French and Spanish merchants from across the Mississippi, and Spain was anxious to maintain her influence in the Illinois country. She also was anxious to send the Potawatomis against the Osages. Intermittent warfare had flared between the Spanish and the Osages in the years following the American Revolution, but in 1793, Spain launched a major campaign, and the Osage reciprocated in kind. In an attempt to crush their enemies, the Spanish enlisted the aid of the Algonquian tribes from Illinois.[1]

The Potawatomis were willing participants in the conflict. Skirmishes between Potawatomi and Osages had occurred when warriors from the Illinois River villages crossed the Mississippi to visit the Spanish, and the Potawatomis were bitter over four scalps taken by the Osages in 1787. Moreover, after the Treaty of Greenville the Potawatomis ostensibly were at peace with the Long Knives, and the war against the Osages offered young warriors an opportunity to assert their manhood. Finally, the Osage war was a relatively "safe" conflict. Accompanied by large numbers of Sacs, Foxes, Kickapoos, and Shawnees, the Potawatomis could cross the Mississippi in safety, attack the Osages in their homeland, and then retreat back into Illinois. The Spanish would supply them with arms yet prevent large numbers of Osages from crossing the river in pursuit.[2]

But the warfare proved "safe" only for the Potawatomis. As both Spanish and American citizens in southern Illinois soon learned, the intertribal conflict often spread into indiscriminate attacks upon whites unlucky enough to encounter Potawatomi war parties returning from Louisiana. Warriors who had been unsuccessful against the Osages hated to return to their villages empty-handed and sometimes substituted white scalps for those of the Osages.[3] Although the Spanish quickly realized they had erred in seeking aid from the warriors across the Mississippi, they were unsure how to end the alliance. In 1794 Spain made peace with the Osages but could not stop the Potawatomis, Sacs, and Kickapoos from continuing their attacks into Louisiana. The Potawatomis still traded with the Spanish, and Potawatomi chiefs assured the Spanish of their fidelity, but Potawatomi war parties continued to cross the river in search of Osage villages.[4]

American officials also opposed the Potawatomi-Osage warfare. Although the western Potawatomis had signed the Treaty of Greenville, some chiefs, such as Main Poc from the Kankakee and Turkey Foot from the Tippecanoe, remained openly hostile to the United States. War parties led by these chiefs ranged across Illinois into

Missouri, as often striking isolated white settlements as the Osages. In the decade between 1795 and the Louisiana Purchase, Potawatomi and Kickapoo raiders plagued southern Illinois, stealing horses, slaughtering livestock, and making travel along the forested horse paths between Vincennes and Kaskaskia extremely hazardous. Solitary travelers feared for their lives upon meeting mounted parties of Potawatomis, and isolated farmers paid a heavy price for venturing away from the populated American Bottom.[5]

In the spring of 1802, while returning from Spanish Louisiana, Turkey Foot and a party of warriors encountered Alexander Dennis and John Vanmeter clearing land along the Mississippi near modern Edwardsville. Well stocked with trade whiskey, and angered over the sight of white men establishing farms in an area they believed their own, Turkey Foot and his warriors killed the two Americans and then fled across the prairie towards the upper Illinois.[6]

The murders of Dennis and Vanmeter were only the latest in a series of similar events occuring since 1795, but the deaths shocked white settlers and forced the government into action. American citizens near Kaskaskia petitioned federal officials, denouncing Turkey Foot and stating that his escapades in southern Illinois constituted a declaration of war against the United States. In reaction, President Jefferson ordered Governor William Henry Harrison to demand that the Potawatomis surrender those warriors responsible for the slayings. But the Potawatomis only ignored the demands, and Turkey Foot remained as irascible as ever.[7]

The Potawatomis' refusal to surrender the warriors convinced the government that it needed a stronger military position in the Northwest. If the United States wished to control the Illinois country, it could not allow the Indians to raid with impunity. Late in 1802, federal officials adopted a twofold plan to remedy the situation. A company of troops was stationed at Kaskaskia, and in the summer of 1803 other soldiers marched from Detroit to establish a new fort at the mouth of the Chicago River. The new post, Fort Dearborn, was raised on a small plot of land ceded by the Potawatomis at the Treaty of Greenville. American troops now occupied the Potawatomi heartland.[8]

The American troops were not the only whites in the region. A potpourri of former French, British, and American traders were scattered along the southern tip of Lake Michigan and eastward toward Detroit. Most were of mixed-blood or French origin. Chevalier had established a post on the Saint Joseph River almost half a century earlier, and a black man, probably of creole origin, Baptiste Point du Sable, had been active at Chicago during the American Revolution. In 1803 at least three French Canadians were trading with the Potawatomis near Chicago when the troops arrived from Detroit. One of them, a man named Ouilmette, had taken a Potawatomi wife. To the northwest, near the site of modern Milwaukee, merchants such as Jacques Viveau, Alexander Lafromboise, and Antoine Le Claire plied their wares to mixed villages of Potawatomis, Winnebagos, and Menominees. Le Claire and Viveau also were married to women of Potawatomi descent. Le Claire earlier had traded among the Potawatomis along the Saint Joseph Valley, where a number of creoles, including Joseph Bertrand, competed for the many muskrat pelts taken from English Lake at the headwaters of the Kankakee.[9]

Other traders were of British or American origin. Among the most prominent was William Burnett, a native of New Jersey, who had moved to the Saint Joseph Valley at the close of the Revolution. Burnett established a trading post and warehouse near the mouth of the river and married Kakima, daughter of Nanaquiba, the old chief who half-heartedly had supported Hamilton's journey down the Wabash in 1778. Burnett, an enterprising man, cleared land and raised crops of corn and wheat, which he shipped to Mackinac for sale. He also maintained warehouses on the Kankakee and near Chicago.[10]

Also active in the region was John Kinzie. Born in Quebec and raised in New York and at Detroit, Kinzie had traded at Sandusky and along the Maumee before coming to the Lake Michigan region. Kinzie had remained friendly to the British and Indians during the border conflicts of the 1790's, and Wayne's army had razed his trading post along the Maumee following Fallen Timbers. Shortly thereafter, he moved to the Saint Joseph Valley and began to trade among the Potawatomi villages near Chicago.[11]

Yet neither the garrison at Chicago nor nearby traders could keep the western Potawatomis at peace. Not satisfied with raids against the Osages and settlers in southern Illinois, the Potawatomis extended their warfare to the lower Wabash tribes and to the Kaskaskias. Since 1796, Main Poc's warriors had prowled the lower Wabash Valley, attacking Wea and Piankashaw hunters or ambushing Cherokee and Chickasaw travelers on their way to Fort Massac. The government made futile attempts to stop the skirmishes, but in the winter of 1804–1805 Potawatomi warriors from Lake Peoria extended the devastation to the remnant of the Kaskaskias, taking several women prisoners in a raid on the Kaskaskia village near Cahokia.[12]

In an attempt to preclude full-scale intertribal warfare, the United States brought delegates from the Potawatomis, Osages, and other tribes to a conference in St. Louis. In October, 1805, the Indians assembled, and after numerous talks by tribal spokesmen a treaty of peace was signed by the Potawatomis, Osages, and several other tribes. Yet the Potawatomis were represented only by two minor chiefs: La Barbue (The Bearded One) and Manamol. Noticeably absent were the great war chiefs Turkey Foot and Main Poc.[13]

The treaty meant nothing. Shortly after it was negotiated, a large war party led by Main Poc left the Kankakee River and crossed the Mississippi above St. Louis. The Osages had been lulled into carelessness by the recent conference, and in early November a band of Little Osages camped near the juncture of the Osage and Missouri rivers. In mid-morning, while the Osage warriors were away hunting deer, Main Poc's war party surprised the encampment. They struck quickly, killing thirty-four women and children and forced the remaining Osages, about sixty women and children, to accompany them back to Illinois. There, many of the captives were given to the Sacs and Foxes.[14]

The Osage warriors, their faces smeared with mud to indicate their sorrow, turned to Governor James Wilkinson for assistance. They argued that they had placed themselves under the protection of the United States and that such protection was meaningless if the Potawatomis were not punished. Wilkinson immediately dispatched letters to Charles Jouett, Indian agent at Chicago, and to Harrison asking them to secure the prisoners' release. Throughout the winter of 1805–1806 Harrison and Jouett pleaded with the Potawatomis, Sacs, and Foxes to give up the Osages, offering trade goods as a ransom for their exchange. In the summer of 1806 many of the Potawatomis near Chicago relinquished their prisoners, as did the Sacs and Foxes, but Main Poc's village held a handful of the unfortunate Osages until the fall of 1807.[15]

Inspired by Main Poc's success, the Potawatomis launched other raids into Missouri. In December, 1805, warriors from Turkey Foot's village killed two white men along the Missouri River, and during the following summer tribesmen in northern Illinois planned another major campaign against the Osages. Convinced that they could not stop the attack, government officials warned the

Osages. In August, 1806, when the Potawatomi war party crossed into Missouri, it was intercepted by Osage scouts, who warned of the party's advance. But the Potawatomis realized they had been discovered and returned to Illinois before the Osages could catch them. In frustration, they killed an American trader as they returned to villages near Chicago.[16]

The eastern Potawatomi were less hostile towards their neighbors. Tribesmen living along the upper Wabash, Elkhart, and Huron rivers remained friendly to the Americans and did not participate in the Osage War. In the years following the Treaty of Greenville, they kept the peace with the Long Knives, returning American prisoners and warning government officials of hostile sentiments among the Ottawas and Chippewas near Saginaw Bay.[17] The Saint Joseph Potawatomis also remained friendly, although some of their young men occasionally joined Main Poc and Turkey Foot. Yet chiefs from the Saint Joseph villages regularly met with the Americans and apologized for the hostilities, complaining that they were trying to keep their young men at home but had been unsuccessful. They also tried to appease the Wabash tribes, ransoming Piankashaw prisoners captured by Main Poc and turning them over to both American and British authorities.[18]

British influence among the Potawatomis continued to alarm the Americans. Many Potawatomi remained friendly to the British, journeying to Amherstburg to receive British gifts and to meet with British agents. Warriors from as far west as Milwaukee participated in the British conferences, but most of the Potawatomis who regularly crossed over into Canada were from villages in southern Michigan and northern Indiana. Although the Americans feared that the British were inciting the Potawatomis against the United States, such fears were exaggerated. The Potawatomis were much more interested in British trade goods.[19]

Attempting to counter British influence, the Americans launched a program of their own. Potawatomis visiting Detroit or Fort Wayne were provided with food and presents. Moreover, in an effort to impress the Potawatomis and their neighbors with the power and numbers of their Great White Father, the government decided to send a delegation of chiefs to Philadelphia. On October 4, 1796, Five Medals and another Potawatomi chief, accompanied by leaders from the Shawnees, Miamis, Ottawas, Chippewas, and Wabash tribes, set sail from Detroit on board the schooner *Swan*. Escorted by a group of government agents and interpreters, the Indians arrived in Philadelphia late in November. There they met with President Washington, who presided at a banquet and then spoke formally to the assembled tribesmen. Washington reminded all the Indians of the terms of the Treaty of Greenville and urged them to relinquish hunting in favor of agriculture. He then directed his address at the Potawatomis. Admitting that the whites had committed crimes against the Indians, Washington promised that such actions would be punished, but he warned the Potawatomis to turn over to the government those tribesmen responsible for crimes against whites. After the meeting with Washington, the Potawatomis and other Indians returned to their homes.[20]

Five Medals' impressions of Washington remain unknown. But the president's pleas to the chief to restrain his warriors from attacking the settlements in Illinois were wasted, for Five Medals' village was located on the headwaters of the Elkhart River in northeastern Indiana, and warriors from his village had not participated in the Osage War. Yet Washington's suggestions on agriculture seemed to interest the chief, for when he returned to Indiana, he found many of his people hungry and ill-prepared for the winter. The fur trade was declining throughout the Potawatomi homeland, and game was scarce. Although the Indians still planted gardens, their meager stores of corn and beans could not sustain them through the cold months. Between 1796 and 1801 the Potawatomis in northern Indiana and southern Michigan suffered poor winter hunts, and Five Medals became convinced that the tribe's economic woes could only be cured through farming. By 1800, Five Medals had persuaded Topinbee (He Who Sits Quietly), a chief from the Saint Joseph, that the Potawatomis should ask the government for agricultural assistance.[21]

In late 1801 the two Potawatomis accompanied Little Turtle and several other Indians to Washington. On the way to the capital the party passed through Baltimore, where they met with a convention of Quakers dedicated to missions on the western frontier. In December, 1801, Five Medals addressed the convention and informed the Friends that the Potawatomis were interested in agriculture but that they needed guidance in clearing lands and establishing farms. The Indians asked the Quakers for assistance and, much to the audience's delight, denounced the burgeoning whiskey trade as an evil being forced on them by unscrupulous traders.[22]

The Indians traveled on to Washington, where they met with government officials in January. In the capital Little Turtle spoke for all the tribes, including the Potawatomis, and again asked for government assistance in establishing farms. The Miami chief also asked officials to keep whites from settling on Indian territory, especially those areas bordering the government lands at Vincennes. He complained that the government's annuity goods often were of a poor quality and asked that the Miami and Potawatomi annuities be paid at Fort Wayne instead of Detroit. Finally, the Miami pleaded that the government supress the liquor trade, which he described as a "fatal poison" among the tribes of the Wabash Valley.[23]

Little Turtle's complaints over annuity distribution were strongly supported by Five Medals and Topinbee. Since the Potawatomis received their annuities at Detroit, many of the villages failed to share in the goods. Tribesmen from Illinois, Wisconsin, and along the Tippecanoe were isolated from the distribution center and rarely obtained any money and merchandise. By moving the annuity payment to Fort Wayne, the distribution would be more centrally located, although the Illinois and Wisconsin tribesmen still would be forced to travel great distances.[24]

Five Medals and Topinbee also were concerned about other problems mentioned by Little Turtle. Although the flow of illegal whiskey had not reached their homes in floodtide proportions, the liquor trade along the Wabash continually increased, and the more responsible chiefs wanted to limit the quantity. During the summer of 1801, Keesass had visited Harrison at Vincennes to discuss this problem and to register a complaint against whites hunting on Indian lands along the Wabash. At the Treaty of Greenville the Wabash tribes had relinquished their claim to a vaguely defined tract of land near Vincennes, but the borders of the tract remained uncertain. As the white population near Vincennes increased, settlers spread onto lands the Indians still considered to be their own. The Potawatomis were not immediately threatened, but they were concerned that the settlement might move north of the Wabash.[25]

Little Turtle's speech obviously pleased both Secretary of War Henry Dearborn and President Thomas Jefferson. They assured the Indians that their grievances would be ameliorated, and Jefferson especially was gratified over the request for farming equipment. In replying to the Indians, he promised the Potawatomis:

> We shall with pleasure see your people become disposed to cultivate the earth, to raise heards [*sic*] of the useful animals and to spin and weave for their food and clothing. These resources are

certain. They never will disappoint you, while those of hunting may fail and expose your women and children to the miseries of cold and hunger. We will with pleasure furnish you with implements for the most necessary arts, and with persons who will instruct how to make use of them.

Following the conference, the Indians returned home via Cincinnati.[26]

The government acted promptly to resolve the Indian complaints. The Potawatomi and Miami annuity distributions were moved from Detroit to Fort Wayne, and an Indian factory was planned for the latter location. Meanwhile, Harrison was ordered to assemble the tribes along the Wabash and to establish a definite boundary between Indian and white lands near Vincennes.[27]

On September 17, 1802, Harrison met at Vincennes with a delegation of chiefs and warriors from the Potawatomis, Miamis, Weas, Piankashaws, and Kickapoos. The purpose of the conference was to establish preliminary guidelines so that the Vincennes tract could be defined more precisely and then ceded at a later date. The Potawatomis were represented by Topinbee, Five Medals, Magaago, and Keesass. At the conference the Indians tentatively agreed to relinquish claims to a tract of land stretching along both sides of the Wabash from Point Coupee, eighteen miles north of Vincennes, to the mouth of the White River. Potawatomi claims to any of that region were nebulous, since their villages reached no further south than Keesass' town, a few miles below the mouth of the Tippecanoe. Yet by 1802 the Potawatomis and Miamis so dominated Indian affairs in Indiana that the lower Wabash tribes sought their approval before taking any action.[28]

The treaty to finalize the Vincennes tract boundaries was negotiated nine months later. In June, 1803, the Potawatomis and other Indians holding lands in Indiana signed a treaty at Fort Wayne which transferred the lands to the federal government. The final treaty was opposed by Little Turtle and a few other Miami chiefs, but it was ratified over their opposition. Yet the Fort Wayne treaty of 1803 was an ominous precedent of government policy in the region. Realizing that white settlement was surging into Indiana, the government had decided to clear the title to as much land as possible. In February, 1803, Jefferson had written to Harrison instructing him to do his best to acquire Indian lands in the Northwest and even suggesting that the tribesmen be put in debt through the factory system so that they would cede their lands as payment. The great American land grab had started anew.[29]

Meanwhile, the government pushed a program of assimilation. In response to Five Medals' and Little Turtle's pleas for farm implements, federal officials initiated a program to foster white methods of agriculture among the tribes near Fort Wayne. Hoes, plows, and livestock were sent to William Wells, the agent at the post, for distribution to the Potawatomis and Miamis. Wells also was instructed to hire white farmers as teachers for the Indians and to employ blacksmiths and carpenters to further the assimilation process.[30]

Government attempts to "civilize" the Potawatomis also were aided by religious organizations. By 1802 the Moravians had established missions among the Delawares on the White River, and several Potawatomis had joined their congregations. More important were the Quakers. In 1803, Five Medals and Little Turtle wrote back to the Quaker assembly they had addressed in Baltimore, again asking for Quaker assistance in learning white farming techniques. The Indians also complained that they needed the Quakers' help to suppress the liquor trade among the Potawatomis near Fort Wayne. The Quakers responded by sending three of their members, Gerard Hopkins, George Ellicott, and Phillip Dennis, to Fort Wayne to talk with the Potawatomis and Miamis and to investigate the possibilities of establishing a mission in the region. On April 5, 1804, they met with Five Medals, Little Turtle, and several other chiefs, who received them favorably. One week later, Wells accompanied the missionaries to a site on the Wabash about thirty-five miles from Fort Wayne, where Dennis decided to set up a model farm as an example to the nearby tribesmen. Hopkins and Ellicott then continued on to Detroit before returning to the East via Lake Erie.[31]

The model farm, known as Dennis Station, proved unsuccessful. Although Dennis was able to persuade a few Potawatomi and Miami warriors to assist him in erecting fences and planting crops, most of the tribesmen took only a passing interest in the venture. By the fall of 1804, Dennis was so discouraged that he discontinued the farm and returned to the east, turning over his harvest to Five Medals and Little Turtle for distribution to their tribesmen.[32]

Three years later the Quakers made another attempt to change the Potawatomis into farmers. In 1807, William Kirk, a missionary who earlier had worked among the Shawnees in Ohio, arrived at Fort Wayne to minister to the neighboring Potawatomis and

Miamis. Kirk had the blessing of President Jefferson and was supported by six thousand dollars in government funds. He hoped to settle among the Potawatomis at Five Medals' village, since the chief continually had expressed an interest in learning white farming methods. Late in May, Kirk met with Five Medals and several Miami chiefs, and the Indians seemed anxious to have the Quakers among them. Yet the mission never materialized. Kirk soon became involved in a bureaucratic dispute with Wells over the administration of the "civilizing program," and Five Medals sided with Wells in the argument. Charges and countercharges were levied, but in the summer of 1807 the Quaker gave up his plans for a mission among the Potawatomis and moved to the Shawnee villages on the Auglaize in Ohio.[33]

In the four years following 1807, Five Medals, Topinbee, and Winamac, a chief from the Tippecanoe, continued their pleas for agricultural assistance, and the government repeatedly sent farm implements to Fort Wayne and Detroit, but the Potawatomis did not become farmers. The interest in agriculture held by a few chiefs such as Five Medals did not permeate the tribe, and most Potawatomi warriors refused to accept the teachings of the missionaries or government agents. Bureaucratic disputes such as the Wells-Kirk controversy hindered the assimilation process, but more important was the growing Potawatomi suspicion of federal land policy in the region.[34]

The Indians' apprehension was valid. The Treaty of Fort Wayne in 1803 was only the first in a series of treaties negotiated by Harrison with the tribes of Illinois and Indiana. By 1806, Harrison had partially acquired a vast acreage in Illinois and southern Indiana through treaties with the Potawatomis, Delawares, Weas, Piankashaws, Miamis, Sacs, Foxes, Kaskaskias, and Kickapoos. Meanwhile, in 1805, at the Treaty of Fort Industry, the Potawatomis, Ottawas, and Chippewas gave up a large region in northern Ohio. The Potawatomis had little claim to any of the areas ceded, and in the years before 1806 they willingly participated in the cessions. The opportunity to acquire government presents and annuities for areas not within their homeland proved to be too strong a temptation. The fur trade continued to decline, and they had refused to become farmers. With a dwindling economic base, the Potawatomis were increasingly dependent on government provisions. A few signatures on a meaningless treaty seemed a small price to pay.[35]

But in 1806 the Potawatomis changed their minds. During the

previous August, Harrison had met with Potawatomis from the Wabash Valley, and they had seemed well disposed toward the United States. Similar assurances of Potawatomi friendship also had been given to General William Hull at Detroit, who met regularly with the Potawatomis from the Huron River. But in June, 1806, reports reached Secretary of War Dearborn that certain tribes in the Old Northwest had become hostile and were planning a general alliance against the Americans. In the same month a French trader near Fort Wayne informed Wells that he believed the Potawatomis, Ottawas, and Chippewas secretly were plotting to attack several posts stretching from Fort Wayne to Mackinac. Wells was apprehensive, but officials in Washington discounted the rumors, for they believed that the Wabash Potawatomis were so loyal they could be used as a stabilizing influence among other tribes.[36]

But the officials were wrong. Although Five Medals and some of the other older village chiefs continued to profess their friendship for the United States, many of the younger Potawatomi warriors had become hostile toward the Americans. Several factors contributed to the alienation. The Potawatomi annuity payments continued to be badly distributed. The western Potawatomis had never shared equally in the annuity distribution, so in 1804 the government decided to pay part of the Potawatomi annuities at Chicago. This move helped to placate the Potawatomis near Lake Michigan, but they still argued that they were receiving less than they should, and Potawatomis near Fort Wayne resented the decrease in their share of the annuities. Meanwhile, in 1805 the government arbitrarily moved the distribution center for the eastern Potawatomis back to Detroit.[37] Such actions should have pleased the Huron River Potawatomis, but since they were the only tribesmen who had claimed the lands in Ohio, they were upset that the annuities from the Treaty of Fort Industry were distributed among the entire tribe. In addition to the confusion over who was to receive the annuities, the government habitually was late in transporting the goods into the west. Finally, there is evidence to suggest that government officials may have allowed Five Medals and other friendly chiefs to appropriate part of each year's annuity before the remainder was distributed among the rest of the tribe.[38]

The continuing traffic in illegal whiskey also contributed to the Potawatomis' alienation. As early as 1801, Harrison had complained that Indians and whites were consuming vast amounts of alcohol, with the resulting drunkedness prompting violence from both sides.

Although Five Medals had railed against the use of liquor, he, like many of his tribesmen, was addicted to it, and the demand for whiskey was so great that both British and American traders used it as a standard commodity in the fur trade. Responsible chiefs such as Topinbee attempted to limit the traffic, but they were unsuccessful, and warriors full of whiskey were hard to control. Many Potawatomis resented the liquor traffic's debilitating effect upon their people, and they blamed the United States government.[39]

Frustration over land sales, annuities, and the whiskey trade made the Potawatomis ready recipients for the doctrines of Tenskwatawa, the Shawnee Prophet. A former alcoholic, in 1805 Tenskwatawa suffered an epileptic seizure in which he claimed to have visited the spirit world, and upon regaining consciousness, he asserted that the Great Spirit had chosen him to spread a new religion. The Prophet expounded a nativistic doctrine, warning his followers against liquor, witchcraft, and the ways of the white man. Interracial marriage was denounced, as was white clothing, private property, and other practices introduced by the Europeans. A native of Wapakoneta, a Shawnee village on the Auglaize River, in 1806 Tenskwatawa and his brother Tecumseh began to spread their new religion among the tribes to the west.[40]

The Prophet's messianic evangelism found converts among many young Potawatomis. In the autumn of 1806, emissaries from the Prophet visited Potawatomi villages as far west as Chicago. The Shawnee messengers carried invitations to a series of intertribal councils to be held on the Auglaize River during the following summer. The Potawatomis were warned that a great darkness would envelope the earth and that only the Prophet could save them from groping blindly in the forest. The means for such salvation would be given to them on the Auglaize. Most of the chiefs were skeptical, but many of the young warriors listened attentively, and in the spring of 1807 many of the Potawatomis left their villages to visit the Prophet in Ohio.[41]

En route to the Auglaize, most of the Potawatomis passed through Fort Wayne, where they were stopped by Five Medals and Wells, who attempted to persuade them to return home. Some of the warriors from the Saint Joseph turned back, but the majority continued on to the Shawnee village. There, near the site of the humiliating Treaty of Greenville, small parties of Potawatomis met with the Prophet throughout the summer of 1807.[42]

The movement of such large numbers of Indians frightened the

Americans. In June, 1807, the *"Chespeake* affair" persuaded many government officials that war with Britain was imminent. Although Hull negotiated another land cession in southeastern Michigan from friendly chiefs of the villages along the Huron and the Raisin, the cession was opposed by many of the Potawatomis who had met with the Prophet, and Indian agents in the west feared that the young warriors might take up the hatchet in support of the British. In the Wabash Valley, Five Medals and Keesass continued to support the United States, but they also were losing control of their young men. Realizing that their relations with the Indians were deteriorating, the Americans blamed their old nemesis, the British.[43]

They were partially correct. In 1807 the British, like the Americans, believed that the two countries were on the brink of war. Vastly outnumbered in the west, the British hoped again to muster the tribes as allies. In October the British invited the Potawatomis near Detroit to meet with them at Amherstberg. Some of the Potawatomis from the Huron River crossed over and met with Thomas McKee, who informed them that war might break out and that their British father expected them to support him. Meanwhile, other British agents sent similar messages to the western Potawatomis.[44]

The growing influence of the Prophet also undermined the American position. In early 1807, messengers from the Shawnee holy man again visited the Potawatomi villages in Illinois, seeking more converts for the new faith. Among their converts was Main Poc. Also known as Wenebeset (Crafty One), Main Poc was a man of alleged religious persuasion, a shaman given to visions and conversing with the spirits. His Potawatomi name (Main Poc) meant "Withered Hand," an allusion to his crippled left hand, from which all the fingers and thumb were missing. Main Poc had been born with this deformity and claimed that it was a special gift from the spirits. His medicine was strong, and many Potawatomis believed him to be invulnerable to injury. An eloquent speaker, Main Poc journeyed to the Sacs and Winnebagos during the summer of 1807, carrying word of the new religion to their villages.[45]

The Prophet was delighted with his new convert. Main Poc's prowess as a war chief was well known to the Shawnee leader, who considered the Potawatomi to be the most influential Indian in Illinois. In the fall of 1807 the Prophet sent messengers to Main Poc, inviting him to come to the Shawnee village on the Auglaize. Main Poc arrived in Ohio during October and remained with the

Prophet for about two months. While among the Shawnees, the war chief invited the Prophet to move his village into western Indiana.[46]

In December, Main Poc and his companions left the Shawnees and journeyed back toward Illinois. As they passed through Fort Wayne, William Wells met with the Potawatomis, attempting to undermine the Prophet's influence. The American agent lavished gifts upon the chief and his followers, enticing them to remain at the fort throughout the winter of 1808. Other Potawatomis also assembled, and by April, Wells reported that he had spent over eight hundred dollars on food and other provisions. Yet Wells thought the money well spent. Main Poc seemed friendly, and the agent believed that he had secured the chief's loyalty. According to Wells, Main Poc referred to himself as a wild horse, recently tamed by the United States, who now would wear a bell so that the Americans could find him and call him in.[47]

But Wells's assessment was premature and far too optimistic. Main Poc had been willing to accept the Americans' hospitality, but he had no intention of remaining at peace. To Wells's surprise, as the Potawatomi chief left Fort Wayne, he informed the agent that he planned to renew his attacks on the Osages. Moreover, other reports confirmed that the Indians remained alienated from the United States. The Potawatomis near Detroit still were friendly to Americans, but they also professed friendship for the British and obviously would support whichever side seemed the stronger. Five Medals complained that his influence among the Potawatomis was diminishing and that the western Potawatomis all supported the Prophet. Meanwhile, friendly Miamis near Fort Wayne reported that the Shawnee holy man was moving his village to the central Wabash.[48]

During the summer of 1808, American officials realized that their influence among the Potawatomis was deteriorating. Warriors from northern Illinois flocked to Prophetstown, the new village near the mouth of the Tippecanoe,[49] while Main Poc continued his preparations to renew the war against the Osages, and warriors from his village threatened the government factor at Chicago over what they believed were exorbitant prices for inferior trade guns. Meanwhile, Potawatomis from the western villages visited the British at Amherstburg.[50]

In an effort to counter the Potawatomi alienation, the government decided to bring Main Poc to Washington. Wells suggested such a course, believing that the Potawatomi chief would be overawed by the experience. The War Department agreed, and late in the fall of 1808 Wells accompanied Main Poc and a small delegation of Potawatomis and other Indians to the capital. They arrived in December, and Jefferson met personally with Main Poc, hoping to win him to the American position. The president urged the chief to take up agriculture so that his people would prosper and admonished him to give up the war against the Osages. Jefferson pointed out that the Osages never crossed the Mississippi to attack the Potawatomis, so why should Main Poc's warriors raid Osage villages? He also complained that the Potawatomi-Osage conflict disrupted commerce on the Missouri and Mississippi rivers. Jefferson ended his plea by assuring Main Poc that his advice was given by one friend to another and was motivated only by "my sincere wish to see you happy and prosperous, increasing in numbers, supplying your families plentifully with food and clothes and relieving them from the constant chance of being destroyed by their enemies."[51]

Main Poc and the other Indians started home in January, 1809. Unfortunately, although Main Poc had adopted some tenets of the Prophet's faith, abstinence was not one of them. As the party traveled through Baltimore, the chief acquired enough whiskey to stay intoxicated for most of the return trip to the west. Wells complained that he was "insufferable," continually threatening the other Indians and causing many costly delays.[52]

Main Poc's party was followed to Washington by a delegation of Huron River Potawatomis, Chippewas, Ottawas, Wyandots, and Shawnees. The Huron River Potawatomis, in conjunction with the other tribes, had met with Hull in November and had agreed to cede a right-of-way for a series of roads in northern Ohio. Once again the Huron River Potawatomis had little claim to the region, but they were willing to share in the sale of the lands and to travel to Washington at government expense.[53]

The spring of 1809 ushered in a brief period of tranquility among the Potawatomi villages. Momentarily impressed by his trip to Washington, Main Poc retired to his home on the Kankakee and spent the next few months quietly. Since the food supplies at Prophetstown were exhausted, many of the Potawatomis who had joined the Prophet also returned to their villages. Rumors of Indian hostility still circulated up and down the Wabash, but those Potawatomis friendly to the United States assured government officials that the tribe had turned from the Prophet and sought friendship with the Americans.[54] A few warriors from the Illinois River joined in a Sac and Sioux raid against the Osages, and others stole about a dozen horses from southern Illinois, but in July, Harrison assured Secretary of War Eustis that only the Kickapoos remained hostile and that the recent threat of a general Indian war had diminished.[55]

But the serenity did not last. President James Monroe's new administration was as anxious to acquire Indian lands as his predecessor's. Realizing that Indian affairs along the Wabash had improved, on July 15, 1809, Secretary of War Eustis ordered Harrison to "take advantage of the most favorable moment for extinguishing the Indian Title to lands lying East of the Wabash and adjoining South on the lines of the Treaties of Fort Wayne and Grouseland." Following Eustis' orders, Harrison sent messages to all the tribes in Indiana to assemble at Fort Wayne in September. The treaty, if successful, would encompass lands claimed by several tribes and would open most of Indiana below the Wabash to white settlement.[56]

Harrison arrived at Fort Wayne on September 15. The Potawatomis began to straggle in a day later. They were led by Winamac, perennial friend of the United States, who earlier had assured Harrison that all the tribes would be willing to cede the lands. Notably absent were such other friendly chiefs as Five Medals and Keesass, who feared retaliation by their younger warriors if they agreed to a land cession. To Harrison's surprise, the Miamis refused to give up their claims to the lands in question. Only after Winamac and several Delawares exerted their influence on behalf of the United States could the Miami representatives be persuaded to sell. The Potawatomis and Delawares agreed to participate in the cession only as "allies" of the Miamis and not as owners of the lands, but the technicalities made little difference to Winamac. Once again his people had given up claims to another tribe's land and would receive a payment in return. In fact, they received more than their fair share of the presents distributed after the treaty. As a token of appreciation for Winamac's support, Harrison increased the Potawatomi portion of the trade goods.[57]

Approximately three million acres passed from Indian hands at the Treaty of Fort Wayne. Part of the Potawatomis were guilty of complicity in the loss. Unquestionably they could use the trade goods, for the past two winters had been hard ones, and many of their people were reduced to wearing rags. Yet Winamac's actions in support of the Americans only served to further split the tribe. Winamac evidently believed that the patronage of the Americans would buttress his position within the tribe, and he was anxious to cultivate Harrison's favor. Keesass and Five Medals also remained friendly to the United States, since their villages were close to American military posts and vulnerable to American expeditions. Like Winamac, they resented the growing influence of Tecumseh and the Prophet, which undermined their status as traditional village chiefs. But the younger, more militant Potawatomis were disgusted with the pro-American leadership and continued to flock to Prophetstown. Angry over the Treaty of Fort Wayne, they listened eagerly to Tecumseh's plea for an intertribal alliance against the Long Knives.[58]

Meanwhile, Winamac continued to serve the United States. Following the Treaty of Fort Wayne, the Potawatomi chief journeyed to Detroit, where he assisted government officials in mediating a dispute between the Miamis and other tribes over lands in northwest Ohio. During the spring and summer of 1810, he tried to keep the Saint Joseph chiefs loyal to the United States and also served as a double agent, reporting on the Prophet's activities and helping Harrison limit the Shawnee's influence. Harrison rewarded Winamac well, but many Potawatomis disliked the chief, envisioning him as little more than a puppet of the Americans.[59]

Yet much of what Winamac reported was not favorable to the United States. Indians continued to flock to Prophetstown, and by June, 1810, the population of the new village on the Tippecanoe was swollen as the Shawnees, Potawatomis, and Kickapoos were joined by Winnebagos, Sacs, Chippewas, Ottawas, Wyandots, and even a few Iowas from across the Mississippi. Estimates of the number of Indians at Prophetstown varied greatly, from 650 to nearly 3,000, but by all accounts they posed a formidable force capable of inundating white settlement in southern Indiana.[60]

In June, Main Poc visited the village, and reports reached Harrison that the Indians were devising a master plan for attacking white military posts. The eastern Potawatomis and Miamis were to attack Fort Wayne; the Kickapoos, Shawnees, and Piankashaws would attack Vincennes; the Ottawas and Chippewas would overwhelm Detroit; the Sacs would assault Mackinac; and Main Poc would lead his warriors against Fort Dearborn. The time of the attacks was unknown, but Harrison was not optimistic. During the summer, tension increased as Potawatomis at Prophetstown drove one of Harrison's spies, a trader named Michael Brouillette, from the village. They also joined with a party of Shawnees and Kickapoos to cross the Wabash and warn settlers off the lands recently ceded at Fort Wayne.[61]

Harrison played for time. He knew the food supply at Prophetstown would not support large numbers of Indians for an extended period. He also hoped that the rest of the Potawatomis could be kept from the Prophet. Five Medals continued to resist invitations by the Shawnee leader to join him at Prophetstown, and the Potawatomis near Detroit still professed friendship to the Americans. At Fort Wayne, John Johnston, the new Indian Agent, met with Indians in the region and seemed assured of their loyalty. The chiefs along the lower Saint Joseph, from the Kankakee portage to Lake Michigan, assembled in council during late June and decided to remain neutral. If the Prophet's influence would decline, then the old chiefs could reassert themselves, and the threat of an Indian war would diminish.[62]

Harrison decided to use the same tactics against the Prophet that he had used against Main Poc. He would send the Shawnee to Washington and overwhelm him with the power and population of the United States. But unfortunately for Harrison, the plan backfired. The Prophet refused his invitation, and instead of the holy man going to Washington, Tecumseh came to Vincennes. The Shawnee chief, accompanied by about seventy-five Shawnees, Potawatomis, Winnebagos, Kickapoos, and Ottawas, arrived in Vincennes on August 12, 1810. He remained with Harrison for ten days, discussing Indian-white relations and vowing that the tribesmen would give up no more lands. On August 20 the conference almost erupted in violence when Tecumseh interrupted a speech by Harrison to call him a liar for stating that the United States was a friend to the Indians. Winamac had assisted Harrison at the conference and was sitting in the grass near the governor's feet. Tecumseh was well aware of the Potawatomi's fidelity to the Americans and had earlier threatened to kill him. Turning to Winamac, the Shawnee chief called him a "black dog" and denounced him in such terms that Winamac became frightened and recharged his pistol. Harrison intervened between the two Indians and attempted to answer Tecumseh's charges, but the angry Shawnee stalked out. Although they met for two more days, Harrison and the Shawnee could come to no agreement. The conference ended on August 22, and the Indians returned to Prophetstown.[63]

The confrontation at Vincennes convinced Tecumseh that there could be no compromise with the Long Knives. In an attempt to strengthen his alliance among the western tribes, the Shawnee chief spent the fall of 1810 visiting Indian villages in Illinois and Wisconsin. During September, Tecumseh rode west to the Potawatomi villages scattered along the Illinois and Fox Rivers. In northern Illinois the Shawnee chief was joined by several Potawatomis, including Billy Caldwell, or Sauganash (Englishman). Caldwell was the son of an Indian woman and William Caldwell, a British officer of Irish descent who had led the Potawatomis at the Battle of the Blue Licks. Born in Canada about 1780, Billy Caldwell had attended school at Detroit and could speak and write both French and English. Although he worked as a trader, Caldwell also was employed by the British Indian Service, and he later served the Crown throughout the War of 1812. Caldwell had visited Prophetstown in 1808, and he took an active interest in Tecumseh's plans. In turn the Shawnee chief occasionally relied upon the lanky mixed-blood to translate and send written communications.[64]

Tecumseh first visited the Potawatomi and Kickapoo villages clustered along the northern shores of Lake Peoria. Those towns were the staging areas for many of the raids against Missouri and southern Illinois, but Gomo, a village chief from the region, recently had visited William Clark in St. Louis and was afraid that the Americans might send troops up the Illinois to his village. He welcomed the visitors, but he was only lukewarm to their proposals. Leaving Lake Peoria, Tecumseh's party ascended the Illinois to the mouth of the Fox River and then turned north, traveling through villages of Potawatomis and Ottawas scattered along the river valley and among the groves of oaks and maples that dotted the prairie. West of Chicago they met with Shabbona (Burly Shoulders), an Ottawa by birth who had risen to a position of leadership among the Potawatomis. Shabbona had been born on the Maumee River in Ohio in about 1775 but had moved to Illinois, where he married a Potawatomi woman. A short, muscular man, Shabbona readily enlisted in Tecumseh's cause and joined the party as it continued through northern Illinois towards Wisconsin. Tecumseh and his Potawatomi followers met with Sacs, Foxes, Menominees, and Winnebagos, finally reaching the Mississippi near Prairie du Chien. The party then turned south to Rock Island, where Shabbona left for his village. In late October, Tecumseh returned to Indiana.[65]

Gomo's reluctance to commit himself to Tecumseh's confederacy resulted from a series of events taking place during the summer of 1810. In July a small party of Potawatomis, led by another chief named Winamac, crossed over into Missouri to raid the Osages. This chief shared the same name with the Potawatomi who served Harrison, but he was consistently hostile to the Americans and in 1812 was to lead the attack upon Fort Wayne. Unsuccessful in their raid against the Osages, the Potawatomis stole some buffalo robes, some deerskins, and several horses from a white settlement in central Missouri. As the Indians fled toward the Mississippi, they were pursued by a party of six white men. The whites followed relentlessly, and on July 21, 1810, the Potawatomis abandoned their robes and deerskins and scattered through a thicket, temporarily eluding their pursuers. The settlers believed that the Indians had fled, and they camped for the night without posting any guard. Early in the morning of July 22 the Potawatomis surrounded the white camp and fired upon its sleeping occupants, killing four of the white men. They then plundered the camp and returned to Illinois.[66]

The attack caused an uproar among white settlers in Illinois and Missouri, and Governor Ninian Edwards of Illinois demanded that Gomo surrender the raiders. Early in September, 1810, Gomo descended the Illinois to St. Louis, where he met with William Clark. Gomo admitted that the Potawatomis were responsible for the raid and that two young men from his village had accompanied Winamac, but he informed Clark that all the raiders had joined the Shawnees at Prophetstown. Gomo blamed the entire incident on the Prophet's influence but assured Clark that the Potawatomis near Peoria remained friendly.[67]

Gomo's assurances of friendship were undercut by Main Poc. As the chief from Peoria journeyed back to his village, Main Poc launched another attack against the Osages. The war chief had spent the summer encamped in western Illinois, where he traveled between Lake Peoria and the Mississippi, helping himself to the possessions of white traders in the region. Late in September, however, he led a large war party of Potawatomis, Sacs, and Kickapoos across the Mississippi, where they surprised a hunting party of Osages. In the resulting skirmish several Osages were killed, but Main Poc was injured, and his warriors retreated, believing that the Osages had found some new and powerful medicine which caused the wound to their leader. The Potawatomi chief could neither ride his horse nor walk, so he was placed in a canoe and carried down the Missouri to the Mississippi. His warriors then crossed over into Illinois, and Main Poc spent the winter on the Mississippi, above Portage des Sioux, recovering from his wounds.[68]

While Tecumseh was absent in Illinois and Wisconsin, the eastern Potawatomis attended two large intertribal conferences sponsored by the government and designed to undermine the Shawnee's influence. In September, 1810, approximately two thousand Indians, including many Potawatomis from the Huron and upper Saint Joseph Rivers, gathered near Detroit, where Hull supplied them with provisions. Hull again advocated the American cause and warned the tribesmen that Tecumseh and the Prophet were trying to destroy the power of their chiefs and thereby gain influence over them. The older chiefs reacted as Hull had envisioned, denouncing the Shawnees and vowing that they would remain neutral in any conflict between the British and the Americans.[69] In October a similar council was organized by Johnston at Fort Wayne. He also supplied the Potawatomis and other Indians in attendance with food and whiskey and reported, upon the conclusion of the meeting, that the Indians were "well disposed" towards the United States.[70]

Such false confidence was not shared by government officials in Illinois. By April, 1811, Main Poc had recovered from his wound and had established a temporary village at Crow Prairie, north of Lake Peoria. The site became a rendezvous for Potawatomi war parties anxious to raid southern Illinois, and in May, two of Main Poc's brothers-in-law led a group of mounted warriors in a sweep through the settlements near Kaskaskia, killing livestock and stealing forty horses. They returned to Peoria unscathed.[71] Later in the month three warriors from Main Poc's village joined a small party of Menominees, who passed down the Illinois River planning to attack the Osages. One of the Potawatomis became ill, and they left the Menominees in southern Illinois. After the Potawatomi recovered, he and his comrades attacked the Cox farm on Shoal Creek, killing Elijah Cox and making his sister, Rebecca, a prisoner. They carried the woman back toward Crow Prairie, but were overtaken by a force of white militia. In the ensuing struggle the woman was wounded but escaped. One of the militia also was wounded, and a Potawatomi was killed. Two weeks later, on June 20, other warriors from Main Poc's village killed one white man and wounded another near modern Hillsboro. They also attacked a ferry on the Mississippi, but were repulsed with the loss of one warrior.[72]

Panic spread throughout southern Illinois. Settlements were deserted and crops abandoned as settlers fled toward Kentucky. Both Clark and Edwards wrote to the War Department, pleading with Eustis to do something to stop Main Poc's attacks. Hoping to contain the Potawatomis above Lake Peoria, Edwards ordered local militia companies to patrol the prairies north of St. Louis and made plans to erect a chain of blockhouses along the Illinois River. Angrily, he denounced Main Poc's people, stating: "Hostility with them is grown into a habit—there is no reason to believe that they will make sufficient satisfaction for the murders they committed and the goods and horses which they stole last year or for the very aggravated and increased instances of similar hostilities in the present year...."[73]

In desperation, Edwards finally attempted to cultivate Gomo's friendship, hoping for a relationship similar to that between Winamac and Harrison. On June 24, 1811, Edwards commissioned Captain Samuel Levering to travel to Gomo's town to speak to the Potawatomis. Levering arrived at Lake Peoria on August 3 and spent the next two weeks conferring with Gomo and other Potawatomis. Gomo again stated that he was sympathetic to the Americans but that he had little authority over the young warriors in the region. He complained that they all supported the Prophet and refused to listen to their traditional chiefs. When asked about the Indians responsible for the recent depredations, Gomo claimed that they were not from his village. Levering met with other village chiefs and headmen from the area, including Little Chief, who mockingly declared that he was astounded that the Americans might think the Potawatomis hostile. The Indians did relinquish two horses which had been stolen and "left" at their villages by other Potawatomis, and they promised to turn over similar horses in the future. Although Levering doubted the sincerity of the Potawatomi promises, he concluded the conference by cautioning them against British influence, and he warned the Indians that any future depredations against the United States would be punished.[74]

Main Poc did not attend the conference near Peoria. Late in the spring he traveled to the Sac villages along the Rock River, enlisting their support in any confrontation with the Long Knives. He then met with the Kickapoos near the mouth of the Kankakee, securing similar agreements from their chiefs. In June, 1811, the Potawatomi war chief left Illinois and journeyed to Amherstburg, where he was warmly received by the British. Main Poc spent the fall and winter in Canada, attempting to lure nearby bands of Ottawas and Chippewas away from the United States.[75]

By the summer of 1811, Tecumseh's influence had spread throughout the Old Northwest. Anxious to enlarge his confederacy, the Shawnee chief decided to seek new converts in the south. In

August, 1811, Tecumseh and a small party of warriors passed through Vincennes en route to the Five Southern Tribes. Harrison envisioned Tecumseh's absence as an opportunity to destroy Prophetstown and to drive the Prophet from the Wabash. In preparation for such a campaign, the governor contacted several friendly chiefs, seeking information of the Prophet and his activities. He also attempted to keep the Potawatomis and Miamis from the British at Amherstburg, warning their chiefs that they must decide, once and for all, between the British and the Americans.[76]

During August and September, Harrison recruited a mixed force of regulars and militia at Vincennes, and on September 27, 1811, he marched up the Wabash toward Prophetstown. On his way to the Indian village the governor erected two small military posts: Fort Harrison near modern Terre Haute, and a smaller blockhouse at the mouth of the Vermilion. The Indians at Prophetstown watched his progress, and in early October, Waubansee (He Causes Paleness), a Potawatomi chief from the Fox River, led an attack on a supply boat being cordelled up the Wabash toward Harrison's camp. There was only one white man on the boat, all the others being on the opposite bank with the rope. Waubansee leapt on board, killed the boatman, and escaped before the Americans could retaliate.[77]

Harrison's friend Winamac had accompanied the governor up the Wabash, and as the Americans neared the mouth of the Tippecanoe, Harrison dispatched the Potawatomi to Prophetstown with a message for the Indians to disperse. Winamac spoke with the Prophet, but returned downstream on the opposite side of the Wabash from Harrison, completely missing the American column. By November 6, Harrison had advanced to within sight of Prophetstown, and in the evening he made camp on a wooded knoll overlooking Burnett's Creek. He planned to meet with the Prophet on the following morning.[78]

As the Americans journeyed up the Wabash toward Prophetstown, many of the Indians in the village became frightened and fled. To strengthen his forces, the Shawnee holy man dispatched Wapewee (White Hair), an old Potawatomi from the Fox River, to the villages along the Illinois. Wapewee pleaded with his kinsmen for assistance, and in late October, Potawatomi warriors from Illinois rode to Prophetstown. They arrived none too soon. Before dawn on the morning of November 7, 1811, the Indians attempted to infiltrate the American camp. A sharp-eyed sentry noticed some movement in the underbrush and fired, hitting a warrior, who cried out in pain. The other Indians, realizing that they were discovered, rushed the camp but were repulsed by the white soldiers. A second attack also failed, but the battle continued until shortly after daylight, when the Indians retreated into a nearby swamp and then dispersed. Harrison remained on the battlefield two days, burning Prophetstown and destroying Indian clothing and foodstuffs. He then withdrew down the Wabash to Vincennes.[79]

Harrison described the battle as a "complete and decisive victory . . . dearly purchased." He had entered the battle with about one thousand officers and men. His casualties were 188, including 62 dead. The Prophet's warriors included Kickapoos, Winnebagos, Shawnees, a few Ottawas and Wyandots, and many Potawatomis. The exact number of Indians is unknown, but they probably totaled between six hundred and seven hundred. They evidently suffered casualties similar to those of the Americans.[80]

The Potawatomis at Prophetstown were led by Shabbona, Waubansee, and the hostile Winamac, the war chief responsible for the Missouri raid of 1810. When the battle ended, they fled to their villages. The American "victory" greatly diminished the luster of the Shawnee holy man. It did not diminish Potawatomi hostility. Frustrated by the steady loss of Indian land, many young Potawatomis no longer followed their traditional village chiefs, who continued to cooperate with the Americans. Although American military power had prevailed at Prophetstown, Harrison retreated back to Vincennes, and Main Poc had proven that warriors could raid the Long Knives with impunity. Tecumseh still offered a vision of Indian unity, and the British promised muskets and powder. Before the Battle of Tippecanoe, most hostile Potawatomis had been concentrated at Prophetstown or on the Illinois. After November, 1811, angry warriors were scattered from Peoria through Amherstburg. For the Potawatomis, the War of 1812 already had started.[81]

8. "Our Most Cruel and Inveterate Enemies"

Harrison's optimism over his alleged victory at Tippecanoe faded during the following winter. Although Five Medals and other friendly chiefs met with Johnston at Fort Wayne, they no longer controlled their warriors and were tied to the United States only through the distribution of annuities. But even the "annuity chiefs" were suspect, for in November, 1811, the government deducted three hundred dollars from their payments to satisfy white claims against the tribe. The deduction rankled the chiefs, and Johnston grumbled that the Potawatomis had become "the most lawless and ungovernable of any [tribe] attached to this agency."[1]

In Illinois, Governor Edwards would have greeted such a minor disagreement as a welcome relief. He was faced with problems of a much more serious nature. Edwards hoped that the destruction of Prophetstown and the scattering of the Prophet's followers would make Gomo more tractable. In December, 1811, he invited the old chief to come to Cahokia for a conference, but Gomo did not reply. The Potawatomi chief was busy at Peoria mediating a dispute between his kinsmen and local traders. During the fall, Shequenebec led a party of Potawatomis from the Fox River down the Illinois Valley, where they established a camp below the mouth of the Sangamon. As the Potawatomis passed through Peoria, they randomly slaughtered twenty cattle and a larger number of hogs belonging to creole merchants at that place. Shequenebec's warriors boasted that the Americans were all cowards, but if any of the whites resisted, they would be tomahawked. Although Gomo opposed the slaughter of the livestock, he did little to stop the pillage, protesting that the butchers were not from his town. Yet when news of Shequenebec's arrival reached the settlements in southern Illinois, a detachment of white militia marched north to intercept them, but the Potawatomis withdrew before the Americans located their camp.[2]

Shequenebec's actions were a portent of things to come. Although Main Poc remained on the River Raisin near Detroit, he dispatched Wabameme (White Pigeon), a chief from the Saint Joseph, to travel through Potawatomi villages in Illinois and Indiana, advising warriors to prepare for war.[3] During the winter many of the Winnebagos who had fought at Prophetstown encamped near Fort Madison on the Mississippi, sniping at the garrison and waylaying white travelers in the region. In February a mixed party of Potawatomis and Kickapoos crossed the Mississippi and killed nine members of the O'Neal family near the mouth of the Salt River in Missouri.[4]

In the spring the Potawatomis turned their attacks toward the Wabash. During April warriors from the villages along the Tippecanoe struck the settlements in Illinois, opposite Vincennes, stealing horses, burning farms, and killing fourteen Americans.[5] On May 5 another war party attacked a farmhouse on the White River in Indiana, killing one settler, and later in the month they raided into Ohio, again killing a white man and stealing horses.[6]

The renewed Potawatomi attacks came as a surprise to many farmers who had moved into southern Illinois and Indiana after the Battle of Tippecanoe. As Indian raiding increased, the settlers fled back across the Ohio into Kentucky, causing local officials and land speculators to clamor for federal assistance. The Illinois militia frantically patroled the prairies north of the settlements, but the war parties eluded them.[7] By May, 1812, white anger against the Indians had reached such a pitch that even the friendly Winamac was advised to stay out of the settlements for fear that he would be murdered.[8]

Attempting to stem the tide of Potawatomi depredations, government agents met with the village chiefs, urging them to keep their young warriors away from the settlements. In late March, Captain Edward Hebert rode to Peoria, carrying an invitation for Gomo and other Potawatomis to meet with Edwards at Cahokia. To Hebert's surprise, Gomo accepted, and in April a large party of Potawatomis, Kickapoos, Ottawas, and Chippewas descended the Illinois to attend the conference. As they passed through settlements near St. Louis, the Indians flew American flags in their canoes, but they were fired upon by a group of whites, who killed an Ottawa and captured two of his fellow tribesmen.[9]

Starting under such unfavorable conditions, the conference at

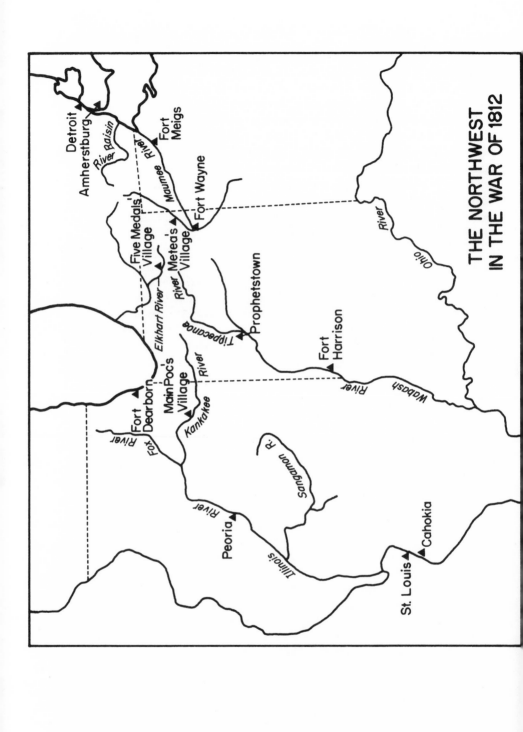

THE NORTHWEST
IN THE WAR OF 1812

Cahokia achieved little success. The Potawatomis were represented by Gomo, White Hair, Pepper (a village chief from Aux Sable Creek), and eighteen other minor chiefs and warriors. Edwards warned the Indians against British influence and tried to assure them that the Americans did not want their lands. But when he asked the Potawatomis for the warriors who had raided against the settlements, the chiefs refused to cooperate. Gomo evaded the request by claiming that the Winnebagos were responsible for the recent attacks and that the Potawatomis who had raided during previous years were not from his village. After the Indians returned to Peoria, Edwards pessimistically reported that Gomo no longer could be trusted and that the Potawatomis probably would follow such pro-British chiefs as Main Poc.[10]

While Gomo, White Hair, and others met with Edwards at Cahokia, Potawatomis along the Wabash and Saint Joseph attended similar conferences with Harrison at Vincennes and with Benjamin Stickney, the new Indian agent, at Fort Wayne. Characteristically, the pro-American chiefs such as Five Medals and Winamac assured white officials that all was well and that the hostiles did not represent the majority of the tribe. The Saint Joseph chiefs also seemed friendly, accepting American presents and promising to remain at peace. Yet they, like Gomo, were aware of Main Poc's plans and did not wish to associate themselves too closely with the Americans. When Stickney invited them to visit President Madison in Washington, they ominously refused.[11]

The refusal also resulted from the Indians' knowledge that Tecumseh had called a multitribal conference to meet on the Mississinewa River in mid-May. At the council, chiefs of the Shawnees, Potawatomis, Wyandots, Miamis, Chippewas, Ottawas, Delawares, Kickapoos, and Winnebagos tried to reconcile differences over their relationships with the Americans. The meeting pitted many of the traditional chiefs against Tecumseh, and the recent Potawatomi raids were the subject of much discussion. The traditional chiefs, especially among the Wyandots, urged the Potawatomis to stop the raids and championed a general policy of restraint regarding the Americans. Tecumseh admitted that some Potawatomis who claimed allegiance to the Prophet had raided the frontier, but he placed the blame on the Potawatomi chiefs, such as Winamac, who were friendly to the Americans. The Shawnee chief asserted that those chiefs had lost all control over their warriors because they continued to carry tales to Harrison and were guilty of "selling land to the white people that did not belong to them." He then admonished the assembled tribes to unite against a common enemy, stating: "Our white brethren are on their feet, their guns in their hands; there is no time for us to tell each other you have done this, and you have done that; if there was, we would tell the prophet that both the red and white people had felt the bad effect of his counsels."[12]

The council settled nothing, but the implications of Tecumseh's plea were not lost on these Potawatomis in attendance. Five Medals left the Mississinewa and hurried to Fort Wayne, where he warned Stickney that he was losing control of the warriors in his village. To his dismay, the chief then learned that a family of friendly Potawatomis from his village had been attacked by whites in Ohio. The Potawatomis had been on a trading expedition to Greenville when they were fired upon as they awakened early in the morning. Two warriors were killed, while two women and one child were taken prisoner. The government released the prisoners, and Stickney "covered" the deaths with presents to relatives, but the incident only reinforced the young warriors' dissatisfaction with Five Medals' pro-American leadership.[13]

Five Medals' position also was threatened by the reestablishment of a new village at Prophetstown. In the spring of 1812, Tecumseh returned to the mouth of the Tippecanoe and began to collect a following of young warriors. Many Potawatomis from northern Indiana and the Illinois River flocked to the Shawnee chief, and since they were short of powder, the warriors spent much of their time making arrows. But both the Indians and the Americans knew that war was imminent, and Tecumseh realized that his warriors must have ammunition if they expected to defend themselves. Therefore, during the middle of June, Tecumseh journeyed to Malden to secure powder from the British and to meet with Main Poc. Before leaving, he dispersed his village at Prophetstown, sending many of his followers west into Illinois, where they would be safe from American intervention. Some of the Potawatomis, accompanied by hostile Kickapoos and Miamis, established new camps along the Illinois River above Peoria. There they awaited the return of Tecumseh and Main Poc, hoping the leaders would bring both guns and powder from Canada.[14]

The growing number of hostile Indians concentrated above Peoria added to the panic of white settlers in Illinois. During June, Thomas Forsyth, an American agent at Peoria, estimated that more than six hundred warriors were lodged within the immediate vicinity of the lake and that another six hundred warriors from northern Illinois could reach the region within ten days. Realizing that he was surrounded by warriors loyal to Main Poc, Gomo cut his ties with the Americans and refused to reaffirm his pledge of friendship toward the United States. Early in July, White Pigeon arrived on the Illinois with messages from Tecumseh advising the Potawatomis that war was imminent. Other messengers informed them that Main Poc soon would return and that he had many kegs of gunpowder. Plans were laid for attacks against southern Illinois and for an assault on Fort Dearborn, at Chicago.[15]

Although news of the declaration of war between the United States and Britain reached the Potawatomis during July, it did not spur immediate action. The tribesmen had expected such a message, but they were hesitant to launch any major campaigns while Main Poc and Tecumseh remained in Canada. A few raiding parties left Lake Peoria and killed three settlers in southern Illinois, but both Indians and whites were unwilling to take the offensive. Meanwhile, the government made a final effort to keep the tribesmen neutral. Potawatomis and other Indians were invited to conferences at Fort Wayne and at Brownstown. Harrison also dispatched Winamac and a party of friendly warriors toward Peoria, hoping the Potawatomis would give up those warriors accused of the depredations in Illinois and Missouri.[16]

All of the American efforts failed. Winamac and his companions were ridiculed by their kinsmen and returned to Indiana emptyhanded. Winamac reported back to Stickney that the Potawatomis in Illinois were friendly, but such statements were only attempts by the chief to save face and to ingratiate himself with the agent. The council at Fort Wayne was moved to Piqua and was poorly attended. It attracted no Potawatomis among an assemblage of 250 Indians. The government had planned to meet with 2,500.[17]

At first the council at Brownstown seemed more successful. During June, Hull had assumed command of a mixed force of militia and regulars in Ohio and had marched north to Detroit. Arriving at the straits unopposed, he strengthened the garrison, and upon hearing of the declaration of war, Hull seized control of Sandwich, opposite Detroit in Canada. He next issued an invitation for Indians in the Detroit region to meet in council, and in mid-July the warriors assembled. Although the Wyandots genuinely championed the Americans cause and urged the tribesmen to remain neutral, the other Indians listened, mouthed platitudes of friendship, but generally were noncommittal. Hull naïvely believed the conference to be a success and reported that the Potawatomis and other Indians had been won over from the British. Ironically however, in reporting news of the conference to the secretary of war, Hull concluded his letter by stating that "Tecumseh and Marpot (Main Poc) are the only chiefs of consequence remaining with the British."[18]

While the lack of action in Indiana and at Detroit seemed to reflect hesitancy on both sides, events to the north and west were pushing the Potawatomis toward a major confrontation. Since the autumn of 1811, Robert Dickson, a red-haired British trader, had been active among the tribes of Wisconsin, distributing presents and enlisting Indians into the British cause. Although Dickson at first held little influence over the Potawatomis near Milwaukee, he gained an important following among the Winnebagos and Menominees at Green Bay. During June, Dickson led large numbers of Indians from northern Wisconsin to Saint Joseph's Island in Lake Huron. On July 17 those Indians supported a small force of British regulars who surprised the American garrison at Mackinac and captured the post. The Americans were completely unprepared, unaware that the war had started. The fall of Mackinac meant that the United States could no longer supply or support Fort Dearborn. Therefore, on July 29 Hull issued orders that the fort should be evacuated.[19]

At Chicago the American position had grown untenable. Throughout the spring and summer of 1812, the Potawatomis in the immediate vicinity of the fort continued to profess their peaceful intentions, but Captain Nathan Heald was suspicious of their loyalty. Friendly tribesmen among the Ottawas and Chippewas warned Heald that the Potawatomis were privately talking of war, and in April the government factor, Matthew Irwin, moved his goods into the fort for protection. Although the Potawatomis did not attack any of the settlers in the region, on April 4 a party of Winnebagos surrounded a farm about three miles from Fort Dearborn and killed two men, one an American and the other a French-Canadian. The Potawatomis did not participate in the raid, yet neither did they express much concern over the murders.[20]

The stalemate at Chicago resulted from Potawatomi indecision over what course to pursue. Almost all of the warriors opposed any further surrender of lands to the Long Knives, yet they differed over their attitudes toward the American traders who were active in the region. Potawatomis from those villages near the fort, especially those villages inhabited by large numbers of mixed-bloods, had established many personal ties with the traders and with the military personnel of the garrison. Led by Chechepinquay (Squinter), known to the whites as Alexander Robinson, these Potawatomis were reluctant to commit themselves to any actions which might harm close friends among the small white community.

But during the summer of 1812 the influence of Robinson and the friendly warriors diminished. They were opposed by Blackbird, son of Siggenauk. who had broken with his father's policies and supported the British. Nuscotomeg (Mad Sturgeon), a war chief from the juncture of the Iroquois and Kankakee rivers, also counseled for war. A brother-in-law to Main Poc, Mad Sturgeon had led raids against Missouri and southern Illinois and was adamantly opposed to the Americans. Blackbird and Mad Sturgeon's arguments were aided by messengers from Main Poc, who circulated among the Potawatomi villages urging the young warriors to strike the Long Knives. In July towns strung along the Fox River were in constant ferment, dancing the war dance and meeting with Sacs and Winnebagos. Young Potawatomis continued to spy upon the fort, and in mid-July they fired on the stockade, killing some livestock.[21]

Hull's order to evacuate Fort Dearborn arrived at Chicago on August 9, 1812. Ironically, the message was carried by Winamac, who, after delivering Hull's orders, met with John Kinzie, the trader, attempting to convince him that an immediate withdrawal was the only chance for success. According to Winamac, if the Americans would evacuate quickly, they could reach Fort Wayne before the hostile Potawatomis had time to gather their forces and intercept them.[22]

But Winamac's pleas fell upon deaf ears. Heald believed that more time was needed to organize the withdrawal, and Hull's orders had instructed him to destroy all surplus arms and ammunition, but to distribute the other goods at the factory to friendly Potawatomis. Heald also needed time to organize the white population of Chicago for the trek to Fort Wayne. On August 13, William Wells arrived with a party of thirty Miamis who had agreed to escort the whites through the Potawatomi country. In the next two days Heald met with friendly tribesmen and distributed the trade goods. Surplus arms and ammunition and a large quantity of whiskey were thrown into the fort's well.[23]

While Heald was preparing for the evacuation, Potawatomis from villages near Lake Michigan hurried to Chicago. At a series of councils, tribal leaders met and argued over what actions should be taken regarding the American withdrawal. Robinson and Mucktypoke (Black Partridge), a chief from the Illinois River, pleaded for a policy of neutrality. Blackbird and Mad Sturgeon continued to argue for war.[24]

Unfortunately for the Americans, the hostile chiefs proved to be more persuasive. The Potawatomis had expected to receive the whiskey and powder within the fort, and when they heard that these commodities had been destroyed, they were infuriated. Moreover, the position of the anti-American faction again was buttressed by messages from Tecumseh and Main Poc urging them to join the British and attack the garrison. Finally, on August 14 the Potawatomis learned that Tecumseh had defeated the Long Knives at the Battle of Brownstown and that Hull had withdrawn from Canada and was hiding behind the walls of Fort Detroit. The news of the British and Indian success was the deciding factor. The warriors agreed to attack the Americans after they left the safety of Fort Dearborn.[25]

Late in the evening of August 14, as Heald was finishing his preparations for the next day's evacuation, Black Partridge met with the officer and returned an American medal given to him by government officials. The Potawatomi chief stated that he no longer could be responsible for his warriors and warned Heald to be wary after leaving the fort in the morning. Just after sunrise on August 15, John Kinzie received a similar message from Topinbee.[26]

But the warnings were ignored. August 15 dawned bright and sunny, and at about nine o'clock Heald started the evacuation. In the lead were William Wells and part of the Miami escort followed by the fort's garrison, the women and children of the officers and settlers, and finally the Chicago militia. Bringing up the rear were the remainder of the Miamis who had accompanied Wells to Chicago. The number of whites remains uncertain, but evidence suggests that there were at least fifty-four officers and enlisted men, nine women, eighteen children, and twelve militia: a total of ninety-six persons. The party traveled south along the shore of Lake Michigan and crossed the Chicago River.[27]

Their journey was paralleled by about five hundred Potawatomis and a few Kickapoos, Sacs, and Winnebagos. Led by Blackbird and Mad Sturgeon, the warriors followed the Americans for about one and one-half miles before taking cover behind a ridge of sand dunes overlooking the beach. There the Potawatomis primed their muskets and waited for the American column to come within range. Wells, who was mounted, discovered the Indians lying near the top of the dunes and galloped back to warn Heald of the ambush. He shouted to the captain to press forward toward a small hill that would be advantageous in repulsing an Indian attack.[28]

Wells's advice came too late. As he fled back toward the soldiers, Blackbird signaled his warriors to attack. Potawatomi warriors surged over the dunes, raking the American column with musket fire. Heald ordered his troops to charge the center of the Potawatomi line, and the soldiers moved forward, pushing the Indians back, but the warriors then outflanked the Americans and fell upon the rear of the column. At the first shots the Miami escort fled, and the rear was protected only by militiamen. The militia retreated toward the center, where they made their stand among some wagons which had been carrying the women and children. A small number of regulars also formed ranks near the militia, but the Americans near the wagons were overwhelmed by warriors who charged down the sand dunes and swarmed through their ranks. The Potawatomis greatly outnumbered their adversaries, and in hand-to-hand fighting near the wagons they killed all the white men but one. They also killed two of the women and twelve of the children.[29]

Meanwhile, Heald and the remainder of the regulars moved toward the hill on the beach. Protected by the sand dunes, other Potawatomis continued to pour their fire down upon the soldiers. After about fifteen minutes, Heald reached the hill, but by then he had lost over half of his command. Finally, both sides ceased firing, and Heald walked toward the dunes, where he met with Blackbird and arranged a truce. The Potawatomi chief demanded that the Americans surrender themselves and pay the tribesmen one hundred dollars for each prisoner still alive. Heald agreed. Blackbird and his warriors then gathered the survivors and marched them back to Fort Dearborn.[30]

The Potawatomi attack took a heavy toll on the Americans. Heald's force suffered fifty-three dead and many wounded. Among the dead was Wells, shot from his horse and then riddled by musket balls as he lay on the beach. The Potawatomis lost about fifteen warriors. Among the wounded was Mad Sturgeon, who suffered a gunshot wound.[31]

Many of the Potawatomis' prisoners did not survive the night. The Indians had lost friends and relatives, and they took revenge on several of the captives, yet friendly Potawatomis interceded to save some of the others. Both Heald and his wife were badly wounded but were taken to William Burnett's trading post near the mouth of the Saint Joseph River. After the hostile warriors departed to join in the attack on Fort Wayne, Alexander Robinson and his wife carried the Healds by canoe to Mackinac, where they were turned over to British authorities. Lieutenant Linai Helm, second in command to Heald, eventually was taken to Lake Peoria, where he was ransomed by Forsyth. During the attack Black Partridge had saved Helm's wife, Margaret, by claiming her as his prisoner, and after the battle both he and Waubansee protected Mrs. Helm and the Kinzie family from unfriendly warriors. They later secured the aid of Jean Baptiste Chandonnai, a mixed-blood, who guided Mrs. Helm and most of the Kinzies to Detroit. Other captives were divided among the different bands. Some were killed. Others were ransomed later in the war.[32]

While the Potawatomis at Chicago planned their attack upon Heald's party, their kinsmen in eastern Michigan assisted the British against Detroit. Even before Hull's surrender, many Potawatomis, led by Main Poc and Shabbona, crossed over into Canada to join Tecumseh and the Redcoats. On July 19, Main Poc was wounded in a skirmish with an American patrol on the Canard River, near Fort Malden. He survived the wound, but it was painful and only increased his bitterness toward the Long Knives. Five days later, other Potawatomis attacked Major James Denny and a small detachment of troops at Petit Cote, a few miles north of the Canard.[33]

After the fall of Mackinac, the British and Indians at Malden took the offensive. Inspired by the victory at the straits, the Potawatomis returned to Michigan hoping to attack Hull's supply column en route from Ohio. On August 5, Potawatomi warriors joined a mixed Indian force led by Tecumseh, who turned back an American detachment at the Battle of Brownstown. Four days later they assisted in the ambush of an American supply column at Monguaga. In the second battle the Potawatomis were led by Caldwell and Main Poc, and in the confusion of the attack they were mistaken by the British for a detachment of Indians serving with the Americans. Seventy Potawatomis under Billy Caldwell were forced to flee from the battlefield, since they received fire from both sides. When the firing ended, Main Poc took his revenge. Angered over his recent wound, he seized an American prisoner and, against the pleas of British officers, buried his tomahawk in the man's skull.[34]

The fall of the American forts at Mackinac and Chicago, coupled with the increased Indian activity along the Detroit River, proved too much for General Hull. Fearing that Detroit would be overrun by large numbers of hostile Indians, he surrendered the fort to the British on August 16, 1812. During the previous evening, large numbers of Potawatomis, Chippewas, and Ottawas had crossed over from Canada and had surrounded the fort on the south and west, effectively cutting off any American retreat. Although the Indians captured a large number of horses from the settlers living near the fort, they took no scalps and turned over all American prisoners to the British.[35]

After the capitulation of Detroit, the Potawatomis turned their attentions toward Fort Wayne. Pierre Moran, or Perish, also known as "the Stutterer," urged the Indians to attack the American post at the forks of the Maumee. Moran, a mixed-blood Kickapoo married to a Potawatomi woman, held influence over several chiefs from northern Indiana. The mixed-blood's counsel found fertile ground in the hostile Winamac, who still smoldered over the Indian defeat at Tippecanoe. Late in August, Winamac sent messengers to the Potawatomi villages in Michigan and Indiana, calling for warriors to attack Fort Wayne. As the Indians assembled near the fort, Potawatomi spokesmen tried to convince Stickney and Captain James Rhea, the officer in command, that the visitors were friendly. But Rhea was panic-stricken by the large number of strange Indians and dispatched frantic pleas for assistance to Governor Return J. Meigs of Ohio. When help did not come, the officer drowned his fears in whiskey, remaining drunk through the middle of September.[36]

Rhea's fears were justified. The many hostile warriors concentrated near Fort Wayne forced even friendly chiefs such as Five Medals to support Winamac. On August 20, Metea (Sulker), a young chief from the Saint Joseph of the Maumee, secretly informed Antoine Bondie, a creole trader, that the Potawatomis intended to attack the American post. Metea offered Bondie refuge in his village, but the trader betrayed the chief's trust and warned the garrison. Eight days later, on August 28, the Potawatomis confirmed Bondie's warning. They killed and scalped Stephen Johnston, a clerk in the Indian factory who had left the post bound for Ohio. They also began to slaughter white livestock in the region.[37]

Fort Wayne soon underwent a state of siege. While the garrison and several white traders remained within the walls, the Potawatomis periodically fired at the stockade, inflicting little damage, but causing much apprehension among the Americans. The Indians also burned several outbuildings located near the pallisade. On September 4 a large number of Potawatomis led by Winamac approached the fort under a flag of truce and met with Rhea. The commander asked them if they intended to make war or if they wished to live in peace with the Americans. Winamac was non-commital, but he reminded Rhea that both Detroit and Mackinac had fallen to the British and that Fort Wayne might suffer a similar fate. The chief's answer frightened the commander, who believed that his post could not survive any attack if the Indians were supported by the British. To ingratiate himself with Winamac, Rhea invited the Potawatomi chief into his quarters, served him wine, and asked the chief to save him if the fort was taken.[38]

Rhea's cowardice encouraged Winamac toward bolder actions. On the following morning, September 5, the Potawatomi chief hid warriors near the fort who killed two soldiers bold enough to venture outside. Later in the day Winamac and a large party of warriors approached the gate and asked to be admitted, stating that they wished to see Stickney so that a truce could be arranged with the Americans. The Indian agent was suspicious and refused entrance to all but Winamac and twelve of his followers, who were searched before they were admitted into the stockade. Meanwhile, a detachment of troops was ordered to stand on guard while the Potawatomis remained inside the walls. Stickney met with the Indians in his quarters, where Winamac disclaimed any responsibility for the deaths of the soldiers. The chief then drew a knife from the folds of his blanket, declaring in Potawatomi, "If my father wishes war, I am a man!" The declaration was the signal for his warriors to kill the agent and open the doors of the fort, but the presence of the troops on guard caused the Potawatomis to hesitate. Stickney was unaware of their intention, but Bondie, who stood behind him, understood the challenge and leaped forward, replying in Potawatomi, "I am a man also!" Realizing that his trickery had failed, Winamac sheathed his knife and led his warriors from the fort.[39]

Frustrated over the collapse of his plans, Winamac again launched a general attack against the stockade. At eight o'clock in the same evening the Potawatomis began firing at the fort from the cover of nearby buildings. They also attempted to set fire to the stockade, shooting burning arrows into the walls, but the Americans easily extinguished the flames.[40] Convinced that he could not capture the fort without assistance, Winamac sent messengers to Detroit, asking for British troops with artillery to batter down the walls. The British were willing to help, but they waited until September 14 before ordering Major Adam Muir to lead a force of more than one thousand men, with three cannon, to the Potawatomis' assistance.[41]

Muir's command had no chance of success. On September 6, while Muir still was waiting at Detroit, William Henry Harrison left Piqua, Ohio, on a forced march, intent upon relieving Fort Wayne. He gathered militia forces along the way, and upon his arrival at the forks of the Maumee, Harrison commanded a detachment of more than twenty-two hundred men. Potawatomi scouts monitored Harrison's advance, reporting back to Winamac that the Long Knives were coming in numbers "as many as the trees in the forest." A few small war parties hurried to meet the Americans, but most of the Indians feared to attack a force of such size. In a small skirmish on September 11, one Potawatomi was killed, and Metea's arm was shattered by a musket ball, but Harrison's army continued their advance. In desperation the Potawatomis renewed their attacks on Fort Wayne, but they still refused to assault the walls without Muir's reinforcements. Finally, before dawn on September 12, Winamac and his warriors withdrew from Fort Wayne and fled north toward Detroit. The siege of Fort Wayne had ended.[42]

Harrison arrived at the post later in the day and promptly made plans to carry the war to the Potawatomis. Originally, the American general had hoped to sweep through northern Indiana, destroying Potawatomi villages along the Tippecanoe, then to attack the towns near Chicago, but on the way from Piqua he had received orders to march on Detroit. Yet the general was angry over the siege and anxious to punish the Potawatomis. On September 14 he dispatched two detachments of troops against Potawatomi villages in the region. One force, led by Brigadier General John Payne, destroyed several Miami villages near the forks of the Wabash. The other party, under the command of Major Samuel Wells, rode north to the Elkhart River, where it planned to surprise Five Medals' town. Wells's detachment arrived on the Elkhart on September 16 but found the village deserted. After burning the town and cutting down the Potawatomi corn fields, the Americans returned to Fort Wayne. A few days later another American force destroyed Little Turtle's town about twenty miles northwest of the fort.[43]

Harrison's attacks against Five Medals' and Little Turtle's towns reflect a mindless reaction on the part of the Americans. Little Turtle was dead, but he steadfastly had supported the government against Tecumseh and the Prophet. Five Medals also had opposed the Shawnees and had tried to cooperate with Stickney to limit their influence. The old Potawatomi chief had taken a limited part in the siege of Fort Wayne, but after the fall of Detroit it would have been dangerous for him to continue championing the American cause. Yet Harrison mistakenly blamed Five Medals for the attack and specifically ordered the troops to destroy his village. Harrison's troops would have been far more justified in attacking Potawatomi villages along the Tippecanoe, since warriors from that region consistently were hostile to the Americans.

After their failure to capture Fort Wayne, most of the eastern Potawatomis abandoned their villages. Short of food, the warriors relied on the British to feed their families. To meet the increasing Indian demand for provisions, in October, 1812, the British established a major depot for food and trade goods at the foot of the rapids on the Maumee River. Matthew Elliott supervised the distribution of the foodstuffs, and by November many Potawatomis had set up temporary camps near the new British post. From the Maumee a few warriors slipped into Ohio or Indiana, where they stole horses. Others accompanied Muir back to Detroit or congregated near Malden.[44]

The hostile Winamac, who had led the unsuccessful attack against Fort Wayne, accompanied Elliott to the Maumee, where he served as a scout against Brigadier General James Winchester's forces in Ohio. On November 22, Winamac and four other Indians accompanied Elliott's son, Alexander, on a reconnaissance patrol up the Maumee Valley. Late in the morning they encountered Logan, a Shawnee chief friendly to the United States, and two other Indians who were serving as scouts for the Americans. Winamac and his party took the pro-American Indians into custody, but Alexander Elliott let the captives keep their firearms. As Winamac and Elliott led their prisoners toward the British position, the Potawatomi tried to convince the young Englishman that Logan's party should be disarmed and bound. Overhearing the discussion, Logan and his companions attempted to escape. Without warning, they turned and fired, killing both Winamac and Elliott. The other British Indians returned the fire, mortally wounding Logan before he and his two companions fled back up the Maumee.[45]

Winamac's death was indicative of Potawatomi fortunes during the autumn of 1812. After relieving Fort Wayne, Harrison was appointed commander of all American forces in the Northwest and immediately assumed the offensive. Late in October he ordered another strike at the Potawatomi villages on the headwaters of the Saint Joseph. Colonel Allen Trimble and five hundred mounted Ohio militia were dispatched to strike White Pigeon's village in southern Michigan. Yet Trimble's force proceeded no farther than Fort Wayne before half of his men deserted. The remainder invaded northern Indiana, where they encountered no Potawatomis, but they did destroy two small vacant villages before returning to Ohio.[46]

Potawatomi villages were also the target of American expeditions in Illinois. Very few Potawatomis from the Illinois River Valley had supported Winamac at the siege of Fort Wayne, but early in the fall of 1812 a few warriors joined with the Kickapoos in an attack on Fort Harrison. Other war parties scattered across southern Illinois, attacking isolated settlements and stealing horses. By late September, southern Illinois once again was paralyzed, and even Governor Ninian Edwards sent his family to Kentucky.[47]

Yet Edwards was heartened by the ability of Forts Harrison and Wayne to repel Indian attacks and by the American advance into the Maumee Valley. Deciding to also take the offensive, he made preparations for a campaign against the Potawatomi villages above Peoria. Edwards planned to attack the villages from two directions. General Samuel Hopkins of Kentucky agreed to recruit two thousand mounted volunteers, march up the Wabash Valley, and then turn west across the prairies, destroying Kickapoo villages along the Sangamon. Meanwhile, Edwards prepared to strike north from the American Bottom, join Hopkins on the Sangamon, and then lead the combined force against the Potawatomi villages above Lake Peoria.[48]

Part of the plan failed. Hopkins moved up the Wabash, but his Kentucky militia deserted by the hundreds. As he turned west into Illinois, Kickapoo scouts reported his advance, and their warriors harassed the Kentucky column, setting fire to the prairie and stealing Hopkins' horses. Confused by the smoke and unfamiliar with the terrain, the Kentuckians became lost and failed to reach the Sangamon. They eventually wandered back to the Wabash and then returned to Kentucky.[49]

Edwards was more successful. He left Camp Russell, near modern Edwardsville, on October 18, leading a force of 362 militia. Marching north to the Salt Fork of the Sangamon, he destroyed two Kickapoo villages while waiting for Hopkins' arrival. When the Kentuckians failed to appear, Edwards continued on to Lake Peoria, where he attacked the villages of White Hair and Black Partridge. If the Potawatomis had been guilty of killing women and children near Fort Dearborn, the Americans took their revenge at Peoria. As the militia swept down on the villages, they shot those Potawatomis who attempted to surrender, causing the other Indians to flee into the swamps bordering the Illinois River. Edwards attempted to pursue them, but the chase was abandoned when the governor and his horse ingloriously tumbled head over heels into a mud hole. The Americans then burned the towns, destroying all the Indians' provisions, and retreated before the Potawatomis north of Lake Peoria could launch a counterattack.[50]

Three weeks after Edwards' raid, another American expedition reached Peoria. Captain Thomas Craig of Shawneetown had hoped to lead a flotilla of Illinois militia up the Illinois River and to rendezvous with Edwards while the latter was at Lake Peoria, but Craig arrived on November 5, and both Edwards and most of the Potawatomis were gone. Angered over his failure to find any Indians, Craig turned his wrath against the creole population of Peoria. Forsyth assured Craig that the creoles had not supported the Potawatomis, but during the evening of November 6 a small party of Indians fired upon Craig's camp, and the captain believed that the creoles were to blame. Denouncing Forsyth and the creole traders as "damned rascals [who] may think themselves well off that they were not scalped," Craig burned their cabins, seized their possessions, and forced the white inhabitants of Peoria to evacuate the village and return to southern Illinois.[51]

The American expeditions in Illinois had little impact upon the Potawatomis. Edwards' raid near Peoria illustrated the vulnerability of Indian villages in the region, and many of the Potawatomis retreated up the river, where they formed new towns near the mouth of Bureau Creek. Yet the Indians remained hostile, and Craig's arrest of Forsyth deprived the government of its lone spokesman in the region. Chiefs such as Gomo and Black Partridge became increasingly pro-British, and Indian depredations against southern Illinois continued. Although the Potawatomis could not launch a major campaign against Kaskaskia or St. Louis, they still posed a serious threat to isolated settlements south of the Sangamon.[52]

The Potawatomis near Detroit proved to be a more serious threat to General James Winchester. Early in January, 1813, Winchester advanced to the Maumee River in preparation for an assault against Detroit. While on the Maumee, he received word that the British had only a token force on the River Raisin and that the French-Canadian settlers in the region would support an American campaign. Against Harrison's instructions, Winchester sent 650 men to Frenchtown, where they defeated a small number of British and Indians on January 18. Winchester then followed his advance guard, arriving on the River Raisin on January 20. At Malden, Proctor learned of the American advance and decided to counterattack. At dawn on January 22, Procter led six hundred white troops and about eight hundred Indians, including many Potawatomis, in an attack against Winchester's camp. The battle was fought in the snow, and the British and Indians eventually gained the upper hand. Late in the morning Winchester surrendered after Procter assured him that American prisoners would have British protection.[53]

Procter failed to keep his promise. After the American surrender, the British commander marched all American prisoners who could walk to his camp on Stony Creek. The wounded captives were left behind on the battlefield under the care of a few interpreters. During the night a mixed party of Potawatomis, Chippewas, Ottawas, Wyandots, and Delawares discovered a cache of whiskey. Drinking heavily, and angry over their defeat of January 18, the Potawatomis and their allies turned on the prisoners, killing them at random. The slaughter ended during the next day, but many of the remaining prisoners were carried off to Indian villages. Some were ransomed. The fate of the others remains unknown.[54]

Following the River Raisin massacre, the Potawatomis retired to their winter camps. The heavy snow and extreme temperatures made winter campaigning hazardous, and the Indians were content to remain by their campfires, repairing weapons and making plans for the spring. The Americans were more active. During February, Harrison advanced to the rapids of the Maumee and immediately began the construction of a fort at that location. Named Fort Meigs after Return J. Meigs, the governor of Ohio, the structure was finished in April, 1813.

It was not completed any too soon. Indian scouts informed Procter of Harrison's advance, and the British commander was anxious to destroy the fort, since Harrison might use it to launch a campaign against Malden. Procter waited until April, when Tecumseh arrived from the Wabash accompanied by newly recruited Potawatomis, Kickapoos, and Winnebagos. With more than twelve hundred warriors supporting his advance, Procter left Malden and moved up the Maumee, arriving opposite Fort Meigs on April 28. He unloaded his artillery and positioned it to fire upon the fort. Meanwhile, the Indians surrounded the American stockade and harassed the garrison with small arms.[55]

The siege of Fort Meigs started on May 1 and soon proved ineffective. Protected behind heavy earth and timber walls, the Americans thwarted British attempts to blow up their powder by covering the magazine with earth as fast as the British artillery uncovered it. The Potawatomis and other tribesmen fired at the walls from the cover of the nearby forest, but they were unwilling to risk a frontal assault. On May 4 Harrison learned that Brigadier General Green Clay was approaching the fort with twelve hundred Kentuckians. Harrison sent orders to the Kentuckians to attack the British artillery opposite the fort, spike the guns, and then retreat to the safety of Fort Meigs, reinforcing the garrison. Early in the morning of May 5 the Kentuckians, led by Lieutenant Colonel William Dudley, landed opposite the fort, captured, yet ineffectively spiked the British artillery, and failed to retreat before the British counterattacked. Sweeping in on the flanks, the Potawatomis and Chippewas cut off the Kentuckians from the river. A fierce hand-to-hand battle ensued, and 150 of the Americans escaped across the Maumee in boats, but the remainder were killed or captured. After the battle the American prisoners were taken to a nearby British camp, where the Potawatomis and Chippewas wished to kill them. The Wyandots and Miamis argued that they should be spared, but while the debate was in progress, some of the Potawatomis began shooting and tomahawking the captives. They did not stop until Tecumseh arrived and ordered them away from the encampment.[56]

On August 9, after the British abandoned the siege of Fort Meigs, the Potawatomis and other tribesmen returned to Michigan. Although the fort remained in American hands, the Indians believed they had achieved a significant victory over Dudley's forces and saw no reason to remain on the Maumee. Moreover, in their triumph over Dudley they had captured large stores of American supplies, and they were anxious to carry such treasure back to their villages. Most of the Potawatomis set up camps along the Huron River or on the River Rouge, where the elderly Five Medals had established a village following the siege of Fort Wayne.[57]

Convinced that part of the Potawatomis had returned to the headwaters of the Saint Joseph, Harrison ordered another military expedition against their villages. During June, 1813, he sent Colonel Richard M. Johnson and a regiment of mounted Kentucky volunteers into northern Indiana, instructing them to again attack Five Medals' town on the Elkhart and then march westward, striking Potawatomi villages near modern South Bend. Johnson and his men proceeded to the Elkhart River, but found Five Medals' town still deserted. They then attempted to march west, but were forced back by flooding along the Saint Joseph. Finally the volunteers turned toward White Pigeon's town in southern Michigan, but found that it also was unoccupied. Discouraged with their lack of success, the Americans returned to Fort Wayne.[58]

The Potawatomis also faced discouragement. In July they halfheartedly supported another attack by Procter against Fort Meigs, and one month later a few warriors fought with the British at Fort Stephenson on the lower Sandusky. Yet both campaigns were desultory affairs in which the Indians and the British had little hope of success. By the summer of 1813, the Americans were gaining the ascendancy in the Northwest as large numbers of reinforcements continued to join Harrison from Ohio and Kentucky. The Potawatomis from camps near Detroit continued to skirmish with Americans in northern Ohio, but they no longer were able to penetrate into the settled areas of Ohio or Indiana.[59]

On September 10, 1813, Captain Oliver H. Perry defeated the British fleet in the Battle of Lake Erie, and the tide of war shifted irrevocably in the Americans' favor. Near Detroit the Potawatomis watched in consternation as Procter first prepared to evacuate Michigan and then Malden. To the Indians, Procter's actions were inexplicable. Although the Americans were in control of northern Ohio, they had not reached Detroit. Moreover, British and Indian forces numbered nearly four thousand, including a large number of western tribesmen who had arrived with Robert Dickson during the summer. On September 18, Procter met with the Indians and informed them that he planned to retreat toward Niagara. Speaking for the assembled warriors, Tecumseh denounced the British officer, calling him a coward and a fat dog who was fleeing with his tail between his legs. Tecumseh then pleaded with Procter to give the Indians arms and ammunition so that they could stand and fight, regardless of the British intentions.[60]

Tecumseh's speech had little effect on the British commander. On September 26 Procter began his slow retreat from Malden, carrying his munitions and supplies in wagons. His withdrawal split the

Potawatomis. Those chiefs and warriors who held an intense personal loyalty toward Tecumseh, Potawatomis such as Mad Sturgeon, Shabbona, and Billy Caldwell, accompanied the Shawnee leader, who retreated with Procter. Most of the Potawatomis, however, remained behind in their camps and villages along the Huron and Rouge rivers. They were angry over the British withdrawal and awaited events in Canada before committing themselves to further action. Main Poc, encamped near Detroit, also remained behind, hoping to attack Harrison's supply columns.[61]

Harrison crossed over into Canada on September 27 and slowly followed Procter toward Moravian Town, a settlement on the Thames River. On October 5, under pressure from the Indians, Procter finally made a stand. The British commander positioned himself in the center with the river on his left and the Indians supporting his right flank. When Harrison's cavalry charged the British, Procter fled, and most of his countrymen surrendered. The Indians fought on. The Potawatomis were near Tecumseh, and there the battle raged the fiercest. Unlike the British, the Indians were fighting for their homes and could retreat no farther. Since Tecumseh had asked Caldwell to stay with Procter, the Potawatomis were led by Shabbona and Mad Sturgeon. From the shelter of the forest the Indians continued to oppose the Americans long after the British surrendered. Finally, Shabbona saw Tecumseh fall and American reinforcements surge toward the Indian position. Convinced that the battle was lost, the Potawatomis retreated through the forest. Some followed Procter towards Niagara, but most slipped through the American lines and returned to their kinsmen near Detroit.[62]

Before Harrison invaded Canada, he had dispatched Brigadier General Duncan McArthur and seven hundred men to Detroit to protect his rear from Main Poc and other hostile Indians. At Detroit, McArthur found that most of the Indians were ready to make peace, especially after they learned of the American victory on the Thames. Accordingly, McArthur extended a temporary armistice to all the tribes in the region, including the Potawatomis. When Harrison returned from Canada, he approved of McArthur's peace with most of the tribes, but opposed any peace with the Potawatomis, whom he still considered to be "our most cruel and inveterate enemies." Finally, however, the American commander was forced to extend the offer of the armistice to the Potawatomis, fearing that their exclusion would force them to rejoin the British and attack the Detroit frontier. Therefore, on October 14 a formal armistice was signed between Harrison and the Potawatomis, Ottawas, Chippewas, Miamis, and Wyandots. Both sides agreed to refrain from hostilities, and the Indians promised to surrender all prisoners. The Indians also agreed to provide hostages to be held in the American settlements until the war should end. Under the terms of the armistice, the Indians could "retire to their usual hunting grounds and there remain unmolested provided they behave themselves peaceably." Among the Potawatomis signing the document were Topinbee, Five Medals, and Main Poc.[63]

Main Poc and his followers had no intention of honoring the agreement. They still remained adamantly opposed to the Americans, but were desperately short of food and other necessities. Since the British had withdrawn, and the Americans had destroyed their cornfields, the Potawatomis were forced to rely on Harrison for provisions to sustain them through the winter. Five Medals genuinely wanted peace, and Topinbee reluctantly cooperated with the Americans, but Main Poc's people drew their rations in silence, biding their time until the return of their British father. The old chief's warriors visited Detroit and listened to the Americans, but they carried intelligence to the British in Canada. Settlers in Michigan complained that they still were stealing horses, and government officials feared that they would renew the war in the spring.[64]

Farther west, on the prairies of Illinois and Wisconsin, the struggle continued without cessation. The armistice at Detroit had no meaning for the western Potawatomis, and they continued to support the British, who supplied them through Mackinac and Wisconsin. In January, 1813, following the American expeditions against Peoria, Main Poc had temporarily returned to Illinois, where he established a camp on the Fox River. Main Poc believed that Craig's raid at Peoria was the initial phase of an American invasion up the river, and he assembled large numbers of Potawatomis above Crow Prairie to meet such an intrusion. Although the invasion failed to materialize, the chief remained in Illinois until May, spreading British influence among the Sacs and sending his warriors in scattered raids against Kaskaskia and Vincennes.[65]

The British cause also was championed by Robert Dickson. In January, 1813, he had been appointed as the agent to all the tribes west of Lake Huron, and he spent the late winter and early spring of 1813 distributing presents and visiting Indian villages in the Lake Michigan area. During March, 1813, he passed through the Potawatomi towns on the lower Saint Joseph en route to Wisconsin, where he met with other Potawatomis, Menominees, Sacs, Foxes, and Winnebagos. He promised the Potawatomis that the British would establish a post at Chicago and would supply them with enough powder to carry on their war against the Long Knives. Dickson also attempted to recruit Potawatomis from Illinois and Wisconsin to assist the British near Detroit. In the spring of 1813 he invited Gomo to Green Bay, lavishing gifts upon the old chief and asking him to lead his warriors against Harrison. Gomo refused, but warriors from the Saint Joseph yielded to Dickson's pleas and traveled to Malden, where they fought under Main Poc and Topinbee.[66]

The impact of Main Poc's and Dickson's influence was evident in the spring of 1813. In a pattern all too familiar to government officials, Potawatomis and Kickapoos from northern Illinois again swept south across the prairie toward the settlements. During March and April, Potawatomis from Mad Sturgeon's village killed a man and his son near the Saline River in southern Illinois, and Gomo led a war party which killed two whites near the mouth of the Little Wabash. Other Potawatomis took scalps near Portage des Sioux and raided into western Indiana. The Kickapoos also sent war parties south, stealing horses and killing travelers near Kaskaskia.[67]

The depredations continued throughout the summer of 1813, and American officials seemed powerless to contain them. American military strength in the west was concentrated with Harrison, and the limited patrols available for Illinois were too sparse to be effective. Small expeditions were sent along the Wabash and Sangamon, burning a few Indian camps, but finding no warriors. In desperation, government agents at St. Louis attempted to enlist the Osages against the Potawatomis and their allies, but the Osages refused to participate in the warfare.[68]

Edwards earlier had recommended that a fort be established at Peoria to contain Indian raiding, and late in the summer of 1813, Governor Benjamin Howard of Louisiana seized upon the idea as the only means to end the Potawatomi forays. During August he collected men and material in southern Illinois, and on September 19 he marched north toward Peoria. Howard's expedition arrived at its destination on September 28, and construction on the fort began immediately. Howard encountered no Indians, but an advance guard had skirmished with a few warriors shortly before the governor's arrival. In search of the hostiles, Howard led a small force to the head of Lake Peoria, where they found several deserted villages. The Americans burned Gomo's town and two others before returning to the construction site. In twelve days the fort was finished and garrisoned, and Howard returned to St. Louis.[69]

Fort Clark, the new post at Peoria, proved to be a success. No longer were the Americans willing to remain in their homes, waiting for Potawatomi raiders to descend upon them. The fort illustrated that the Long Knives had taken the offensive and were willing to establish a new post in the Potawatomi homeland. After October, 1813, a few Potawatomi war parties still managed to reach southern Illinois, but their numbers declined as more and more warriors realized that the British were beaten. Black Partridge, Gomo, and Senachewine or Petacho (Swift Water), Gomo's brother, moved back to Lake Peoria late in the fall of 1813 and made peace with Captain Joseph Phillips, the commander of the garrison. Early in January, 1814, Black Partridge and a small party of warriors journeyed to St. Louis, where they assured William Clark that they no longer would support the British. As a pledge of their good intentions, nine of the warriors agreed to remain among the Americans as hostages.[70]

The growing friendship between the Peoria Potawatomis and the Americans caused much consternation in Wisconsin. Robert Dickson knew that the Potawatomis at Detroit had signed an armistice with the Americans, and he was afraid that the entire tribe had gone over to the United States. In March, 1814, after the Potawatomis welcomed Forsyth back to Peoria, Dickson believed that his suspicions had been confirmed. He also feared that the Peoria Potawatomis were conspiring against his life with Potawatomis near Milwaukee. To regain the initiative, Dickson attempted to kill or capture Forsyth, sending a party of Winnebagos to Peoria, but the Potawatomis warned Forsyth, and the Winnebago mission failed.[71]

Dickson's mistrust of the Potawatomis increased when he learned that the Americans had seized several British traders and killed one of his agents active among the Potawatomis along the Saint Joseph. In early January, 1814, a party of American Indian agents and interpreters led by Robert Forsyth surprised and captured Joseph Bailly and three other traders living among the Saint Joseph villages. The Potawatomis did not oppose the seizure, and Dickson accused them of compliance in the action. Later, in the spring, one of Dickson's agents, Charles Chandonnai, was killed when he tried to rally the same Potawatomis against an American party visiting in their towns. The Americans were led by Jean Chandonnai, the British agent's nephew, who had arrived from Detroit in an effort to persuade the Saint Joseph Potawatomis to attend an American conference to be held at Greenville. A confrontation between the two relatives occurred, and the younger Chandonnai shot and killed his uncle. Once again the Potawatomis took no part in the incident, but they allowed the Americans to leave unharmed.[72]

Yet Dickson's fears regarding the Saint Joseph Potawatomis were premature. Although some of the friendly chiefs such as Topinbee, Five Medals, and Metea attended the conference held at Greenville in July, 1814, most of the Potawatomis refused to participate. During the summer Main Poc established a temporary camp on Yellow River in north-central Indiana, and his warriors raided near Fort Harrison.[73] The chief spent the summer conferring with Mad Sturgeon, Moran, and Chebass (Little Duck), a hostile chief from the Saint Joseph. All of the pro-British chiefs visited Mackinac, and Chebass led a small party of warriors who helped the British repulse Major George Croghan's ill-fated attack on this island during August.[74]

Angered by the Potawatomis' continued violation of the truce, the government decided to move against the hostiles. In August, 1814, Secretary of War John Armstrong ordered McArthur to raise one thousand mounted volunteers and to march through northern Indiana, destroying the Potawatomi villages along the Saint Joseph and Kankakee. McArthur also was instructed to erect an American post at the mouth of the Saint Joseph to prevent the British from shipping arms and ammunition to the Indians.[75]

Learning of the proposed expedition, Potawatomis near Fort Wayne warned their kinsmen on the Saint Joseph, where the news was viewed with alarm. After a council at Topinbee's village, from which Topinbee was excluded, the hostile chiefs sent messages to the villages in northern Illinois, asking for assistance. They also dispatched runners to the Ottawas along the Grand River, urging them to journey to the Saint Joseph to meet McArthur's expedition. British traders pledged supplies of powder, and by late September more than eight hundred warriors had assembled along the lower Saint Joseph River.[76]

But the attack never came. The American expedition formed too slowly, and McArthur could raise no more than six hundred men. Fearing that his command would be overwhelmed along the Saint Joseph, McArthur changed his plans. In October he marched

north toward Detroit, destroying the lodges of several friendly Potawatomis on the Huron River, and then crossed into Canada, where
he raided British food depots along the Thames and the Grand
River.[77]

When McArthur's expedition failed to appear, the large numbers
of warriors along the Saint Joseph dispersed back to their villages.
Throughout the winter of 1814–15, Potawatomis from the Saint
Joseph and the Kankakee visited Mackinac, asking the British for
food and blankets, but they received few presents. By 1815 the
British were hard pressed to supply their regular troops and had
few provisions available for the Indians. The hard-core British
chiefs such as Main Poc, Chebass, Moran, and Mad Sturgeon maintained their ties to the Crown, but most of the other Potawatomis
now realized that the war was lost and were anxious to make peace
with the Americans.[78] By mid-winter, the weather was especially
severe, and many of the villages suffered chronic food shortages. On
January 10, White Pigeon was captured by an American patrol near
Fort Wayne, where he had come to surrender and ask for supplies.
Aware of the Potawatomi shortages, government officials used food
and other provisions as a weapon in their struggle to gain control
over the tribe. Agents were ordered to offer supplies to all Potawatomi chiefs who would bring their people over to the Americans.[79]

The government's "food offensive" was particularly successful in
Illinois, where Robert Dickson inadvertently aided the American
cause. Convinced that all Potawatomis were conspiring to kill him,
the British agent did not differentiate between friendly and hostile
bands and refused to give British provisions to any member of the
tribe. This refusal forced many of the Potawatomis living along the
Fox River to move closer to Peoria, where Gomo, Black Partridge,
and Pepper had reestablished friendly relations with the garrison at
Fort Clark. Potawatomis in the Peoria region traded actively with
the soldiers, exchanging fresh game and fish for flour and other
staples. The Americans were generous with their supplies, and the
Potawatomis near the fort passed the winter in relative comfort. In
repayment they provided the garrison with information about
Dickson's activities or warned the soldiers of hostile war parties.[80]
Even the murder of a party of friendly Potawatomis by a detachment of rangers did not bring about any rupture in the good relations. The government apologized and "covered" the dead Potawatomis with trade goods, and the Indians remained at peace.[81]

Throughout the winter of 1814–15 rumors reached the white

settlements in Illinois and Indiana that the spring would bring a renewal of Indian warfare. A few small war parties slipped south in February, but before the hostile chiefs could raise large numbers of warriors, they learned that the war was over. News of the Treaty of Ghent reached the British and Americans during March, and both sides notified the Indians as soon as possible. Yet a few of the hostile chiefs refused to accept the message. On the Saint Joseph River, Chebass seized one American messenger and held him prisoner while threatening the life of two others if they dared to spread such rumors in his village. Other chiefs met in council and decided to send Main Poc to Mackinac to ask the British if the American messengers were correct.[82]

To Main Poc's chagrin, the rumor proved true. At Mackinac the British informed Main Poc, Blackbird, and an assemblage of other chiefs and warriors that they must lay down their tomahawks and accept the Americans as friends. Main Poc returned to the Saint Joseph unreconciled and joined with Chebass and Moran in an attempt to raise enough warriors to attack the settlements near Vincennes, but they were unsuccessful. The Potawatomis along the Saint Joseph were anxious for peace and no longer wished to antagonize the Long Knives. Even Mad Sturgeon refused their overtures, and in May he journeyed to Fort Wayne, where he met with Stickney, professing his friendship to the United States and claiming that he always had opposed raids against the settlements.[83]

The peacemaking progressed more quickly in Illinois. Gomo died during April, 1815, but his brother, Senachewine, assumed the chieftainship and continued the dead leader's policies. When news of the peace reached Illinois, the Potawatomis at Peoria carried government invitations to all their kinsmen on the Illinois River, asking them to attend a peace conference at Portage des Sioux during the summer. On July 18, Senachewine, Black Partridge, White Hair, and four other Potawatomis met with government officials and signed a treaty of peace and friendship with the United States which stated that both parties would be "on the same footing upon which they stood before the war." The Potawatomis also agreed that "every injury or act of hostility . . . shall be mutually forgiven" and that "perpetual peace and friendship" would govern their relations with the United States. Convinced that they could once again return to their old way of life, the Potawatomis went back to their villages above Peoria.[84]

While the Illinois River Potawatomis were signing the treaty at

Portage des Sioux, government agents planned a similar treaty at Spring Wells, near modern Detroit. During the summer of 1815, Stickney sent several invitations to the Potawatomis along the Saint Joseph and Tippecanoe to meet with treaty commissioners in August. Main Poc and Moran spurned the offer, but Chebass, finally convinced that peace was inevitable, accepted the proposal, and in July he visited Stickney at Fort Wayne. Chebass assured both Stickney and Major John Whistler, the commanding officer at Fort Wayne, that he would no longer oppose the Americans and that he would use his influence to bring the other Saint Joseph Potawatomis to the treaty. Whistler provided him with supplies to take back to his village, and the chief returned to his people. Chebass kept his promise, and in August he joined with Topinbee to lead a large delegation of Saint Joseph Potawatomis to Spring Wells.[85]

The treaty proceedings began on August 22, 1815. The commissioners, Harrison, McArthur, and John Graham, a government surveyor from Indiana, met with chiefs and warriors from the Potawatomis, Ottawas, Chippewas, Wyandots, Shawnees, Miamis, Delawares, and Senecas. The commissioners were instructed to secure a peace with the tribes, but not to negotiate for any new land cessions. After two weeks of formal meetings, the Potawatomis and other Indians agreed to resume relations with the United States under the same conditions that had prevailed before the war, but they were forced to accept all of the land cessions negotiated by the government between 1795 and 1811. The Potawatomis also promised to break their ties with the British and to "place themselves under the protection of the United States, and no other power whatsoever."[86]

Among the Potawatomis signing the document were Topinbee, Chebass, Five Medals, Metea, and Mad Sturgeon. Main Poc refused to attend the conference and returned to his camp on the Yellow River in Indiana. In ill health, and unable to adjust to the new peace, the old Potawatomi drank heavily and died while hunting in Michigan during the spring of 1816.[87]

Following the treaties, the Potawatomis returned to their villages and assumed their old way of life. Many were unaware of the importance of the Treaty of Ghent. Although the British remained in Canada and still welcomed them at Malden, the Potawatomis could no longer rely upon the Redcoats for support against the Americans. The United States emerged from the War of 1812 self-confident and surging with a new nationalism that would send hordes of land-hungry settlers into the Old Northwest. Although the Potawatomis had slowly acculturated with many of the old values of the French traders and had made feeble attempts at agriculture under Quaker tutelage, they were unprepared for the changes that would innundate them after 1815. Yankee farmers would plow up their prairies and Protestant missionaries would proselytize their children. But the Potawatomis could no longer strike back in the time-honored manner of warriors. Main Poc's death in 1816 is significant in that the incorrigible old warrior was the last of the traditional war chiefs. His way of life had ended. The new leaders among the tribe would be men skilled in diplomacy, not warfare. Some would be full-bloods, and some would be of mixed lineage, but all would be masters at accommodation.

No-taw-kah (Rattlesnake), by George Winter. In 1836 Notawkah and two other chiefs sold the reservation on the Yellow River that they shared with the old chief Menominee. Although Notawkah and his comrades left the reservation, Menominee refused to move. *Courtesy Tippecanoe County Historical Society*

Keewaunay Council, by George Winter. Winter's painting depicts Abel
C. Pepper urging Potawatomi leaders at Keewaunay's village in 1837

to remove. *Courtesy Western History Collections, University of Oklahoma Library*

Me-no-quet, a Distinguish'd Pottowattomie Chief, by J. O. Lewis. A Wabash Potawatomi, Menoquet was a chief from a village on the upper Tippecanoe River. *Courtesy Western History Collections, University of Oklahoma Library*

Sun-a-get, or Hard Times, by J. O. Lewis. Sun-A-Get's costume, combining white clothing and the horned headdress, is indicative of Potawatomi acculturation in the 1830's. *Courtesy Western History Collections, University of Oklahoma Library*

Senator John Tipton led the force of Indiana volunteers that surrounded Menominee's village and forced the old chief and his followers to remove to the west. *Courtesy Indiana Historical Society Library*

Pach-e-po, a Pottowattomie Chief, by J. O. Lewis. In 1839 Pashpoho
was imprisoned for the accumulated debts his followers owed merchants near Rochester, Indiana. Released from prison, Pashpoho and
his villagers removed to the west in 1840. *Courtesy Amon Carter Museum, Fort Worth*

Leopold Pokagon, by Van Sanden. A chief from the Saint Joseph River, Pokagon and his followers remained on their small farms in Michigan and were not removed to the west. *Courtesy Northern Indiana Historical Society*

9. "The Ploughshare Is Driven Through Our Tents"

The years immediately following the Treaty of Ghent did not hold profound changes for the Potawatomis. They returned to their villages, planted their corn, and spent the winter dispersed in small hunting camps scattered through the forests. Peace brought a resurgence of the fur trade, and the United States attempted to keep British traders from visiting the Potawatomi villages by reestablishing the Indian factory at Chicago. Private traders also swarmed into the Potawatomi homeland, and the demand for furs increased. Warriors along the Kankakee, Fox, and Saint Joseph trapped muskrats and raccoons, while their kinsmen near Peoria brought in deerskins taken along the Little Mackinaw and the Sangamon. But the animals were few. The fur bearers had been severely depleted before the war, and the deer herds suffered from the incursions of large white hunting parties which entered Potawatomi hunting lands from the south and east. Potawatomi hunters still scoured the timber, but they often returned with no meat, and their traplines were empty.[1]

Because the fur trade declined, the Potawatomis were forced to rely more heavily on government annuities. Before the War of 1812, the tribe received a small annuity of about two thousand dollars per year, but because of the war they were given only a partial annuity in both 1811 and 1812, and from 1813 to 1816 they received none at all. The government paid them all back annuities in one lump sum during the summer of 1816, and the money and goods provided a welcome relief from the poverty of the immediate postwar period, but it soon was spent and had little lasting impact. The Potawatomis therefore faced an uncertain future. They continually needed more of the white man's goods to sustain life, but they continually had fewer resources with which to buy such materials.[2]

They sought solace from the British. His Majesty's Indian Department continued to invite the Potawatomis and other tribesmen to Canada, where it lent a sympathetic ear to the Indians' problems and presented them with gifts of food, clothing, and trade goods. The Potawatomis eagerly accepted such presents, and in the years following 1815 they frequently crossed over to Malden or Saint Joseph Island to meet with their former allies. In addition, a few Potawatomi chiefs, including Metea and Moran, received regular British payments after 1815. Metea, who had been wounded opposing Harrison's relief of Fort Wayne, received a British pension for his disability, and Moran evidently was employed by the British as a source of intelligence during the postwar period.[3]

The continuing Potawatomi-British friendship caused much consternation among the Americans. In the immediate postwar period the white frontier was flooded with rumors of another Indian conflict, and the settlers willingly believed that the British were involved.[4] To counter the British "threat" the United States expanded its Indian service in the Old Northwest, reestablishing the agency at Chicago and creating new agencies at Green Bay and Prairie du Chien. A subagency also was established at Peoria. To provide a military deterrent to any Indian hostilities, the government also erected a series of military posts. Although Fort Clark was abandoned, new forts were built at Chicago, Green Bay, Prairie du Chien, and Rock Island.[5]

The proliferation of new posts and agencies contributed to the political fragmentation of the Potawatomis. As government agents at various locations met with different chiefs and leaders, the agents tended to view the chiefs at their agencies as the principal chiefs of the tribe. At Fort Wayne, Stickney and Whistler continued to consult with Five Medals and Metea, since both chiefs were co-operative and had a large following among Potawatomis living in northeastern Indiana and south-central Michigan. Charles Jouett, the newly appointed agent at Chicago, ascribed to Topinbee and Chebass the primary leadership of the tribe. In 1819, after Jouett resigned, the new agent, Doctor Alexander Wolcott, pushed Alexander Robinson and Billy Caldwell as the most important Potawatomi leaders. At Peoria, Indian Agent Richard Graham supported Senachewine and Shabbona. The resulting confusion over tribal leadership was more perplexing to the Americans than to the Potawatomis, since the Indians' conception of chieftainship was flexible and emphasized the roles of different leaders at different times, but the government's attempt to work simultaneously through different Indians did contribute to intratribal bickering.[6]

Much of the bickering centered upon the distribution of annuities. With the exception of a small proportion of the annuity paid to Senachewine's people at Peoria, the entire tribal annuity was paid to the Potawatomis at Detroit. All of the tribe were encouraged to attend the annuity payment and to share in the goods and money, but many of the Potawatomis living west of Chicago refused to travel so far, and even the chiefs from the Wabash complained to Stickney that they wanted their payment at Fort Wayne. Those Potawatomis not in attendance accused their kinsmen of keeping all the annuity and grumbled that they had not received their fair share. At Chicago, Jouett took up their cause and petitioned the government to move the Potawatomi annuity payment to his post, since "five out of six of the whole nation lie within this agency." Indian agents at Fort Wayne championed a similar proposal, but Jouett proved more persuasive, and in 1818 the government agreed to pay part of the annuities at Chicago. Topinbee and Robinson were pleased, but the Potawatomis near Fort Wayne and Detroit were angry.[7]

The tribal fragmentation and growing dependence upon annuities made the Potawatomis susceptible to the government's aggressive land policies in the postwar period. In the treaties ending the War of 1812, federal officials had scrupulously avoided any attempts at further land cessions, but such hesitancy ended after 1815. Ohio, Indiana, and Illinois all were anxious to clear Indian title from their territory and petitioned the federal government for such action. Federal officials responded to their pleas, and with peace restored, the United States resumed its land-grabbing tactics which earlier had been championed by William Henry Harrison.[8]

The first postwar cession of Potawatomi lands occurred in 1816. In the treaties at the end of the war, the Potawatomis agreed to recognize those land cessions made through 1811. At first the chiefs evidently believed that such recognition extended only to those cessions made by their tribe and not to any Potawatomi lands relinquished by other Indians. In the autumn of 1815, however, Richard Graham informed the Potawatomis along the Illinois River that the terms of the peace treaty also applied to the Sac and Fox cession of western Illinois in 1804. Graham told the Indians that the government intended to use the region for military bounty lands and that surveyors would begin mapping the area in the spring. Senachewine,

Black Partridge, and other chiefs at Peoria adamantly repudiated the Sac and Fox cession, claiming that the Potawatomis had lived in the region for half a century. They warned both Graham and William Clark at St. Louis that they would oppose any survey, and in the spring, when surveyors crossed into the lands between the Illinois and Mississippi rivers, the Potawatomis harassed them, destroying their equipment and threatening their lives.[9]

Faced with the threat of renewed Indian warfare in Illinois, the government resorted to bribery. Federal officials knew that the Potawatomis along the Illinois River needed trade goods, so in the summer of 1816 they invited the Indians to a council at St. Louis. In August, Ninian Edwards, William Clark, and Auguste Chouteau, a fur trader from Missouri, met at St. Louis with "the chiefs and warriors of the united tribes of Ottawas, Chippewas, and Potawatomies, residing on the Illinois and Melwakee Rivers, and their waters, and on the southwestern parts of Lake Michigan." In the resulting treaty, the Potawatomis relinquished all claim to the Sac and Fox cession in western Illinois below a line drawn due west from the tip of Lake Michigan to the Mississippi. They also ceded a small region in northeastern Illinois, bordering on Lake Michigan. In return the government guaranteed the Potawatomis title to the remaining lands in northern Illinois and to parts of southern Wisconsin. The Potawatomis retained the right to hunt in the Sac and Fox cession until such lands were claimed by white citizens. They also accepted an annuity of one thousand dollars in trade goods for twelve years.[10]

The treaty of August 24, 1816, is important in that it was the first of twenty-eight such agreements signed by the tribe in the quarter-century following the War of 1812. Moreover, with the exception of the treaty negotiated at Detroit in November, 1807, the 1816 treaty at St. Louis marks the first time that the Potawatomis had ceded any of their own homeland. In previous cessions the tribe had relinquished claims to territory occupied by other Indians, but had not given up lands surrounding Potawatomi villages. The treaty in 1816 also marks the first attempt by the government to purchase lands and deliver annuities to specific "bands" within the tribe instead of the entire tribe as a political entity. Earlier, federal officials may have negotiated with a few chiefs representing only one or two villages of Potawatomis, but the government viewed such individuals as spokesmen for the entire tribe, and all the Potawatomis supposedly shared in the annuities. After 1815, conditions changed.

On occasion, the different villages of Potawatomis began to meet with the government separately, each claiming large areas of tribal homeland and each trying to gain the lion's share of the annuities. The Potawatomis would bargain away their birthright, selling their lands piecemeal for the Americans' trade goods, money, and promises.[11]

The treaty at St. Louis was followed by two others within the next two years. In September, 1817, the Potawatomis, Ottawas, Chippewas, Wyandots, Senecas, Delawares, and Shawnees met with government commissioners at Fort Meigs, near the Rapids of the Maumee. The commissioners' primary objective was to clear the title to the remaining Indian lands in Ohio, and the Potawatomis were invited because they had improperly participated in the Fort Industry treaty in 1805. Most of the Potawatomis in attendance were from the Saint Joseph, Wabash, and Detroit regions and were led by Metea and Winamac. Notably absent were Topinbee, Chebass, and the chiefs from Illinois. The chiefs at the treaty not only gave their assent to the major cession of lands in Ohio, but also relinquished a small tract in northwestern Ohio and south-central Michigan bordering the lands ceded in 1807. In exchange they received another annuity of thirteen hundred dollars in specie for fifteen years. The terms of the treaty specified that the money was to be paid at Detroit. The western Potawatomi had acquired their annuity increase in 1816; now the eastern bands received one of their own.[12]

One year later the tribe ceded additional lands in the Wabash Valley. This land cession was negotiated at Saint Mary's, in eastern Ohio, in October and was one of a series of treaties signed at that place in the fall of 1818. During the previous winter the Senate had rejected part of the Fort Meigs treaty, and the commissioners were forced to renegotiate with the Wyandots, Senecas, Shawnees, and Ottawas over provisions involving individual reservations in Ohio. Although the Potawatomi cession at Fort Meigs was not renegotiated, the government invited the Potawatomis, Weas, Delawares, and Miamis to sell their lands along the Wabash, and during September and October, representatives of many tribes assembled at Saint Mary's. Indiana was anxious to open the Wabash Valley to white settlement, and the government appropriated large sums of money for gifts to tribal delegations and important leaders. The Potawatomis attending the conference received nineteen hundred dollars in "presents" plus an unknown additional share of six thousand dollars dispensed as bribes to individual chiefs.[13]

The government's cajolery achieved its purpose. Unlike the previous treaty, the Saint Mary's negotiations were attended by leading chiefs from most of the villages in Michigan and Indiana. Topinbee, Chebass, Moran, Mad Sturgeon, Metea, and Five Medals all signed the agreement exchanging approximately 1,550 square miles of land along the Wabash in western Indiana and extreme eastern Illinois for a perpetual annuity of twenty-five hundred dollars in silver. Ironically, however, the fragmentation over annuity payments continued. The Potawatomis demanded that half of the new annuity be paid at Detroit and the other half at Chicago.[14]

Encouraged by their success in acquiring Potawatomi lands in Indiana, the government decided to attempt the purchase of all the remaining Potawatomi lands in Michigan. On June 1, 1820, Secretary of War John C. Calhoun appointed Cass and Solomon Sibley, a politician from Michigan, to serve as commissioners for the treaty. Cass spent a year preparing for the treaty negotiations, working through Alexander Wolcott, the newly appointed Indian agent at Chicago. Although the proposed cession was in Michigan, Wolcott and Cass contrived to hold the treaty at Chicago, since the Saint Joseph's Potawatomis would be forced to leave their villages and "the sense of attachment to, and reluctance to part with things and places long dear to them would be less strong when those things and places were at a distance than if directly in their view." Once again, government funds were obtained to bribe influential chiefs, while large stores of food, whiskey, and trade goods were assembled at Chicago.[15]

Nearly three thousand Potawatomis, with a scattering of Ottawas and Chippewas, assembled at Chicago during August, 1821. The negotiations started on August 17 and lasted almost two weeks. Much to the commissioners' surprise, the Potawatomis seemed reluctant to negotiate. Cass assured them that they could keep part of their lands as reservations and occupy any ceded area until it was purchased by individual white settlers, but his promises fell upon deaf ears. Speaking for the Potawatomis, Metea informed the commissioners that they had willingly ceded small portions of land in the past, but they were taken aback by the size of the proposed cession. The chief complained that the whites were crowding onto Potawatomi lands so quickly that "the plowshare is driven through our tents before we have time to carry out our goods and seek another habitation."[16]

For the next two weeks Cass used all of his power of persuasion to gain the lands for the United States. He reminded the tribesmen that their annuities would be increased and that their chiefs would receive extra funds for their cooperation. He refused to dispense the customary whiskey, stating that drinking might hamper the negotiations, but if the treaty were concluded he promised to give the Potawatomis enough alcohol "to make every man, woman, and child in the nation drunk." Cass would not accept the Potawatomi refusal and warned the Saint Joseph tribesmen that the remainder of the trade goods would be distributed only to the other Potawatomis if the Saint Joseph leaders continued in their recalcitrance.[17]

Topinbee, Chebass, Congee (Bear Paws) and others spoke for the Potawatomis, but by far the greatest opponent of the cession was Metea. Henry Schoolcraft, an eyewitness to the negotiations, described the chief as a man of forty years, with a sullen dignity but an unpleasant personal appearance because of his crippled arm and a large scar across his face. Yet Schoolcraft admitted that Metea was a superb orator with a gift for language and a forthright presentation. According to Schoolcraft, Metea's "voice is not unpleasant, nor can his manner be considered as vehement . . . he is by far the best speaker in his nation."[18]

But Metea's oratory failed. The Ottawas and Chippewas at the treaty urged the Potawatomis to accept the government's offer, as did many of the traders and mixed-bloods among the tribe. The promises of presents, enlarged annuities, and plentiful whiskey proved too great a temptation, and on August 29 the Potawatomis capitulated. Metea opposed the cession to the last, but Topinbee, a tired old man much given to drinking, grew impatient and finally pleaded with Cass, "We care not for the land, the money, or the goods, it is the whiskey we want—give us the whiskey."[19]

In the treaty, the Potawatomis ceded to the United States all of their lands in southwestern Michigan from the Saint Joseph River east to the boundaries of the lands ceded in 1807 and 1817 and stretching as far north as the Grand River. They also relinquished their claim to a small strip of lands in northern Indiana extending from South Bend to the Ohio line. In return, the United States agreed to pay the Potawatomis an additional annuity of five thousand dollars in specie for twenty years and to appropriate one thousand dollars annually to support a blacksmith and teacher among the tribe. Withheld from the cession were a number of small tracts and reserves awarded to particular villages or individuals.

Most of the individual reserves, which could not be sold without the permission of the president, were granted to mixed-bloods and reflected the growing importance of these people in tribal councils. Among the recipients of the reserves were the Burnets, Chandonais, Beaubiens, Bertrands, Le Claires, and La Framboises, families resulting from marriages between traders and Potawatomi women. These individuals, realizing that the tribe was giving up most of its remaining lands in Michigan, were anxious to acquire valuable tracts of real estate for themselves. Many possessed the rudiments of a formal education, and in the years to come they would serve as catalysts between the two cultures, mediating Indian-white problems while reaping rewards from both sides.[20]

The mixed-bloods' acculturation was facilitated by their contact with white missionaries. Although the Catholic mission at Saint Joseph closed in the 1770's, priests from the settlements in Illinois and Indiana and at Detroit continued to visit the Potawatomis, baptizing infants, administering the sacraments, and occasionally accompanying mixed-blood children back to the settlements, where they were enrolled in Catholic schools. Billy Caldwell had attended a Jesuit school in Detroit during the 1780's, and other mixed-blood children also learned to read and write (often in French) and to master simple problems in mathematics. Moreover, most of the mixed-blood families, and some of the full-bloods, maintained their semblance of faith, remaining Catholic in form, if not in substance.[21]

During the postwar period this religion-sponsored acculturation increased. Spurred on by the Second Great Awakening, and inspired by the nationalism of the postwar years, the Protestants marched forth into the wilderness hoping to evangelize the "red heathens" and prepare them for "a glorious inheritance in the kingdom of Immanuel." Equating Christianity with nineteenth-century American society, the Protestants were as anxious to "civilize" the Indians as to "save" them.[22]

The most active Protestant missionary among the Potawatomis was Isaac McCoy, a Baptist missionary from Kentucky. In 1820 McCoy established a mission school at Fort Wayne which soon enrolled twenty-six students, including several Potawatomis. Among McCoy's students was Abraham Burnett, the son of William Burnett and nephew of Topinbee; the boy was brought to the school by his mother.[23] At Fort Wayne, McCoy also was visited by Menominee, a minor chief from a village on the Yellow River who had emerged as a religious leader among the Potawatomis along the Saint Joseph and the Tippecanoe. Menominee had combined some of the Shawnee Prophet's old tenets, including abstinence from alcohol, with Roman Catholicism in an attempt to create a new religion that would help his tribesmen accommodate to the changes swirling around them.[24]

Menominee invited McCoy to visit the Potawatomi towns, and in June, 1821, the missionary, guided by Abraham Burnett, passed through villages on the Yellow River before arriving at Burnett's trading post near the mouth of the Saint Joseph. McCoy was aware that the treaty at Chicago would soon take place, and he was able to convince the chiefs along the Saint Joseph that they should ask for a mission school at the treaty. Believing that such an institution would aid in "civilizing" the Potawatomis, the treaty commissioners granted the request, and the treaty provided a government payment of one thousand dollars for fifteen years and two sections of land, one on the Grand and the other on the Saint Joseph River, as sites for teachers and blacksmiths.[25]

Evidence suggests that the Potawatomis were much more interested in acquiring a blacksmith than a missionary and preferred a Catholic over a Baptist, but McCoy received the appointment. In December, 1822, after a disagreement over the mission site was settled, McCoy moved his school to a new location about a mile from the Saint Joseph River, just west of modern Niles, Michigan. A school, a blacksmith's shop, and four log houses were built, and on January 27, 1823, McCoy began his ministry among the Saint Joseph Potawatomis.[26]

Carey Mission, named after William Carey, a Baptist missionary to India, at first met with success. Topinbee moved his village to a new location a few miles southwest of the mission, and the Indians welcomed the missionaries into their homeland. The school received financial support from the federal government's "civilization" fund as well as money and other assistance from the Baptists. New buildings were added to the establishment, and new students were recruited for the school. In an effort to establish a model community for the surrounding Potawatomis, and to make the mission self-supporting, land was cleared and crops were planted. By 1825 the school was "prosperous and flourishing," with approximately seventy pupils, the majority of them mixed-bloods.[27] Robert Simmerwell, a combination teacher-blacksmith, translated several texts and catechisms into Potawatomi, and the students learned such "sophisticated" subjects as geography and ancient history. In addition, Potawatomi boys were taught agricultural skills through their chores on the mission farm, while girls learned to weave and sew in the best traditions of nineteenth-century American society.[28]

The missionaries made some gains in attracting adult Potawatomis to their establishment. By offering the Indians an evening meal, they were able to entice some of the warriors to periodically work on the farm, and McCoy reported that thirty families within the vicinity of Carey had fenced their farms, with missionary assistance, and were "improving, more or less rapidly." Moreover, a small congregation of Potawatomis, including the chief Muccose (Young Bear), occasionally attended McCoy's religious services, and a few Indians, mainly students, "descended into the dews of heaven," or were baptized.[29]

Yet the mission failed to attract large numbers of Potawatomis. Although a few of the students excelled and were sent east to more advanced schools in New England or enrolled in the Choctaw Academy at Great Crossings, Kentucky, many of the Potawatomi children eventually tired of the rigid schedule and strict discipline of the school and withdrew from the mission. Awakened by a trumpet blast at five in the morning (earlier in the summer) and forced to spend their day in manual labor, school, and prayer meetings, it is not surprising that few Potawatomi youngsters found the white man's world appealing. With few exceptions, those Potawatomis who remained in school for long periods of time were mixed-bloods, and even these successful students refused to accept the missionaries' value system. They learned to read and write the white man's language, but they became traders, not farmers.[30]

After 1826 the mission declined. The traders in the region opposed the institution, since they wished the Potawatomis to continue trapping and supplying pelts for the fur trade. During the middle 1820's the government decided upon a policy of removal, and McCoy became more interested in finding a site for a new mission in the west than in maintaining his establishments in Michigan. Moreover, treaties in 1826 and 1827 opened much of northern Indiana and the remaining Potawatomi lands in Michigan to white settlement. As the whites moved in, the liquor trade increased, and the missionaries were unable to compete with the whiskey.[31]

The abundance of illegal whiskey in the Indian country caused many problems. It was cheaply produced, readily available, and commonly sold to the Potawatomis. In 1817 Richard Graham complained of the volume of contraband alcohol being traded to the Indians at Peoria, and during the next decade the traffic increased. The major distribution points were at Peoria, at Fort Wayne, along the Kankakee, and ironically, on the lower Saint Joseph, near Carey Mission. The rotgut whiskey had a devastating impact upon the Potawatomis. Many Indians, including chiefs such as Topinbee, drank to excess and suffered the debilitating effects of such an addiction. After the 1821 treaty Cass kept his promise and distributed enough whiskey "to make every man, woman, and child in the nation drunk," and the resulting debacle caused the death of almost a dozen Indians. At Carey, McCoy continually complained that a Squire Thompson and other traders openly sold liquor to the Potawatomis. He reported that Topinbee's death in the summer of 1826 occurred after the old chief became intoxicated and fell off his horse.[32]

The whiskey trade also caused many of the Potawatomis to squander their annuities. Since the traders knew when the annuity payments would be made, they followed the Potawatomis to the payments and then offered whiskey in return for the money and trade goods. After plying the Indians with liquor, the traders often fleeced them out of all they had received. The whiskey peddlers then followed the Potawatomis back to their villages, where the practice continued. At Carey, Simmerwell complained:

> They purchase anything the Indians choose to part with. A silver mounted gun has been purchased for the value of two raccoons in liquor. Clothes and utensils purchased for liquor are again bartered in fur. Maguakwak brought me a gun to repair for which he gave to Thompson eighty muskrats. Tomahawks have been brought to the shop by our white neighbors to be worked up for their use, [and] work that I have done for the Indians [I have] seen in the stores of the whiskey sellers.[33]

More important than the loss of annuities were the problems engendered between the Potawatomis and their white neighbors. In the decade following the War of 1812, white settlement moved north onto the prairies of Illinois and Indiana. Many of the settlers were not averse to squatting on Indian land, but they resented the Indians hunting among their settlements. Moreover, although they often sold whiskey to the Potawatomis, they were quick to complain when drunken warriors threatened their property. These complaints were channeled through state officials, who then asked the federal government to remove the Potawatomis to the west.[34]

A focal point of such contention emerged at Peoria. By the early 1820's, the white population at Peoria and along the Sangamon River had increased, the former mixed-blood and French community being supplanted by Anglo-Saxons from southern Illinois. Although the Potawatomis resented the influx of Americans, they traded with them, and Forsyth lamented, "It is truly shameful that such quantities of whiskey are sold and traded with the Indians on this river, almost every settler's home is a whiskey shop, and will buy from the Indians the most trifling articles for whiskey." When James Latham, the subagent at Peoria, attempted to suppress the traffic, white citizens in the region tried to have him removed.[35] Yet the same citizens complained that the Potawatomis, while intoxicated, were stealing vegetables from their gardens and killing their hogs and cattle. Forsyth investigated the charges against the Indians and concluded that many of them were false. Although the Potawatomis occasionally were guilty of stealing horses and killing hogs, most of the horses had been returned, and many of the hogs had been killed by other white men. Yet public clamor against the Potawatomis increased, adding weight to the argument that the Indians should be removed from their homeland.[36]

By the 1820's the Potawatomis had accepted many of the physical trappings of white culture. Deerskin hunting shirts and dresses had been discarded for garments of brightly colored calico or flannel, and although some men still wore buckskin leggings, many others preferred cloth trousers similar to their white neighbors'. Both sexes continued to wear moccasins, but their winter dress now included a trade blanket instead of a buffalo robe or a bearskin. Potawatomi men no longer shaved their heads in the traditional manner of warriors, choosing instead to wrap their hair in a cloth turban modeled after those of the Shawnees. They were wholly dependent upon the traders for the many necessities of life and purchased much the same hardware and dry goods as did white settlers. An inventory of merchandise at the Indian factory in Chicago resembles that of a typical frontier general store and includes such items as hats, ruffled shirts, horse bells, combs, needles, buttons, kettles, tobacco, salt, lead, powder, ribbons, a variety of soft goods, and many other articles too numerous to mention. Many of the more affluent Indians, especially the mixed-bloods, constructed log cabins, although the majority of the tribe continued to live in the more traditional wigwams.[37]

But if the Potawatomis accepted the products of American technology, they rejected the American ideal of becoming small yeoman farmers. The repeated attempts by both government and religious leaders to transform the tribe into a nation of small, self-sustaining farmers met with little success. A few families near Carey Mission temporarily tried the white man's road, but they abandoned their efforts after a short period. Most of the tribe continued to plant their gardens, raising small crops of corn, beans, and pumpkins, but they remained horticulturists, not agriculturists.[38]

Disgruntled missionaries and government officials charged that the tribe had made no strides toward "white civilization" and that they "adhered with tenacity to the manners of their forefathers while everything around them has changed." But such charges were untrue. Indeed, the Potawatomis continued to reject the role of small farmers, but they had adopted many ideals of another group of white men: the French traders.[39]

With a few exceptions, such as Burnett and Bailey on the Saint Joseph and Kinzie at Chicago, the majority of the merchants who exchanged trade goods for Potawatomi fur and annuities were men with French surnames. In the 1820's both Chicago and Detroit contained large creole populations, and Fort Wayne was so heavily French-Canadian that an American observer complained, "The business of a town of this kind differs so materially from that carried on in our cities, that it is almost impossible to fancy ourselves still within the same territorial limits."[40]

To the Potawatomis, the French trader, not the Anglo farmer, represented a goal for acculturation. The trader was a man of wealth and enjoyed economic and political influence, yet was not tied down to a farm and the back-breaking labor required to maintain it. Moreover, compared to American farmers, traders represented a more accessible goal, for many of the creoles also had acculturated toward the Potawatomis, marrying Indian women and adopting certain facets of Potawatomi culture.[41]

By the 1820's some of the Potawatomis, especially the mixed-bloods, had acculturated toward the creole image. Acquiring valuable experience through the fur trade, they combined that knowledge with a mission-school education to emerge as the new economic and political leaders of the tribe. Their experience among the whites equipped them to meet the Americans on white terms, yet adherence to Indian ways enabled them to maintain their tribal identity. Some of the new leaders were active as traders. At Chicago, both Robinson and Caldwell bought and sold fur as well as other items, and many of William Burnett's children followed a similar vocation on the St. Joseph. A few full-bloods also worked as traders, while others, in true engagé fashion, served as porters between the Saint Joseph and Kankakee rivers.[42]

Many of the more acculturated Potawatomis eventually sought employment with the government. Alexander Robinson, Gabriel Godfroy, Antoine Le Claire, Abraham Burnett, Joseph Ogee, and Naoquet or Luther Rice all served as interpreters. In 1825 Billy Caldwell was appointed justice of the peace at Chicago. He also served as an election judge during that year.[43]

Because the mixed-bloods were literate and were tied to the government, Indian agents attempted to work through such individuals in dealing with the tribe. Topinbee died in 1826, followed by Metea one year later. Chebass's influence declined, leaving few chiefs of tribal stature. Since the government periodically needed tribal spokesmen with whom to negotiate, officials began to turn to the mixed-bloods. In turn, these individuals' stature within the tribe appreciated because of their ability in negotiating with the government and because they began to control the flow of government presents and annuities. This change in leadership was opposed by some of the village chiefs, including Senachewine at Peoria, but these more traditional leaders had little support outside their villages and were unable to stop the transition.[44]

The emergence of the new leadership occurred during the last half of the 1820's and is reflected in several treaties negotiated during that period. In October, 1826, tribal leaders met with treaty commissioners Cass, Tipton, and James B. Ray, governor of Indiana, and ceded two tracts of land in Indiana. One cession followed the north banks of the Wabash and Maumee from the mouth of the Tippecanoe to the Ohio line; the other included a small area in northwestern Indiana between Lake Michigan and the Saint Joseph River. The Potawatomis also agreed to relinquish a strip of land for the construction of a road between the Wabash and Lake Michigan. In return, the Indians received an additional annuity of $2,000 in silver for twenty-one years, a blacksmith, a gristmill and miller at government expense, and an annual payment of 160 bushels of salt. The government agreed to appropriate approximately $2,000 for the education of Potawatomi boys at the Choctaw Academy, "as long as Congress . . . may think proper," and to pay a total of $9,573 in claims against the tribe held by various traders.[45]

At first the Potawatomis had been reluctant to negotiate. Led by Metea and Aubbeenaubbee, a heavy-set old chief from the Tippecanoe, the Potawatomis had rejected suggestions that they remove to the west and had refused to sell any more lands to the Americans. But they eventually succumbed to more than thirty thousand dollars in trade goods, distributed as "presents" at the treaty negotiations, and to the pressure of the mixed-bloods. Many mixed-bloods and traders attended the proceedings, and although none signed the document, Cass admitted that they "materially aided us during the negotiations." In return for their assistance, the mixed-bloods shared in the presents and were awarded small tracts or reserves within the ceded lands. This practice had been initiated at the Chicago treaty in 1821, but in 1826 it was amplified and extended. Many of the mixed-bloods who had received tracts at Chicago, supposedly to be used as farms, were awarded additional reservations in 1826. Yet little of the land was ever cultivated by the Potawatomis. It was held until a later date and then sold to white settlers or back to the government.[46]

During the next two years the Potawatomis made other land cessions in Indiana and Michigan. In 1827, Potawatomis on small reservations in eastern Michigan agreed to "consolidate" on similar-sized reservations along the Saint Joseph River. One year later, in September, 1828, Potawatomis from southwestern Michigan, northern Indiana, and Illinois met with government officials at Carey Mission and agreed to relinquish a large tract of land in northeastern Indiana and a small area in Michigan between the Saint Joseph River and Lake Michigan. In return they received additional annuities and more than forty thousand dollars' worth of presents to be parceled out to the different villages in 1828 and 1829. Ironically, the treaty also contained a provision in which the government tacitly admitted that its acculturation program had failed. The second article of the agreement provided that the government would clear and fence Potawatomi land, provide the Indians with livestock and farm utensils, and then *hire government laborers to farm for the Indians.*[47]

Again, the influence of the new leadership was apparent. Although few mixed-bloods signed the treaty, the negotiations were conducted by Leopold Pokagon, a young chief from the Saint Joseph who was under the influence of traders Joseph Bertrand and

Alexis Coquillard. Individual reservations were awarded to nineteen persons, most of whom were of mixed-blood lineage or were married to traders. Another article of the treaty provided that approximately eleven thousand dollars should be appropriated to pay debts owed to traders by members of the tribe.[48]

Federal officials also made plans to acquire Potawatomi lands in Illinois and Wisconsin. In 1825 the government sponsored a large intertribal conference at Prairie du Chien at which tribal claims to the upper Mississippi Valley were differentiated. Few Potawatomis attended the conference, but the tribe reasserted its claim to a tract of land in extreme northwestern Illinois and southwestern Wisconsin.[49] Known as the Fever River District, the lands were rich in lead deposits, and after 1825 the region was overrun by white miners. Although there were no Potawatomi villages in the area, the miners clashed with the Winnebagos, and in June, 1827, a small number of Winnebagos led by Red Bird killed a handful of whites near Prairie du Chien. When news of the attacks reached the settlements, whites panicked, and government officials sent militia units and federal troops to the Wisconsin frontier to "inflict exemplary chastisement" upon the Winnebagos. Although Red Bird and his followers surrendered, the turmoil spilled over among the Potawatomis in northern Illinois. The resulting confusion strengthened the position of the mixed-blood community at Chicago.[50]

In June, 1827, while Red Bird and his followers were planning their attacks in Wisconsin, the Potawatomis within the Chicago agency assembled at Chicago to receive their annuities. Among the crowd of Indians was Mawgehset, or Big Foot, a village chief from Lake Geneva in southern Wisconsin. The Potawatomis at Big Foot's village had intermarried with the Winnebagos and knew of Red Bird's plans to attack the Americans. At the request of the Winnebagos, Big Foot met secretly with the other chiefs and presented them an invitation from the Winnebagos and the Sioux to join in a war against the Long Knives. The other Potawatomis refused the war belt and dispersed to their villages, but Big Foot and his warriors remained at Chicago. They committed no depredations, but they aroused the suspicion of the whites when they refused to help fight a fire which engulfed part of the deserted barracks at Fort Dearborn.[51]

Big Foot and his warriors eventually returned to Lake Geneva, but when news of the Winnebago attacks reached Chicago, the Americans became alarmed. To calm their white neighbors, Caldwell, Robinson, Shabbona, and Shamagaw (Soldier), a village chief from the Kankakee, volunteered to travel to Lake Geneva to investigate Big Foot's intentions. They reached Big Foot's village late in July, but the chief was absent, so the four Potawatomis proceeded on to the Winnebago village on Lake Koshkonong. Before arriving at the Winnebago camp, the Potawatomis decided that Shabbona should enter the village alone, since he was well known to the Winnebagos and would arouse less suspicion than the entire party. The other Potawatomis agreed to remain hidden near the village until Shabbona's return.[52]

When Shabbona entered the Winnebago village, the Winnebagos became alarmed and seized him, threatening his life and accusing him of being an American spy. Shabbona replied that he had been absent when Big Foot delivered the war message at Chicago and that he had journeyed to Wisconsin so that he might hear the message personally. The Winnebagos kept Shabbona all night, but in the morning they decided to release him if he would promise to return directly to his village in northern Illinois and not report back to the whites in Chicago. Shabbona agreed, but the Winnebagos did not trust the Potawatomi and assigned an escort of Winnebago warriors to return with him to his village. As the party left the Winnebago village and passed the hiding place of his comrades, Shabbona loudly complained about what had happened so that Caldwell and the others might be informed. After Shabbona and his Winnebago escort were gone, the Potawatomis slipped away and returned to Chicago, where they reported the events to the Americans.[53]

Meanwhile, other Winnebago emissaries met with the Potawatomis near Peoria, but Senachewine, Waubansee, and Shickshack (Nine) also refused the war message and vowed their friendship to the whites.[54] Although the threat of hostilities soon ended, government officials used the events surrounding Red Bird's War as an excuse to urge that Indian title to lands in northern Illinois be extinguished. Governor Edwards of Illinois falsely accused the Potawatomis of joining the Winnebagos and demanded that they be removed beyond the Mississippi.[55]

Edwards was particularly anxious to remove the Potawatomis from the Peoria area. Although Senachewine and other Potawatomi leaders on the Illinois River remained friendly to the United States, the region was filling with white population, and the whiskey trade along the river continued unabated. In May, 1828, a clash between some Potawatomis and a whiskey peddler occurred near the mouth of the Spoon River, resulting in the death of at least one Indian. A government investigation placed much of the blame upon the settlers, but the clamor against the Potawatomis increased.[56]

Reacting to public opinion, and anxious to clear Indian title to the Fever River district, Cass met with a delegation of Potawatomis and Winnebagos at Green Bay in August, 1828, and made preliminary arrangements for a land cession to be negotiated during the following summer. The Potawatomis and Winnebagos agreed to assemble at Rock Island in June, 1829, but during the spring of that year the Winnebagos changed their minds and demanded that the treaty be held at Prairie du Chien. Not wishing to jeopardize the good will of the Winnebagos, the government agreed to their demands. Yet, federal officials failed to notify the Potawatomis of the change until many had assembled to leave for Rock Island.[57]

Angry over the change, Senachewine and many of the Potawatomis near Peoria refused to travel to Prairie du Chien, but the treaty was well attended by a large number of tribesmen from northern Illinois and Wisconsin. Led by Caldwell, Robinson, and several other mixed-bloods, the Potawatomis gave up two large tracts of lands in northern Illinois and southwestern Wisconsin, including the Fever River district. In return they received $20,000 in presents, an additional perpetual annuity of $16,000 to be paid at Chicago, the promise of another gift of $12,000 in goods, and several smaller items. The government also agreed to pay $11,600 owed by the tribe to traders in Illinois and Wisconsin. Reserved from the ceded territories and from other government lands were fourteen tracts of land which were assigned to individual Indians. Eleven of the fourteen reservations went to mixed-bloods, including Robinson and Caldwell. Another was awarded to Shabbona for his service during the Red Bird uprising.[58]

At Peoria, Senachewine protested against the treaty, claiming that those Potawatomis who sold the lands were not the same people to whom the lands had been guaranteed in the 1816 treaty. He complained that the lands had been ceded by "strangers" who were under the influence of government agents at Chicago and that the land belonged to the Potawatomis near Peoria and could not be sold by Caldwell and Robinson. The government at first ignored Senachewine's pleas, but his protest was supported by Pierre Menard, Jr., the subagent at Peoria and son of one of the treaty commissioners. In 1830 William Clark investigated the protests, and although the government refused to invalidate the land cession, it did agree that the Potawatomis near Peoria were entitled to part of the presents and annuities.[59] In 1831 Senachewine and several other chiefs from the Illinois River attended the annuity payments at Chicago, but they were dissatisfied with their portion of the annuity. Senachewine died during that year, but his son, Nauntay, complained about the apportionment, and the government agreed to take a census of Potawatomis in Illinois and to divide the annuities proportionately.[60]

Meanwhile, white settlers continued to pour into the lands along the Illinois Valley, and state officials increased their demands that the Potawatomis leave all ceded lands near Peoria and withdraw across the Mississippi or onto tribal lands in northern Illinois. The Potawatomis again protested that they wished to stay "on land given to us by the Great Spirit," but desperately short of provisions, and harassed by white settlers, most of the Potawatomis near Peoria agreed to move to the Rock River late in 1831.[61]

The confusion over Potawatomi census numbers, land claims, and annuity payments reflected the shifting population patterns that had occurred since the War of 1812. In 1815, large numbers of Potawatomis still were concentrated in the Fort Wayne and Detroit areas, but in the years following the war, many of these Potawatomis gradually moved westward, establishing new villages along the Saint Joseph, Tippecanoe, and Eel rivers. In Illinois, the Fox, Kankakee, and Illinois river valleys continued to hold many Potawatomi villages, with the Indians encamped as far south as Peoria. Other Potawatomis were dispersed across southeastern Wisconsin, with a few mixed villages of Potawatomis, Sacs, Winnebagos, and Menominees scattered as far north as the Green Bay region.[62]

Population figures for the tribe vary and are inaccurate because of the inability of agents to obtain precise information and because the agents had difficulty in ascertaining band or village membership. In 1825, official government reports list only 106 Potawatomis in Michigan and 3,900 others in Illinois and Indiana, excluding approximately 300 other tribesmen near Milwaukee. Such a figure is low, since a report by Alexander Wolcott at Chicago indicates that there were more than 3,300 Potawatomis within his agency, not including those Indians at Peoria, on the Tippecanoe and Eel rivers, and in eastern Michigan. Tipton's payroll for the Wabash and Elkhart Potawatomis lists at least 600 Indians who were not within

Wolcott's jurisdiction, while Menard indicates that there were almost 850 such Potawatomis attached to his subagency at Peoria. At least half of the Indians at Peoria probably drew part of their annuities at Chicago, but the others were not included with Wolcott's census. Therefore, the Potawatomi population in the Old Northwest probably approached 6,000 people during the late 1820's.[63]

In an attempt to distribute annuities and to negotiate with different chiefs and villages, government officials devised a system of band nomenclature which added to the confusion. At the turn of the century, the Potawatomis had divided themselves into three general bands: the Potawatomis of the Huron River, the Potawatomis of the Saint Joseph, and the Potawatomis of the Wabash. But as the tribe gave up their lands in eastern Michigan and northeastern Indiana and began to concentrate along the Saint Joseph, Tippecanoe, and Illinois rivers, the old divisions broke down. Moreover, individual Indians continually moved from village to village, changing village or band affiliations and increasing the frustration of the Indian agents.[64]

By 1830 most of the Huron Potawatomi had left eastern Michigan, either resettling along the Saint Joseph or moving east into Ontario. The Saint Joseph band remained a viable entity, but its membership overlapped that of the Wabash and Prairie bands. Although Potawatomis living along the Elkhart River were nominally attached to their kinsmen on the Saint Joseph, they also were included by government officials with the Wabash band. Meanwhile, Cass, Tipton, Wolcott, and others referred to the Indians living on the Tippecanoe, Kankakee, and Iroquois rivers in western Indiana and eastern Illinois as Prairie Potawatomis. But these Potawatomis also overlapped with both the Wabash and Saint Joseph bands.[65]

To add to the confusion, the government negotiated treaties in 1816, 1821, 1825, 1828, and 1829 with the "United Tribes of Potawatomi, Chippewas and Ottawas" living on the Illinois River and as far north as Wisconsin. These Indians, whose membership also included Potawatomis from the Saint Joseph and Prairie bands, were centered at the tip of Lake Michigan but extended west to the Rock River and as far south as Peoria. Ironically, after the 1829 treaty at Prairie du Chien, the Potawatomis at Peoria claimed that they were not affiliated with the united tribes near Chicago.[66]

Other terminology also appears in government documents, further complicating official nomenclature. Those Indians near Lake Michigan are sometimes referred to as the "Potawatomis of the

Lakes," while in 1828 Wolcott reported that a disagreement had arisen between "my Potawatomis of the Prairie and those of the woods." According to Wolcott, the Woods Potawatomis lived on the Saint Joseph and in northern Indiana.[67]

The Potawatomi band nomenclature that emerged from this period was used much more often by government officials than by the Indians. Individual Potawatomis had always lived within the fabric of a loose political structure and would continue to do so throughout their remaining years in their homeland. Ironically, the flexibility of village membership, which was denounced as primitive by government officials, proved to be advantageous for the Indians. It not only provided an escape mechanism for intravillage disputes, but it also enabled many Indians to claim simultaneous membership in different bands and to share in all of the bands' annuities.

Government efforts to remove the Indians from Illinois were directed at other tribes besides the Potawatomis. In 1804 a few Sac and Fox chiefs had signed a treaty at Vincennes, Indiana, relinquishing tribal lands in western Illinois and southern Wisconsin. Although they had reconfirmed the treaty on subsequent occasions, many of the Sacs and Foxes disclaimed the document and refused to leave Illinois. Led by Black Hawk, these Indians continued to occupy their ancestral homes near Rock Island until they were forced into Iowa by the Illinois militia during the summer of 1831. Dissatisfied with conditions in Iowa, on April 6, 1832, Black Hawk led approximately two thousand Sacs and Foxes back across the Mississippi into Illinois. Most of the Indians were old men, women, and children, and the Sacs and Foxes only wished to reoccupy their old village near Rock Island, but many white officials interpreted the entrance into Illinois as a hostile act, and Governor John Reynolds called out the state militia. For all practical purposes, the Black Hawk War had started.[68]

The Potawatomis soon became involved. Traditional ties between the Sacs and Foxes and the Potawatomis had been strengthened during the 1820's. After the War of 1812, when the Sacs and Foxes journeyed to Malden to receive British presents, they passed through Potawatomi villages in Illinois and Michigan. The Potawatomis had welcomed the travelers, and in 1827 the Sacs invited part of the Potawatomis in Michigan to settle among them on the Mississippi. The Potawatomis declined the offer, but two years later several chiefs from the Illinois River met with Black Hawk's band

and agreed to support the Sacs in their opposition to removal. Meanwhile, as the Potawatomis were forced away from Peoria, some formed new villages on the Rock River, where they were in close contact with Black Hawk's people. Other Potawatomis moved to the village of Wabokieshiek (White Cloud), the Winnebago Prophet, also on the Rock River. The prophet had close ties with the old Sac war chief and had been instrumental in Black Hawk's decision to return to Illinois.[69]

Black Hawk believed that the Potawatomis and Winnebagos would support him against the Americans. He knew that many of the Illinois River Potawatomis were angry over the 1829 treaty and that several Potawatomis had been beaten by whites along the Spoon River during the previous winter. As the Sac war chief moved up the Rock River Valley, he rejected government requests that he return to Iowa and counseled with the Winnebagos before meeting with several Potawatomi chiefs at the mouth of the Kishwaukee River on May 14, 1832.[70]

The meeting did not bode well for the Sacs and Foxes. The Potawatomis realized that their villages were so near the white settlements that any act of hostility on their part would bring quick retribution from American military forces. Moreover, the new Potawatomi leadership, especially the chiefs at Chicago, knew that their stature depended upon their ability to serve as middle-men between the tribe and the government. Since April 6, Caldwell, Robinson, and Shabbona consistently had endeavored to keep any of their tribesmen from joining with Black Hawk's band. Caldwell had journeyed to Potawatomi villages scattered along the Rock River, urging his kinsmen to reject Black Hawk's invitations and to move their women and children east toward Chicago. Meanwhile, other Potawatomi leaders met with Thomas Owen, the Indian agent at Chicago, to assure the official of the tribe's fidelity.[71]

At the Kishwaukee, the Potawatomis again listened to Black Hawk's appeals, but once more they refused any assistance. They informed the chief that rumors of British support were entirely false and that the Potawatomi villages were so short of corn that they had none to spare for Black Hawk and his followers. Although the Sac chief was disappointed by the Potawatomi refusal, he treated the chiefs cordially and prepared a feast for them. Unfortunately for the Indians, the feast was interrupted when Sac scouts brought news that between three hundred and four hundred mounted militiamen were approaching within eight miles of the Sac encampment. The

Potawatomis quickly withdrew, while Black Hawk sent a small delegation of warriors to discuss surrender terms with Major Isaiah Stillman, the commander of the Americans. Although the Sacs carried a white flag, the frightened militiamen fired upon the warriors, touching off a skirmish, known as "Stillman's Run," in which the Americans panicked and fled toward Dixon's Ferry, leaving eleven of their comrades dead upon the prairie.[72]

The Battle of Stillman's Run was a tragedy for both the whites and the Indians. Although the Sacs forced the Americans to retreat, the skirmish ended any chances for Black Hawk and his people to return to Iowa in peace. Shocked by exaggerated accounts of the American defeat, government officials mobilized all their power in an effort to crush the hapless Sacs and Foxes. The American defeat also had a profound impact upon a few Potawatomis. Shabbona, at his village thirty-five miles east of Dixon's Ferry, realized that the Sac and Fox victory might encourage some of Black Hawk's warriors to raid among the American settlements north of the Illinois River. He also was afraid that a few disaffected Potawatomis might join with the Sacs against the Americans. Between May 16 and 19, Shabbona, his son, and a nephew rode among the settlements warning the Americans of the impending danger and urging them to withdraw towards the larger towns along the Illinois River.[73]

Shabbona's warnings were genuine. Unfortunately, not all of the whites heeded them. On Indian Creek, in modern LaSalle County, William Davis had established a small farm, blacksmith shop, and gristmill. To supply waterpower for the mill, Davis had dammed the creek, preventing fish from the Fox River from passing upstream. The milldam angered a small village of Potawatomis who lived about six miles upstream from Davis and who depended upon fish for much of their food supply. Both Shabbona and Waubansee had attempted to ameliorate the dispute, and Meaueus, the leader of the village, agreed to fish below the dam, but the Potawatomis remained angry. After Stillman's Run, Shabbona twice warned Davis that he might be in danger, but the blacksmith was determined to remain at his home and collected several families, numbering twenty-three persons, at that location. At midafternoon on May 20 the whites were surpised by a war party of approximately forty Potawatomis, accompanied by a few Sacs, who forced their way into the Davis cabin. Led by two Potawatomi warriors, Toquamee (Autumn) and Comee, the Indians killed fifteen of the settlers and took two young women, Sylvia and Rachel Hall, prisoner.[74]

After the attack the Indians carried the women north to Black Hawk's camp near the Turtle River in southern Wisconsin. The captives remained unharmed, and on May 28 they were ransomed by White Crow, an old Winnebago, who then turned the women over to the Americans. Toquamee, Comee, and one other Potawatomi were later charged with murder, but they were acquitted when the Hall women could not positively identify them as members of the war party.[75]

The Indian Creek attack caused widespread panic among settlers as far east as Michigan and Indiana. Michigan mobilized its state militia and investigated rumors that the Sacs were planning to flee to the Potawatomi villages along the Saint Joseph. In Indiana, armed volunteers patrolled the prairies from the Kankakee to Vincennes. Governor Reynolds of Illinois, anxious to clear his state of all Indians, issued a proclamation declaring that the state had been invaded by "powerful detachments" of Sacs, Foxes, Winnebagos, and Potawatomis and that all the tribes were to be considered hostile. Those settlers who had dared to remain on their farms now fled in terror toward the larger towns, while reports reached officials in Washington that northern Illinois was full of "scenes of bloodshed and devastation unsurpassed in the history of Indian warfare in the western country."[76]

Such reports were much exaggerated. After Stillman's Run, Black Hawk had retreated up the Rock River valley, planning to turn westward and escape into Iowa. Meanwhile, General Atkinson and approximately four thousand regulars and volunteers followed the Sacs toward Wisconsin while the government massed one thousand other troops under Winfield Scott at Chicago. Although a handful of dissident Potawatomis may have accompanied the Sacs for a few days, most of the tribe continued to cooperate with the government.

Anxious to separate themselves from any association with the hostiles, Potawatomis from northern Illinois and southern Wisconsin deserted their villages and flocked to temporary camps on the Des Plaines River about twelve miles from Chicago. Owen provided them with small rations of food, and Potawatomi warriors served as scouts for the white community at Chicago, exploring the region along the Fox River and reporting the advance of Sac war parties. Two days after the attack upon Indian Creek, a small party of Potawatomi scouts was captured by Sacs and Kickapoos near the Fox River. The hostiles held the Potawatomis prisoner for several hours and then released them. Meanwhile, other Potawatomis, including

Big Foot, sent messages to Black Hawk, asking the Sacs to return to their own lands. The Potawatomis complained that they wanted no part in the conflict and that the disruption kept them from planting their corn.[77]

As Black Hawk continued his flight toward the Mississippi, other Potawatomis enlisted with Atkinson and guided his troops across northern Illinois and Wisconsin. Led by Caldwell, Robinson, and Shabbona, these Indians left Chicago and joined the army late in June, 1832. It was hazardous duty. Not only were the Potawatomis in danger from meeting hostile Sacs, but they also were continually threatened by many members of the army they were serving. Volunteer and militia units from downstate Illinois were unfamiliar with the Potawatomis and were prone to consider any Indian they met to be hostile. To provide some security from being shot by their comrades in arms, the Potawatomis wore white headbands. Most of the warriors, however, saw little action and were mustered out of the army on July 22, 1832.[78]

With the exception of the lone attack upon Indian Creek, the Potawatomis remained loyal to the United States throughout the Black Hawk War. Awed by American military power, and led by chiefs such as Caldwell and Robinson, the Potawatomis refused to participate in an uprising they knew was doomed to failure. Anxious to gain favor with the government, more than ninety warriors had accompanied the Americans against the hapless Sacs and Foxes. Whites at Chicago were almost unanimous in praising Potawatomi fidelity, and Owen was angered by Reynolds' irresponsible proclamation that the tribe had joined with Black Hawk. An extensive investigation exonerated the Potawatomis from any collaboration with the Sacs and Foxes. Unfortunately, however, Governor Reynolds and other officials would use the Black Hawk War to support their case for Indian removal. White resentment toward the Sacs and Foxes would be transferred to the Potawatomis, and Potawatomi fidelity would be forgotten in the rising demand that all Indians be removed beyond the Mississippi.

10. Removal

During the 1820's, while most government officials continued to argue for the assimilation of the Indians into white society, a growing minority of Americans believed that the Indians should be removed to the west. Although government and religious organizations continued their efforts at assimilation, by the late 1820's many officials in the Office of Indian Affairs feared that the Potawatomis were acquiring all of the white vices while rejecting the "virtues of Christian civilization." In 1827, Superintendent of Indian Affairs Thomas L. McKenney, a former champion of assimilation, journeyed through the Indian country and reported that the government's "civilization" program was failing. The Potawatomis and their neighbors were not becoming farmers, but continued to "catch fish, and plant patches of corn; dance, paint, hunt, get drunk, when they can get liquor, fight, and often starve." To save the Indians from complete debauchery, McKenney and other dignitaries decided to remove the tribesmen beyond the Mississippi. In the west the Potawatomis could be protected from negative white influences and could pursue their traditional way of life until they were ready to join white society.[1]

McKenney's position received strong support from President Andrew Jackson. Although Jackson may have held paternal feelings toward the tribesmen, he also was receptive to local politicians who were anxious to rid their states of the Indians.[2] In addition, missionaries such as Isaac McCoy also urged the president to remove the Potawatomis. With Carey Mission declining, and the Baptists unable to compete with whiskey peddlers, McCoy hoped to consolidate the Potawatomis with other tribes in Kansas, where they could be nurtured in a "new Canaan," free from the "floods of ardent spirits" that flowed down the Saint Joseph Valley.[3]

In 1828, as a first step toward removal, federal officials appointed McCoy to lead a mixed party of Potawatomis, Ottawas, Chickasaws, Choctaws, and Creeks in an exploration of modern Kansas and Oklahoma. Most of the Potawatomis opposed the venture, but McCoy enlisted three Saint Joseph tribesmen, Jean B. Chandonnai, Nagauwatuk (Noise Maker), and Shawanikuk (Southern Thunder), to accompany him west. Joined by a few Ottawas, McCoy and the Potawatomis spent August and September traveling through western Missouri and onto the plains of Kansas, where the Indians camped along the Marais des Cygnes River, and met with a party of recently emigrated Shawnees. In October, McCoy and the tribesmen journeyed back to St. Louis, where the missionary made plans to guide the southern Indians into Oklahoma. Unimpressed with Kansas, the Potawatomis and Ottawas returned to their villages in Michigan.[4]

The 1828 exploring trip did not induce the Potawatomis to move west. For four years following the journey, Potawatomi leaders successfully parried government suggestions that they choose new homes in Missouri or Kansas. But after the passage of the Removal Bill in 1830 and the Black Hawk War two years later, such evasion became impossible. Although the Potawatomis had assisted the government against the Sacs and Foxes, their support was ignored or forgotten. Angry over the recent loss of lives and property, white frontiersmen blamed all Indians indiscriminately, and when the war ended, all Indians would be forced to pay. For the Potawatomis, the price was removal.

Even before the Black Hawk War had ended, government officials made plans for another major Potawatomi land cession. Realizing that the war had left the Indians vulnerable, during July, 1832, Secretary of War Lewis Cass appointed Jonathan Jennings, John Davis, and Marks Crume to meet with the Potawatomis and Miamis and to secure as much Indian land as possible in Illinois, Indiana, and Michigan. Although the Miamis refused to attend the conference, Potawatomis from the three states assembled on the Tippecanoe River in Indiana during October, 1832.[5]

The negotiations soon bogged down under a morass of conflicting claims between different villages over who owned the prairie region stretching along the Kankakee River. Part of the area in Illinois had been ceded by the Kickapoos in 1819, but the Potawatomis had violently opposed the Kickapoo cession and continued to assert a claim to the region.[6] Finally, in an effort to satisfy all the Indians in attendance, the commissioners signed three separate treaties with three different "bands." The Potawatomis of "the Prairie and Kankakee" band gave up their title to lands in eastern Illinois; Potawatomis from villages in Indiana relinquished claims to their lands in that state; and in a third treaty another group of Potawatomis, primarily from the Saint Joseph River, gave up all claims to lands in Illinois, Indiana, and Michigan.[7]

The commissioners were anxious to complete the treaty negotiations, and they readily succumbed to Potawatomi pressure for small reservation within the ceded lands. The three treaties provided for more than 120 reservations for various villages and individual Indians. As in earlier treaties, the influence of the mixed-bloods was apparent, and many of the individual reservations went to Indians with French surnames. Although Caldwell and Robinson did not sign the treaty or obtain any reservation, the third article of the Prairie Potawatomi treaty provided that Caldwell would receive a lifetime annuity of six hundred dollars, while Robinson and Antoine LeClaire, another mixed-blood from Chicago, would receive similar annuities of two hundred dollars apiece.[8]

The treaties reflected the growing skill of the tribe in negotiating with the government. Potawatomi chiefs were well aware of the government's desire to acquire the remaining Indian lands in Illinois and Indiana, and they held out for a better price than in previous treaties. The three agreements negotiated during the fall of 1832 increased tribal annuities by $50,000 and provided that the Potawatomis would receive $168,000 in trade goods, to be distributed immediately after the negotiations were completed. Another $80,000 in trade goods were to be paid to the tribe during 1833.[9]

The large expenditures for trade goods also indicated the continued influence of the Indian traders, both with the Potawatomis and with the treaty commissioners. Since the goods were purchased immediately after the treaty, Indian traders within the three-state region reaped handsome profits from the negotiations. Some of the profits resulted from dishonesty. Evidence suggests that many of the traders banded together to establish artificially high prices for shoddy merchandise. Nor were the commissioners free from blame. Not only did they purchase the goods at inflated prices, but they also again raised the price of the merchandise on invoices they turned in to the federal government, evidently pocketing the difference between the price paid to the traders and the sum on their official report.[10]

From the government's viewpoint, the Tippecanoe treaties proved unsatisfactory for several reasons. The large number of small reservations granted to Potawatomis within the ceded lands would plague future attempts to remove the Indians to the West. Instead of single negotiations for large tracts of Potawatomi territory, the United States would be forced to bargain endlessly with individual tribesmen for the small reservations. The process would be both costly and time-consuming. In addition, the treaty commissioners had been ordered to urge the Potawatomis to remove beyond the Mississippi, but only one of the treaties mentioned removal, and that document couched the policy in such general terms that it offered the Indians government assistance "if they shall at anytime hereafter wish to change their residence." Moreover, the treaty of October 20 guaranteed the Prairie Potawatomis the right to hunt on their former lands in Illinois until such lands were purchased by white farmers. Therefore, following the treaty negotiations, these Potawatomis returned to their villages in eastern and northern Illinois.[11]

They did not spend the winter in peace. White frontiersmen were anxious to establish preemption claims on the newly ceded lands, and during the winter they swarmed onto the prairies along the Kankakee. Many of the new settlers were veterans of the Black Hawk War who distrusted all Indians, and they exaggerated reports of Indian hostilities.[12] White farmers along the Illinois River complained that the Potawatomis were burning haystacks, killing livestock, and threatening American lives. A bridge across the Winnebago inlet on the Peoria-Galena road was mysteriously set afire, and settlers feared a Potawatomi plot to disrupt communications in northern Illinois. Reacting to the alarm, Governor Reynolds appointed a commission to investigate the rumors. After meeting with panic-stricken settlers in the Indian Creek region, the commissioners ordered all Potawatomis to leave the area and reported back toReynolds, "It is the opinion of reflecting men, whom we consulted and in whose opinion we entirely concur, that unless suitable measures be taken to drive the Indians to their own country, or to awe them into peaceful behavior, some seriously hostile steps toward the whites, in the course of the present winter may be foreboded." To forestall such "hostile steps," Reynolds requested that troops be sent to force the Potawatomis north toward Chicago.[13]

The troops were not needed. The Potawatomis in northern Illinois had approached the settlements hoping to barter furs and trade goods to the whites for food. Since the Indians had been forced to congregate near Chicago during the Black Hawk War, they had not planted any corn and were desperately short of food during the winter. They undoubtedly killed a few hogs belonging to Americans, but when asked to leave the Indian Creek region, most retreated toward Chicago.[14]

Other Potawatomis, led by Quiquito (Moving Sun), a chief from the Kankakee River, fled into Indiana. Suffering from hunger, these Potawatomis sought refuge with William Marshall, the Indian agent at Logansport. In the previous summer Marshall had fed a large number of Indians during the Black Hawk War, and after Quiquito's arrival at Logansport, the Indian agent again provided the tribesmen with rations of bread to sustain them through the winter. Discouraged over conditions in Illinois, Quiquito informed Marshall that his people finally were ready to remove beyond the Mississippi. The chief stated that his followers wished to live near Kannekuk, or the Kickapoo Prophet, in the vicinity of Fort Leavenworth, Kansas. During the 1820's many of the Prairie Potawatomis had become disciples of the Kickapoo holy man, and in 1833, when the Kickapoos were removed, a small party of Potawatomis had accompanied them west. Quiquito promised Marshall that his people would be willing to leave in the spring as soon as the grass was high enough to provide forage for their horses.[15]

Marshall relayed Quiquito's message to Washington, where officials were elated over the prospect of Potawatomi removal. In response, the War Department appointed Abel C. Pepper, a Democratic politician from Rising Sun, Indiana, to conduct Quiquito's people west. Pepper was ordered to travel to Logansport, assemble an exploring party, and then select lands in Kansas suitable for the Potawatomis' new home. After returning from Kansas, Pepper planned to collect all the Potawatomis interested in removal and lead them west.[16]

Pepper arrived in Logansport on April 11, 1833, and found a large number of Indians awaiting removal. Besides Quiquito's band of 256 Prairie Potawatomis, many Wabash Potawatomis, Kickapoos, and Weas also had assembled. Since Pepper did not have sufficient funds to feed all the Indians, he ordered them back to their villages, but instructed them to reassemble during the first week in June, when the removal would start west. Meanwhile, the government selected two other Democrats, Lewis Sands and Rudolphus Schoonover, to assist Pepper with the venture.[17]

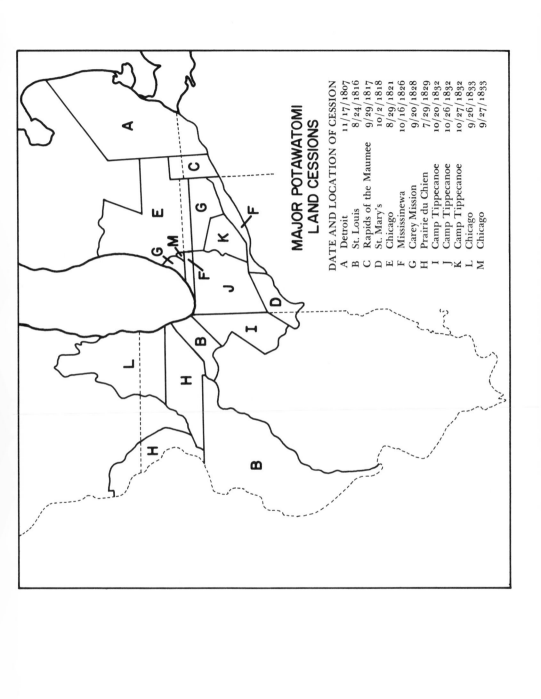

MAJOR POTAWATOMI
LAND CESSIONS

DATE AND LOCATION OF CESSION
A   Detroit   11/17/1807
B   St. Louis   8/24/1816
C   Rapids of the Maumee   9/29/1817
D   St. Mary's   10/2/1818
E   Chicago   8/29/1821
F   Mississinewa   10/16/1826
G   Carey Mission   9/20/1828
H   Prairie du Chien   7/29/1829
I   Camp Tippecanoe   10/20/1832
J   Camp Tippecanoe   10/26/1832
K   Camp Tippecanoe   10/27/1832
L   Chicago   9/26/1833
M   Chicago   9/27/1833

To provide a paymaster for the trip, the War Department appointed Lieutenant William R. Montgomery as "disbursing agent" and ordered him to report to Indiana. Unfortunately, Montgomery was at sea when the appointment was made, and his orders did not reach him until after June 1. Although Montgomery finally started west, he did not arrive in Logansport until July 20, six weeks after the removal had been scheduled to start. Meanwhile, Pepper, Sands, and Schoonover were forced to supervise and feed a growing assemblage of Indians. Since the Potawatomis expected to go west in early June, more than four hundred Indians assembled at the debarkation camp. But after several weeks of waiting, when the removal failed to materialize, many Indians became disgruntled and returned to their villages.[18]

The exploring party also encountered difficulties. Pepper had planned to leave in April, but a series of minor problems delayed his departure, and the exploring party did not start for the west until June 30. Pepper and the Indians traveled no farther than western Illinois before encountering news that St. Louis was full of cholera. The Potawatomis refused to enter the city, so Pepper went on alone. Although the agent did not contract cholera, he came down with "bilous fever," and when he returned to the Potawatomi camp, the warriors became frightened and decided to go back to their homes. Too sick to accompany them, Pepper remained in Alton, Illinois, recovering from his illness. Although the agent eventually returned to Indiana, a relapse of his condition prevented him from resuming his duties at Logansport.[19]

Meanwhile, the number of Potawatomis in the removal camp at Logansport continued to decline. Some became angry over the delay and left the camp in frustration. Others learned that the government was planning another treaty, to be held at Chicago in September, 1833, and they decided to attend the negotiations before leaving their homeland. Although Montgomery finally arrived at the removal camp on July 20, he found only 145 Indians willing to go west. He also encountered hostility from Lewis Sands, who denounced him for the late arrival and quarreled with the disbursing agent over who should assume jurisdiction over the removal.[20]

Finally, on July 27, approximately two months behind schedule, Sands and Montgomery started the remaining Potawatomis west. The Indians requested additional wagons to transport their possessions, but Montgomery angrily refused. In response, about seventy tribesmen deserted the removal and returned to their village along the Iroquois River in eastern Illinois. The other Potawatomis were marched across the prairies to Alton, where they boarded a steamboat which carried them to Fort Leavenworth, Kansas. Only sixty-seven Potawatomis completed the removal.[21]

The failure of the 1833 removal engendered a series of charges and countercharges by both Sands and Montgomery in which each blamed the other for the small number of Indians transported west. Montgomery argued that Pepper and Sands had promised the Potawatomis an unrealistic departure date and that the removal could not possibly have started in June. Sands countered with charges that Montgomery spent entirely too much time en route to the removal camp, including a five-day stopover in Indianapolis, before proceeding on to Logansport. Yet the upcoming treaty at Chicago was more important than the actions of either agent in limiting the number of Potawatomis who went west. The Indians knew that in addition to their annuities, many presents would be distributed at the treaty negotiation. Although Montgomery assured the Potawatomis that they would receive their fair share of such merchandise in the west, many of the Indians were skeptical about such promises and preferred to attend the treaty negotiations in person.[22]

While Sands and Montgomery moved Quiquito's people west, other government agents finalized plans for the treaty at Chicago. On April 8, 1833, Lewis Cass had appointed Governor George B. Porter of Michigan Territory, Indian Agent Thomas J. V. Owen, and William Weatherford, a native of Morgan County, Illinois, to meet with the Potawatomis and to acquire the remaining tribal lands east of the Mississippi. During the summer, the commissioners sent messages to the Potawatomi villages, and by September 14, 1833, more than six thousand Indians had assembled at Chicago. At first the Potawatomis seemed reluctant to sell. Speaking for the tribesmen, Aptakisic (Half Day), a chief from the Fox River, informed the commissioners that the Potawatomis had no intention of exchanging their lands along the western shore of Lake Michigan for unknown areas in the West. Claiming that the tribesmen had assembled only to receive their annuities, Aptakisic requested that the payments be made so that the Indians could return to their statement, they knew the Potawatomis eventually would sell their lands and were only attempting to get a high price. For several days the Indians and the commissioners exchanged speeches, but on September 19 the Potawatomis announced that they had chosen Caldwell and Robinson to act as their spokesmen, and the negotia- villages and harvest their corn.[23]

Although the commissioners expressed surprise at Aptakisic's tions became more serious. After meeting for another week, the mixed-bloods and the government agents came to an agreement. The treaty was signed on September 26, 1833.[24]

The Potawatomis gave up the rest of their homeland. The cession stretched from northeastern Illinois as far west as the Rock River and as far north as the southern tip of Lake Winnebago in Wisconsin. In return, the tribe received five million acres along the east bank of the Missouri River in modern Iowa and Missouri. The government agreed to pay $150,000 in claims against the tribe held by various traders; an additional annuity of $14,000 for twenty years; $100,000 in trade goods; $150,000 for houses, farm buildings, and implements in the west; and $70,000 for "purposes of education and the encouragement of the domestic arts." Since no individual reservations were allowed within the land cession, the commissioners also agreed to pay $100,000 to more than two hundred Potawatomis (mostly mixed-bloods) "in lieu of reservations." Caldwell, Robinson, Shabbona, and Joseph Laframboise received additional cash payments of up to $5,000. In a separate agreement, negotiated on September 27, the "Woods Potawatomis" relinquished all claims to tribal reservations along the Saint Joseph River and at Nottawasippi, in southern Michigan.[25]

This last great assemblage of Potawatomis in their homeland provided a colorful spectacle at Chicago. As in earlier treaties, warriors brought their families to the negotiations, and the prairies surrounding the frontier village were covered with Indian camps. Potawatomi men, women, and children, all dressed in their best, filled the streets of Chicago, where they conversed with friends and renewed old acquaintances. Since the government provided food for the duration of the negotiations, much of the drudgery of everyday life was gone, and the town was filled with a carnival atmosphere.[26]

Unfortunately, Chicago also was full of whiskey. Alcohol was so plentiful that drunken brawls resulting in serious injury or death were a common occurrence. The Potawatomis were guilty of such rowdiness, but they were joined by a collection of frontier riffraff who one observer described as "more pagan than the red men." According to Charles Latrobe, a British traveler, most of the whites at Chicago consisted of

> Horse dealers, and horse stealers,—rogues of every description . . . half-breeds, quarter-breeds, and men of no breed at all;—dealers in pigs, poultry and potatoes;—men pursuing Indian claims, some

for tracts of land, others . . . , for pigs which the wolves had eaten;—creditors of the tribe or of particular Indians, who know they have no chance of getting their money, if they do not get it from government agents;—sharpers of every degree; pedlars, grog-sellers; Indian agents and Indian traders of every description. . . . The little village was in an uproar from morning to night, and from night to morning. . . .[27]

The "little village" also was the scene of extensive fraud and collusion. Porter awarded two of his friends, John Kinzie and Benjamin Kercheval, a virtual monopoly for supplying trade goods at the treaty proceedings, and the merchants were allowed to set highly inflated prices on all merchandise sold. Yet government security was so loose that trade goods worth more than twenty thousand dollars were pilfered from warehouses before they could be distributed to the Potawatomis.[28] Moreover, in examining the claims of merchants against the tribe and in bestowing cash grants in lieu of reservations, Porter awarded over one hundred thousand dollars to the Kinzie-Forsyth families. Other traders charged Porter with fraud, and during the following winter the government started an investigation of the payments, but Porter died of cholera in July, 1834, and the investigation was abandoned.[29]

When the Chicago treaty reached Congress, the Senate balked at its ratification. Not only were many senators angry over the alleged fraud, but the state of Missouri waged a strong campaign in opposition to the treaty. The agreement awarded the Potawatomis approximately thirty-one hundred square miles of well-watered, fertile lands between the western boundary of Missouri and the Missouri River. Located in what now is extreme northwestern Missouri, this tract, known as the Platte Country, had been omitted from the state when Missouri achieved statehood in 1820. Officials in Missouri were anxious to annex the region and opposed its inclusion within those lands granted to the Potawatomis. In the Senate, Missourians Lewis F. Linn and Thomas Hart Benton blocked the treaty and amended the document so that the Platte Country was deleted from the new Potawatomi lands in the west. In exchange, a similar acreage was added to Potawatomi lands in Iowa, and the Senate conditionally ratified the amended treaty in May, 1834.[30]

But before the treaty could become final, the Potawatomis had to agree to the change. They were reluctant to do so. Cass sent the altered treaty to Chicago, and Owen spent the summer of 1834 trying to convince the Potawatomis to accept the amendment.

Although the tribesmen from Michigan and Indiana steadfastly refused to sign the new document, in October, 1834, Caldwell, Robinson, Waubansee, and four other Potawatomis from northern Illinois agreed to exchange the Platte Country for a tract of lands along the Little Sioux River in northern Iowa. In return, the government agreed to pay Caldwell's followers an additional ten thousand dollars upon their removal to Iowa. Since the original treaty had been signed by more than 120 Potawatomis, and the amended agreement bore the signatures of only Caldwell and six others, the Potawatomis in Michigan and Indiana raised a storm of protest. Yet the Senate accepted the new agreement as valid, and the treaty was finally ratified in February, 1835.[31]

The amended treaty also provided that the government pay the expenses for an exploring party of Potawatomis who would visit Iowa before the tribe's removal. In the spring of 1835, Caldwell's followers in northern Illinois and southern Wisconsin agreed to send a party west. They also agreed that upon the party's return they would remove to their new lands in Iowa. During August, forty Potawatomis, including Caldwell, Robinson, and Big Foot, explored the newly acquired lands along the Little Sioux River. They also visited the Platte Country. The Potawatomis were unhappy over the lands in Iowa, complaining that there were no trees and that the region was too near the Sioux. In contrast, they were pleased with the Platte Country, where they were welcomed by many of Quiquito's followers, who had recrossed the Missouri River from Kansas and had established villages in the region.[32]

Upon their return to the east, Caldwell and his companions reported unfavorably upon the lands in Iowa. The report was not welcome among Indian agents at Chicago. They had spent the summer preparing the Potawatomis in northern Illinois for removal and had collected nearly one thousand Indians who were prepared to remove west. Uncertain over their destination, the Potawatomis decided to draft an appeal to President Andrew Jackson, asking him to allow them to settle temporarily in the Platte Country until they could find other lands in Iowa more to their liking. Captain John B. F. Russell, the military disbursing agent, feared that the removal would fail, so he convinced the Indians that they should cross the Mississippi before sending their appeal to the president. Russell argued that such actions would convince Jackson that the Potawatomis were already removing and would make him more receptive to their plea. Russell also promised the Indians that they could settle in the Platte Country and remain there until their plea was answered.[33]

Russell's argument saved the removal. Late in September, 1835, Caldwell led about 700 Potawatomis west toward Iowa. The party crossed the prairies of northern Illinois, traveling about twelve miles per day and camping each evening in one of the hardwood groves that dotted the region. On October 21 they reached the Mississippi at Yellow Banks, near modern Oquawka, Illinois. Although Russell, Caldwell, and about 250 Indians crossed the river and continued on to the Platte Country, the other Potawatomis turned north into Iowa, where they spent the winter along the Skunk River.[34]

After crossing the Mississippi, Caldwell's party met in council and decided to petition the government to allow them to remain in the Platte Country for twenty years. During the winter of 1835–36, they sent a delegation of six chiefs, led by Alexander Robinson, to Washington. The Potawatomis met with Commissioner of Indian Affairs Elbert Herring, who insisted that they must accept the lands in Iowa. However, Herring did give them permission to remain in the Platte Country until they could select sites for permanent villages near Council Bluffs.[35]

The Potawatomi occupancy of the Platte Country encountered stiff opposition from white Missourians. Many settlers believed that the region soon would be annexed to Missouri, and they crossed over into the area, clearing land and erecting cabins. During February, 1836, troops from Fort Leavenworth forced the settlers back into Missouri, but the military actions angered state officials, and Senators Benton and Linn and Congressman Albert G. Harrison redoubled their efforts to have the Platte Country annexed to their state.[36]

Meanwhile, the Potawatomi population in the disputed region increased. In the summer of 1836, many of the tribesmen who had spent the winter on the Skunk River in Iowa rejoined Caldwell in the Platte Country, and at Chicago, Removal Agent Gholson Kercheval prepared to bring another party of Potawatomis west. During late summer, about 750 tribesmen from the Fox River valley in Illinois assembled at a removal camp on the Des Plaines River. On September 20 the Potawatomis set out for Missouri, traveling across northern Illinois toward Quincy, where they hoped to cross the Mississippi. The removal was plagued by hardship. Although Kercheval and other agents had planned well, the Potawatomis trekked west through continual rain, which soaked their baggage and turned the primitive roads into quagmires. En route to the Mississippi, measles broke out among the emigrants, causing much illness and the death of a child. The Indians arrived at Quincy on October 17 and crossed the river three days later, in the midst of a blizzard. On October 24 Kercheval's party was overtaken by a large number of Potawatomis led by Shabbona and Waubansee, who had followed in the rear of their kinsmen all the way from northern Illinois. The two parties joined in eastern Missouri and proceeded on to the Platte Country, where they settled among Caldwell's followers in mid-November.[37]

With the arrival of Kercheval's party, the Potawatomi population in the Platte Country swelled to nearly sixteen hundred Indians, and friction between the Potawatomis and white Missourians continued. While Kercheval had assembled his removal in Illinois, a gang of white horse thieves from Missouri swept through the Platte Country, stealing several Potawatomi horses. Caldwell's warriors pursued the outlaws and recovered most of the animals, but in the resulting skirmish one Indian and two whites were killed. A government investigation exonerated the Potawatomis, but Governor Daniel Dunkin of Missouri threatened to drive the Potawatomis across the Missouri River with six hundred volunteers. Although federal troops from Fort Leavenworth turned back the Missourians, relations between the Potawatomis and Missouri did not improve.[38]

The growing tension in Missouri prodded the federal government into action. Indian agents knew that in 1837 the Platte Country would be annexed to Missouri, and they feared that further Potawatomi-white clashes might occur if the Indians remained in the region. Government officials believed that Caldwell and his followers would eventually move to Iowa, but Quiquito's people, the Potawatomis from the Kankakee and Iroquois rivers, threatened to move back into Kansas. Moreover, many Potawatomis remaining in Michigan and Indiana remained bitter over the amended treaty at Chicago and vowed that they would never settle among Caldwell's tribesmen. Therefore, in an effort to attract all Potawatomis west of the Mississippi, yet keep them out of the Platte Country, the government decided to establish another large Potawatomi reservation in Kansas. Since exploring parties of Saint Joseph and Wabash tribesmen were familiar with the region along the Marais de Cygnes River, in February, 1837, federal officials offered the Potawatomis "a tract of country, on the Osage [Marais des Cygnes] River southwest of the Missouri River, sufficient in extent, and adapted to their habits and wants." In Washington a group of Wabash and Prairie chiefs accepted the offer, and Anthony Davis, the former Potawatomi agent at Fort Leavenworth, was appointed in charge of the new subagency.[39]

Meanwhile, federal officials took steps to lure Caldwell's followers into Iowa. In April, 1837, the government established another new subagency at Council Bluffs and appointed Dr. Edwin James, a former army physician, to supervise the facility. Indian agents hoped the new subagency would draw Caldwell into Iowa, for in March, Missouri had annexed the Platte Country, and white settlers poured into the region. But the Potawatomis remained in the Platte Country, refusing all government suggestions that they move to Iowa or Kansas.[40]

Angry over the Potawatomi refusal to leave Missouri, the government adopted stronger measures. Federal officials had fed the Potawatomis since their arrival in the west, but in June, 1837, the provisions abruptly were cut off. Since Indian agents had urged the Potawatomis to leave the region, they had discouraged the Indians from planting any gardens, and the new policy left the tribesmen facing starvation. Meanwhile, the War Department made plans to use military personnel to force the Indians from Missouri. Major General Alexander Macomb ordered Brigadier General Henry Atkinson, at Jefferson Barracks near St. Louis, to proceed to Fort Leavenworth and remove Caldwell's people to Iowa.[41]

Before Atkinson could act, Major General Edmund P. Gaines intervened. In command of the Western Department of the U.S. Army, Gaines spent the summer of 1837 inspecting posts on the frontier. In early July he arrived at Fort Leavenworth, learned that the Potawatomis still were in Missouri, and decided to take matters into his own hands. To win the confidence of the Indians and to keep them from slaughtering white livestock, Gaines ordered officials at Fort Leavenworth to resume furnishing the Potawatomis with food. He found that Quiquito's followers were making plans to remove to Kansas, but that the other Potawatomis claimed they had insufficient food and no transportation for the trip to Iowa. To spur their removal, Gaines promised Caldwell that the government would provide food in Iowa and would transport old and infirm Potawatomis to Council Bluffs via steamboats. Convinced that the problem was solved, Gaines waited until Atkinson arrived at Fort Leavenworth and then continued on his tour of inspection.[42]

When Atkinson reached Fort Leavenworth in mid-July, he immediately followed Gaines's plan for removal. During the third week in July, Atkinson assembled Caldwell's followers near the Blacksnake Hills, at the site of modern Saint Joseph, Missouri, where the 165 Potawatomis who could not travel overland were loaded aboard two steamboats and carried upriver to Council Bluffs. The other Indians journeyed north across the Missouri-Iowa border and arrived at their new home in mid-August. Approximately 1,450 Potawatomis resettled in Iowa.[43]

The other Potawatomis in western Missouri and eastern Kansas followed Davis to the new subagency along the Marais des Cygnes. They were joined by a few Potawatomis who earlier had lived among the Kickapoos and by a scattering of Saint Joseph and Wabash tribesmen who had followed their kinsmen west. In September, 1837, the population of the new Osage River Subagency numbered 681 Indians.[44]

Ironically, while Gaines and Atkinson were removing the Potawatomis from the Platte Country, the federal government again changed its mind about the Potawatomis' final destination in the west. Since white settlers rapidly were moving into Iowa, federal officials feared they soon would inundate the new Potawatomi lands near Council Bluffs, causing a recurrence of earlier Potawatomi-white problems in the east. Indian agents also were apprehensive that the resettlement of the Potawatomis in Iowa might precipitate an intertribal war with the Sioux, which would force the government to station large numbers of troops along the Missouri. Therefore, in July, 1837, Commissioner of Indian Affairs Carey A. Harris wrote to Atkinson, instructing him to move all the Potawatomis to Kansas. Although the letter arrived too late to prevent Caldwell's people from going to Iowa, its message supposedly served as a directive for all future Potawatomi removals.[45]

While the Potawatomis from northern Illinois were settling in the Platte Country, their kinsmen in the east also made plans for removal. During the spring of 1834 many of the tribesmen who had left Sands's and Montgomery's removal party expressed a renewed interest in going west. In the summer of 1833 these Potawatomis had fled to their homes on the Iroquois River, but in April, 1834, they informed trader Gurdon S. Hubbard of Danville that they would like to join Quiquito's people in Kansas.[46]

The tribesmen on the Iroquois were led by Wabanim (White

Dog) and Michicaba (Snapping Turtle). Michicaba had accompanied Sands and Montgomery west, but in the fall of 1833 he returned to Illinois and spent the winter months encouraging his kinsmen to remove to Kansas. At Logansport, Indian Agent William Marshall supported the chief's efforts, furnishing Michicaba's followers with food and promising them that they could go west during the summer of 1834. In May, Marshall wrote to Washington asking that the removal be implemented as soon as possible. But much to Marshall and Michicaba's surprise, Commissioner Herring replied that the Potawatomis would have to wait until a removal party of at least five hundred Indians could be assembled. Michicaba protested that although he had gathered fewer than two hundred Potawatomis, they were all the Indians that would remove, and if the journey did not start soon, his people would become angry and refuse to go west.[47]

Marshall feared that Herring's decision would jeopardize all future Potawatomi removals, so he decided to bypass the commissioner's directive. Marshall recently had visited Washington, where he had discussed Indian affairs with Secretary of War Lewis Cass. In the discussion, Cass had mentioned that any number of Indians could be removed if the cost were small enough. Since Cass was Herring's superior, Marshall relied upon his conversation with the secretary for authority to move the Potawatomis west. Late in June, Marshall appointed William Gordon as acting assistant agent for removal and instructed him to take the Potawatomis to Kansas. Gordon proceeded to Wabanim and Michicaba's camp, where he found 188 Indians. On July 11, 1834, the Potawatomis started west. Traveling across Illinois, the Indians crossed the Mississippi at St. Louis and then journeyed on to Fort Leavenworth. They joined with Quiquito's people in early September.[48]

Meanwhile, Abel C. Pepper made plans to remove the "Wabash Potawatomis." During the summer of 1834, while Michicaba's people were on the way to Kansas, Pepper met with five chiefs from villages on the Tippecanoe and Eel rivers. The Potawatomis agreed to accompany Pepper in another exploring trip of the West, but they refused to visit the new lands in Iowa. Angry that Caldwell was negotiating to relinquish the Platte Country, the Wabash chiefs vowed that they would never remove to northern Iowa or occupy lands contiguous to the Chicago Potawatomis. Instead of visiting the lands along the Missouri, the Wabash Potawatomis demanded that they be taken to the region explored by McCoy's party in 1828.

During August, 1834, Pepper and the chiefs journeyed to St. Louis, where Superintendent William Clark tried to persuade them to go to Council Bluffs, but the Potawatomis refused. Finally Pepper gave in, and the exploring party crossed Missouri and then followed the Marais des Cygnes River onto the plains. The Indians were satisfied with the country and expressed a desire to settle in the region after they were removed from the east. In September the party returned to Indiana.[49]

Encouraged by the success of the exploring party, federal officials continued their preparations to move the Wabash Potawatomis west. But their efforts soon bogged down under a morass of confusion over the many small reservations granted by the Tippecanoe treaties in 1832. The primary problem was that many of the reservations had not been located. Since the large Indian land cessions never had been plotted, the government postponed the assignment of individual reservations until the region had been surveyed. Officials were anxious that the small Potawatomi reservations should be awarded in sections and that they should conform with official section lines. But before the survey was completed, the former Indian lands were overrun by white squatters anxious to preempt the best farmlands. Therefore, when the survey was finished, government agents attempting to assign the individual reservations found that almost every desirable section already contained some type of white dwelling. Although compromises finally were arranged, both the Potawatomis and the squatters remained dissatisfied.[50]

Ironically, however, by the mid-1830's many of the claims to individual reservations already had passed from Potawatomi hands. Since many of the Indians owed large sums of money to traders, they had signed their claims to reservations over to the merchants in payment of their debts. Most of the traders hoped to speculate with the land, and they were determined that the tracts be located on fertile soil. To assure the success of their speculation, the traders bribed land office agents not to record any preemption claims on certain choice locations. Those squatters interested in preempting the good lands countered with bribes of their own and lodged angry protests with President Jackson that the honest "settlers of the Western Wilds" were being uprooted by the "machinations of a set of speculators." The government investigated the charges and tried to award the lands to the best claimants, but many of the traders believed they had been cheated.[51]

Although most of the reservations granted to individual Indians soon passed into white hands, the Potawatomis generally retained those small tracts of land awarded to villages or "bands." The Tippecanoe treaties had established small reservations of from one to thirty-six sections for seventeen different villages, and earlier treaties had provided similar reservations for some of the tribesmen in Michigan. A few of these small reservations already had been sold to the government, but federal officials were anxious to purchase the others. Indian agents believed that as long as the Potawatomi villages held any lands in the east, those reservations would attract Indians opposed to moving west. To facilitate the removal of the Potawatomis from Indiana, Cass instructed Marshall to purchase as many of the "village reservations" as possible. He also informed the Indian agent that President Jackson wanted no fanfare or prolonged treaty negotiations which would prove expensive to the United States.[52]

Following Cass's directive, in December, 1834, Marshall met with several villages of Wabash Potawatomis and eventually purchased their claims to four small reservations. Two of the tracts were never surveyed, but the other two reservations belonged to villages led by Muckose (Little Bear) and Mota and were located in the Tippecanoe Valley between Maxinkuckee Lake and modern Warsaw, Indiana. Potawatomis from these villages received small payments in cash and trade goods, and they agreed to give up their reservations within three years. The lands were purchased for about fifty cents per acre and Marshall assured Cass that they were worth at least four times that amount. Yet only the treaty with Mota's people specifically provided for removal after the three-year period.[53]

In 1835 Marshall resigned from the Indian service, and the responsibility for obtaining the remaining small reservations was assigned to Pepper. During the spring and summer of 1836, Pepper met with several village chiefs and negotiated a series of treaties through which the Potawatomis gave up six small reservations along the Tippecanoe and Yellow rivers. The Indians received one dollar per acre for their lands and agreed to remove from Indiana within two years of the treaty date. The Potawatomis also agreed that a commissioner should be appointed by the governor to examine all claims against them held by traders. The Indians promised to pay all just claims from the proceeds of the recent sale of their reservations.[54]

Potawatomi indebtedness to the traders reflected the economic deterioration of the tribe. By 1836 the remaining reservations in

Indiana were surrounded by white settlement. Although the Indians continued to grow small fields of corn, hunting was so poor that most Potawatomis were forced to rely heavily upon the traders for food and other necessities. The tribe continued to receive a yearly annuity, but few of the Indians saved their money, and the funds were spent long before the year ended. To survive, the Potawatomis purchased food and other items on credit, promising to pay the traders from their future annuities. In the fall, when the annuities were paid, the traders presented the Indian agents with vouchers for the Potawatomi debts, and the agents paid the bills before distributing the remainder of the annuity to the Indians. This practice was encouraged by John Tipton, who served as Indian agent in Indiana between 1823 and 1832, and had been continued by his successors. By 1835, however, the Wabash Potawatomis had so extended their credit that their annuities failed to pay for their debts. In response, the merchants to whom the Indians were indebted contested with each other over whose bill should be paid. They also presented exaggerated claims, hoping to receive at least part of the figure in payment. But in 1835 the government announced it no longer would deduct funds from the Potawatomi annuities for debt payments. Although Pepper attempted to negotiate between the Potawatomis and their creditors, many of the merchants were dissatisfied. One year later, when the traders learned that funds from the sale of the small reservations would be used to pay Potawatomi debts, they flocked to the annuity payment, determined to press their claims against the Indians.[55]

Meanwhile, Pepper attempted to purchase the remaining Potawatomi reservations in Indiana. At first he was unsuccessful. The Tippecanoe treaties had awarded the tracts to villages led by chiefs such as Kinkash, Checawkose (Little Crane), Ashkum, (More and More), and Weesionas, but those chiefs refused to sell. Angry over the refusals, Pepper decided to buy the reservations from other Indians. On September 23, 1836, Pepper bought the lands from another group of Potawatomis whom he designated as "the Chiefs warriors, and headmen of the Patawattamies of the Wabash." Although the Indians who sold the reservations had little specific claim to the lands, the government recognized the treaty as valid, and it was ratified by the Senate.[56]

In late September, 1836, when the Potawatomis in Indiana assembled for their annuities, the "payment ground" on the Tippecanoe River swarmed with angry men. Ashkum, Checawkose, and the other chiefs whose reservations had been sold by their kinsmen denounced the recent cessions and threatened the lives of those leaders who had signed the document. The protests were supported by about fifty Potawatomis from the Saint Joseph, who were led by Alexis Coquillard, a trader from the South Bend region. Coquillard was one of more than three hundred white men, mostly merchants, who were determined to press their claims on the commissioners. Since Pepper had negotiated the recent cessions with "the Chiefs warriors, and headmen of the Pattawattamies of the Wabash," he foolishly allowed the same Indians to designate the commissioners who would judge the validity of the claims against the tribe. These chiefs, led by Iowa, Pashpoho, Wewesah, Kewawnay (Prairie Chicken), and Pepinawah, were heavily indebted to, and under the influence of, several local merchants. As commissioners, the chiefs selected George W. Ewing and Cyrus Taber. Both men were traders with large claims against the tribe.[57]

The annuity payment took place on September 25, 1836. Although the Saint Joseph tribesmen attempted to claim part of the money, Pepper refused, telling them that they would receive their annuity payment at Chicago. The Wabash Potawatomis received a annuity of sixty-three thousand dollars. The Indians set aside sixteen thousand dollars for themselves and designated most of the remainder for the payment of their debts. Ewing and Taber, who were adjudicating the claims, promptly turned in their own vouchers and claimed twenty-four thousand dollars: sixteen thousand for Ewing and eight thousand for Taber. They also awarded eight thousand dollars to Joseph Barron, a government interpreter and trader who was a close friend.[58]

Ewing and Taber's actions brought a storm of protest from the other Potawatomi creditors. They all had expected to share in the funds, but after the first three claims, over two-thirds of the money was gone. Led by Alexis Coquillard, the other traders besieged the annuity cabin, threatening to tear the building down and seize the funds for themselves. Coquillard climbed onto the roof of the cabin but was forced off by one of Ewing's employees, who threatened to "blow out his brains" if he continued his actions. The Potawatomis also took sides, with the chiefs who had cooperated with Pepper generally supporting Ewing and Taber. The other Indians, especially Ashkum and the Saint Joseph warriors, backed Coquillard.[59]

Pepper and Captain I. P. Simonton, the military disbursing

agent, eventually restored order, but all payments were suspended until a new group of commissioners could be appointed. On the following morning Pepper selected five "gentlemen of high character in the community": Ebenezer Ward, William Polke, R. B. Stevenson, S. B. Bathelet, and E. V. Cicott, who redistributed the money. Ironically, several of the new commissioners also were traders, but their claims were smaller and they were less greedy than Ewing and Taber. To prevent any further "disturbances," three companies of militia arrived from Logansport and patrolled the grounds for several days.[60]

The 1836 annuity payment sparked a myriad of claims and counter-claims by the traders in attendance. Foremost in protest was Ewing, who argued that his firm should have been awarded the entire sum that he first had allowed. Other traders lodged similar protests, and in 1837 the government appointed Judge John W. Edmonds to investigate both the events at the annuity payment and the resulting hodgepodge of claims against the Indians. During the summer and fall of 1837, Edmonds held a court of inquiry at Logansport, attempting to ascertain the validity of all claims against the Wabash Potawatomis. In December, 1837, he reported back to the commissioner of Indian affairs upon which claims should be paid, but his decision still dissatisfied many of the claimants, and they continued to protest to the government well into the 1840's.[61]

The events surrounding the 1836 annuity payments had an important impact upon future Potawatomi removals. Although the federal government preferred to remove all the Potawatomis to one location in the west, after 1836 many of the Wabash Indians refused to consider joining with their northern kinsmen. Since Ashkum and several of the Saint Joseph Potawatomis had threatened their lives, Iowa and many of the Wabash leaders asked to be removed to Kansas, where they would be out of the reach of "the Catholic and hostile British Indians of the North." Iowa's request contributed to the government's decision to establish the Osage River Subagency in Kansas. Meanwhile, several of the chiefs whose reservations had been illegally sold eventually succumbed to government pressure and agreed to the cession, but others, led by Menominee, continued to protest and vowed they never would leave their homes. Finally, many of the traders who were dissatisfied with the claims settlement worked against government attempts to move the Potawatomis west. Embittered that the second group of commissioners had disqualified some of his vouchers, Ewing wrote to Secretary of War Benjamin Butler and warned that the Potawatomis would never "get out of Indiana until we are paid if it is in my power to prevent them."[62]

Undaunted by Ewing's threat, Indian agents spent the spring of 1837 preparing the Potawatomis for another trek west. At Logansport, Pepper and Sands met with the Wabash Indians and offered to take them to Kansas. Meanwhile, Gholson Kercheval visited Potawatomi villages in southern Wisconsin, northern Illinois, and Michigan. Kercheval planned to assemble the northern Potawatomis at Chicago and lead them to Council Bluffs. Government officials especially were anxious to remove the Indians from Michigan, for in January, 1837, a series of minor scuffles had occurred between whites and Potawatomis near Coldwater. Although the Potawatomis had ceded all tribal lands in Michigan, many Indians held individual reservations, and other tribesmen still wandered through the Saint Joseph Valley.[63]

Kercheval achieved only limited success. Although many of the remaining Potawatomis in Illinois and Wisconsin agreed to the removal, their kinsmen on the Saint Joseph were more reluctant to go west. The Indian agent spent several weeks among the villages in Michigan and finally convinced some of the tribesmen to make the journey, but others refused to be enrolled. The Indians informed Kercheval that they planned to move their lodges onto the individual reservations still held by their friends. Others made preparations to join with Menominee at his village on the Yellow River in Indiana. Unfortunately for Kercheval, he spent all of his efforts attempting to enroll the Potawatomis for removal and failed to answer correspondence from the Indian Office. Angered over Kercheval's lack of communication, Harris fired him on July 14, 1837.[64]

Kercheval was replaced by Lewis Sands. Sands earlier had assisted Pepper in assembling the Wabash Potawatomis, but upon his promotion, he hurried to Illinois. At Chicago, Sands's new position inflated his ego and made him unbearable. He soon alienated many of the Potawatomis from Illinois and Wisconsin, and hundreds of Indians deserted the removal camp on the Des Plaines River. Some of the tribesmen fled north to the Ottawas. Many others sought refuge in Canada. Big Foot's followers withdrew from the removal and announced that they preferred to go to Council Bluffs unassisted. Yet Sands still envisioned a removal party of more than 1,000 Indians, and he hired ten assistants and a large number of wagons to transport the Potawatomis west. On August 15, 1837, he collected all of the Saint Joseph tribesmen who would remove, about 170 Indians, and started them west toward northern Illinois. Sands planned to join with the Potawatomis on the Des Plaines and then march all the tribesmen to Shabbona's Grove, about twenty-five miles west of the Fox River, where the Potawatomi annuities would be distributed before the Indians went west.[65]

The Potawatomis arrived at Shabbona's Grove early in September. In addition to the removal party, comprising of 170 tribesmen from the Saint Joseph and about 300 Indians from the camp on the Des Plaines, many other Potawatomis also assembled to share in the annuities. But the annuities were not what the Indians expected. Although the government had promised to pay most of the Potawatomi annuity in specie, the financial panic of 1837 prevented federal officials from acquiring the coins. Therefore, when the tribesmen gathered, Sands and Disbursing Agent Lieutenant James T. Sprague informed the Potawatomis that half their annuity would be paid in specie, but that the other half would be paid in trade goods purchased by the government in the east. Sands assured the tribesmen that their Great Father knew what they needed, and if they accepted the goods the government would transport the merchandise west. If they refused the goods, however, the merchandise would be given to other Indians, and the Potawatomis would have to wait until the government had enough specie to make the payment. Moreover, the specie payment would be made in one lump sum in the West, where the assembled Indians would have to share it with all other members of their tribe.[66]

The Potawatomis were surprised and angered by the government offer. Although Alexander Robinson was not part of the removal party, he was present for the annuity payment, and he spoke for all the Indians, denouncing the government's actions. Yet the Potawatomis could not refuse the agents' terms. Winter was approaching and they were en route to the west. If the tribesmen rejected the government's proposition, they would arrive in their new homes impoverished and uncertain of ever recovering their lost annuities. At least the government blankets would cover them during the coming winter. On September 4 they accepted the trade goods.[67]

The duplicity of the annuity payment was indicative of the entire removal. As the Potawatomis removed west, they were plagued by autumn rains, and when the Indians reached Quincy, they found the river bottoms under water and ferriage across the

Mississippi painfully slow. Arriving in Missouri, the tribesmen encountered more rainfall, and when they approached the Chariton River near Keytesville, they were forced to wade through waist-deep water for more than a mile before they even reached the stream. The bridge across the main channel was so flimsy that it collapsed while the Potawatomis were crossing it, but fortunately, none of the Indians were drowned.[68]

On October 25, 1837, the Indians reached the Platte River in western Missouri. There the removal split into two groups. Although Commissioner Harris had ordered Sands to take all of the Potawatomis to Kansas, most of the Indians preferred to join Caldwell in Iowa and refused to go to the Osage River Subagency. Led by Patogoshuk (Lead in a Heap), 287 tribesmen from northern Illinois turned north to Council Bluffs. The younger Topinbee, a son of the chief who had died in 1826, led the remaining 164 Saint Joseph Potawatomis to the new reservation in Kansas.[69]

Sands and his white associates were of little assistance on the removal. Although the Potawatomis were forced to camp in rain, the whites secured food and lodging in frontier taverns. As the Indians marched west, freighters employed to haul their possessions stole part of the goods, hiding them in the forest to be recovered on the return trip from Missouri. In 1833 Sands had quarreled with Montgomery. In 1837 he quarreled with every one. His assistants charged him with drunkenness, incompetency, and fraud. The Potawatomis charged that the removal agents had forced several Indian women to prostitute themselves to obtain daily rations during the removal. Upon the conclusion of the journey, Sands and a physician accompanying the removal became involved in a drunken brawl. Sands lost and was bedridden for two days. When he returned to the East, Sands was discharged from the Indian service.[70]

Ironically, while Sands and his ten assistants removed 450 Indians, almost twice as many Potawatomis journeyed west on their own. Less than one month after Patogoshuk's people reached Council Bluffs, Big Foot and about 800 Potawatomis from northern Illinois and southern Wisconsin arrived on the Des Moines River, where they established new villages. Big Foot's followers removed west at their own expense, although they sought government assistance after settling in Iowa.[71]

Although Sands's discharge brought praise from the Potawatomis at Council Bluffs, he was sorely missed along the Wabash. Before his transfer to Chicago, Sands had assisted Pepper in organizing the

Wabash Potawatomis for their journey to Kansas. At first the Wabash tribesmen seemed ready to remove. Naswakay (Counselor) spoke for the Potawatomis and assured the agents that his people would go west in August. But after Sands's departure, Indian interest in the journey diminished.[72] The Potawatomis claimed that they were reluctant to go west without Sands, but Pepper believed their hesitancy stemmed from other reasons. The removal agent charged that local traders had undermined the removal and that Father Louis Deseille, a priest active among the Potawatomis in Menominee's village, had persuaded the Indians to remain in Indiana.[73]

By late August, only fifty-two Indians agreed to make the journey. Several of these tribesmen had signed the questionable treaties of September, 1836, and since their lives had been threatened, they were anxious to leave Indiana. On August 23, 1837, under the supervision of George Proffit, the Potawatomis left their removal camp near Logansport and started west. In Illinois they encountered both cholera and the heavy rains that plagued the northern removal, but they crossed the Mississippi at St. Louis and arrived at the Osage River Subagency in late October.[74]

Pepper's charges that Father Deseille had undermined the 1837 removal reflected the growing influence of the Catholic church among the Potawatomis remaining in northern Indiana and Michigan. As Carey Mission declined, priests from Detroit and Vincennes sought converts among the Potawatomi villages, and in 1830 Father Frederick Rezé journeyed to the Saint Joseph, where he baptized thirteen tribesmen, including Pokagon. Although Rezé returned to Detroit, Pokagon accompanied him, and the chief persuaded the Jesuits to send Father Stephen T. Badin as a permanent missionary to the Saint Joseph villages. Badin found that many of the Potawatomis still retained certain tenets of Roman Catholicism taught to their fathers by the French. During the early 1830's the missionary established two churches in the Saint Joseph Valley and baptized a growing number of converts. In 1833 Badin was joined by Father Deseille, who spread the evangelism to the Potawatomis along the Yellow River. Deseille was especially successful in Menominee's village, and during the following year he baptized the old chief and several of his followers.[75]

Deseille also championed a policy of assimilation among the Yellow River Potawatomis. Attempting to convert Menominee's people into small farmers, the priest hoped to integrate the tribesmen into frontier society. Although he did not openly oppose removal, Deseille did encourage the Potawatomis to retain their reservations.[76]

The priest's attempt at assimilation clashed with government removal policy. Since Pepper was using all his influence to remove the Indians west, the agent envisioned Deseille as a direct threat to his success. In 1835 Pepper wrote to the priest and warned him against meeting with the Potawatomis "without the consent of the proper authority." Deseille replied that his "business with the Indians [was] only about their spiritual concerns" and invited the agent to attend any of the religious services held among the Indians. Pepper was temporarily satisfied, but when Deseille and Menominee asked for permission to establish a Catholic school on Yellow River, the agent again grew suspicious and denied the request.[77]

During the winter of 1835–36, officials in Washington inadvertently strengthened Menominee's determination to remain in Indiana. In November, 1835, Menominee and several other chiefs journeyed to the capital, where they met with federal officials who promised the Indians they could remain on their reservations as long as they owned the land. In February, 1836, Menominee received a similar promise in writing from Secretary of War Cass. Meanwhile, Cass instructed Pepper to purchase the remaining Potawatomi reservations in Indiana. Cass and the other officials evidently believed that Menominee could be persuaded to relinquish his land and that the government would not be obligated to honor its promises.[78]

They completely misjudged Menominee. The old chief and his followers shared a reservation of twenty-two sections awarded to Menominee and three other chiefs by the Tippecanoe treaty of October 26, 1832. Although Pepper successfully purchased other reservations during the spring of 1836, Menominee steadfastly refused to sell. Finally, in August, 1836, just before the troubled annuity payments, Pepper negotiated a treaty for the reservation with Notawkah (Rattlesnake), Pepinawah, and Mackahtahmoah (Black Wolf), the three chiefs who shared the land with Menominee. Yet Menominee did not take part in the transaction and charged that the treaty was fraudulent, since the reservation had been awarded to all four Indians. Pepper believed that Deseille encouraged the protest, and his suspicion of the priest deepened after the disturbance at the 1836 annuity payments. Since the Coquillard family was closely associated with the Catholic effort on the Saint

Joseph, Pepper believed that Coquillard's opposition to the annuity payments also had been inspired by Deseille.[79]

Although Menominee and his followers continued to protest the illegal sale of their reservation, their pleas for justice were ignored. During the summer of 1837, while Sands and Proffit led other Potawatomis west, Menominee and his people remained in Indiana. Deseille undoubtedly encourged their lack of cooperation, but Pepper's charges that the priest had undermined the entire 1837 removal were much exaggerated. Still, the agent was determined to force Deseille from Menominee's village, and in May, 1837, Pepper wrote to the priest, ordering him to leave the Yellow River or be prosecuted for acts against the government. Deseille withdrew to the Saint Joseph, where he died during the following September.[80]

Although Father Benjamin Marie Petit soon replaced Deseille on the Yellow River, Pepper did not envision the new priest as a threat to removal, and the agent spent the spring of 1838 making preparations to take the remaining Potawatomis west. Once again, two removals were planned. Pepper intended to collect Indians from Indiana and southern Michigan at a removal camp near Menominee's village, just north of Twin Lakes. Meanwhile, Isaac S. Berry, another removal agent, was instructed to assemble the Potawatomis still living in Illinois and Wisconsin at another removal camp on the Des Plaines River. Pepper spent $750 bribing Iowa and other influential leaders to urge removal among their followers, and by August, 1838, most of the remaining Wabash Potawatomis agreed to leave Indiana.[81]

Pepper was less successful among the tribesmen along the Yellow and Saint Joseph Rivers. On the Saint Joseph many of Pokagon's people still retained their small individual reservations and were determined to stay in Michigan. Others had purchased small acreages from nearby whites, holding the property under state and federal law. With no legal justification for removing Pokagon's followers, the government decided to allow them to remain in Michigan, but federal officials warned the Indians that they no longer would be "protected" by the government or share in tribal annuities.[82]

Menominee's people posed a more serious problem. The old chief continued to assert that he had not sold his reservation, and he refused all offers to enroll his followers for removal. Moreover, his village attracted many landless Potawatomis who also were determined to remain in the east. Since the three chiefs who had ceded the reservation had agreed to vacate the lands by August 6, 1838, when that date arrived, Pepper demanded that Menominee and his people leave their village. The chief refused, charging:

> The president does not know the truth. He, like me, has been imposed upon. He does not know that you made my young chiefs drunk and got their consent and pretended to get mine. . . . He would not drive me from my home and the graves of my tribe, and my children, who have gone to the Great Spirit, nor allow you to tell me that your braves will take me, tied like a dog . . . the President is just, but he listens to the words of young chiefs who have lied; and when he knows the truth, he will leave me to my own. I have not sold my lands. I will not sell them. I have not signed any treaty, and will not sign any. I am not going to leave my lands. . . .

But unfortunately, the old chief's impassioned speech had little effect upon the scores of white settlers who were poised on the borders of his reservation. After August 6, Menominee's lands were overrun by squatters anxious to preempt the best farmland. Angered by the intrusion, the Potawatomis destroyed a squatter's hut and threatened the owner's life. The whites retaliated by burning down a dozen Indian cabins.[83]

Afraid that blood would be shed, Pepper called for military assistance. Governor David Wallace of Indiana authorized Senator John Tipton to raise one hundred armed volunteers and to remove the Potawatomis west by force. On August 29, 1838, while Pepper lured Menominee to a council, Tipton and the volunteers quickly surrounded the chief's village. Menominee and several other leaders were placed in custody, and the remaining Potawatomis were forced to enroll for removal. During the next five days, Pepper and the volunteers brought in other tribesmen from Michigan and northern Indiana. The Wabash Potawatomis also assembled at the removal camp, and on September 4, 1838, more than 850 Indians started west for Kansas.[84]

The trip west was a disaster. Menominee refused to make the journey and was forced from his village at gunpoint. The food issued to the emigrating Indians was so bad that many of the volunteers refused to eat it and demanded government funds to purchase their own rations. Unfortunately for the Potawatomis, Illinois and Indiana were in the grip of a typhoid epidemic, and as the tribesmen trekked west, nearly three hundred Indians suffered from the disease. So many Potawatomis became ill and fell behind that a separate and smaller removal followed in the wake of the original party, collecting dropouts and herding them west. Before the Indians reached Kansas, they left forty-two of their kinsmen buried along the trail.[85]

The Potawatomis crossed the Mississippi near Quincy on October 8 and proceeded on into Missouri. Late in October, the second removal party overtook the original emigrants, and the Indians arrived at the Osage River Subagency on November 4, 1838. They numbered about 750 tribesmen. Besides the dead, others had slipped away from the removal and had returned to Indiana.[86]

Meanwhile, on the Des Plaines River near Chicago, Isaac Berry assembled 163 Potawatomis from northern Illinois and Wisconsin. The northern emigration left the Des Plaines in early August and proceeded on to Iowa. Unlike Menominee's removal, the Indians from northern Illinois did not contract typhus, and the journey west was uneventful. They arrived at Council Bluffs on September 18, 1838.[87]

The Potawatomis who fled from Menominee's removal returned to southern Michigan and northern Indiana. They also returned to deprivation. Although they joined with other tribesmen scattered across their former homeland, none of the Indians received any annuities. Even their corn crops, planted during the summer of 1838, had been seized and harvested by white settlers. Most of the refugees spent the winter of 1838–39 shivering in poorly constructed bark huts and living off the meager credit extended to them by the few traders still willing to provide such assistance. In April, 1839, some of the wandering tribesmen tried to return to the old Nottawasippi reservation near Coldwater, Michigan, but found their former lands occupied by white farmers. Several minor incidents occurred, and during the summer, Indian Agents Isaac Ketchum met with the Potawatomis and offered to take them to Kansas. The Indians refused, and Ketchum reported that they never would remove as long as they could find sanctuary among the Chippewas and Ottawas north of Grand River. Ketchum recommended that the government use troops, similar to the volunteers who had removed Menominee, to force the Potawatomis west of the Mississippi.[88]

Yet federal officials waited several months before taking any action. During the spring, Pepper had resigned his position as superintendent of emigration, leaving the removal effort leaderless. Finally, in September, 1839, the government appointed Samuel Milroy, a former agent to the Miamis, as Pepper's replacement. Milroy attempted to organize a removal during the autumn of 1839, but he met with little success. Most of the Potawatomis left in Indiana were led by Checawkose, and the chief refused to start for the west at such a late season. However, he promised Milroy to remove in the spring if the emigration started before his women planted their corn.[89]

Other Potawatomis, led by Pashpoho, were willing to remove, but their village on the Yellow River contained only seventy tribesmen, and Milroy was reluctant to transport such a small number west. Throughout October, Milroy and William Polke, an agent who had assisted in Menominee's removal, visited scattered Potawatomi camps, seeking additional emigrants. Although some of the Indians seemed willing to go west, Milroy's efforts were handicapped by events beyond his control. On October 22, 1839, a bank in Delphi, Indiana, in which Milroy had deposited all removal funds, failed, and the money was lost. To add insult to injury, two days later Pashpoho was arrested and imprisoned by local officials at Rochester for failure to pay certain debts owed by his people to nearby merchants. Milroy secured the chief's release, but during the last week in October the agent postponed the removal until the following spring.[90]

The winter of 1839–40 was a hard one for the Indians. Although the government cancelled the removal, Milroy refused to supply the Potawatomis with any provisions, and the tribesmen spent the season huddled in hunting camps along the Kankakee River in western Indiana. To the north, the Potawatomis living near Coldwater, Michigan, faced similar problems and sustained themselves by poaching stray livestock they found wandering in the forest. Yet Milroy's refusal to supply the Indians achieved the desired effect. By the spring of 1840 most of the Potawatomis remaining in Indiana were ready to move to Kansas.[91]

The government made elaborate plans for their removal. To assure that local traders would support the venture, officials again promised the merchants that the government would investigate all claims against the tribe and would urge the Indians to pay their debts. Moreover, Alexis Coquillard was enlisted as a removal agent and given the contract for provisions for the journey west. In February, Secretary of War Joel Pointsett appointed Brigadier General Hugh Brady as the superintendent of the removal and empowered him with "all the necessary measures for carrying it into full effect." Pointsett also warned the general to "neglect no military precautions which may seem . . . expedient . . . and to ensure the success of the operation." Brady and Coquillard spent the early summer of 1840 assembling Potawatomis at the removal camp near South Bend. Many of the Indians were anxious to leave, and on August 17, 1840, under the direction of Brady's son, S. P. Brady, they left for Kansas. Although the Potawatomis were short of clothing, the government supplied them with blankets, and the removal proceeded well. They crossed the Mississippi near Quincy and arrived at the Osage River Subagency on October 6. The party consisted of 524 Potawatomis, including Pashpoho, Checawkose, and Abram Burnett.[92]

Although most of the Indiana Potawatomis went west with Pashpoho and Checawkose, many tribesmen still wandered across southwestern Michigan. Pokagon's followers remained on their farms along the Saint Joseph, and Brady made no attempts to move them west. But other Indians continued to congregate near the old Nottawasippi Reservation, and they refused all offers of removal. Led by Mackahtamoah and Pamtipee, the tribesmen were resented by settlers in the region, and during the spring of 1840 several incidents between whites and Potawatomis occurred. One of the clashes caused the death of a settler named Wisner, and local officials arrested a Potawatomi known as "the Net" and charged him with murder. To facilitate Potawatomi removal, Governor William Woodbridge of Michigan ordered the prisoner released, but the Indians still refused to go to Kansas.[93]

Angry over the Potawatomis' stubbornness, Brady resorted to force. During August he assembled an expedition of two hundred regulars and about one hundred volunteers and made plans to surround Mackahtamoah and Pamtipee's village. But before he could act, a few local traders informed the Indians of Brady's plans and embellished the report with rumors that the troops were infected with smallpox and had been ordered to shoot the Indians. Frightened by the warning, the Potawatomis abruptly left their village and fled into the nearby forests. When Brady arrived at Nottawasippi, he found the village deserted and ordered his troops into the woods after the Indians. For two months the soldiers scoured the forests and prairies of southern Michigan. Special rewards were offered for Mackahtamoah and Pamtipee. The latter, an elderly man, was captured twice and escaped twice. Although part of the Indians made their way north to the Ottawas above Grand River, by mid-October Brady had collected about 440 Potawatomis, who were kept under guard at a removal camp near Marshall, Michigan.[94]

On October 15, 1840, the reluctant emigrants were started toward their new homes in Kansas. Brady placed Major Robert Forsyth in charge of the removal, but since "not 20 of the 439 Indians moved willingly," the general and the troops were forced to accompany the Potawatomis as far west as Peru, Illinois, where the Indians were loaded on steamboats. The vessels carried the Potawatomis to Westport, Missouri, where the tribesmen debarked in mid-November. They arrived at the Osage River Subagency on November 25, 1840.[95]

The Potawatomi occupancy of new lands in the west was only a part of the great Indian removals of the 1830's and 1840's. Convinced that assimilation had failed, some government leaders thoroughly believed that removal was in the Indians' best interest. Since the fur trade had diminished and most of the Potawatomis had little interest in becoming farmers, they no longer had any economic base in their former homelands. Although the Potawatomis received government annuities, the funds were insufficient to support the many members of the tribe. Moreover, an agriculturally oriented frontier society would not tolerate large numbers of semi-nomadic hunters in its midst. The Potawatomis planted small cornfields, but they also allowed most reservation land to remain in its natural state, a virtual crime to the land-hungry settlers of the region. But if some officials were motivated by concern for the Indians, others were more sympathetic to frontier politics. Since white settlers wanted the lands and demanded that the Potawatomis be removed, many federal policy makers succumbed to state and local pressures. At best, Jacksonian politics was a risky business, and whites voted; Indians did not.

Regardless of the motivation behind white policy, the removal period was a disastrous time for many Potawatomis. Some of the problems were caused by the Indians. Bribes must be accepted, as well as offered, and leaders such as Caldwell, Robinson, and Iowa sometimes profited at their kinsmen's expense. Moreover, some of the Indians who fled removal placed themselves in jeopardy, since they had no means of acquiring food or shelter in their old homelands. But much of the suffering resulted from fraud and incompetency by the government. The purchase of Menominee's reservation was an illegal act by both state and federal statutes, and the events surrounding the Tippecanoe treaties also were fraught with criminality.

More important were the actual journeys west. Although some proceeded well, many other removals brought undue suffering to the Potawatomis enrolled in them. Subjected to fraud and chaotic planning, the Potawatomis often were marched west under the supervision of political hacks more interested in making money than in the welfare of their charges. Billy Caldwell's people were allowed to settle in the Platte Country even though federal officials knew the region soon would be annexed to Missouri. Lewis Sands had proven his incompetence in 1833, yet he was retained by the Indian Office until after the disastrous 1837 removal. Both those incidents, and many others, could be excused as typical bureaucratic blunders, yet just where did the responsibility for such malfeasance in office end? Were the president and his cabinet or other high-ranking officials accountable for the operations of government during their administrations? Of course they were. To attempt the removal of large numbers of Indians through disorganized planning and with dishonest and ill-trained personnel was to invite disaster. To believe that such removals would take place smoothly was inexcusable ignorance.

Epilogue

After 1840 most of the Potawatomis were gone from the Old Northwest. Although scattered families still roamed through their old homeland, the vast majority of the tribe either had removed or had fled to Canada. The exact number of Indians seeking refuge in Canada is unknown, but more than two thousand Indians eventually crossed over the border. The largest migration took place between 1835 and 1840 as the Potawatomis fled the forced removals to Iowa and Kansas, but other Indians continued to enter Canada during the next decade. Most of the migrants left the United States by crossing the Saint Clair River above Detroit. Others fled north along the western shore of Lake Michigan, passed through Mackinac, and sought sanctuary at Manitoulin Island. By the last half of the nineteenth century, small communities of Potawatomis dotted the northeastern shores of Lake Huron from Manitoulin Island to Sarnia, about forty miles north of Detroit. Other tribesmen settled on Walpole Island at the mouth of the Saint Clair River. Today, the descendants of these Potawatomi refugees still live in upper Canada.[1]

Some of the Potawatomis who eventually fled to Canada were Indians who had returned from the removals to the west. Dissatisfied with Iowa or Kansas, several groups of Potawatomis straggled back across the Mississippi and wandered aimlessly through their old homelands. Although a few of the Indians reappeared in Michigan and Indiana, most returned to Wisconsin, where they sought assistance from the Winnebagos and Menominees. Whites in Wisconsin resented their return, and government agents complained that the Potawatomis were roving through the countryside, living off white gardens and killing white livestock. In 1848 a detachment of federal troops forced part of the refugees back into Iowa, but other Potawatomis remained in Wisconsin, and state officials clamored for their permanent removal to the west.[2]

Three years later, Alexis Coquillard secured a government contract to remove all the returned Potawatomis to Kansas. During the summer of 1851, Coquillard collected a few tribesmen from Indiana and Michigan and accompanied them to Theresa, Wisconsin, where he established a removal camp and informed the Wisconsin Potawatomis that he would take them west. Many of the Wisconsin Potawatomis were starving, and they accepted Coquillard's offer. By late July, Coquillard's encampment contained more than six hundred Indians. Many of the tribesmen were Potawatomis who had returned from the west, but the others were Indians who previously had refused to remove and had fled to northern Wisconsin. During the first week in August, Coquillard started his charges west. They crossed the Mississippi at Dubuque, Iowa, and arrived at the new Potawatomi reservation in Kansas in early September.[3]

Not all of the Wisconsin Potawatomis accompanied Coquillard. Some of the tribesmen were fugitives from earlier removals in Michigan, and they sought refuge in the forests west of Green Bay. Throughout the last half of the nineteenth century they wandered across northeastern Wisconsin. Some eventually acquired homesites under the Indian Homestead Act of 1884, while others received lands through congressional action in the early twentieth century. Many of these Potawatomis now live at Wisconsin Rapids; near Laona, in Forest County; and across the border in upper Michigan's Menominee County.[4]

Pokagon's followers also refused to emigrate, and since they held lands in the Saint Joseph Valley, they were allowed to remain in the east. Although most of their lands now have passed into white hands, the descendants of Pokagon's people still reside in scattered communities near Dowagiac and Hartford in southwestern Michigan.[5]

Other Potawatomis, including refugees from Brady's removal and remnants of the "Potawatomis of the Huron," continued to roam through southern Michigan. In 1848 the state of Michigan purchased 160 acres of land in Calhoun County and established a tiny reservation for these people. Today, a small group of Potawatomi families live on the tract, which is located a few miles north of modern Athens.[6]

In the west, both the Council Bluffs and Osage River subagencies were abolished in 1846, and one year later the Potawatomis were consolidated onto a new reservation on the Kansas River. But the factionalization that had plagued the tribe during the removal period continued, and in 1861 the Wabash Potawatomis, or "Mission Band," demanded that the reservation be divided and that their share of the lands be distributed to individuals. The government agreed, but within six years almost all of the redistributed land had passed into white hands, and the Mission Band was destitute. Finally, in 1867, the landless Potawatomis accepted a new reservation in Oklahoma. Although their Oklahoma lands were alloted by the Dawes Act, the former Mission Band, now known as the "Citizens Band," continue to reside near Shawnee, Oklahoma. The Kansas Potawatomis, or "Prairie Band," still occupy a small reservation near Mayetta, Kansas.[7]

Notes

CHAPTER ONE

1. W. Vernon Kinietz, *The Indians of the Western Great Lakes, 1615–1760*, 308; Frederick W. Hodge (ed.) , *Handbook of American Indians North of Mexico*, Bulletin 30 of the Bureau of American Ethnology, II, 289.

2. David I. Bushnell, Jr., *Tribal Migrations East of the Mississippi*, Smithsonian Miscellaneous Collections, LXXXIX, No. 12, 1–3; Donald J. Berthrong, *Indians of Northern Illinois and Southwestern Michigan*, 1–2; William W. Warren, "History of the Objibways," *Collections of the Minnesota Historical Society*, V, 81–82.

3. Charles F. Hockett, "The Position of Potawatomi in Central Algonkian," *Papers of the Michigan Academy of Science, Arts, and Letters*, XXVIII, 524; Charles Callendar, *Social Organization of the Central Algonkian Indians*, Milwaukee Public Museum Publication in Anthropology No. 7, 1–2; James E. Fitting and Charles Cleland, "Late Prehistoric Settlement Patterns in the Upper Great Lakes," *Ethnohistory*, XVl (Fall, 1969) , 297; George Irving Quimby, *Indian Culture and European Trade Goods: The Archaeology of the Historic Period in the Western Great Lakes Region*, 22–23.

4. Louise P. Kellogg, *The French Regime in Wisconsin and the Old Northwest*, 94–95; George T. Hunt, *The Wars of the Iroquois: A Study in Intertribal Trade Relations*, 109; Reuben G. Thwaites (ed.) , *The Jesuit Relations and Allied Documents*, XXIII, 225.

5. Hunt, *Wars of the Iroquois*, 87–116; Francis Parkman, in *The Jesuits in North America*, describes the Huron-Iroquois contest in vivid detail. For years some anthropologists and historians confused the Mascoutens and Potawatomis. The separate identity of the Mascoutens is clarified in David Baerris, Erminie Wheeler-Voegelin, and Remidios Wycoco-Moore, "The Identity of the Mascoutens," in *Indians of Northeastern Illinois*, 249–99.

6. Kellogg, *French Regime in Wisconsin*, 88; Hunt, *Wars of the Iroquois*, 119–20.

7. Nicolas Perrot, "Memoir on the Manners, Customs, and Religion of the Savages of North America," in *The Indian Tribes of the Upper Mississippi Valley and Region of the Great Lakes*, ed. by Emma Helen Blair, I, 148–50.

8. Pierre-Espirit Radisson, "Radisson's Account of His Third Journey," in *Early Narratives of the Northwest*, ed. by Louise Phelps Kellogg, 44–45; Claude Allouez, "Journal of Father Allouez's Journey to Lake Superior," in *ibid.*, 123. Also see Pierre François Xavier Charlevoix, *History and General Description of New France*, trans. and ed. by John Gilmary Shea, III, 104, and Kellogg, *French Regime in Wisconsin*, 114.

9. Claude Charles Le Roy Bacquerville de-la Potherie, "History of the Savage

Peoples Who Are Allies of New France," in Blair, *Indian Tribes of the Upper Mississippi*, I, 316.

10. *Ibid.*, 15–16, 301–10.

11. *Ibid.*, 310–16.

12. *Ibid.*, 316–17.

13. *Ibid.*; Kellogg, *French Regime in Wisconsin*, 127 fn. 50; la Potherie, "History of the Savage Peoples," in Blair, *Indian Tribes of the Upper Mississippi*, I, 321–322.

14. *Ibid.*, 336–42.

15. Thwaites, *Jesuit Relations*, LIV, 197, 205–207; LV, 187; Claude Allouez, "Father Allouez's Journey into Wisconsin, 1669–1670," in Kellogg, *Early Narratives of the Northwest*, 147–53; Kellogg, *French Regime in Wisconsin*, 162.

16. La Potherie, "History of the Savage Peoples," in Blair, *Indian Tribes of the Upper Mississippi*, I, 343.

17. *Ibid.*, 343–44.

18. *Ibid.*, 344–48; "Saint-Lusson's Proces-Verbal," June 14, 1671, in *The Collections of the State Historical Society of Wisconsin*, XI, 26–28; Simon-Francois Daumont, Sieur de Saint-Lusson, "Report of the Taking Possession of the Countries Situated Toward Lakes Huron and Superior, June 14, 1671," Margry Translation, Burton Historical Collection, Detroit Public Library, part 1, 136–138 (microfilm).

19. Thwaites, *Jesuit Relations*, LVIII, 37–41; Jacques Marquette, "Unfinished Journal of Father Jacques Marquette, addressed to the Reverend Father Claude Dablon, Superior of Missions," in Kellogg, *Early Narratives of the Northwest*, 262; Francis Borgia Steck, *The Joliet-Marquette Expedition*, 152.

20. Thwaites, *Jesuit Relations*, LVIII, 37–41, 267, 287; "Perrot Memoir," in Blair, *Indian Tribes of the Upper Mississippi*, I, 188–89; *Wisconsin Historical Collections*, XVI, 29–30; Hjaalmar R. Holand, "The Sign of the Cross," *Wisconsin Magazine of History*, XVIII (December, 1933), 157–64.

21. Holand, "Sign of the Cross," 163; Francis Parkman, *La Salle and the Discovery of the Great West*, 126–29.

22. Louis Hennepin, "Hennepin's Narrative," in *Collections of the Illinois State Historical Library*, I, 53–56.

23. *Ibid.*, 57–59; Parkman, *La Salle and the West*, 130.

24. "From La Potherie," *Wisconsin Historical Collections*, XVI, 100–101; Father Engarlaran to Lefevte de la Barre, governor of New France, August 26, 1683, *ibid.*, 110–11.

25. "Perrot Memoir," in Blair, *Indian Tribes of the Upper Mississippi*, I, 151–57; Charlevoix, *History of New France*, III, 161–62; Thwaites, *Jesuit Relations*, LIV, 265.

26. "Statement by La Salle on the Illinois Country, 1680," *Illinois Historical Collections*, XXIII, 15.

27. "Relation of Henri de Tonty Concerning the Exploration of La Salle from 1678 to 1683," in Potawatomi File, Great Lakes–Ohio Valley Indian Archives Project, Glenn A. Black Laboratory of Archaeology, Indiana University; Louise Phelps Kellogg, "A Wisconsin Anabasis," *Wisconsin Magazine of History*, VII, (March, 1924), 332–38; Robert A. Goldstein, *French-Iroquois Diplomatic and Military Relations, 1606–1701*, 119; Reverend Father de Lamberville to Count de Frontenac, September 20, 1682, in *Documents Relative to the Colonial History of the State of New York*, ed. by Edward B. O'Callaghan, IX, 192. Also see Hunt, *Wars of the Iroquois*, 156–57.

28. La Potherie, "History of the Savage Peoples," in Blair, *Indian Tribes of the Upper Mississippi*, II, 16.

29. *Ibid.*, 20.

30. *Ibid.*, 21–25; Cadwallader Colden, *The History of the Five Indian Nations Depending on the Province of New York in America*, 58–65; Henry de Tonty, "Tonty's Memoir," in Kellogg, *Early Narratives of the Northwest*, 310; Goldstein, *French-Iroquois Relations*, 152–54. The strength of the French force is unknown.

31. La Potherie, "History of the Savage Peoples," in Blair, *Indian Tribes of the Upper Mississippi*, II, 54–60.

32. *Ibid.*; Kellogg, *French Regime in Wisconsin*, 245–48.

33. La Potherie, "History of the Savage Peoples," in Blair, *Indian Tribes of the Upper Mississippi*, II, 60; "An Account of the Most Remarkable Occurrences in Canada from the Month of September, 1694, to the Sailing of the Vessels in 1695," *New York Colonial Documents*, IX, 620; Kellogg, *French Regime in Wisconsin*, 249–53.

34. Kellogg, *French Regime in Wisconsin*, 257–60.

35. Charlevoix, *History of New France*, IV, 277–78; *Wisconsin Historical Collections*, XVI, 166–67.

36. Charlevoix, *History of New France*, V, 67; "An Account of the Most Remarkable Occurrences in Canada from the Departure of the Vessels in 1696 to the 15th of October, 1697," *New York Colonial Documents*, IX, 673.

37. Charlevoix, *History of New France*, V, 69; "An Account of the Most Remarkable Occurrences in Canada from the Departure of the Vessels in 1696 to the 15th of October, 1697," *New York Colonial Documents*, IX, 673–75.

38. "An Account of the Most Remarkable Occurrences in Canada from the Month of September, 1694, to the Sailing of the Vessels in 1695," *New York Colonial Documents*, IX, 623; letter by Francis Buisson de St. Cosme, January 2, 1699, in Kellogg, *Early Narratives of the Northwest*, 345; Berthrong, *Indians of Illinois and Michigan*, 15–17. St. Cosme was a priest in Wisconsin.

39. Antoine Denis Raudot, "Memoir Concerning the Different Indian Nations of North America," in Kinietz, *Indians of the Western Great Lakes*, 313, 381; Albert Ernest Jenks, "The Wild Rice Gatherers of the Upper Lakes: A Study in American Primitive Economics," *Nineteenth Annual Report of the Bureau of American Ethnology*, 1063; Huron H. Smith, *Ethnobotany of the Forest Potawatomi Indians*, Bulletin of the Public Museum of the City of Milwaukee, Vol. VII, pt. 1, 24; "Allouez Wisconsin Memoir," in Kellogg, *Early Narratives of the Northwest*, 145.

40. Smith, *Ethnobotany of the Forest Potawatomi*, 24; La Potherie, "History of the Savage Peoples," in Blair, *Indian Tribes of the Upper Mississippi*, I, 303–306; Kinietz, *Indians of the Western Great Lakes*, 313–14.

41. Robert E. and Pat Ritzenthaler, *The Woodland Indians of the Western Great Lakes*, 61–62; Smith, *Ethnobotany of the Forest Potawatomi*, 23; "Allouez Wisconsin Memoir," in Kellogg, *Early Narratives of the Northwest*, 146.

42. Jacques Charles Sabrevois de Bleury, "Memoir on the Savages of Canada as Far as the Mississippi, Describing Their Customs and Trade," *Wisconsin Historical Collections*, XVI, 366–68; Ritzenthaler, *Woodland Indians*, 60–61.

43. La Potherie, "History of the Savage Peoples," in Blair, *Indian Tribes of the Upper Mississippi*, I, 305–306; Ritzenthaler, *Woodland Indians*, 17–21.

44. Kinietz, *Indians of the Western Great Lakes*, 312–13; William H. Keating, *Narrative of an Expedition to the Source of St. Peters River*, I, 85–86; Ritzenthaler, *Woodland Indians*, 56–60.

45. *Wisconsin Historical Collections*, III, 302; Kinietz, *Indians of the Western Great Lakes*, 312–13; Ritzenthaler, *Woodland Indians*, 58–60; James Van Stone, "Canadian Trade Silver from Indian Graves in Northern Illinois," *Wisconsin Archaeologist*, LI (March, 1970), 21–30.

46. Ruth Landes, *The Prairie Potawatomi: Tradition and Ritual in the Twen-*

tieth Century, 36; Alanson Skinner, *The Mascoutens or Prairie Potawatomi*, Bulletin of the Public Museum of the City of Milwaukee, VI, 17–29; Robert Ritzenthaler, *The Potawatomi Indians of Wisconsin*, Bulletin of the Public Museum of the City of Milwaukee, XIX, No. 3, 141–42; Callendar, *Social Organization of the Central Algonkians*, 30–31, 81–83, 93–97.

47. Landes, *Prairie Potawatomi*, 29–30; Callendar, *Social Organization of the Central Algonkians*, 94–95.

48. Ritzenthaler, *Woodland Indians*, 28–36; Callendar, *Social Organization of the Central Algonkians*, 25; Keating, *Narrative of an Expedition*, I, 93.

49. Skinner, *Mascoutens*, 34; Ritzenthaler, *Woodland Indians*, 37–38.

50. Landes, *Prairie Potawatomi*, 182–84; Ritzenthaler, *Woodland Indians*, 36–37.

51. Landes, *Prairie Potawatomi*, 251–55; Ritzenthaler, *Woodland Indians*, 41–43; Keating, *Narrative of an Expedition*, I, 112–14.

52. Keating, *Narrative of an Expedition*, I, 172–73; Skinner, *Mascoutens*, 52; Ritzenthaler, *Woodland Indians*, 43–44; Thwaites, *Jesuit Relations*, LXI, 149; Landes, *Prairie Potawatomi*, 57–59.

53. "Allouez Wisconsin Memoir," in Kellogg, *Early Narratives of the Northwest*, 127; Landes, *Prairie Potawatomi*, 51, 89, 192–94; Ritzenthaler, *Woodland Indians*, 101–106.

54. Landes, *Prairie Potawatomi*, 26, 46–48; Callendar, *Social Organization of the Central Algonkian*, 95–96.

55. Keating, *Narrative of an Expedition*, I, 85, 118–19; Kinietz, *Indians of the Western Great Lakes*, 311–12; "Allouez Wisconsin Memoir," in Kellogg, *Early Narratives of the Northwest*, 123–24.

56. George Winter, *The Journals and Indian Paintings of George Winter, 1837–1839*, plate XXVII; Ritzenthaler, *Woodland Indians*, 88–91, 117–27.

57. For conflicting views of Potawatomi political structure, see David Baerris, "Chieftainship Among the Potawatomi," *Wisconsin Archaeologist*, LIV (September, 1973), 114–34, and James A. Clifton, "Potawatomi Leadership Roles: On *Okama* and Other Influential Personages," in *Proceedings of the 1974 Algonquian Conference, Mercury Series*.

58. Onontio was the Potawatomi name for the governor of New France.

CHAPTER TWO

1. Charlevoix, *History of New France*, V, 141–42.

2. *Ibid.*, 143; Goldstein, *French-Iroquois Relations*, 195–96.

3. "Ratification of the Peace Between the French and the Indians," *New York Colonial Documents*, IX, 722–24; Goldstein, *French-Iroquois Relations*, 196–97.

4. Claude Aveneau to Cadillac, June 4, 1702, *Michigan Historical Collections*, XXXIII, 123; Erminie Wheeler-Voegelin, "Before the Claims Commission: An Ethnohistorical Report on the Indian Use and Occupancy of Royce Area 66," 115. This report is a multilith copy of materials prepared for the Indian Claims Commission and can be found in the Great Lakes Indian Archives. Also see Frances Krauskopf, "The French in Indiana, 1700–1760" (Ph.D. diss., Indiana University, 1953), 30; and Erminie Wheeler-Voegelin and David Stout, *Indians of Illinois and Northwestern Indiana*, 45–46.

5. Kellogg, *French Regime in Wisconsin*, 271–72; François Clairambault d'Aigremont to Count de Pontchartrain, November 14, 1708, *Michigan Historical Collections*, XXXIII, 431–32; William J. Eccles, *The Canadian Frontier, 1543–1760*, 136. D'Aigre-

mont was a French official investigating conditions in the west. Pontchartrain was intendant of finance in France.

6. D'Aigremont to Pontchartrain, November 14, 1708, *Michigan Historical Collections*, XXXIII, 432–35; speech by Miscouaky (Ottawa chief) to Vaudreuil, September 26, 1706, *ibid.*, 288–89; C. M. Burton, "Fort Pontchartrain de Detroit—1701–1710—Under Cadillac," *ibid.*, XXIX, 285 fn. 1. Vaudreuil was appointed governor of New France after Callieres died in 1703.

7. Jean Joseph Marest to Vaudreuil, October 30, 1706, *Michigan Historical Collections*, XXXIII, 267; Jean LeBlanc to the governor general, June 23, 1707, *ibid.*, 382. Marest was a Jesuit among the Ottawas. LeBlanc, also known as Otoutagon, was a chief among the Ottawas. Also see Krauskopf, "French in Indiana," 31, and Wheeler-Voegelin, "Before the Claims Commission: Royce Area 66," 115.

8. Vaudreuil to Pontchartrain, October 25, 1711, *New York Colonial Documents*, IX, 858; Krauskopf, "French in Indiana," 36.

9. Vaudreuil to Pontchartrain, October 31, 1710, *Wisconsin Historical Collections*, XVI, 263.

10. "Words of the Marquis de Vaudreuil to the Savages Who Come Down from the Upper Country," *Michigan Historical Collections*, XXXIII, 503–506; Howard H. Peckham, *The Colonial Wars, 1682–1762*, 72.

11. La Potherie, "History of the Savage Peoples," in Blair, *Indian Tribes of the Upper Mississippi*, I, 321–22; Bernard de la Harpe, "Historical Journal of the Establishment of Louisiana by France," *Wisconsin Historical Collections*, XVI, 181–83; Kellogg, *French Regime in Wisconsin*, 275–76.

12. Wheeler-Voegelin, "Before the Claims Commission: Royce Area 66," 116; Kellogg, *French Regime in Wisconsin*, 276.

13. Dubuisson to Vaudreuil, June 15, 1712, *Wisconsin Historical Collections*, VXI, 269, 278; Thwaites, *Jesuit Relations*, LXVI, 285. Also see Charlevoix, *History of New France*, V, 257.

14. Dubuisson to Vaudreuil, June 15, 1712, *Wisconsin Historical Collections*, XVI, 267–72.

15. *Ibid.*, 272–83.

16. *Ibid.*, 283–84. Also see William A. Hunter, "Refuge Fox Settlements Among the Senecas," *Ethnohistory*, III (Winter, 1956), 11–12.

17. Marest to Vaudreuil, June 21, 1712, *Michigan Historical Collections*, XXXIII, 553–55; Vaudreuil to French ministers, October 15, 1712, *ibid.*, 570; Wheeler-Voegelin and Stout, *Indians of Illinois and Northwestern Indiana*, 48–49.

18. "Memoir on the Indians of Canada as Far as the River Mississippi, with Remarks on Their Manners and Trade," *New York Colonial Documents*, IX, 888; Milo Milton Quaife (ed.), *The Western Country in the 17th Century: The Memoirs of Antoine Lamothe Cadillac and Pierre Liette*, 64. Also see Wheeler-Voegelin, "Before the Claims Commission: Royce Area 66," 116.

19. Vaudreuil to the Council of Marine, October 14, 1716, *Wisconsin Historical Collections*, XVI, 341–43; Louis Phelps Kellogg, "The Fox Indians Under the French Regime," *Proceedings of the State Historical Society of Wisconsin at its Fifty-Fifth Meeting*, 164.

20. Vaudreuil to the Council of Marine, October 14, 1716, *Wisconsin Historical Collections*, XVI, 343; Kellogg, *French Regime in Wisconsin*, 288.

21. Kellogg, *French Regime in Wisconsin*, 290–92.

22. Vaudreuil to the Council of Marine, March 11, 1720, *Wisconsin Historical Collections*, XVI, 382; speech of the Ottawas and Potawatomis at Montreal, June 24,

1717, *Michigan Historical Collections*, XXXIII, 584; Burt Anson, *The Miami Indians*, 34.

23. Sabrevois to Vaudreuil, April 8, 1717, *Michigan Historical Collections*, XXXIII, 583.

24. Vaudreuil to the Council of Marine, October 12, 1717, *ibid.*, 590–91. Alphonse de Tonty was a younger brother of Henry de Tonty, who had served as a lieutenant to La Salle.

25. *Ibid.*, 591; "Talk of the Poutouatamis and the Reply of M. de Vaudreuil, June 24, 1717," *ibid.*, 586–87.

26. Kellogg, *French Regime in Wisconsin*, 292; Wheeler-Voegelin, and Stout, *Indians of Illinois and Northwestern Indiana*, 50–51. A few of the Potawatomis may have remained in the Saint Joseph Valley. See Valentine B. Deale, "The History of the Potawatomis Before 1722," *Ethnohistory*, V (Fall, 1958) , 337.

27. Unknown to Claude de Ramezay, January 10, 1723, *Wisconsin Historical Collections*, XVI, 422; George Paré and Milo Milton Quaife (eds.) , "The St. Joseph Baptismal Register," *Mississippi Valley Historical Review*, XIII (September, 1926) , 201–13; Krauskopf, "French in Indiana," 75–77. Ramezay served as acting governor of Canada, 1725–27.

28. Vaudreuil to the Duke of Orleans, October 12, 1717, *Michigan Historical Collections*, XXXIII, 590; Vaudreuil to the Council of Marine, October 28, 1719, *Wisconsin Historical Collections*, XVI, 380–81.

29. Kellogg, *French Regime in Wisconsin*, 302–304.

30. Vaudreuil to the Council of Marine, October 22, 1720, *Wisconsin Historical Collections*, XVI, 392–93; "Proceedings of the Council Regarding the Letter of Governor Vaudreuil, December 2, 1721," *ibid.*, 395–97.

31. Vaudreuil to the Council of Marine, October 22, 1720, *ibid.*, 393; "Proceedings of the Council Regarding the Letter of Governor Vaudreuil, December 2, 1721," *ibid.*, 397.

32. Vaudreuil to the minister of the colonies, October 11, 1723, *ibid.*, 433; "Speeches of the Foxes at a Council Held at the House of Monsieur De Montigny in the Presence of the Missionary, September 6, 1722," *ibid.*, 419; Krauskopf, "French in Indiana," 110; Kellogg, "Fox Indians," 166–70.

33. Kellogg, "Fox Indians," 169–70.

34. Thwaites, *Jesuit Relations*, LXVII, 207–11; A. M. Gibson, *The Kickapoos: Lords of the Middle Border*, 18–19.

35. Constant Marchand de Lignery to Beauharnois, August 30, 1728, *Wisconsin Historical Collections*, XVII, 31–39; Beauharnois and others to the French minister of war, September 1, 1728, *ibid.*, V, 94; Beauharnois to the French minister, July 21, 1729, *ibid.*, XVII, 62–65. Lignery led the campaign into Wisconsin in 1728.

36. Beauharnois to the French minister, October 12, 1729, *ibid.*, 81; Beauharnois to the French minister, September 1, 1729, *ibid.*, 67–70.

37. Pierre Paul Sieur de Marin to Beauharnois, May 11, 1730, *ibid.*, 88–100. Marin commanded a French post at Green Bay.

38. Jean Baptiste St. Ours Deschaillons to Beauharnois, August 22, 1730, *Michigan Historical Collections*, XXXIV, 67–68. Deschaillons was the commander at Detroit.

39. *Ibid.*

40. Beauharnois to the French minister, September 9, 1730, *Wisconsin Historical Collections*, XVII, 109–12; De Villiers to Beauharnois, September 23, 1730, *ibid.*, 113–15. Although the first of these two letters is dated September 9, it obviously was finished at a later date.

41. De Villiers to Beauharnois, September 23, 1730, *ibid.*, 116.

42. *Ibid.*, 117.

43. *Ibid.* The exact location of this engagement has been the subject of much speculation by historians and antiquarians. Kellogg, in *The French Regime in Wisconsin*, 326 fn. 29, places the encounter about 150 miles south-southeast of Starved Rock, near the headwaters of the Kaskaskia. Stanley Faye, in "The Fox Fort—1730," *Journal of the Illinois State Historical Society*, XXVIII (October, 1935), 137–47, states that the battle took place near the Vermillion River of the Illinois, probably in Livingston County, Illinois. John H. Burham, in "Mysterious Battle Grounds in McLean County, Illinois," *Transactions of the Illinois State Historical Society for the Year 1908*, 190, claims that the encounter occurred near the headwaters of the Sangamon in McLean County.

44. "Memorandum by De Noyan Concerning the Present Condition in Canada, 1730," *Michigan Historical Collections*, XXXIV, 74, 82; Boishebert to Beauharnois, February 2, 1732, *Wisconsin Historical Collections*, XVII, 148–52; Beauharnois to the French minister, May 1, 1733, *ibid.*, 172–73; Boishebert to Beauharnois, November 7, 1732, *ibid.*, 173–74. De Noyan was a French military officer. Louis Henri Deschamps, Sieur de Boishebert, assumed command at Detroit in 1730.

45. "Yearly Report of Beauharnois and Hocquart Relating to Affairs in the Upper Country, October 7, 1734," *Wisconsin Historical Collections*, XVII, 206–207; De Noyelles to Beauharnois, no date, *ibid.*, 221–29; Hocquart to the controller general. October 26, 1735, *Michigan Historical Collections*, XXXIV, 130–33. Gilles Hocquart was intendant of Canada from 1728 to 1748. De Noyelles led the French expedition to Iowa.

46. Beauharnois to the French minister, October 17, 1726, *Wisconsin Historical Collections*, XVII, 259; Beauharnois to the French minister, October 16, 1737, *ibid.*, 275–76; Kellogg, *French Regime in Wisconsin*, 338–39.

CHAPTER THREE

1. Sieur de Vincennes to the French minister, no date, in Jacob Piatt Dunn, *The Mission to the Wabash*, 307; Beauharnois to the French minister, May 30, 1733, *Wisconsin Historical Collections*, XVII, 181; Arrell M. Gibson, *The Chickasaws*, 40–48. Vincennes was a French officer stationed on the Wabash.

2. Sieur de Bienville and Edme Gatien Salmon to Jean Frederic Phelypeaux, Comte de Maurepas, April 8, 1734, in Dunbar Rowland and A. G. Sanders (ed.), *Mississippi Provincial Archives: French Dominion*, 1729–1740, III, 656–67. Bienville was governor of Mississippi. Salmon was intendant of Louisiana. Maurepas was minister of marine. Also see Beauharnois to the French minister, May 30, 1733, *Wisconsin Historical Collections*, XVII, 181–82; Beauharnois to the French minister, July 24, 1733, *Michigan Historical Collections*, XXXIV, 108; Gibson, *Chickasaws*, 49–50.

3. "Account of the Battle Fought by D'Artaguette with the Chickasaws, March 25, 1736," in Caroline and Eleanor Dunn (trans. and eds.), *Indiana's First War: An Account Made by Bienville of His Expedition Against the Chickasaws*, 109; copy of a list of Indian parties at the Piankashaw Post, April 24–September 6, 1736, Potawatomi File, Great Lakes Indian Archives; Krauskopf, "French in Indiana," 193–199; Gibson, *Chickasaws*, 50–54.

4. Gibson, *Chickasaws*, 54–55.

5. Salmon to Maurepas, May 4, 1740, in Rowland and Sanders, *Mississippi Provincial Archives*, I, 441; Gibson, *Chickasaws*, 55–56.

6. Memoir on the Indians and their relations, *Wisconsin Historical Collections,* XVII, 337; Beauharnois to the French minister, September 26, 1741, *ibid.,* 366; "Inventory of Supplies Furnished to the Indians, September 5, 1743–July 1, 1746," Potawatomi File, Great Lakes Indian Archives; Krauskopf, "French in Indiana," 220, 227, 235.

7. Mactigue Macarty to Antoine Louis Rouille, May 20, 1753, *Illinois Historical Collections,* XXIX, 187. Macarty was a French officer in Illinois. Rouille was minister of marine between 1749 and 1754. Also see Frances Krauskopf (trans. and ed.), *Ouiatanon Documents,* 148; Eccles, *Canadian Frontier,* 150–54, and Kellogg, *French Regime in Wisconsin,* 373–76.

8. Beauharnois to the French minister, October 6, 1738, *Michigan Historical Collections,* XXXIV, 151–54.

9. "Memorandum on What Has Taken Place in the Affair Between the Hurons of Detroit and the Outawacs, Poutawatamis, Sauteux and Missisagues of That Post . . . ," 1738–41, *Michigan Historical Collections,* XXXIV, 195–202; "Memorandum to Serve as Instructions for the Chevr. de Beauharnois . . . ," June 14, 1741, *ibid.,* 205–206. Also see Charles Augustus Hanna, *The Wilderness Trail,* II, 165.

10. William Trent, *Journal of Captain William Trent,* ed. by Alfred T. Goodman, 17. Trent was a British trader. Also see Albert T. Volwiler, *George Croghan and the Westward Movement, 1741–1782,* 35–36. Volwiler suggests that Croghan instigated the conspiracy.

11. Trent, *Trent's Journal,* 18; "Extracts from the Diary of Events for the Year 1747, Sent by the Governor and Intendant of New France to the French Minister," *Wisconsin Historical Collections,* XVII, 458.

12. "Extracts from the Diary of events, 1747," *Wisconsin Historical Collections,* XVII, 458–69, 484–86; Count de Raymond to the French minister, November 2, 1747, *ibid.,* 475; Anson, *Miami Indians,* 43.

13. Speech by the St. Joseph Potawatomis to Beauharnois, July 16, 1742, *Wisconsin Historical Collections,* XVII, 393–94; reply by Beauharnois, July 22, 1742, *ibid.,* 393–96.

14. Extracts from the Potier Gazette, in Ernest J. Lajeunesse (ed.), *The Windsor Border Region,* 38. Pierre Potier was a missionary among the Hurons at Detroit. Also see "Journal of Occurrences in Canada," 1746, 1747, *New York Colonial Documents,* X, 91, 122; "Abstract of the Different Movements at Detroit," 1745–46, *ibid.,* 34; report by Boishebert on Indian affairs, November 1747, *ibid.,* 84; and "Extracts from the Diary of Events, 1747," *Wisconsin Historical Collections,* XVII, 490–91. Boishebert was in charge of all Indian affairs in New France at this time.

15. "Journal of Events at Quebec," 1747, *New York Colonial Documents,* X, 151; "Extracts from the Diary of Events, 1747," *Wisconsin Historical Collections,* XVII, 468, 486–91.

16. La Galissonniere to the French minister, October 23, 1748, *Wisconsin Historical Collections,* XVII, 509–12; Vaudreuil to Maurepas, March 20, 1748, *Illinois Historical Collections,* XXIX, 54; Hanna, *Wilderness Trail,* II, 166–67; Anson, *Miami Indians,* 43.

17. "Extracts from the Diary of Events, 1747," *Wisconsin Historical Collections,* XVII, 479; La Galissonniere to Maurepas, October 23, 1748, *New York Colonial Documents,* X, 181–82.

18. Wilbur Jacobs, "Presents to Indians Along the French Frontiers in the Old Northwest, 1748–1763," *Indiana Magazine of History,* XLIV (September, 1948), 252; Kellogg, *French Regime in Wisconsin,* 379.

19. Minutes of the Provincial Council, June 23, 1748, *Pennsylvania Colonial Records,*

V, 289–90; "Report of a Treaty at the Court House in Lancaster," *ibid.*, 307–14; "Message from the President and Council to the Assembly," *ibid.*, 329–30; Anson, *Miami Indians*, 48–49.

20. Charles de Raymond to the Marquis de Jonquiere, September 5, 1749, *Illinois Historical Collections*, XXIX, 110; Raymond to La Jonquiere, October 11, 1749, *ibid.*, 120–23. Raymond was the commander at Fort Miamis. La Jonquiere succeeded La Galissonniere as governor of New France.

21. A. A. Lambing (ed.), "Celoron's Journal," *Ohio Archaeological and Historical Publications*, XXIX, 335–96. Also see R. David Edmunds, "Pickawillany: French Military Power versus British Economics," *Western Pennsylvania Historical Magazine*, LVIII (April, 1975), 174–75.

22. Raymond to La Jonquiere, January 5, 1750, in Krauskopf, *Ouiatanon Documents*, 214; Raymond to La Jonquiere, May 22, 1750, *Illinois Historical Collections*, XXIX, 205–209; Nicholas Wainwright, *George Croghan, Wilderness Diplomat*, 30–31.

23. Raymond to La Jonquiere, May 14, 1750, *Illinois Historical Collections*, XXIX, 68; reports by Raymond, March–April, 1750, *ibid.*, 166–78; La Jonquiere to the French minister, September 20, 1750, *Wisconsin Historical Collections*, XVIII, 68; La Jonquiere to the French minister, September 17, 1751, *ibid.*, 84.

24. Celoron to Vaudreuil, August 4, 1751, *Illinois Historical Collections*, XXIX, 286; Celoron to Vaudreuil, April 23, 1751, *ibid.*, 247–48.

25. Examination of Morris Turner and Ralph Kilgore, *Pennsylvania Colonial Records*, V, 482–84; Benjamin Stoddart to Governor Hamilton, *ibid.*, 549–50. Turner and Kilgore were British traders captured by the French who later escaped and brought back news of the proposed raid to the British. Stoddart was the British commander at Oswego who learned of the expedition from French *coureurs de bois*.

26. La Jonquiere to Rouille, October 25, 1751, *Illinois Historical Collections*, XXIX, 419; La Jonquiere to Celeron, October 29, 1751, *ibid.*, 385–88. Also see Baron de Longueuil to the French minister, April 21, 1752, *Wisconsin Historical Collections*, XVIII, 107. Longueuil served as acting governor of Canada after La Jonquiere died on March 17, 1752, until August of the same year.

27. François Marchand des Ligneris to Vaudreuil, October 25, 1751, *Illinois Historical Collections*, XXIX, 416–17. Des Ligneris was the French commandant at Ouiatanon. Also see La Jonquiere to Rouille, October 29, 1751, *ibid.*, 417–21, and French minister to Ange du Quense, May 15, 1752, *Wisconsin Historical Collections*, XVIII, 119. Du Quense served as governor of Canada from 1752 to 1755.

28. Martin Kellogg to William Johnson, April 13, 1752, *Pennsylvania Colonial Records*, V, 574; Longueuil to the French minister, April 21, 1752, *Wisconsin Historical Collections*, XVIII, 110–11. Kellogg was a British trader.

29. Lawrence Henry Gipson, *The British Regime Before the American Revolution*, IV, 221.

30. *Wisconsin Historical Collections*, XVIII, 128–30 fnn. 67, 68; Trent, *Trent's Journal*, 86–89; Sewell Elias Slick, *William Trent and the West*, 19–20; Emily Blasingham, "The Miami Prior to the French and Indian War," *Ethnohistory*, II (Winter, 1955), 6.

31. Trent, *Trent's Journal*, 47–49; De Ligneris to unknown, October 3, 1752, in Krauskopf, *Ouiatanon Documents*, 218–19; Anson, *Miami Indians*, 52–53.

32. La Jonquierre to Rouille, September 16, 1751, *Illinois Historical Collections*, XXIX, 349; "Extracts from the Diary of Events, 1747," *Wisconsin Historical Collections*, XVII, 479; J. Joe Bauxar, "The Historic Period," in *Illinois Archaeology*,

Bulletin No. 1 of the Illinois Archaeological Survey, 54. The problem of internal dissension within Potawatomi villages is discussed in Clifton, "Potawatomi Leadership Roles," 15–27.

33. La Jonquiere to Rouille, September 25, 1751, *Illinois Historical Collections*, XXXIX, 359–60; La Jonquiere to Rouille, October 15, 1750, *Wisconsin Historical Collections*, XVIII, 84. Also see Emily Blasingham, "The Depopulation of the Illinois Indians," *Ethnohistory*, III (Fall, 1956), 204–206.

34. La Jonquiere to the French minister, September 25, 1751, *Wisconsin Historical Collections*, XVIII, 89.

35. Macarty to Vaudreuil, September 2, 1752, *Illinois Historical Collections*, XXIX, 654–55; Blasingham, "Depopulation of the Illinois," 207–209. The Cahokia and Michigamea were small tribes within the Illinois Confederacy.

36. Kellogg, *French Regime in Wisconsin*, 425; Peckham, *Colonial Wars*, 140.

37. "Augustin Grignon's Recollections," *Wisconsin Historical Collections*, III, 212; Kellogg, *French Regime in Wisconsin*, 425–26.

38. "Account of the Affair at the Belle Riviere, July 6–9, 1755," Potawatomi File, Great Lakes Indian Archives; Peckham, *Colonial Wars*, 143–44.

39. "Account of the Affair at the Belle Riviere," Potawatomi File, Great Lakes Indian Archives; Peckham, *Colonial Wars*, 145.

40. Stanley Pargellis, "Braddock's Defeat," *American Historical Review*, XLI (January, 1936), 257–59, 269; William A. Hunter, *Forts on the Pennsylvania Frontier, 1753–58*, 120.

41. Pargellis, "Braddock's Defeat," 263, 269; Peckham, *Colonial Wars*, 145–46.

42. "Account of the Affair at the Belle Riviere," Potawatomi File, Great Lakes Indian Archives; Peckham, *Colonial Wars*, 146–47.

43. Contrecoeur to Vaudreuil, July 26, 1755, Potawatomi File, Great Lakes Indian Archives; "Journal of Occurrences in Canada from October 1755, to June, 1756," *New York Colonial Documents*, X, 401; John H. Krenkel, "British Conquest of the Old Northwest," *Wisconsin Magazine of History*, XXXV (Autumn, 1951), 50.

44. Vaudreuil to Jean-Baptiste Machault d'Arnouville, August 8, 1756, *New York Colonial Documents*, X, 437; entry for November 21, 1756, in Montcalm's journal, *Wisconsin Historical Collections*, 164 fn. 6; Krenkel, "British Conquest," 49–50; Peckham, *Colonial Wars*, 151–59.

45. Kellogg, *French Regime in Wisconsin*, 430–31; Peckham, *Colonial Wars*, 51.

46. Conference between Vaudreuil and the Indians, 1756, *New York Colonial Documents*, X, 512; Kellogg, *French Regime in Wisconsin*, 431; Edward P. Hamilton (ed.), *Adventure in the Wilderness: The American Journals of Louis Antoine de Bougainville, 1755–1760*, 61.

47. Hamilton, *Adventure in the Wilderness*, 45–46.

48. *Ibid.*, 48–50, 55–61, 102, 105, 114.

49. *Ibid.*, 117–21, 131–32, 154; Kellogg, *French Regime in Wisconsin*, 432; James Smith, *An Account of the Remarkable Occurrences in the Life and Travels of Colonel James Smith*, 44.

50. Hamilton, *Adventure in the Wilderness*, 142–43.

51. *Ibid.* Also see Francis Parkman, *Montcalm and Wolfe*, II, 170–71.

52. Hamilton, *Adventure in the Wilderness*, 143–62; Parkman, *Montcalm and Wolfe*, II, 186–88.

53. Hamilton, *Adventure in the Wilderness*, 162–69; Parkman, *Montcalm and Wolfe*, II, 193.

54. Hamilton, *Adventure in the Wilderness*, 169–71; Parkman, *Montcalm and Wolfe*, II, 194–96; Peckham, *Colonial Wars*, 163.

55. Parkman, *Montcalm and Wolfe*, 197–201; Peckham, *Colonial Wars*, 163. After the massacre, Montcalm protected the survivors in the French camp for five days before delivering them to Fort Edward.

56. "Detail of the Campaign of 1757,.from the 30th of July to the 4th of September," *New York Colonial Documents*, X, 630; Montcalm's journal, *Wisconsin Historical Collections*, XVIII, 205; François Pouchot, *Memoir upon the Late War in North America Between the French and English*, I, 92.

57. Montcalm's journal, *Wisconsin Historical Collections*, XVIII, 205; Wheeler-Voegelin, "Before the Claims Commission: Royce Area 66," 212–13.

58. Nicholas Wainwright (ed.), "George Croghan's Journal, 1759–1763," *Pennsylvania Magazine of History*, LXXI (October, 1947), 322; François Pouchot, "Journal of the Siege of Fort Niagara," *New York Colonial Documents*, X, 987–82; Peckham, *Colonial Wars*, 181–82.

59. Pouchot, "Journal of the Siege of Fort Niagara," 986–90; Peckham, *Colonial Wars*, 182–83.

60. Wainwright, "George Croghan's Journal," 324, 336–40, 362–63; "List of the Indian Nations at the Pittsburgh Council, November 5, 1759," Potawatomi File, Great Lakes Indian Archives; "Minutes of a Conference Held in Pittsburgh," July, 1759, *Minutes of the Provincial Council of Pennsylvania*, VIII, 383–91; "At a Council Held in Philadelphia," December 4, 1759, *Pennsylvania Colonial Records*, VIII, 415–21.

61. George Croghan to Horatio Gates, May 20, 1760, Potawatomi File, Great Lakes Indian Archives; Wainwright, "George Croghan's Journal," 280–383; "At a Conference Held by the Honourable Brigadier General Monckton with the Western Indians," August 12, 1760, *Pennsylvania Archives, First Series*, III, 744–51. Also see "Indian Intelligence, Fort Pitt, June 17, 1760," Sylvester K. Stevens and Donald H. Kent (eds.), *The Papers of Henry Bouquet*, Vol. 21655, 94. These nineteen volumes are numbered 21643–21655. Some have two parts.

62. "Indian Conference at Detroit, December 3–5, 1760," Stevens and Kent, *Papers of Henry Bouquet*, Vol. 21655, 96–101; Wainwright, "Croghan's Journal," 394–95.

63. "Indian Conference at Detroit, December 3–5, 1760," Stevens and Kent, *Papers of Henry Bouquet*, Vol. 21655, 97–101.

CHAPTER FOUR

1. Wilbur R. Jacobs, *Wilderness Politics and Indian Gifts: The Northern Colonial Frontier, 1748–1763*, 52–55, 72–73; Howard H. Peckham, *Pontiac and the Indian Uprising*, 72–73.

2. Campbell to Bouquet, December 23, 1760, *Michigan Historical Collections*, XIX, 50.

3. Campbell to Bouquet, June 1, 1761, *Michigan Historical Collections*, XIX, 70; Peckham, *Pontiac*, 74–75; Anthony R. C. Wallace, *The Death and Rebirth of the Seneca*, 114–15.

4. Donald Campbell, "Report of an Indian Council near Detroit," July, 1761, in Stevens and Kent, *Papers of Henry Bouquet*, Vol. 2165, 125.

5. *Ibid.*, 126–27; Campbell to Bouquet, July 7, 1761, *Michigan Historical Collections*, XIX, 86–87.

6. Wainwright, "George Croghan's Journal," 412–13; Robert Monckton to Bouquet, July 13, 1761, *Michigan Historical Collections*, XIX, 94; Peckham, *Pontiac*, 76–78.

7. "Minutes of a Conference with the Indian Tribes at Detroit, September 9–11, 1761," in Alexander Flick *et al.* (eds.), *The Papers of Sir William Johnson*, III, 474–93;

Bouquet to Monckton, October 5, 1761, *Michigan Historical Collections*, XIX, 114; Peckham, *Pontiac*, 81.

8. L. H. Beeson, "Fort St. Joseph—The Mission, Trading Post and Fort Located About One Mile South of Niles, Michigan," *Michigan Historical Collections*, XXVII, 186; Peckham, *Pontiac*, 89–90.

9. William R. Riddell (ed.), "French Report on the Western Front," *Journal of the Illinois State Historical Society*, XXIV (October, 1931), 580; "Speech of the Puant Chief," August 20, 1760, Flick, *Papers of Sir William Johnson*, VI, 327; "Extract of a Letter to Governor Murray, Giving Some Account of the Indian Trade in the Upper Country," August 10, 1761, *Michigan Historical Collections*, XIX, 14; Peckham, *Pontiac*, 90. James Murray was acting governor of Canada in 1761.

10. Amherst to Bouquet, January 16, 1762, *Michigan Historical Collections*, XIX, 127–28; Campbell to Bouquet, July 3, 1762, *ibid.*, 153–54. Also see Campbell to Bouquet, August 26, 1762, in Stevens and Kent, *Papers of Henry Bouquet*, Vol. 21648, part 2, 74–75.

11. Thomas Hutchins, "A Tour from Fort Cumberland North Westward Round Part of the Lakes Erie, Huron, and Michigan, Including Parts of the Rivers St. Joseph, the Wabash, and the Miamis, with a Sketch of the Road from Thence by the Lower Shawnace Town to Fort Pitt" (manuscript), Huntingdon Library. A copy of this manuscript can be found in the Potawatomi File, Great Lakes Indian Archives. Also see entries for April 4–September 24, 1762, in Thomas Hutchins' journal, in Stevens and Kent, *Papers of Henry Bouquet*, Vol. 2165, 167–74.

12. Alexander McKee to Bouquet, November 8, 1762, in Stevens and Kent, *Papers of Henry Bouquet*, Vol. 21648, part 2, 158; Croghan to Bouquet, December 10, 1762, *ibid.*, 176–77; Peckham, *Pontiac*, 95–97. McKee was a trader from Pennsylvania who later became a British Indian agent.

13. Pierre Joseph Neyon, Sieur de Villiers to Jean Jacques D'Abbadie, December 1, 1763, *Wisconsin Historical Collections*, XVIII, 259–60. De Villiers was the commander at Fort Chartres. D'Abbadie was governor of Louisiana. Also see McKee to Bouquet, November 8, 1762, in Stevens and Kent, *Papers of Henry Bouquet*, Vol. 21648, part 2, 158; Croghan to Bouquet, December 10, 1762, *ibid.*, 176–77; Bouquet to Amherst, December 12, 1762, *ibid.*, Vol. 21634, 116–17; and Peckham, *Pontiac*, 102–103.

14. Entry for April 27, 1763, in Milo Milton Quaife (ed.), "The Journal of Pontiac's Conspiracy," *The Siege of Detroit in 1763*, 7–17. Although the exact authorship of this journal remains unknown, it probably was written by Robert Navarre, a French settler at Detroit. Also see Peckham, *Pontiac*, 107–11. Historians have disagreed over the role of Pontiac in the rebellion. Francis Parkman, in *The Conspiracy of Pontiac*, ascribes the entire conflict to the carefully laid plans of the Ottawa chief. Parkman indicated that Pontiac successfully agitated the western tribes against the British and then planned the attacks on British posts through a well-organized conspiracy. See *ibid.*, 153–55. Peckham indicates that the Ottawa exercised great influence over the Detroit tribes and planned the attack upon Detroit, but he does not believe that Pontiac organized a conspiracy throughout the Northwest. Wilbur Jacobs, in "Was the Pontiac Uprising a Conspiracy?" *Ohio State Archaeological and Historical Quarterly*, LIX (January, 1950), 26–37, also argues that there was no well-planned conspiracy, but sees Pontiac channeling Indian grievances into a war of independence against the British.

15. Quaife, "Journal of Pontiac's Conspiracy," 21–26; Thomas Hutchins, "A Tour from Fort Cumberland," Potawatomi File, Great Lakes Indian Archives; Wheeler-

Voegelin, "Before the Claims Commission: Royce Area 66," 275.

16. Quaife, "Journal of Pontiac's Conspiracy," 28–46; Peckham, *Pontiac*, 121–25; James MacDonald to Bouquet, July 12, 1763, *Michigan Historical Collections*, XIX, 213–14. MacDonald was an officer at Detroit. Peckham includes a good discussion of those people who possibly could have informed Gladwin of the plot.

17. Quaife, "Journal of Pontiac's Conspiracy," 59–61.

18. *Ibid.*, 65–67.

19. *Ibid.*, 86–88; "Copy of an Embassy Sent to the Illinois by the Indians at Detroit by the Couriers Godfrey and Chene," *Michigan Historical Collections*, XXVII, 644–45.

20. Quaife, "Journal of Pontiac's Conspiracy," 130 fn. 63; Cezar Cormick, "Intelligence from Detroit," in Stevens and Kent, *Papers of Henry Bouquet*, Vol. 21655, 204; Peckham, *Pontiac*, 145. Cormick was a trader at Detroit.

21. "Extract of a Court of Enquiry Held by Order of Major Henry Gladwin to Enquire into the Manner of the Taking of Forts St. Dusky, St. Josephs, Miamis, and Presqu' Isle," July 6, 1763, *Michigan Historical Collections*, XXVII, 636–37.

22. *Ibid.*; Peckham, *Pontiac*, 159; Richard Winston to English merchants at Detroit, June 19, 1763, Stevens and Kent, *Papers of Henry Bouquet*, Vol. 21655, 207–208. Winston was one of the British traders hidden by Chevalier. Chevalier evidently was playing a middle role between the Indians and the British. Although he resented the competition of British traders at Saint Joseph, he was afraid to become involved in the rebellion and hid the traders in order to gain the good will of Gladwin.

23. "Copy of Intelligence Brought to Fort Pitt by Mr. Calhoun, June 1, 1763," *Michigan Historical Collections*, XIX, 186; Macdonald to Bouquet, July 12, 1763, *ibid.*, 217; Edward Jenkins to Gladwin, June 1, 1763, *ibid.*, XXVII, 635–36; George Etherington to Gladwin, July 18, 1763, *Wisconsin Historical Collections*, XVIII, 255–56. Thomas Calhoun was a British trader. Jenkins was the commanding officer at Fort Ouiatanon. Etherington was the commanding officer at Michilimackinac.

24. Bouquet to Amherst, June 23, 1763, *Michigan Historical Collections*, XIX, 195; Johnson to Amherst, July 11, 1763, *ibid.*, 211–12; John Christie to Bouquet, July 10, 1763, *ibid.*, 209–10; Quaife, "Journal of Pontiac's Conspiracy," 121–22. Christie was commanding officer at Presque Isle.

25. Quaife, "Journal of Pontiac's Conspiracy," 101–10; Peckham, *Pontiac*, 156.

26. Christie to Lieutenant Francis Gordon, June 3, 1763, *Michigan Historical Collections*, XIX, 188–89; Peckham, *Pontiac*, 156. Gordon commanded at Fort Venango.

27. Cuyler's report quoted in Parkman, *Conspiracy of Pontiac*, 207–209 fn. 6; Christie to Gordon, June 3, 1763, *Michigan Historical Collections*, XIX, 188–89; MacDonald to Bouquet, July 12, 1763, *ibid.*, 216.

28. Quaife, "Journal of Pontiac's Conspiracy," 130–31; Peckham, *Pontiac*, 181.

29. Quaife, "Journal of Pontiac's Conspiracy," 135; Peckham, *Pontiac*, 184.

30. Quaife, "Journal of Pontiac's Conspiracy," 133–34; Peckham, *Pontiac*, 183–84.

31. Quaife, "Journal of Pontiac's Conspiracy," 137–38; Peckham, *Pontiac*, 184.

32. Quaife, "Journal of Pontiac's Conspiracy," 150–51; Peckham, *Pontiac*, 189; Parkman, *Conspiracy of Pontiac*, 221–22.

33. Quaife, "Journal of Pontiac's Conspiracy," 150–52; Parkman, *Conspiracy of Pontiac*, 222.

34. Quaife, "Journal of Pontiac's Conspiracy," 158–76.

35. Quaife, "Journal of Pontiac's Conspiracy," 179; Peckham, *Pontiac*, 196–97.

36. Quaife, "Journal of Pontiac's Conspiracy," 184–85; Peckham, *Pontiac*, 198. Crawford had been captured on the Wabash River in June. See Thomas Calhoun, "Indian Intelligence," May 27, 1763, *Michigan Historical Collections*, XIX, 186.

Abraham had been taken by the Hurons near Detroit on May 13. He feigned insanity, and the Hurons gave him to the Potawatomis.

37. Quaife, "Journal of Pontiac's Conspiracy," 185–86, 197–98.

38. Bouquet to Amherst, August 27, 1763, *Michigan Historical Collections*, XIX, 227; Quaife, "Journal of Pontiac's Conspiracy," 200.

39. Entries for August 11 and August 14, 1763, in Jehu Hay, "Diary of the Siege of Detroit, 1763–1765," William L. Clements Library, Ann Arbor, Michigan; Peckham, *Pontiac*, 205, 210.

40. Gladwin to Thomas Gage, April 12, 1764, Gage Papers, Clements Library; Peckham, *Pontiac*, 232.

41. De Villiers to the Indians, September 27, 1763, *Michigan Historical Collections*, XXVII, 653–54; Peckham, *Pontiac*, 240.

42. Erminie Wheeler-Voegelin and J. A. Jones, *Indians of Western Illinois and Southern Wisconsin*, 73; Peckham, *Pontiac*, 235.

43. Chevalier to Gladwin, November 24, 1763, Gage Papers, Clements Library; entry for February 23, 1764, in Hay, "Diary of the Siege of Detroit," Clements Library; Gage to William Johnson, April 25, 1764, Flick, *Papers of Sir William Johnson*, IV, 408–409.

44. Gladwin to Gage, March 24, 1764, Gage Papers, Clements Library; Gladwin to Gage, April 12, 1764, *ibid.*; George McDouall to Bouquet, March 24, 1764, Stevens and Kent, *Papers of Henry Bouquet*, Vol. 21650, part 2, 68.

45. Gladwin to Gage, June 7, 1764, Gage Papers, Clements Library; Dederick Brehm to Bouquet, May 1, 1764, Stevens and Kent, *Papers of Henry Bouquet*, Vol. 21650, part 1, 123. Lieutenant Brehm served at Detroit.

46. Gladwin to Gage, May 12, 1764, Gage Papers, Clements Library; Gage to the Earl of Halifax, July 21, 1764, *New York Colonial Documents*, VII, 656; Johnson to the boards of trade, August 30, 1764, *ibid.*, 648–49; "Nations at the General Meeting, July, 1764," Flick, *Papers of Sir William Johnson*, IV, 481.

47. Bouquet to Gage, August 27, 1764, *Michigan Historical Collections*, XXVII, 271–72; Peckham, *Pontiac*, 257–60.

48. Bradstreet to Gage, August 28, 1764, Gage Papers, Clements Library; Bradstreet to Gage, September 12, 1764, *ibid.*; "Congress with the Western Nations," September 7–10, 1764, Flick, *Papers of Sir William Johnson*, IV, 526–33.

49. Thomas Morris, "Journal of Captain Thomas Morris," in Reuben G. Thwaites (ed.), *Early Western Travels*, 1748–1846, I, 301–302, 323–24; John Montresor, "Journals of Captain John Montresor," Potawatomi File, Great Lakes Indian Archives; Louis St. Ange to D'Abbadie, August 12, 1764, *Illinois Historical Collections*, X, 293–96.

50. Entries for November 23–26, 1764, in Hay, "Diary of the Siege of Detroit," Clements Library; "Intelligence from Fort Pitt, December 20, 1764," Stevens and Kent, *Papers of Henry Bouquet*, Vol. 21655, 254–55; Johnson to the Lords of Trade, May 24, 1765, *New York Colonial Documents*, VII, 711.

51. Entry for December 14, 1764, in Hay, "Diary of the Siege of Detroit," Clements Library; "Conference with the Potawatomis, January 26, 1765," Gage Papers, *ibid.*; Gage to Halifax, April 27, 1765, Clarence E. Carter, *The Correspondence of General Thomas Gage with the Secretaries of State, 1763–1775*, I, 57.

52. Johnson to the Lords of Trade, May 24, 1765, *New York Colonial Documents*, VII, 711; St. Ange to D'Abbadie, April 7, 1765, *Illinois Historical Collections*, X, 468–71; St. Ange to D'Abbadie, February 21, 1765, *ibid.*, 439–41.

53. Fraser to Gage, May 26, 1765, Gage Papers, Clements Library; Peckham, *Pontiac*, 270–73.

54. Fraser to Gage, May 15, 1765, *Illinois Historical Collections*, X, 491–92; Fraser to Campbell, May 17, 1765, *ibid.*, 493–94; Fraser to unknown, May 17, 1765, Gage Papers, Clements Library.

55. George Croghan, "Croghan's Journal, 1765," in Thwaites, *Early Western Travels*, I, 126–48.

56. *Ibid.*, 153–61; Peckham, *Pontiac*, 288.

57. Campbell to Gage, August 2, 1765, Gage Papers, Clements Library; Croghan, "Croghan's Journal," 164–66. The two Potawatomis taken hostage by Campbell at Detroit in January, 1765, were released at this time.

58. "Proceedings at a Conference with Pontiac and Chiefs of the Ottawas, Pautawattamies, Hurons and Chippewaes Begun Tuesday, July 23, 1766," *New York Colonial Documents*, VII, 854–67; Peckham, *Pontiac*, 288–90.

CHAPTER FIVE

1. Statement by Hugh Crawford, July 22, 1765, *Illinois Historical Collections*, X, 484; speech by Machioquisse, August 14, 1786, Flick, *Papers of Sir William Johnson*, XII, 585–86; "Report of the Various Indian Tribes Receiving Presents in the District of Ylinoa or Illinois, 1769," Louise Houck (ed.), *The Spanish Regime in Missouri*, I, 44; *Wisconsin Historical Collections*, XVIII, 398 fn. 97; Wheeler-Voegelin and Jones, *Indians of Western Illinois*, 72–77; Wheeler-Voegelin and Stout, *Indians of Illinois and Northwestern Indiana*, 112–13.

2. Entry for August 31, 1766, in Harry Gordon's journal, *Illinois Historical Collections*, XI, 300; Croghan to Gage, January 16, 1767, *ibid.*, 487–89; Johnson to Gage, January 29, 1767, *ibid.*, 503. Gordon was a British officer in Illinois. Also see Turnbull to Gage, October 19, 1766, Gage Papers, Clements Library, and Johnson to Gage, December 12, 1766, Flick, *Papers of Sir William Johnson*, XII, 227–28.

3. Campbell to Gage, April 10, 1766, Gage Papers, Clements Library; Campbell to Johnson, February 24, 1766, *Illinois Historical Collections*, XI, 157–58.

4. Campbell to Gage, April 18, 1766, Gage Papers, Clements Library; Turnbull to Gage, May 12, 1767, *ibid.*; Gage to Johnson, June 16, 1766, Flick, *Papers of Sir William Johnson*, V, 271–72; Robert Rogers to Johnson, September 23, 1766, *ibid.*, XII, 193–94; Edward Cole to Johnson, June 30, 1766, *Illinois Historical Collections*, XI, 330. Cole was an Indian trader in Illinois.

5. Turnbull to Gage, August 3, 1767, Gage Papers, Clements Library; Jehu Hay to Croghan, August 13–August 17, 1767, Flick, *Papers of Sir William Johnson*, V, 618–21; Hay to Croghan, August 28, 1767, *ibid.*, 643–44. Also see George Pare, "The St. Joseph Mission," *Mississippi Valley Historical Review*, XVII (June, 1930), 46.

6. Howard H. Peckham (ed.), *George Croghan's Journal of His Trip to Detroit in 1767*, 40–45; Turnbull to Gage, February 23, 1768, Gage Papers, Clements Library; Hay to Croghan, February 17, 1768, *ibid.*

7. Turnbull to Croghan, March 1, 1768, Gage Papers, Clements Library; Gordon Forbes to Gage, June 23, 1768, *ibid.*; Clarence Edwin Carter, *Great Britain and the Illinois Country, 1763–1774*, 63; John Campbell to Baynton, Wharton, and Clark, April 8, 1768, Microfilm Roll 3, 845–46, Baynton, Wharton, and Morgan Papers, Pennsylvania State Archives, Harrisburg. Captain Forbes commanded at Fort Chartres. Campbell was a trader. Baynton, Wharton, and Morgan was a trading company located in Philadelphia.

8. Entries for March 25–28, 1771, in "John Wilkins' Journal of Transactions and Presents Given to the Indians," Potawatomi File, Great Lakes Indian Archives; Gage

to Johnson, August 14, 1771, Flick, *Papers of Sir William Johnson*, VIII, 224–25; Henry Basset to Gage, December 24, 1772, *ibid.*, 672–73; Gage to Johnson, March 31, 1773, *ibid.*, 749. Basset assumed command at Detroit in 1772.

9. "Proceedings of Sir William Johnson with the Six Nations, April 9, 1773," *New York Colonial Documents*, VII, 367–68; Henry Basset to General Frederick Haldimand, September 30, 1773, *Michigan Historical Collections*, XIX, 313; "Speech of the Potawatomi Chiefs at Detroit, May 22, 1773," Flick, *Papers of Sir William Johnson*, VIII, 803–805; Pedro Piernas to Don Luis de Unzaga, July 30, 1772, in Lawrence Kinniard (ed.), *Spain in the Mississippi Valley, 1765–1794: Annual Report of the American Historical Association for 1945*, I, 206. Basset succeeded Turnbull as commander at Detroit. Haldimand succeeded Gage as commander in chief of British forces in North America. Piernas commanded Spanish forces at St. Louis. Unzaga was governor of Louisiana.

10. John Porteous to unknown, August 16, 1767, John Porteus Papers, Burton Collection; "The Road from Detroit to the Illinois," in Jacob Piatt Dunn (ed.), *Documents Relating to the French Settlements on the Wabash*, 435–38. Also see Wheeler-Voegelin, "Before the Indian Claims Commission: Royce Area 66," 274.

11. Hamilton to the Earl of Dartmouth, August 29–September 2, 1776, *Michigan Historical Collections*, X, 269–70; John D. Barnhart (ed.), *Henry Hamilton and George Rogers Clark in the American Revolution*, 28; "Information from John Hamilton and John Bradley to the Commissioners, September 13, 1776," Potawatomi File, Great Lakes Indian Archives. Hamilton and Bradley were American agents among the Delawares.

12. "Message from the Delaware Council, February 26, 1777," Potawatomi File, Great Lakes Indian Archives; George Germain to Haldimand, March 26, 1777, *Michigan Historical Collections*, IX, 347–48. Lord George Germain was the British secretary of state. Also see Barnhart, *Henry Hamilton and George Rogers Clark*, 29, and Jack M. Sosin, *The Revolutionary Frontier, 1763–1783*, 109.

13. Hamilton to unknown, June 15, 1777, *Michigan Historical Collections*, X, 277; "Extract of a Council Held at Detroit, June, 1777," *Wisconsin Historical Collections*, XXII, 7–13. Also see John D. Barnhart (ed.), "Lieutenant Governor Henry Hamilton's Apologia," *Indiana Magazine of History*, LII (December, 1956), 383–96.

14. Barnhart, *Henry Hamilton and George Rogers Clark*, 33; Sosin, *Revolutionary Frontier*, 109–11; "Proclamation by Henry Hamilton," January 5, 1778, Potawatomi File, Great Lakes Indian Archives.

15. "Orders of Council, January 2, 1778," *Illinois Historical Collections*, VIII, 33; Patrick Henry to Clark, January 2, 1778, *ibid.*, 34–35; Clarence Walworth Alvord, *The Illinois Country, 1673–1818*, 324–25. Also see Sosin, *Revolutionary Frontier*, 116–17.

16. Clark to the inhabitants of Vincennes, July 13, 1778, *Illinois Historical Collections*, VIII, 50–53; Alvord, *Illinois Country*, 326–28.

17. Hamilton to Haldimand, September 5, 1778, *Michigan Historical Collections*, IX, 466; *Wisconsin Historical Collections*, XVIII, xix. Also see William H. English, *Conquest of the Country Northwest of the Ohio, 1778–1783, and the Life of George Rogers Clark*, I, 205; Clark to George Mason, November 19, 1779, *ibid.*, 420–21. Mason was a resident of Virginia.

18. Arent Schuyler De Peyster to unknown, June 13, 1777, *Michigan Historical Collections*, X, 276–77; "Augustin Grignon's Recollections," *Wisconsin Historical Collections*, III, 229; Sieur de Rocheblave to Edward Abbott, June 1, 1777, in Edward G. Mason, *Early Chicago and Illinois*, 392–93. Also see Clark to Mason, November 19, 1779, in English, *Conquest and Clark*, I, 423–26. De Peyster was the British commander

at Mackinac. Rocheblave was a British Indian agent. Abbott was the British commander at Vincennes.

19. De Peyster to unknown, June 6, 1777, *Michigan Historical Collections*, X, 275; Patrick Henry to Virginia delegates in Congress, November 16, 1778, *Illinois Historical Collections*, VIII, 72; Clark to John Brown, 1791, *ibid.*, 252–55; Louise Phelps Kellogg, *The British Regime in Wisconsin and the Old Northwest*, 155–56.

20. Hamilton's journal, in Barnhart, *Henry Hamilton and George Rogers Clark*, 104.

21. "Council at Detroit," June 14, 1778, *Michigan Historical Collections*, IX, 442–52; Hamilton to Haldimand, September 22, 1778, *ibid.*, 479; De Peyster to Haldimand, August 15, 1778, *ibid.*, 368; Hamilton's journal, in Barnhart, *Henry Hamilton and George Rogers Clark*, 104.

22. De Peyster to Langlade and Gautier, October 26, 1778, Edward E. Ayer Manuscripts, Newberry Library, Chicago; De Peyster to Haldimand, October 24, 1778, *Michigan Historical Collections*, IX, 374–76; De Peyster to Haldimand, January 29, 1779, *ibid.*, 377–78.

23. "Extract of a Council Between Hamilton and the Indians," September 24, 1778, *Michigan Historical Collections*, IX, 482–83; Hamilton to Haldimand, November 1, 1778, *Wisconsin Historical Collections*, XI, 178–81; Hamilton to Haldimand, December 4, 1778, *Illinois Historical Collections*, I, 220; Hamilton's journal, in Barnhart, *Henry Hamilton and George Rogers Clark*, 114–49.

24. Hamilton to Haldimand, December 18, 1778, *Illinois Historical Collections*, I, 232; Hamilton to Haldimand, January 24, 1779, *ibid.*, 393; Hamilton's journal, in Barnhart, *Henry Hamilton and George Rogers Clark*, 112, 156–57, 171–73.

25. Hamilton to John Stuart, January 13, 1779, quoted in Robert R. Rea, "Henry Hamilton and West Florida," *Indiana Magazine of History*, LIV (March, 1958), 55; De Peyster to Haldimand, March 29, 1779, *Wisconsin Historical Collections*, XI, 125; Clark to John Brown, 1791, *Illinois Historical Collections*, VIII, 281–89; Hamilton's journal, in Barnhart, *Henry Hamilton and George Rogers Clark*, 177–88.

26. John Long, "John Long's Journal," in Thwaites, *Early Western Travels*, II, 181–84; "Memorial and Petition by Mathew Lessey and Others," 1779, *Michigan Historical Collections*, X, 367; Joseph Bowman to Mechikigie, April 20, 1779, *Illinois Historical Collections*, VIII, 311–13; Clark to Nanalobi (Nanaquiba), April 20, 1779, *ibid.*, 313–15. The petitioners were traders from Mackinac whose goods were seized by the Potawatomis. Major Bowman was in command of American forces at Cahokia. Mechkigie was a chief of the Potawatomis at Chicago.

27. Bowman to Clark, May 28, 1779, *Illinois Historical Collections*, II, 610; Clark to Brown, 1791, *ibid.*, VIII, 295–97; Chevalier to Haldimand, February 28, 1779, *Michigan Historical Collections*, XIX, 375.

28. Lieutenant Colonel Mason Bolton to Haldimand, May 20, 1779, *Michigan Historical Collections*, XIX, 415–16; De Peyster to Haldimand, May 2, 1779, *ibid.*, IX, 379–80; De Peyster to Haldimand, June 1, 1779, *Wisconsin Historical Collections*, XI, 133; Clark to Brown, 1791, *Illinois Historical Collections*, VIII, 300. Also see Kellogg, *British Regime in Wisconsin*, 159. Bolton was a British officer at Niagara.

29. De Peyster to Langlade, July 1, 1779, *Wisconsin Historical Collections*, XVIII, 375–76; De Peyster to Haldimand, July 9, 1779, *ibid.*, 391.

30. "Lieutenant Bennet's Report," *ibid.*, 398.

31. *Ibid.*, 399; "Council Between Bennet and the Potawatomis," August 3, 1779, *Michigan Historical Collections*, X, 348–53.

32. "Lieutenant Bennet's Report," *Wisconsin Historical Collections*, XVIII, 398–

401; Bennet to De Peyster, August 9, 1779, *ibid.*, 392–93.

33. "Remarks on Board His Majesty's Sloop *Felicity* by Samuel Roberts on Piloting Her on Lake Michigan," *Wisconsin Historical Collections*, XI, 210–11; Kellogg, *British Regime in Wisconsin*, 160.

34. Thomas Quirk to Clark, August 22, 1779, *Illinois Historical Collections*, VIII, 359; Clark to Jefferson, September 23, 1779, *ibid.*, 364–66; Chevalier to unknown, March 13, 1780, *Michigan Historical Collections*, X, 380–81. Quirk was a captain in the Illinois-Virginia regiment of volunteers.

35. James A. James, "The Significance of the Attack on St. Louis, 1780," *Proceedings of the Mississippi Valley Historical Association*, II, 205–206.

36. Pierre Provost to Clark, February 20, 1780, *Illinois Historical Collections*, VIII, 394–95; John Montgomery to Clark, May 30, 1780, Potawatomi File, Great Lakes Indian Archives; Chevalier to unknown, March 13, 1780, *Michigan Historical Collections*, X, 380–81. Provost was a French trader sympathetic to the American cause. Montgomery was the commander of American forces in Illinois.

37. Lieutenant Governor Patrick Sinclair to Haldimand, July 8, 1780, *Michigan Historical Collections*, IX, 558; Sinclair to Haldimand, July 30, 1780, *ibid.*, 563; James, "Attack on St. Louis," 209–10. Sinclair became commander at Mackinac in 1779 after De Peyster was transferred to Detroit.

38. Kellogg, *British Regime in Wisconsin*, 169; Sinclair to Bolton, June 4, 1780, *Michigan Historical Collections*, XIX, 529–30.

39. Proclamation by Montgomery, Cato, Winston, and St. Germain, May 6, 1780, *Illinois Historical Collections*, I, 456–57; Sinclair to Haldimand, July 8, 1780, *Michigan Historical Collections*, IX, 558. Winston and Cato were citizens of Kaskaskia. Jean St. Germain was a French official sent to the United States to keep the Indians pro-American.

40. Chevalier to unknown, April 30, 1780, *Michigan Historical Collections*, X, 391–93; De Peyster to Bolton, May 16, 1780, *ibid.*, XIX, 519–20; De Peyster to Haldimand, May 17, 1780, *ibid.*, X, 395–96; Theodore Calvin Pease, "The Revolution at Crisis in the West," *Journal of the Illinois State Historical Society*, XXIII (January, 1931), 676–77.

41. De Peyster to Sinclair, May 18, 1780, *Michigan Historical Collections*, IX, 582–83; De Peyster to Haldimand, June 1, 1780, *ibid.*, X, 398–99.

42. De Peyster to Bolton, July 6, 1780, *Michigan Historical Collections*, XIX, 540; De Peyster to Haldimand, August 31, 1780, *ibid.*, X, 424; Joseph Louise Ainse to Sinclair, June 30, 1780, *ibid.*, 406. Ainse was a British Indian agent.

43. De Peyster to Sinclair, September 17, 1780, *Michigan Historical Collections*, IX, 617; Sinclair to Haldimand, August 2, 1780, *ibid.*, 569–70; memorial by Ainse, October 5, 1780, *ibid.*, X, 435–37. Volumes X and XI of the *Michigan Historical Collections* contain extensive correspondence regarding the removal of Chevalier.

44. De Peyster to Haldimand, January 8, 1781, *Michigan Historical Collections*, X, 450–51; Sinclair to Captain Robert Matthews, February 23, 1781, *ibid.*, IX, 629. Matthews was Haldimand's secretary. Also see Arthur Clinton Boggess, *The Settlement of Illinois, 1778–1830*, 37–38.

45. Francisco Cruzat to Governor Bernado Galvez, November 13, 1780, in Kinniard, *Spain in the Mississippi Valley*, I, 397; Cruzat to Galvez, January 10, 1781, quoted in Lawrence Kinniard, "The Spanish Expedition Against Fort St. Joseph in 1781, A New Interpretation," *Mississippi Valley Historical Review*, XIX (September, 1932), 187–89. Much has been written on the expedition and the reasons behind it. See Clarence M. Alvord, "The Conquest of St. Joseph Michigan, by the Spaniards in

1781," *Missouri Historical Review*, II (July, 1908), 195–210, and Frederick J. Taggart, "The Capture of St. Joseph, Michigan, by the Spaniards in 1781," *Missouri Historical Review*, V (July, 1911), 214–28.

46. Cruzat to Don Estevan Miro, August 6, 1781, Kinniard, *Spain in the Mississippi Valley*, I, 431–32. Miro was acting governor of Louisiana.

47. *Ibid.*, 432–34.

48. "Indian Council at Detroit," March 11, 1781, *Michigan Historical Collections*, X, 453–55.

49. De Peyster to Alexander McKee, May 8, 1780, *Michigan Historical Collections*, X, 394; "Indian Conference at Detroit," August 11, 1781, *ibid.*, 506–508; Andrew Thompson to De Peyster, September 21, 1781, *ibid.*, 515–16; "Indian Council at Detroit," May 15, 1782, *ibid.*, 576–78. Thompson was a captain among Butler's Rangers.

50. De Peyster to McKee, June 11, 1782, *Michigan Historical Collections*, X, 584; De Peyster to McKee, June 13, 1782, *ibid.*, 586; Randolph C. Downes, *Council Fires on the Upper Ohio*, 273–74.

51. Consul Wilshire Butterfield, *History of the Girtys*, 167–75; Reginald Horsman, *Matthew Elliott, British Indian Agent*, 36–39.

52. Antoine Chesne to De Peyster, August 16, 1782, *Michigan Historical Collections*, X, 628; Beverly W. Bond, Jr., *The Foundations of Ohio*, 235; James Alton James, *The Life of George Rogers Clark*, 268–71; Butterfield, *History of the Girtys*, 195–98. Chesne was a British Indian agent.

53. De Peyster to Haldimand, September 4, 1782, *Michigan Historical Collections*, X, 634; Butterfield, *History of the Girtys*, 198. Estimates of the losses suffered by both sides in the Battle of the Blue Licks vary greatly. James, in *Life of Clark*, 274, states that the British and Indians lost only 7 men, but agrees that the Americans suffered about 70 killed. Jack Sosin, in *Revolutionary Frontier*, 140, indicated that the British and Indians killed 140 Americans.

54. "Indian Council at Detroit," April 24, 1783, in Arent Schuyler De Peyster, *Miscellanies by an Officer, 1774–1813*, II, 12–14.

55. "Copy of a Report by Ephriam Douglass to the Secretary of War, 1783," *Pennsylvania Archives, First Series*, X, 83–90; De Peyster to Brigadier General Allen MacLean, July 7, 1783, *Michigan Historical Collections*, XX, 138; MacLean to De Peyster, July 8, 1783, *ibid.*, 138–39. MacLean was in command at Niagara. Also see Horsman, *Matthew Elliott*, 42–43.

56. "Minutes of the Transactions with Indians at Sandusky," August 26–September 7, 1783, *Michigan Historical Collections*, XX, 174–183.

57. The Potawatomi word for the English was "Sauganash."

CHAPTER SIX

1. Entry for October 15, 1783, in Gailland Hunt (ed.), *Journals of the Continental Congress, 1774–1789*, XXV, 680–95. The best discussion of American Indian policy during this period can be found in Reginald Horseman, *Expansion and American Indian Policy, 1783–1812*.

2. Downes, *Council Fires*, 289–97; entry for August 8, 1785, in David I. Bushnell, ed., "Journal of Samuel Montgomery," *Mississippi Valley Historical Review*, II (September, 1915), 264; "Copy of a Speech of Peteasuva to the American Messengers," November 8, 1785, *Michigan Historical Collections*, XXIV, 24–25. Montgomery was an American messenger sent to the Indians. Peteasuva was a Shawnee chief.

3. Downes, *Council Fires*, 279–82.

4. Arthur Campbell to Patrick Henry, May 21, 1785, in William P. Walker *et al.* (eds.), *Calendar of the Virginia State Papers and Other Manuscripts,* IV, 30; Cruzat to Miro, July 19, 1786, in Kinniard, *Spain in the Mississippi Valley,* I, 173–74; John Reynolds, *Pioneer History of Illinois,* 153; John Burnett to John Sayer, June 26, 1786, in Wilbur M. Cunningham (ed.), *Letter Book of William Burnett,* 14; Downes, *Council Fires,* 298. Campbell was a citizen of Kentucky. Burnett was a trader among the Potawatomis on the Saint Joseph. Sayer was an agent for a merchandising firm in Montreal.

5. "Information of Captain Teunise," July 6, 1786, Josiah Harmar Papers, Clements Library: "Report by the United States in Congress Assembled," October 20, 1786, *Pennsylvania Archives, First Series,* XI, 72–73; "Speech of the United Indian Nations, at Their Confederate Council, November 28–December 18, 1786," *American State Papers: Indian Affairs,* I, 8–9. Captain Teunise was a Delaware Indian.

6. David Duncan to Harmar, June 17, 1787, Harmar Papers, Clements Library; "Report of the Secretary of War to Congress, July 10, 1787," in Clarence Edwin Carter (ed.), *The Territorial Papers of the United States,* II, 31–35; secretary of Congress to Governor St. Clair, October 26, 1787, *ibid.,* 78–79. Duncan was a Pennsylvania trader.

7. St. Clair to the secretary of war, January 27, 1788, in Carter, *Territorial Papers,* II, 89–90; St. Clair to the secretary of war, July 5, 1788, *ibid.,* 119–20. Also see Thomas Hughes, *A Journal of Thomas Hughes,* 164. Hughes was a British soldier stationed at Detroit.

8. St. Clair to Knox, December 13, 1788, in William Henry Smith (ed.), *The St. Clair Papers,* II, 106; Harmer to Knox, January 13, 1788, Harmer Papers, Clements Library; Ebenezer Denny, "Military Journal of Major Ebenezer Denny," in *Memoirs of the Historical Society of Pennsylvania,* VII, 331–34. The treaties can be found in Charles Kappler, ed., *Indian Treaties, 1778–1883,* II, 18–25. Denny was an American military officer.

9. St. Clair to the secretary of war, January 18, 1789, Smith, *St. Clair Papers,* II, 108–109; Lord Dorchester to Lord Sydney, June 25, 1789, *Michigan Historical Collections,* XII, 10; Lord Dorchester to Lord Sydney, July 15, 1789, *ibid.,* 11. Lord Dorchester, or Guy Carleton, was governor of Canada. Thomas Townshend, or Lord Sydney, was secretary of state for the Home Department, 1783–89.

10. John Francis Hamtramck to Harmar, March 28, 1789, in Gayle Thornbrough (ed.), *Outpost on the Wabash,* 159; William Burnett to Mr. Hand, February 2, 1790, in Cunningham, *Letter Book of William Burnett,* 34. Also see Milo Milton Quaife (ed.), "Henry Hay's Journal from Detroit to the Miami River," in *Proceedings of the State Historical Society of Wisconsin at its Sixty-Second Annual Meeting,* 251. Both Hand and Hay were British traders at Detroit.

11. Secretary of war to Harmar, December 19, 1789, Harmar Papers, Clements Library; St. Clair to Hamtramck, January 23, 1790, in Smith, *St. Clair Papers,* II, 130; Hamtramck to Harmar, March 17, 1790, Thornbrough, *Outpost on the Wabash,* 222–25; "Antoine Gamelin's Journal," *American State Papers: Indian Affairs,* I, 93–94. Gamelin was one of the messengers dispatched up the Wabash.

12. James Wilkinson to Harmar, April 7, 1790, Harmar Papers, Clements Library; Hamtramck to Harmar, May 16, 1790, *ibid.;* John Cleve Symmes to Jonathan Dayton, April 30, 1790, in Beverly W. Bond, Jr. (ed.), *The Correspondence of John Cleve Symmes,* 126–27; Jacob Burnet, *Notes on the Early Settlement of the Northwestern Territory,* 83–91. Both Symmes and Dayton were land speculators in Ohio.

13. St. Clair to Winthrop Sargent, June 10, 1790, Carter, *Territorial Papers,* III,

311; St. Clair to the secretary of war, August 23, 1790, *American State Papers: Indian Affairs*, I, 92–93; Harmar to Hamtramck, July 15, 1790, Thornbrough, *Outpost on the Wabash*, 236–38. Sargent was St. Clair's secretary.

14. Hamtramck to Harmar, August 2, 1790, Harmar Papers, Clements Library; Sargent to Hamtramck, July 16, 1790, Carter, *Territorial Papers*, III, 320–21; Sargent to St. Clair, August 17, 1790, *ibid.*, II, 300–301.

15. "St. Clair to the Chiefs and Warriors of the Ottawa Nations," October 7, 1790, *Michigan Historical Collections*, XXIV, 101–102; Anson, *Miami Indians*, 114–15.

16. Denny, "Military Journal," 348–50; Harmar to St. Clair, October 18, 1790, Northwest Territory Papers, Indiana Historical Society Library; Paul Woehrman, *At the Headwaters of the Maumee: A History of the Forts of Fort Wayne*, 31–32.

17. Elliott to McKee, October 23, 1790, *Michigan Historical Collections*, XXIV, 108–109; journal of Captain John Armstrong, quoted in Basil Meek, "General Harmar's Expedition," *Ohio Archaeological and Historical Quarterly*, XX (January, 1911), 83–84. Armstrong commanded the regulars accompanying Hardin.

18. Diary of General Harmar, Harmar Papers, Draper Manuscripts, 2W343; Information of Captain Matthew Elliott, October 28, 1790, *Michigan Historical Collections*, XXIV. 133–34; Francis Paul Prucha, *The Sword of the Republic: The United States Army on the Frontier, 1783–1846*, 21.

19. Prucha, *Sword of the Republic*, 21.

20. Hamtramck to Harmar, November 2, 1790, Thornbrough, *Outpost on the Wabash*, 259–64; Hamtramck to Harmar, Harmar Papers, Draper Manuscripts, 2W372; Hamtramck to Harmar, September 21, 1790, Harmar Papers, Clements Library; Hamtramck to Harmar, November 28, 1790, *ibid.*

21. Hiram Beckwith, "Fort Wayne Manuscript," Potawatomi File, Great Lakes Indian Archives; Burnet, *Notes on the Northwestern Territory*, 111–12; Butterfield, *History of the Girtys*, 249–55; William Burnett to Andrew Todd, February 6, 1791, Cunningham, *Letter Book of William Burnett*, 45; Burnett to Hand, February 6, 1791, *ibid.*, 47–48. Todd was a merchant in Montreal.

22. Entries for March 9–April 7, 1791, in "Journal of What Happened at the Miamis and the Glaize with the Ouias and Piconns," *Michigan Historical Collections*, XXIV, 220–22; Reynolds, *Pioneer History of Illinois*, 175; Hamtramck to Sargent, Winthrop Sargent Papers, Massachusetts Historical Society, Boston (microfilm); Symmes to Dayton, June 19, 1791, Bond, *Correspondence of Symmes*, 143.

23. Report of Brigadier General Scott, June 28, 1791, *American State Papers: Indian Affairs*, I, 131–32; Lieutenant Colonel–commandant Wilkinson's Report, *ibid.*, 133–35; R. David Edmunds, "Wea Participation in the Northwest Indian Wars, 1790–1795," *The Filson Club History Quarterly*, XLVI (July, 1972), 247–49.

24. "McKee's Speech to the Indians," July 1, 1791, in Ernest A. Cruikshank (ed.), *The Correspondence of Lieutenant Governor John Graves Simcoe*, I, 369; Alured Clark to Simcoe, August 17, 1791, *ibid.*, 55. Simcoe was lieutenant governor of Upper Canada. Also see Detroit merchants to Johnson, August 10, 1791, *Michigan Historical Collections*, XXIV, 306–307; "Lord Dorchester's Speech to the Indians," August 15, 1791, in *Collections of the Massachusetts Historical Society, Third Series*, V, 159–63; Horsman, *Matthew Elliott*, 66–67.

25. Instructions by Henry Knox, March 21, 1791, *Michigan Historical Collections*, XXIV, 187–97; Downes, *Council Fires*, 317.

26. McKee to Thomas Smith, July 15, 1791, *Michigan Historical Collections*, XXIV, 86; William Darke to Mrs. Sarah Darke, November 1, 1791, *ibid.*, 231–33; Milo Milton Quaife (ed.), "A Picture of the First United States Army: The Journal of Captain

Samuel Newman," *Wisconsin Magazine of History*, II (September, 1918), 44–73; Frazer Wilson, "St. Clair's Defeat," *Ohio Archaeological and Historical Quarterly*, XI (July, 1902), 36. Both Darke and Newman served under St. Clair.

27. "Winthrop Sargent's Diary While with General Arthur St. Clair's Expedition Against the Indians," *Ohio Archaeological and Historical Quarterly*, XXXIII (July, 1924), 238–52; St. Clair to the secretary of war, November 9, 1791, *American State Papers*, I, 136–37.

28. Simon Girty to McKee, October 28, 1791, *Michigan Historical Collections*, XXIV, 329–30; Butterfield, *History of the Girtys*, 261; Beckwith, "Fort Wayne Manuscript," Potawatomi File, Great Lakes Indian Archives.

29. "Winthrop Sargent's Diary," 257–58; St. Clair to the secretary of war, November 9, 1791, *American State Papers: Indian Affairs*, I, 137; Wilson, "St. Clair's Defeat," 39.

30. "Winthrop Sargent's Diary," 258–62; St. Clair to the secretary of war, November 9, 1791, *American State Papers: Indian Affairs*, I, 137–38; Sargent to St. Clair, February 5, 1792, Sargent Papers, Massachusetts Historical Society.

31. "Causes of the Failure of the Expedition Against the Indians in 1791, Under the Command of Major General St. Clair," *American State Papers: Military Affairs*, I, 36–38; Francis Vigo to Winthrop Sargent, April 1, 1792, Sargent Papers, Massachusetts Historical Society; Prucha, *Sword of the Republic*, 26. Vigo was a merchant at Vincennes.

32. Instructions to Captain Peter Pond and William Steedman, January 9, 1792, *American State Papers: Indian Affairs*, I, 227; Wilkinson to the Indians, April 3, 1792, Ayer Manuscripts, Newberry Library; Henry Knox to Captain Alexander Trueman, April 3, 1792, *Michigan Historical Collections*, XXIV, 414–16; speech by Knox to the Indians, April 4, 1792, *ibid.*, 394–96; Woehrmann, *At the Headwaters of the Maumee*, fnn. 38–39; Butterfield, *History of the Girtys*, 265. Pond, Steedman, and Trueman were messengers sent to the Indians.

33. Major John Smith to Captain François Le Maistre, October 20, 1790, *Michigan Historical Collections*, XXIV, 108; "Statement by Major John Smith Relative to Indians near Detroit," January 23, 1791, *ibid.*, 167; "Indian Speech to Major Hamtramck," no date, *American State Papers: Indian Affairs*, I, 241. Smith was a British officer stationed at Detroit. Le Maistre was a British officer stationed at Quebec.

34. "A Journal of the Proceedings at a Council Held with the Indians of the Wabash and Illinois at Post Vincents, by Brigadier General Putnam," in Rowena Buell (ed.), *The Memoirs of Rufus Putnam*, 335–62; "List of the Signers of the 1792 Treaty," Potawatomi File, Great Lakes Indian Archives; "A Treaty of Peace and Friendship," *American State Papers: Indian Affairs*, I, 338; Wheeler-Voegelin and Jones, *Indians of Western Illinois and Southern Wisconsin*, 103–104.

35. Dwight Smith, "Wayne's Peace with the Indians of the Old Northwest, 1795," *Ohio Archaeological and Historical Quarterly*, LIX (July, 1950), 244; John Jordan (ed.), "Narrative of John Heckewelder's Journey to the Wabash in 1792," *Pennsylvania Magazine of History and Biography*, XII, No. 2 (1888), 173–84; Wheeler-Voegelin and Jones, *Indians of Western Illinois and Southern Wisconsin*, 104–105.

36. Instructions to Captain Hendrick Aupaumut, Chief of the Stockbridge Indians, May 8, 1792, *American State Papers: Indian Affairs*, I, 233; "Proceedings of a General Council of the Several Indian Nations . . . at the Glaize," September 30, 1792, Cruikshank, *Correspondence of Simcoe*, I, 218–29; "Journal of William Johnson," October, 1792, *Michigan Historical Collections*, XXIV, 470–72; Downes, *Council Fires*, 321.

37. Western Indians to Washington, Cruikshank, *Correspondence of Simcoe*, I, 283–84; speech by Knox to the Indians, December 12, 1792, *Michigan Historical Collections*, XXIV, 518–19; John Adair to James Wilkinson, November 6, 1792, *American State Papers: Indian Affairs*, I, 335; Hiram Beckwith, "Fort Wayne Manuscript," Potawatomi File, Great Lakes Indian Archives; deposition by Joseph Collins, February 16, 1793, *ibid.* Colonel John Adair led the Kentuckians at the battle near Fort St. Clair. Collins was an American spy among the Potawatomis.

38. Instruction to Lincoln, Randolph, and Pickering, April 26, 1793, *American State Papers: Indian Affairs*, I, 340–42; Washington to the heads of departments, March 22, 1793, Carter, *Territorial Papers*, II, 447–49; Secretary of war to the Indian commissioners, April 29, 1793, *ibid.*, 454–55.

39. "Speech of the Confederate Indian Nations at the Glaize to Lieutenant Colonel England, Commanding at Detroit," no date, *Michigan Historical Collections*, XXIV, 43–44; Simcoe to the Indians, June 22, 1793, *ibid.*, 551–54; Horsman, *Matthew Elliott*, 80.

40. "Minutes of a Council at Niagara," July 7, 1793, Cruikshank, *Correspondence of Simcoe*, I, 378–82; Benjamin Lincoln, "Journal of a Treaty Held in 1793, with the Indian Tribes Northwest of the Ohio, by Commissioners of the United States," *Massachusetts Historical Collections, Third Series*, V, 137–42; Reginald Horsman, "The British Indian Department and the Abortive Treaty of Lower Sandusky, 1793," *Ohio Historical Quarterly*, LXX (July, 1961), 202–203.

41. Brant to Simcoe, July 28, 1793, *Michigan Historical Collections*, XXIV, 571–72; Dwight L. Smith (ed.), "William Wells and the Indian Council of 1793," *Indiana Magazine of History*, LVI (September, 1960), 217–26; Brant to McKee, August 4, 1793, *Correspondence of Simcoe*, V, 66–67; Western Indians to the commissioners of the United States, July 27, 1793, *ibid.*, 491–92.

42. Speech of the commissioners to the Indians, July 31, 1793, *American State Papers: Indian Affairs*, I, 352–53; reply by the Indians, August 13, 1793, *Michigan Historical Collections*, XXIV, 587–92; commissioners to the Indians, August 16, 1793, *ibid.*, 592–93; Horsman, *Matthew Elliott*, 87–88.

43. Prucha, *Sword of the Republic*, 29–35; Downes, *Council Fires*, 324–25.

44. Israel Chapin to secretary of war, December 11, 1793, Anthony Wayne Papers, Clements Library; Simcoe to Henry Dundas, November 10, 1793, Cruikshank, *Correspondence of Simcoe*, II, 99–101; entries for November 5 and November 14, 1793, in Alexander McKee's journal, *ibid.*, 128; Thomas Pasteur to Wayne, January 14, 1794, Donald J. Berthrong Collection, Bizzell Memorial Library, University of Oklahoma, Norman; Dundas was a British official in England. Duggan was employed by the British Indian Department at Detroit.

45. Speech by Lord Dorchester, February 10, 1794, Cruikshank, *Correspondence of Simcoe*, II, 149–150; Pasteur to Wayne, March 8, 1794, Potawatomi File, Great Lakes Indian Archives; Simcoe to Lord Dorchester, April 29, 1794, *Michigan Historical Collections*, XXIV, 659–60; Horsman, *Matthew Elliott*, 93–95.

46. McKee to Joseph Chew, June 9, 1794, Cruikshank, *Correspondence of Simcoe*, II, 262; McKee to Chew, June 10, 1794, *ibid.*, 263; Horsman, *Matthew Elliott*, 95–97. Joseph Chew was secretary of the Department of Indian Affairs in Montreal.

47. Wayne to Knox, July 7, 1794, in Richard C. Knopf (ed.), *Anthony Wayne, A Name in Arms: The Wayne-Knox-Pickering-McHenry Correspondence*, 345–48; McKee to Chew, July 7, 1794, *Michigan Historical Collections*, XX, 364–65.

48. Wayne to Pasteur, July 5, 1794, Berthrong Collection, University of Oklahoma; McKee to Colonel Richard England, July 10, 1794, Cruikshank, *Correspondence of*

Simcoe, II, 315; Dwight Smith (ed.) , *From Greenville to Fallen Timbers: A Journal of the Wayne Campaign*, 277; Reginald Horsman, "The British Indian Department and the Resistance to General Anthony Wayne," *Mississippi Valley Historical Review*, XLIV (September, 1962) , 276. England was in command at Detroit.

49. Richard C. Knopf (ed.) , "A Precise Journal of General Wayne's Last Campaign," *Proceedings of the American Antiquarian Society*, LXIV (October, 1954) , 279–87; McKee to Simcoe, July 26, 1794, Cruikshank, *Correspondence of Simcoe*, II, 344; McKee to England, August 15, 1794, *Michigan Historical Collections*, XXV, 14; Wayne to William McMahan, June 28, 1794, Wayne Papers, Clements Library.

50. Captain William Doyle to Langlade, July 26, 1794, *Wisconsin Historical Collections*, XVIII, 45; "William Clark's Journal of General Wayne's Campaign," *Mississippi Valley Historical Review*, I, (December, 1914) , 425; Smith, *From Greenville to Fallen Timbers*, 281 fn. 92; Horsman, *Matthew Elliott*, 103.

51. Knopf, "Journal of Wayne's Last Campaign," 290; Wayne to the secretary of war, August 28, 1794, *American State Papers: Indian Affairs*, I, 491; Horsman, *Matthew Elliott*, 103.

52. Wayne to the secretary of war, August 28, 1794, *American State Papers: Indian Affairs*, I, 491; "William Clark's Journal," 428–30; McKee to Chew, August 27, 1794, *Michigan Historical Collections*, XX, 370–72; Thomas Case, "The Battle of Fallen Timbers," *Northwest Ohio Quarterly*, XXXV (Spring, 1963) , 54–68.

53. Horsman, "The British and the Resistance to Wayne," 282.

54. "William Clark's Journal," 430–31; Milo Milton Quaife (ed.) , "General James Wilkinson's Narrative of the Fallen Timber Campaign," *Mississippi Valley Historical Review*, XVI (June, 1929) , 86 fn. 5; deposition of Thomas Stephens, October, 1794, Potawatomi File, Great Lakes Indian Archives. Stephens was an American held prisoner by the Ottawas.

55. Richard C. Knopf (ed.) , "Two Journals of the Kentucky Volunteers, 1793 and 1794," *Filson Club History Quarterly*, XXVII (July, 1953) , 268; Guillame La Mothe to Chew, July 19, 1794, *Wisconsin Historical Collections*, XVIII, 442–43; Horsman, *Matthew Elliott*, 104. La Mothe was an interpreter at Mackinac.

56. Wayne to the Indian sachems, September 12, 1794, *Michigan Historical Collections*, XII, 143–44; Woehrmann, *At the Headwaters of the Maumee*, 44–48.

57. Horsman, *Matthew Elliott*, 106–109; "Proceedings of a Council Held at Brown's Town, October 11–14, 1794," *Michigan Historical Collections*, XXV, 40–46.

58. Hamtramck to Wayne, December 29, 1794, *Michigan Historical Collections*, XXXIV, 734; "Council with the Indians, January 19–21, 1795," Potawatomi File, Great Lakes Indian Archives; Wayne to secretary of war, January 24, 1795, *American State Papers: Indian Affairs*, I, 559–60; Antoine Laselle to Jacques Laselle, January 31, 1795, Cruikshank, *Correspondence of Simcoe*, III, 281. Antoine and Jacques Laselle were Indian traders.

59. Speech by Okia, March 12, 1795, Potawatomi File, Great Lakes Indian Archives; speech by Cashakoa, March 12, 1795, *ibid.*; "Preliminary Articles of Peace Signed by the Potawatomi of the Huron," March 12, 1795, *ibid.*; Hamtramck to Wayne, May 16, 1795, *ibid.*

60. Pasteur to Wayne, February 15, 1795, Potawatomi File, Great Lakes Indian Archives; Thomas Bodley to Wayne, June 12, 1795, *ibid.*; Hamtramck to Wayne, April 10, 1795, *ibid.*; Dwight Smith (ed.) , "Notes on the Wabash River in 1795," *Indiana Magazine of History*, L (September, 1954) , 287–89. Bodley was an American officer who traveled on the Wabash.

61. Pasteur to Wayne, March 15, 1795, Potawatomi File, Great Lakes Indian

Archives; excerpt from James T. Hair, *Gazetteer of Madison County*, 250–52, *ibid.*; John Mills to Wayne, June 2, 1795, John Mills File, Chicago Historical Society; May Allinson, "The Government of Illinois," *Transactions of the Illinois State Historical Society for the Year 1907*, 289–90.

62. John Edgar and François Canis to Wayne, March 31, 1795, Potawatomi File, Great Lakes Indian Archives; J. Hammill to Major Thomas Doyle, April 30, 1795, Berthrong Collection, University of Oklahoma; Norman Caldwell, "Fort Massac: The American Frontier Post," *Journal of the Illinois State Historical Society*, XLIII (Winter, 1950), 272. Edgar and Canis were American citizens of Kaskaskia. Doyle and Hammill were officers at Fort Massac.

63. Wayne to St. Clair, June 5, 1795, Smith, *St. Clair Papers*, II, 274–75, 343–44 fn. 1; St. Clair to Wayne, Potawatomi File, Great Lakes Indian Archives; Sargent to justices of the peace, April 21, 1795, Carter, *Territorial Papers*, III, 433–34.

64. Richard C. Knopf (ed.), "A Surgeon's Mate at Fort Defiance: The Journal of Joseph Gardener Andrews for the Year 1795," *Ohio Historical Quarterly*, LXVI (April, 1957), 168–71; Wayne to Pickering, June 17, 1795, Knopf, *Anthony Wayne*, 427–28; Samuel Drake to Wayne, June 30, 1795, Berthrong Collection, University of Oklahoma; John Mills to Sargent, July 16, 1795, Sargent Papers, Massachusetts Historical Society.

65. "Minutes of a Treaty with the Indians," June–August, 1795, *American State Papers: Indian Affairs*, I, 564–82; "A Treaty of Peace Between the United States and the Tribes of Indians," Kappler, *Indian Treaties*, II, 39–45.

CHAPTER SEVEN

1. Baron de Carondelet to Zenon Trudeau, December 22, 1792, in Kinniard, *Spain in the Mississippi Valley*, III, 102. Carondelet was governor-general of Louisiana. Trudeau was the commandant at St. Louis. Also see John Joseph Mathews, *The Osages: Children of the Middle Waters*, 265–82, and Carl Chapman, "The Indomitable Osage in Spanish *Illinois* (Upper Louisiana), 1763–1804," in John F. McDermott, *The Spanish in the Mississippi Valley*, 287–318.

2. "Minutes of an Indian Council at Michilimackinac, July 7, 1787," *Michigan Historical Collections*, XI, 494–96; northern Indians to Trudeau, 1793, in Kinniard, *Spain in the Mississippi Valley*, III, 110–11; Trudeau to Carondelet, March 2, 1793, in A. P. Nasatir (ed.), *Before Lewis and Clark: Documents Illustrating the History of Missouri, 1785–1804*, I, 167–68.

3. Trudeau to Carondelet, May 6, 1793, in Nasatir, *Before Lewis and Clark*, I, 173–74; Trudeau to Carondelet, September 28, 1793, *ibid.*, 197–99.

4. Entry for August 15, 1794, in "Journal of Lorimer During the Threatened Genet Invasion of Louisiana, 1793–1795," in Houk, *Spanish Regime in Missouri*, II, 94. Lorimer was a trader at Saint Genevieve. Also see Trudeau to Carondelet, April 30, 1795, in Nasatir, *Before Lewis and Clark*, I, 322; Trudeau to Gayoso de Lemos, December 20, 1797, *ibid.*, II, 528; and Mathews, *The Osages*, 265–82. Manuel Gayoso de Lemos succeeded Carondelet as governor-general of Louisiana.

5. Henry Vanderburgh to Winthrop Sargent, April 2, 1797, Winthrop Sargent Papers, Massachusetts Historical Society; Jonathan Jones to Sargent, May 9, 1798, *ibid.*. Vanderburgh was a citizen of Vincennes.

6. John Reynolds, *My Own Times, Embracing Also the History of My Life*, 74.

7. Reynolds, *Pioneer History of Illinois*, 280; president to the secretary of war, August 30, 1802, Carter, *Territorial Papers*, VII, 71–72. Also see secretary of war to

Harrison, April 23, 1802, "Records of the Secretary of War Relating to Indian Affairs, Letters Sent," Microfilm M15, Roll 1, 205, National Archives, Washington, D.C., and secretary of war to Harrison, September 3, 1802, *ibid.*, 265–268.

8. Secretary of war to Harrison, September 3, 1802, M15, Roll 1, 265–68, National Archives. Also see Milo Milton Quaife, *Chicago and the Old Northwest*, 126–36. Quaife's volume contains a very good description of the founding of this post.

9. "Narrative of Andrew J. Vieau, Sr.," *Wisconsin Historical Collection*, XI, 218; "Antoine Le Clair's Statement," *ibid.*, 238–42. Also see Quaife, *Chicago and the Old Northwest*, 142–45, and "Licenses Granted by the Governor to Indian Traders," Hyacinth Lasselle Papers, Indiana State Library, Indianapolis.

10. Bert Anson, "The Early Years of Lathrop M. Taylor, the Fur Trader," *Indiana Magazine of History*, XLIV (December, 1948), 369–70; Wilbur Cunningham, *Land of Four Flags*, 89–93. Also see day book of William Burnett, 1796–97, William Burnett Papers, Burton Collection; Wilbur Cunningham (ed.), *Letter Book of William Burnett*; and Joseph Bailly's journal, Porter County Historical Society, Valparaiso, Indiana.

11. Quaife, *Chicago and the Old Northwest*, 145–48. Also see Juliette Kinzie, *Wau-Bun, the Early Day in the Northwest*. This volume contains much information on the history of the Kinzie family.

12. Speech of the Wabash Indians, February 18, 1796, Potawatomi File, Great Lakes Indian Archives; Zebulon Pike to Wayne, July 5, 1796, Berthrong Collection, University of Oklahoma; "Report by Thomas Forsyth," in Blair, *Indian Tribes of the Upper Mississippi*, II, 203 fn. 76; Jean Ducoigne to John Lalime, March 2, 1805, Carter, *Territorial Papers*, XIII, 103–104. Forsyth was a trader and Indian agent. Ducoigne was the chief of the Kaskaskias. Lalime was an interpreter at Chicago.

13. Speech of La Barbue, October 15, 1805, Berthrong Collection, University of Oklahoma; Wilkinson to the secretary of war, October 22, 1805, Carter, *Territorial Papers*, XIII, 243–44; "A Treaty Between the Tribes," *ibid.*, 245–47.

14. Wilkinson to Dearborn, November 26, 1805, Berthrong Collection, University of Oklahoma; Wilkinson to Dearborn, December 3, 1805, *ibid.*; Zebulon M. Pike, "A Dissertation on . . . a Late Tour . . . in the Years 1806 and 1807," in Donald Jackson (ed.), *The Journals of Zebulon Montgomery Pike*, II, 33.

15. Wilkinson to Dearborn, December 23, 1805, Berthrong Collection, University of Oklahoma; Dearborn to Jouett, October 13, 1806, M15, Roll 2, 258, National Archives; Dearborn to Harrison, August 18, 1807, *ibid.*, 330. Also see Wilkinson to Pike, June 26, 1806, in Jackson, *Journals of Pike*, I, 285 and 287 fn. 1.

16. Harrison to Dearborn, January 16, 1806, in Logan Esarey (ed.), *Messages and Letters of William Henry Harrison*, I, 184–86; Jouett to Wilkinson, July 10, 1806, in Jackson, *Journals of Pike*, II, 115; Wilkinson to Pike, August 6, 1806, *ibid.*, 134; Pike to Wilkinson, August 28, 1806, *ibid.*, 144. Also see Dearborn to Jouett, October 13, 1806, M15, Roll 2, 268, National Archives.

17. Hamtramck to Wayne, September 24, 1795, Potawatomi File, Great Lakes Indian Archives; Hamtramck to Wayne, October 10, 1795, *ibid.* Also see Burnett to Hamtramck, March 30, 1796, Berthrong Collection, University of Oklahoma; and entry for August 29, 1795 in Wayne's orderly book, *Michigan Historical Collections*, XXXIV, 640.

18. Topinbee to Hamtramck, March 21, 1796, Potawatomi File, Great Lakes Indian Archives; Captain Hector McLean to Major James Green, July 12, 1799, *Wisconsin Historical Collections*, XII, 106. Both Green and McLean were British officers serving at Amherstburg.

19. "Goods Recommended to be Given to the Indians by Matthew Elliott," September 20, 1797, *Michigan Historical Collections*, XIX, 545; McLean to McKee, October 28, 1797, *ibid.*, 565; Peter Audrain to Sargent, June 28, 1797, Sargent Papers, Massachusetts Historical Society; Indian Council at Amherstburg, June 8, 1805, *Michigan Historical Collections*, XXIII, 39–42. Audrain was a citizen of Detroit.

20. Wayne to James McHenry, August 8, 1796, in Knopf, *Anthony Wayne*, 515–16; Wayne to McHenry, October 3, 1796, *ibid.*, 532–33. McHenry succeeded Knox as secretary of war. Also see David Strong to Wayne, September 7, 1796, Berthrong Collection, University of Oklahoma; F. Clever Bald, *Detroit's First American Decade*, 63–64; and John C. Fitzpatrick (ed.), *The Writings of George Washington*, XXXV, 299–302. The second Potawatomi chief who made the journey is unknown.

21. Burnett to Augustin Charboiller and Edward Young, May 17, 1796, Cunningham, *Letter Book of Burnett*, 70; Burnett to Robert Innes and Co., December 20, 1798, *ibid.*, 112; Burnett to George Gillespie, May 31, 1801, *ibid.*, 143. Charboiller, Young, Innes, and Gillespie all were traders at Mackinac or Detroit.

22. James Henry to William Wells, December 24, 1801, Northwest Territory Papers, Indiana Historical Society Library, Indianapolis; *A Brief Account of the Proceedings of the Committee Appointed by the Yearly Meeting of Friends, Held in Baltimore, for Promoting the Improvement and Civilization of the Indian Natives*, 25; Gerrard Hopkins, *A Mission to the Indians from the Indian Committee of Baltimore Meeting to Fort Wayne in 1804*, 167–73.

23. Speech by Little Turtle, January 4, 1802, M15, Roll 1, 138–42, National Archives.

24. Return Jonathan Meigs to Anthony Wayne, August 30, 1796, Berthrong Collection, University of Oklahoma; Dearborn to Hamtramck, November 4, 1801, Hamtramck Papers, Burton Collection; Harrison to Charles Jouett, January 15, 1803, William Henry Harrison Papers, Indiana Historical Society Library.

25. Harrison to the secretary of war, July 15, 1801, Lasselle Papers, Indiana State Library; Wilkinson to Sargent, November 17, 1797, Sargent Papers, Massachusetts Historical Society.

26. "Conference Held with Little Turtle and Chiefs of the Miamis, Potawatomis and Weas, January 7, 1802," M15, Roll 1, 135–37, National Archives; speech by Jefferson to the chiefs of the Miamis, Potawatomis, and Weas, January 7, 1802, *ibid.*, 142–43; Dearborn to John Wilkins, January 11, 1802, *ibid.*, 145. Wilkins was a clerk in the War Department.

27. Secretary of war to Harrison, January 23, 1802, M15, Roll 1, 146–47, National Archives; secretary of war to William Wells, June 4, 1802, *ibid.*, 220–22; secretary of war to Harrison, July 24, 1803, *ibid.*, 253–54.

28. Harrison to the secretary of war, February 26, 1802, Esarey, *Messages and Letters of Harrison*, I, 41–46; Harrison's address at the Indian council, August 12, 1802, *ibid.*, 52–54; minutes of an Indian conference, September 17, 1802, *ibid.*, 56–57.

29. "Articles of a Treaty Made at Fort Wayne," June 7, 1803, Kappler, *Indian Treaties*, II, 64–66; Harrison to the secretary of war, March 3, 1803, Esarey, *Messages and Letters of Harrison*, I, 76–84; secretary of war to Harrison, February 21, 1803, M15, Roll 1, 328–31, National Archives. Also see Bernard Sheehan, *Seeds of Extinction: Jeffersonian Philanthropy and the American Indian*, 171.

30. Woehrmann, *At the Headwaters of the Maumee*, 116–18. Woehrmann's volume contains the best account of attempts to acculturate the Potawatomis of the Fort Wayne region. Also see secretary of war to William Lyman, temporary agent for Indian affairs, July 14, 1804, M15, Roll 1, 92–97, National Archives, and secretary of war to Wells, February 28, 1806, *ibid.*, Roll 2, 177.

31. Entry for November 14, 1802, "Diary of the Little Indian Congregation on the White River for the Year 1802," in Lawrence Henry Gipson (ed.) , *The Moravian Indian Mission on White River*, 201; William H. Love, "A Quaker Pilgrimage," *Maryland Historical Magazine*, IV (March, 1909) , 1–24; Hopkins, *Mission to the Indians*, 45–90; Woehrmann, *At the Headwaters of the Maumee*, 114–16.

32. Woehrmann, *At the Headwaters of the Maumee*, 116; Otho Winger, "The First School of Agriculture in Indiana" (manuscript) , Otho Winger Papers, Indiana State Historical Library.

33. Kirk to Dearborn, May 28, 1807, Potawatomi File, Great Lakes Indian Archives; John Johnston to Dearborn, May 31, 1807, *ibid.*; Jonathan Smith to Wells, July 8, 1807, M15, Roll 2 ,324, National Archives. Johnston was the Indian factor at Fort Wayne. Smith was a clerk in the War Department. The best discussion of the controversy can be found in Woehrmann, *At the Headwaters of the Maumee*, 119–35.

34. Address of the Miamis, Potawatomis, and Eel Rivers to the president of the United States, August 23, 1807, Potawatomi File, Great Lakes Indian Archives; memorial by John Johnston for the Committee of Friends from Baltimore, May 26, 1808, *ibid.*; Dearborn to Wells, March 18, 1808, M15, Roll 2, 362, National Archives. Also see Woehrmann, *At the Headwaters of the Maumee*, 136–41, and Joseph A. Parsons, "Civilizing the Indians of the Old Northwest, 1800–1810," *Indiana Magazine of History*, LVI, (September, 1960) , 212–16.

35. These treaties can be found in Kappler, *Indian Treaties*, II, 67–89.

36. Hull to Dearborn, October 28, 1805, *Michigan Historical Collections*, XL, 77–78; Quaife, *Chicago and the Old Northwest*, 193. Also see Dearborn to Harrison and Hull, June 4, 1806, M15, Roll 2, 233, National Archives, and Dearborn to Harrison, August 18, 1806, *ibid.*, 248.

37. Harrison to Charles Jouett, January 15, 1803, Potawatomi File, Great Lakes Indian Archives; Dearborn to Wells, October 17, 1804, M15, Roll 2, 18, National Archives; Dearborn to Wells, *ibid.*, 131; Dearborn to Jouett, May 12, 1806, *ibid.*, 220.

38. Harrison to the secretary of war, July 10, 1805, in Esarey, *Messages and Letters of Harrison*, I, 147–51; secretary of war to Hull, March 24, 1807, M15, Roll 2, 243–44, National Archives. Also see John Johnston to the superintendent of Indian trade, October 10, 1806, Records of the Superintendent of Indian Trade, Letters Received, Microfilm T58, Roll 1, National Archives, and Wells to Dearborn, September 10, 1807, Potawatomi File, Great Lakes Indian Archives.

39. Harrison to the secretary of war, July 15, 1801, Lasselle Papers, Indiana State Library; Dearborn to Wells, May 13, 1804, M15, Roll 2, 4, National Archives; Alexander McKee to the Potawatomis, November, 1804, in Esarey, *Messages and Letters of Harrison*, I, 111–12. Also see Burnett to Wells, March 2, 1806, Solomon Sibley Papers, Burton Collection.

40. Hodge, *Handbook of American Indians*, 729–30.

41. McHenry to St. Clair, April 30, 1799, Edward E. Ayer Manuscripts, Newberry Library, Chicago; *The Western Sun*, September 19, 1807, in Potawatomi File, Great Lakes Indian Archives; Henry R. Schoolcraft, "Discourse Delivered Before the Historical Society of Michigan," in *Historical and Scientific Sketches of Michigan*, 103–106. Also see Glenn Tucker, *Tecumseh: Vision of Glory*, 111–14.

42. Wells to the secretary of war, April 19, 1807, Potawatomi File, Great Lakes Indian Archives; Wells to the secretary of war, July 14, 1807, in Carter, *Territorial Papers*, VII, 465–66. Also see Walter Havighurst, *Wilderness for Sale: The Story of the First Western Land Rush*, 25–26.

43. Harrison to the secretary of war, September 5, 1807, in Esarey, *Messages and Letters of Harrison*, I, 247–49; Wells to Dearborn, October 20, 1807, Potawatomi File,

Great Lakes Indian Archives; Hull to Dearborn, August 4, 1807, in *Michigan His-torical Collections*, XL, 169–70; Hull to Dearborn, November 18, 1807, in *ibid.*, 219–20. Also see "Articles of a Treaty Made at Detroit, November 17, 1807," in Kappler, *Indian Treaties*, II, 92–94.

44. Hull to Dearborn, November, 1807, in *Michigan Historical Collections*, XL, 247–52; Hull to unknown, November 8, 1807, in Carter, *Territorial Papers*, VII, 498–99; Jouett to the secretary of war, *ibid.*, 496–97. Also see Horsman, *Matthew Elliott*, 157–58.

45. Charles Reaume to Captain J. Dunham, June 4, 1807, in *Michigan Historical Collections*, XL, 136–37; Jouett to the secretary of war, August 22, 1807, Carter, *Territorial Papers*, VII, 472. Also see Blair, *Indian Tribes of the Upper Mississippi*, II, 203 fn. 76. Reaume was a trader and American magistrate at Green Bay. Dunham was an American officer at Mackinac.

46. Wells to the secretary of war, January 7, 1808, Potawatomi File, Great Lakes Indian Archives; Wells to the secretary of war, April 20, 1808, Carter, *Territorial Papers*, VII, 555–58.

47. Wells to Dearborn, January 7, 1808, Potawatomi File, Great Lakes Indian Archives; Wells to the secretary of war, April 20, 1808, Carter, *Territorial Papers*, VII, 555–58; Wells to Dearborn, April 2, 1808, Berthrong Collection, University of Oklahoma.

48. Wells to the secretary of war, April 20, 1808, Carter *Territorial Papers*, VII, 555–58; Wells to Dearborn, April 22, 1808, *ibid.*, 558–59; Wells to Dearborn, April 23, 1808, *ibid.*; Esarey, *Messages and Letters of Harrison*, I, 284. Also see William Claus to Francis Gore, February 14, 1808, *Michigan Historical Collections*, XIX, 42, and Claus to Gore, February 27, 1808, *ibid.*, XV, 44. Claus was a British Indian agent. Gore was lieutenant governor of Upper Canada.

49. Deposition of Billy Caldwell, August 1, 1816, Caldwell File, Chicago Historical Society; Tucker, *Tecumseh*, 124. Also see Harrison to Dearborn, May 19, 1808, Esarey, *Messages and Letters of Harrison*, I, 290–91, and statement by John Conner, June 18, 1808, Berthrong Collection, University of Oklahoma. Connor was sent by government officials to investigate the new Indian village.

50. Delaware chiefs to Harrison, in Esarey, *Messages and Letters of Harrison*, I, September 9, 1808; Quaife, *Chicago and the Old Northwest*, 193. Also see superintendent of Indian trade to John Johnston, January 3, 1808, Records of the Superintendent of Indian Trade, Letters Sent, Microfilm M16, Roll 1, 295–99, National Archives; superintendent of Indian trade to Mathew Irwin, September 9, 1808, *ibid.*, 231–35. Irwin recently had been appointed government factor at Chicago. Also see entry for July 16, 1808, in the diary of Colonel William Claus, in *Michigan Historical Collections*, XXII, 58.

51. Wells to the secretary of war, June 5, 1808, Potawatomi File, Great Lakes Indian Archives; Jonathan Smith to William Wells, August 2, 1808, M15, Roll 2, 389, National Archives; Thomas Jefferson to Marpock, December, 1808, *ibid.*, 397–400.

52. Woehrmann, *At the Headwaters of the Maumee*, 190.

53. "Articles of a Treaty Made and Concluded at Brownstown . . . November 25, 1808," in Kappler, *Indian Treaties*, II, 99–100; Jefferson to the Wyandots, Ottawas, Chippewas, Potawatomis, and Shawnees, January, 1809, in J. A. Washington (ed.), *Collected Writings of Thomas Jefferson*, VIII, 232–39.

54. Wells to Harrison, April 8, 1809, in Esarey, *Messages and Letters of Harrison*, I, 337–41; Harrison to the secretary of war, April 18, 1809, *ibid.*, 340–41; Harrison to the secretary of war, April 26, 1809, *ibid.*, 342–43.

55. Harrison to Eustis, July 5, 1809, Berthrong Collection, University of Oklahoma;

John Bradbury, "Travels in the Interior of America," in Thwaites, *Early Western Travels*, V, 48–49. Also see Nathaniel Pope to Indian agents, May 25, 1809, Governor's Correspondence, Illinois State Archives, Springfield. Pope was governor of Illinois.

56. Eustis to Harrison, July 15, 1809, M15, Roll 3, 2–3, National Archives; Woehrmann, *At the Headwarters of the Maumee*, 192.

57. "Journal of the Proceedings at the Indian Treaty at Fort Wayne and Vincennes, September 1 to October 27, 1809," in Esarey, *Messages and Letters of Harrison*, I, 363–77; William Wells, "A Correct Statement of the Number of Indians That Attended at the Treatys of Fort Wayne in June, 1803, and in September, 1809," Potawatomi File, Great Lakes Indian Archives; Harrison to Eustis, November 3, 1809, Ratified Indian Treaties, Microfilm M668, Roll 3, 384–92, National Archives. Also see Harrison to Eustis, October 3, 1809, in Gayle Thornbrough (ed.), *Letter Book of the Indian Agency at Fort Wayne, 1809–1815*, 66–69.

58. "A treaty Between the United States . . . and the Indians," September 30, 1809, Kappler, *Indian Treaties*, II, 101–102.

59. "Proceedings of a Council Held at Detroit in the Month of November, 1809," in Potawatomi File, Great Lakes Indian Archives; secretary of war to Johnson, May 12, 1810, M15, Roll 3, 25–26, National Archives; John Badollet to Albert Gallatin, June 24, 1810, in Gayle Thornbrough (ed.), *The Correspondence of John Badollet and Albert Gallatin, 1804–1836*, 151. Badollet was register of the Vincennes Land Office. Gallatin was treasurer of the United States. Also see Harrison to the secretary of war, May 15, 1810, in Esarey, *Messages and Letters of Harrison*, I, 420–21; Harrison to the secretary of war, July 4, 1810, in *ibid.*, 438–40; and extract from the *Western Sun*, July 14, 1810, in Potawatomi File, Great Lakes Indian Archives.

60. Harrison to the secretary of war, June 14, 1810, in Esarey, *Messages and Letters of Harrison*, I, 422–30; Harrison to the secretary of war, June 26, 1810, *ibid.*, 433–36; Woehrmann, *At the Headwaters of the Maumee*, 197.

61. Harrison to the secretary of war, June 14, 1810, in Esarey, *Messages and Letters of Harrison*, I, 422–30; Harrison to the secretary of war, August 1, 1810, *ibid.*, 453–54. Also see statement by John Shaw, June 24, 1810, Potawatomi File, Great Lakes Indian Archives. Shaw was the subagent at Fort Wayne.

62. Harrison to Johnston, June 16, 1810, Potawatomi File, Great Lakes Indian Archives; Hull to Eustis, July 20, 1810, *ibid.*; Woehrmann, *At the Headwaters of the Maumee*, 198; Harrison to the secretary of war, July 4, 1810, in Esarey, *Messages and Letters of Harrison*, I, 438–40.

63. Harrison to the secretary of war, August 6, 1810, in Esarey, *Messages and Letters of Harrison*, I, 456–59; speech by Tecumseh, August 20, 1810, *ibid.*, 463–68; Harrison to the secretary of war, August 22, 1810, *ibid.*, 460–63. Also see Tucker, *Tecumseh*, 162–67.

64. Hodge, *Handbook of American Indians*, II, 408; Alta P. Walters, "Shabonee," *Journal of the Illinois State Historical Society*, XVIII (October, 1924), 386.

65. Much confusion exists regarding Shabbona's early life. See Hodge, *Handbook of American Indians*, II, 517–18; Walters, "Shabonee," 388–89; "Chicago Indian Chiefs," *Bulletin of the Chicago Historical Society*, I (August, 1935), 109–11; Nehemiah Matson, *Memories of Shaubena*, 17–20; Virgil J. Vogel, *Indian Place Names in Illinois*, 132–35.

66. Deposition by James Moredaugh, August 17, 1810, Ninian Edwards Papers, Chicago Historical Society; deposition by Stephen Cole, September 21, 1810, *ibid.*; Benjamin Howard to Ninian Edwards, November 15, 1810, *ibid.* Moredaugh and Cole were the survivors of the attack. Edwards was governor of Illinois Territory.

Howard was governor of Missouri Territory. Also see Louise Houk, *A History of Missouri*, III, 98–100, and Ninian W. Edwards, *History of Illinois from 1778 to 1833*, 37–38. There is much confusion over the two Winamacs. Hodge lists them separately, but like many other writers, he intermingles and confuses their biographies during the first two decades of the nineteenth century. The friendly Winamac consistently served the Americans and survived the War of 1812 to die in 1821. The hostile Winamac was a steadfast ally of Tecumseh and Main Poc and was killed in a skirmish in November, 1812.

67. Potawatomi speech, September 13, 1810, Ninian Edwards Papers, Chicago Historical Society; declaration by Wanatee, chief of the Sac Nation, October 16, 1810, *ibid.*; Clark to the secretary of war, September 12, 1810, Carter, *Territorial Papers*, XIV, 412–14; Clark to Edwards, November 14, 1810, in E. B. Washburne (ed.), *The Edwards Papers*, 57.

68. Depositions by citizens of Illinois, April–June, 1810, Carter, *Territorial Papers*, XVI, 116–19; Blair, *Indian Tribes of the Upper Mississippi*, II, 203–204. Also see Clark to Eustis, January 22, 1811, Potawatomi File, Great Lakes Indian Archives, and Draper's notes, Draper Manuscripts, 26S90.

69. Speeches by the chiefs at the council at Brownstown, September 26, 1810, Potawatomi File, Great Lakes Indian Archives; Hull to Johnston, September 27, 1810, Thornbrough, *Letter Book at Fort Wayne*, 83–86.

70. Johnston to Eustis, October 20, 1810, Potawatomi File, Great Lakes Indian Archives; Johnston to Harrison, October 14, 1810, Berthrong Collection, University of Oklahoma; "An Exact Account of the Number of Indians Who Attended a Council at Fort Wayne, October 1, 1810," Thornbrough, *Letter Book at Fort Wayne*, 90–91. Also see Woehrmann, *At the Headwaters of the Maumee*, 201–202.

71. Lalime to Clark, May 26, 1811, In Esarey, *Messages and Letters of Harrison*, I, 511; Lalime to Johnston, July 7, 1811, *ibid.*, 530–31. Also see Clark to Eustis, July 3, 1811, Potawatomi File, Great Lakes Indian Archives, and Edwards to Eustis, June 7, 1811, in Edwards, *History of Illinois*, 285–86.

72. Deposition by Rebecca Cox, June 13, 1811, Potawatomi File, Great Lakes Indian Archives; Clark to Eustis, July 3, 1811, *ibid.*; Wells to Eustis, August 27, 1811, *ibid.* Also see Edwards to Eustis, June 20, 1811, in Edwards, *History of Illinois*, 286–87, and Edwards to Eustis, July 6, 1811, in Carter, *Territorial Papers*, XVI, 164–66.

73. Clark to Eustis, July 3, 1811, Potawatomi File, Great Lakes Indian Archives; Edwards to the secretary of war, June 27, 1811, in Carter, *Territorial Papers*, XVI, 162–63; Edwards to the secretary of war, July 6, 1811, *ibid.*, 164–66.

74. A good description of Levering's journey, the conference, and the speeches of the participants can be found in Edwards, *History of Illinois*, 38–55. Also see Clark to Eustis, July 3, 1811, Potawatomi File, Great Lakes Indian Archives; Thomas Forsyth to William Clark, Thomas Forsyth Papers, Missouri Historical Society. Forsyth was a trader who became Indian agent at Peoria. For a discussion of Gomo's role during these years, see R. David Edmunds, "The Illinois River Potawatomis in the War of 1812," *Journal of the Illinois State Historical Society*, LXIII, (January, 1970), 341–462.

75. Clark to Eustis, May 24, 1811, Potawatomi File, Great Lakes Indian Archives; Lalime to Clark, June 2, 1811, *ibid.* Also see Matthew Irwin to the secretary of war, May, 1811, in Carter, *Territorial Papers*, XVI, 159–60; Edwards, *History of Illinois*, 39; and Eustis to the Indians, October 8, 1811, in *Michigan Historical Collections*, VIII, 601.

76. Harrison to Eustis, August 7, 1811, in Esarey, *Messages and Letters of Harrison*,

I, 548–51; extract of Harrison to Johnson, September, 1811, *ibid.*, 583–84; Harrison to the Indian chiefs, September 4, 1811, *ibid.*, 576–77; Indian chiefs to Harrison, September 4, 1811, *ibid.*, 577–82.

77. Harrison to the secretary of war, September 25, 1811, Esarey, *Messages and Letters of Harrison*, I, 589–92; Harrison to Eustis, October 11, 1811, Potawatomi File, Great Lakes Indian Archives; Reynolds, *My Own Times*, 136; Woehrmann, *At the Headwaters of the Maumee*, 207–208.

78. Harrison to Eustis, November 18, 1811, *American State Papers: Indian Affairs*, I, 776–79.

79. *Ibid.*; Forsyth to Clark, November 1, 1811, Forsyth Papers, Missouri Historical Society; J. Wesley Whickar, "Shabonee's Account of Tippecanoe," *Indiana Magazine of History*, XVII (December, 1921), 353–63. Also see Alec Gilpin, *The War of 1812 in the Old Northwest*, 16–18 and Almeda McCollough (ed.), *The Battle of Tippecanoe: Conflict of Cultures.*

80. Harrison to Eustis, November 8, 1811, Esarey, *Messages and Letters of Harrison*, I, 614–15; Harrison to Eustis, November 26, 1811, Potawatomi File, Great Lakes Indian Archives; Johnston to Eustis, November 28, 1811, *ibid.*; Gilpin, *War of 1812 in the Old Northwest*, 18–20.

81. Harrison to Eustis, January 14, 1812, Potawatomi File, Great Lakes Indian Archives.

CHAPTER EIGHT

1. Speech by the Indians in council at Fort Wayne, November 22, 1811, Potawatomi File, Great Lakes Indian Archives; entry for November 30, 1811, in Thornbrough, *Letter Book of Fort Wayne*, 100–101; Robert McAfee, *History of the Late War in the Western Country*, 39.

2. Edwards to the principal chiefs of the Pottawottamies residing on the Illinois River, December 14, 1811, in Edwards, *History of Illinois*, 292; Edwards to Eustis, May 6, 1812, *ibid.*; Clark to Eustis, November 23, 1811, Potawatomi File, Great Lakes Indian Archives; Edwards to Eustis, January 25, 1812, in Washburne, *Edwards Papers*, 294–95.

3. Josiah Snelling to Harrison, January 18, 1812, Potawatomi File, Great Lakes Indian Archives; Wells to Eustis, February 10, 1812, in Esarey, *Messages and Letters of Harrison*, II, 21–22; Edwards to Eustis, March 3, 1812, in Carter *Territorial Papers*, XVI, 193–94. Captain Snelling was in command at Fort Harrison.

4. Edwards to Eustis, March 3, 1812, in Carter, *Territorial Papers*, XVI, 193–94; John Johnson to Howard, March 9, 1812, *ibid.*, XIV, 534–35; Howard to Eustis, March 19, 1812, *ibid.*, 531–32. Also see Draper's notes, Draper Manuscripts, 25S32–33.

5. Harrison to Eustis, April 14, 1812, Potawatomi File, Great Lakes Indian Archives; Harrison to Eustis, April 29, 1812, in Esarey, *Messages and Letters of Harrison*, II, 41–44; Badollet to Gallatin, April 29, 1812, in Thornbrough, *Correspondence of Badollet and Gallatin*, 226–28, Stickney to Eustis, May 7, 1812, in Thornbrough, *Letter Book of Fort Wayne*, 116–17.

6. Harrison to Eustis, May 6, 1812, in Esarey, *Messages and Letters of Harrison*, II, 44–45; Harrison to Eustis, May 13, 1812, in *ibid.*, 48–49; Also see Johnston to Return Jonathan Meigs, May 22, 1812, in Richard C. Knopf (ed.), *Return Jonathan Meigs, Jr., and the War of 1812 in the Northwest*, 170.

7. Edwards to Eustis, February 10, 1812, in Edwards, *History of Illinois*, 300–302; Howard to Eustis, January 13, 1812, in Richard C. Knopf (ed.), *Letters to the Secre-*

tary of War, 1812, Relating to the War of 1812 in the Northwest, part 1, 11; militia officers to Eustis, February 7, 1812, *ibid.*, 37; Stanley Griswold to Eustis, March 5, 1812, *ibid.*, 73–75.

8. Harrison to Eustis, April 29, 1812, in Esarey, *Messages and Letters of Harrison*, II, 41–44; Badollet to Gallatin, May 19, 1812, in Thornbrough, *Correspondence of Badollet and Gallatin*, 230–32; Stickney to Harrison, May 29, 1812, in Thornbrough, *Letter Book of Fort Wayne*, 131–33.

9. Edwards to Hebert, March 12, 1812, in Edwards, *History of Illinois*, 55; Clark to Edwards, April 11, 1812, Potawatomi File, Great Lakes Indian Archives; Draper's notes, Draper Manuscripts, 26S37; Clark to Eustis, April 12, 1812, Berthrong Collection, University of Oklahoma.

10. Speech by Edwards, April 16, 1812, in Edwards, *History of Illinois*, 56–60; speech by Gomo, April 16, 1812, *ibid.*, 60–64; Edwards to Eustis, April 24, 1812, in Carter, *Territorial Papers*, XVI, 215.

11. Draper's notes, Draper Manuscripts, 26S50; Stickney to Harrison, April 18, 1812, in Thornbrough, *Letter Book at Fort Wayne*, 102–107; minutes of a conference with the Indians, April 18, 1812, *ibid.*, 108–10; Stickney to Nathan Heald, April 29, 1812, *ibid.*, 114–15. Heald was the commander at Fort Dearborn. Also see Tucker, *Tecumseh*, 235.

12. Speeches of the Indians at Massassinway, May 15, 1812, in Esarey, *Messages and Letters of Harrison*, II, 50–53; Tucker, *Tecumseh*, 236–38.

13. Speech of Five Medals, May 12, 1812, in Thornbrough, *Letter Book of Fort Wayne*, 120–21; Stickney to Meigs, May 15, 1812, *ibid.*, 124–25; Stickney to Eustis, May 25, 1812, *ibid.*, 130–31; J. Munger to Meigs, May 14, 1812, in Knopf, *Return Jonathan Meigs*, 176–77.

14. William Claus to Major General Brock, June 16, 1812, in E. A. Cruikshank (ed.), *Documents Relating to the Invasion of Canada and the Surrender of Detroit, 1812*, 32–33; Stickney to Hull, June 20, 1812, in Thornbrough, *Letter Book at Fort Wayne*, 140–43; Forsyth to Edwards, June 8, 1812, Forsyth Papers, Missouri Historical Society.

15. Forsyth to Howard, June 9, 1812, in Carter, *Territorial Papers*, XIV, 570–71; William Russell to Eustis, July 1, 1812, *ibid.*, XVI, 238–40; Forsyth to Edwards, July 13, 1812, *ibid.*, 250–53; report of Antione LeClair, July 14, 1812, *ibid.*, 253–55. Russell was in command of the Illinois Rangers, a mounted militia organization.

16. Reynolds, *My Own Times*, 131–32; Eustis to Meigs and others, July 1, 1812, Potawatomi File, Great Lakes Indian Archives; Hull to Eustis, in Cruikshank, *Documents Relating to the Invasion of Canada*, 78; Stickney to Hull, July 8, 1812, in Thornbrough, *Letter Book at Fort Wayne*, 158–59.

17. Stickney to Hull, July 8, 1812, in Thornbrough, *Letter Book at Fort Wayne*, 158–59, 170 fn. 80. Also see Woehrmann, *At the Headwaters of the Maumee*, 216.

18. Hull to Eustis, July 14, 1812, in *Michigan Historical Collections*, XL, 413–15; Hull to Eustis, July 21, 1812, in Cruikshank, *Documents Relating to the Invasion of Canada*, 78. Also see Gilpin, *War of 1812 in the Old Northwest*, 79.

19. Kellogg, *British Regime in Wisconsin*, 281–85; Hull to Heald, July 29, 1812, quoted in Quaife, *Chicago and the Old Northwest*, 216 fn. 583.

20. Irwin to Eustis, March 10, 1812, in Carter, *Territorial Papers*, XVI, 195; Irwin to Heald, April 12, 1812, in Knopf, *Letters to the Secretary of War*, part 1, 127; Heald to John Whistler, April 15, 1812, *ibid.*, 134.

21. John Kinzie to Thomas Forsyth, July 7, 1812, in Carter, *Territorial Papers*, XVI, 248–50; report by Antoine LeClair, July 14, 1812, *ibid.*, 253–55; Heald to Porter Hanks,

July 13, 1812, in Cruikshank, *Documents Relating to the Invasion of Canada*, 55.

22. Mentor L. Williams (ed.), "John Kinzie's Narrative of the Fort Dearborn Massacre," *Journal of the Illinois State Historical Society*, XLVI, (Winter, 1953), 347–48.

23. Quaife, *Chicago and the Old Northwest*, 215–20. Quaife's volume contains the most accurate, detailed account of the Fort Dearborn Massacre. In appendices to his volume, Quaife examines and evaluates the conflicting descriptions of the massacre collected from the white survivors.

24. Quaife, *Chicago and the Old Northwest*, 221–23. Henry Rowe Schoolcraft, *Historical and Statistical Information Respecting the History, Condition, and Prospects of the Indian Tribes of the United States*, V, 530–31.

25. Quaife, *Chicago and the Old Northwest*, 220, 393; Forsyth to Howard, September 7, 1812, in Carter, *Territorial Papers*, XVI, 261–65; Tucker, *Tecumseh*, 252–58; McAfee, *History of the Late War*, 101.

26. Quaife, *Chicago and the Old Northwest*, 220–21; Kinzie, *Wau-Bun*, 175.

27. Quaife, *Chicago and the Old Northwest*, 225–26.

28. *Ibid.*, 226.

29. *Ibid.*, 226–28.

30. *Ibid.*, 229–31.

31. *Ibid.*, 230–31.

32. Quaife devotes an entire chapter to the fate of the white survivors, See *Chicago and the Old Northwest*, 232–61. Mrs. Kinzie erroneously states that Billy Caldwell arrived shortly after the attack and saved several of the survivors. All the available evidence, however, indicates that Caldwell was in Michigan or Canada at this time.

33. John Parish (ed.), *The Robert Lucas Journal of the War of 1812 During the Campaign Under General William Hull*, 37, 43. Lucas was a participant in the skirmish. Also see Milo M. Quaife (ed.), *War on the Detroit: The Chronicles of Thomas Vercheres De Boucherville and the Capitulation by an Ohio Volunteer*, 81–84, 246–49. Vercheres was a Canadian merchant.

34. Colonel Henry Proctor to Brock, August 11, 1812, in *Michigan Historical Collections*, XV, 129–30; Hull to the secretary of war, August 13, 1812, in Cruikshank, *Documents Relating to the Invasion of Canada*, 139–41; Tucker, *Tecumseh*, 255–59; Quaife, *War on the Detroit*, 90–92.

35. Quaife, *War on the Detoit*, 108–10; Horsman, *Matthew Elliott*, 195–96; Brock to Lieutenant General Sir George Prevost, August 16, 1812, in *Michigan Historical Collections*, XV, 132.

36. Rhea to Meigs, August 22, 1812, in Knopf, *Return Jonathan Meigs*, 32; Stickney to Cass, June 23, 1816, in Potawatomi File, Great Lakes Indian Archives; Harrison to Meigs, September 5, 1812, William Henry Harrison Papers, Indiana Historical Society Library; Woehrmann, *At the Headwaters of the Maumee*, 225–30.

37. Daniel Curtis to Jacob Kingsbury, September 21, 1812, in Howard H. Peckham (ed.), "Recent Documentary Acquisitions to the Indiana Historical Society Library Relating to Fort Wayne," *Indiana Magazine of History*, XLIV (December, 1948), 414; Wallace A. Brice, *History of Fort Wayne*, 214–15. Second Lieutenant Curtis was a member of the garrison at Fort Wayne. Colonel Kingsbury was an officer stationed in Rhode Island.

38. Bert Griswold, *Fort Wayne, Gateway to the West, 1802–1813*, 57–58; Curtis to James Witherell, October 4, 1812, in Charles E. Slocum, *History of the Maumee River Basin from the Earliest Account to Its Organization into Counties*, 277–79.

39. Brice, *History of Fort Wayne*, 215–16; Woehrmann, *At the Headwaters of the Maumee*, 228–29.

40. Curtis to Kingsbury, September 21, 1812, in Peckham, "Recent Documentary Acquisitions," 415–16; Woehrmann, *At the Headwaters of the Maumee*, 228–29.

41. Gilpin, *War of 1812 in the Old Northwest*, 141; Tucker, *Tecumseh*, 276–77.

42. Harrison to Eustis, September 5, 1812, Potawatomi File, Great Lakes Indian Archives; McAfee, *History of the Late War*, 123–25; Bert Griswold, *The Pictorial History of Fort Wayne, Indiana*, 180; Woehrmann, *At the Headwaters of the Maumee*, 241.

43. Harrison to Eustis, September 21, 1812, in Esarey, *Messages and Papers of Harrison*, II, 143–47; Milo M. Quaife (ed.) , "A Diary of the War of 1812," *Mississippi Valley Historical Review*, I (September, 1914) , 276–77. The unknown author of this diary served as one of Wells's scouts. Also see McAfee, *History of the Late War*, 128–31.

44. Muir to Proctor, September 30, 1812, in *Michigan Historical Collections*, XV, 151–54; Edward Dewar, deputy assistant quartermaster general, to Lieutenant Colonel Robert McDonall, October 19, 1812, *ibid.*, 169–71; Johnston to Harrison, Potawatomi File, Great Lakes Indian Archives; Horsman, *Matthew Elliott*, 201–202.

45. Harrison to Eustis, December 14, 1812, in Esarey, *Messages and Papers of Harrison*, II, 246–47; entry for November 22, 1812 in Elias Darnell, *A Journal Containing an Accurate and Interesting Account of the Hardships, Sufferings, Battles, Defeat and Captivity of Those Heroic Kentucky Volunteers and Regulars, Commanded by General Winchester, in the Years 1812–1813*, 35–36; Brice, *History of Fort Wayne*, 236–37.

46. Gilpin, *War of 1812 in the Old Northwest*, 140–41; Harrison to Eustis, October 26, 1812, Potawatomi File, Great Lakes Indian Archives; Woehrmann, *At the Headwaters of the Maumee*, 248–49.

47. Zachary Taylor to Harrison, September 10, 1812, Potawatomi File, Great Lakes Indian Archives; Forsyth to Howard, September 7, 1812, in Carter, *Territorial Papers*, XVI, 261–65; Edwards to Eustis, September 21, 1812, in Knopf, *Letters to the Secretary of War*, part 3, 172. Also see Edmunds, "Illinois River Potawatomis in the War of 1812," 354.

48. Edwards to Eustis, November 18, 1812, in Edwards *History of Illinois*, 69–71; Reynolds, *My Own Times*, 136–37.

49. Hopkins to Harrison, October 6, 1812, in Esarey, *Harrison Papers*, II, 162–63; Isaac Shelby to Harrison, November 1, 1812, *ibid.*, 192–93; Hopkins to John Gibson, October 26, 1812, in Knopf, *Letters to the Secretary of War*, part 4, 67. Shelby was governor of Kentucky. Gibson was the acting governor of Indiana Territory.

50. Edwards to Eustis, November 18, 1812, in Edwards, *History of Illinois*, 69–72; Reynolds, *My Own Times*, 136–41.

51. Craig to Edwards, December 10, 1812, in Washburne, *Edwards Letters*, 86–90; memorial to Congress from the inhabitants of Peoria, December 20, 1813, in Carter, *Territorial Papers*, XVI, 379–83; Forsyth, "Journal of a Voyage from St. Louis to the Falls of St. Anthony in 1814," in *Wisconsin Historical Collections*, VI, 197; Alvord, *Illinois Country*, 445. Also see Ernest E. East, "Lincoln and the Peoria French Claims," *Journal of the Illinois State Historical Society*, XLII (March, 1949) , 40–56.

52. Petition to Congress by the territorial legislature, November 30, 1812, in Carter, *Territorial Papers*, XVI, 271–72; Edwards to the secretary of war, March 12, 1813, *ibid.*, 312; Edwards to Eustis, December 4, 1812, in Knopf, *Letters to the Secretary of War*, part 4, 130; Edwards to unknown, February 16, 1813, Berthrong Collection, University of Oklahoma.

53. Winchester to Harrison, Jan. 19, 1813, in Esarey, *Messages and Letters of Harrison*, II, 315–16; Winchester to the secretary of war, January 23, 1813, *ibid.*, 327–29; Procter to Major General Roger Sheaffe, January 25, 1813, in *Michigan Historical*

Collections, XV, 227–29; Alexander C. Casselman (ed.), *Richardson's War of 1812,* 132–33.

54. "Narrative of Timothy Mallary," in Darnell, *Journal,* 81–90; "Curocher's Narrative of Captain Hart's Massacre," in *Michigan Historical Collections,* VIII, 644–47; Isaac Baker to Winchester, February 25, 1813, in Esarey, *Messages and Letters of Harrison,* II, 371–75; letter by unknown, February 13, 1813, in Richard C. Knopf (ed.), *The National Intelligencer Reports the War of 1812 in the Northwest,* part 2, 27–28. Ensign Baker was one of the American prisoners.

55. Harrison to Shelby, February 11, 1813, Harrison Papers, Indiana Historical Society; Harrison to the secretary of war, April 21, 1813, in Esarey, *Messages and Letters of Harrison,* II, 422–23; McAfee, *History of the Late War,* 256–57.

56. Clay to Harrison, May, 1813, in Knopf, *National Intelligencer Reports the War,* 111–12; Harrison to the secretary of war, May 5, 1813, in Esarey, *Messages and Letters of Harrison,* II, 431–33; Peter Chambers to Noah Freer, April 24–May 5, 1813, in *Michigan Historical Collections,* XV, 289–91. Major Chambers was a British officer at Fort Meigs. Freer was a military secretary in Canada. Also see McAfee, *History of the Late War,* 264–77.

57. Procter to Prevost, May 14, 1813, in *Michigan Historical Collections,* XV, 293–96; Procter to McDonall, May 14, 1813, *ibid.,* 297; Harrison to the secretary of war, May 9, 1813, in Esarey, *Messages and Letters of Harrison,* II, 438–40; McAfee, *History of the Late War,* 281.

58. Johnson to Harrison, June 14, 1813, Potawatomi File, Great Lakes Indian Archives; Harrison to the secretary of war, July 2, 1813, in Esarey, *Messages and Letters of Harrison,* II, 480–82; Brice, *History of Fort Wayne,* 252–54.

59. Harrison to Duncan McArthur, July 2, 1813, McArthur Papers, Burton Collection, Detroit Public Library; Procter to Prevost, August 9, 1813, *Michigan Historical Collections,* XV, 347–50; Harrison to the secretary of war, August 1, 1813, in Esarey, *Messages and Letters of Harrison,* II, 506–507; George Croghan to Harrison, August 5, 1813, *ibid.,* 514–16. Croghan commanded Fort Stephenson.

60. Orders of evacuation, September 27, 1813, in "Reports and Correspondence from Canadian Archives," *Historical Society of North West Ohio Quarterly Bulletin,* II, (October, 1930), 11; Horsman, *Matthew Elliott,* 213; Tucker, *Tecumseh,* 299–300.

61. Harrison to the secretary of war, September 30, 1813, Potawatomi File, Great Lakes Indian Archives; McArthur to the secretary of war, October 6, 1813, *Michigan Historical Collections,* XL, 535–36; Brice, *History of Fort Wayne,* 269.

62. Harrison to the secretary of war, October 9, 1813, in Esarey, *Messages and Letters of Harrison,* II, 558–65; Procter to Francis De Rottenburg, October 23, 1813, *Michigan Historical Collections,* XV, 427–29. Major General De Rottenburg was the military commander in Upper Canada. Also see William Hickling, *Caldwell and Shabonee,* 4, 7–8; Matson, *Memories of Shaubena,* 26–29; Draper's notes, Draper Manuscripts, 26S70; and Forsyth to Edwards, March 31, 1816, *Wisconsin Historical Collections,* XI, 345–47.

63. McArthur to unknown, October 15, 1813, in Draper's notes, Draper Manuscripts, 26S124–25; Harrison to the secretary of war, Potawatomi File, Great Lakes Indian Archives. Also see "Terms of an Armistice with the Indians," in Esarey, *Messages and Letters of Harrison,* II, 577–79, and Brice, *History of Fort Wayne,* 277.

64. Lewis Cass to John Armstrong, October 21, 1813, Potawatomi File, Great Lakes Indian Archives; Cass to William Woodbridge, Woodbridge Papers, Burton Collection, Detroit Public Library. Armstrong was secretary of war. Woodbridge was acting governor of Michigan Territory. Also see Elliott to the deputy superintendent of general Indian affairs, March 25, 1814, in *Michigan Historical Collections,* XV, 524,

and report by William Claus, May 14, 1814, *ibid.,* 553. Claus was a British Indian agent.

65. Procter to Major General Roger Shaeffe, January 13, 1813, *Michigan Historical Collections,* XV, 215–16; Edwards to the secretary of war, Potawatomi File, Great Lakes Indian Archives. Shaeffe served as commander of Upper Canada from late 1812 till the summer of 1813. Also see report of Auguste LaRoche and Louis Chevalier, April 4, 1813, in Carter, *Territorial Papers,* XIV, 652–54, and Forsyth to Howard, May 7, 1813, *ibid.,* XVI, 324–27. LaRoche and Chevalier were spies employed by Forsyth.

66. Forsyth to Howard, February 12, 1813, Potawatomi File, Great Lakes Indian Archives; Dickson to Noah Freer, March 16, 1813, *Michigan Historical Collections,* XV, 259. Freer was the military secretary to Prevost. Also see Donald Jackson, *Black Hawk: An Autobiography,* 65–66:; Ernest Allen Cruikshank, "Robert Dickson, the Indian Trader," *Wisconsin Historical Collections,* XII, 144–45; and Reginald Horsman, "Wisconsin in the War of 1812," *Wisconsin Magazine of History,* XLVI (Autumn, 1962).

67. Edwards to Shelby, March 17, 1813, Edward E. Ayer Manuscripts, Newberry Library, Chicago; Forsyth to William Clark, July 20, 1813, Forsyth Papers, Missouri Historical Society. Also see statement by John Ketcham, no date, in Esarey, *Messages and Letters of Harrison,* II, 280–81, and Reynolds, *Pioneer History of Illinois,* 408.

68. Benjamin Stephenson to Edwards, May 20, 1813, in Carter, *Territorial Papers,* XVI, 333–35; Edwards to the secretary of war, May 24, 1813, *ibid.,* 331–33; William Russell to Governor Thomas Posey, July 25, 1813, in Esarey, *Messages and Letters of Harrison,* II, 497–99; Russell to Pierre Andre, August 5, 1813, Hyacinthe Lasselle Papers, Indiana State Library. Stephenson, Russell, and Andre were rangers patroling the Illinois-Indiana frontier.

69. Edwards to the president, October 16, 1811, in Edwards, *History of Illinois,* 288; Clark to the secretary of war, January 6, 1814, September 12, 1813, William Clark Papers, Missouri Historical Society; Howard to Armstrong, October 28, 1813, in Carter, *Territorial Papers,* XVI, 370–73; Draper's notes, Draper Manuscripts, 26S126–27.

70. Clark to John G. Comegys, November 20, 1813, Clark Papers, Missouri Historical Society; Clark to the secretary of war, in Carter, *Territorial Papers,* XVI, 727–28. Comegys was a merchant from Kentucky. Also see "Minutes of a Council between Clark and the Potawatomis Chief, Black Patridge," January 2, 1814, Potawatomi File, Great Lakes Indian Archives, and Jackson, *Black Hawk,* 75–77.

71. Dickson to Lawe, February 4, 1814, *Wisconsin Historical Collections,* XI, 290–91; Dickson to Lawe, February 11, 1814, *ibid.,* X, 103–104; "Remarks on the Bad Intentions of the Pottawatomies, March 2, 1814, *ibid.,* 108–111. Also see Forsyth to Clark, March 31, 1814, Clark Papers, Missouri Historical Society, and Forsyth to Clark, May 5, 1814, *ibid.*

72. Anthony Butler to the secretary of war, January 23, 1814, Potawatomi File, Great Lakes Indian Archives; John Whistler to McArthur, July 1, 1814, *ibid.* Butler commanded Fort Detroit. Whistler commanded Fort Wayne. Also see *Wisconsin Historical Collections,* X, 112 fn. 1; XIX, 159–160 fn. 12.

73. McArthur to the secretary of war, June 29, 1814, McArthur Papers, Burton Collection; "Journal of Treaty Proceedings," *American State Papers: Indian Affairs,* I, 829–36; "A Treaty of Peace and Friendship," Kappler, *Indian Treaties,* II, 105–106; Joseph Barron to Posey, October 24, 1814, Potawatomi File, Great Lakes Indian Archives. Joseph Barron was an interpreter who worked for the government.

74. Kinzie to Cass, September 22, 1814, in Carter, *Territorial Papers,* X, 489–90; Lieutenant Colonel Robert McDonall to Prevost, July 20, 1814, *Michigan Historical*

Collections, XXIII, 558; "Minutes of a Council Held at Mackinac, January 29, 1815," *ibid.*, 469–71.

75. Secretary of war to McArthur, August 2, 1814, in Carter, *Territorial Papers*, X, 471.

76. Louis Grignon to Lewis Crawford, September 6, 1814, *Wisconsin Historical Collections*, XI, 304; McArthur to James Monroe, October 12, 1814, Potawatomi File, Great Lakes Indian Archives; McArthur to Monroe, September 26, 1814, in Carter, *Territorial Papers*, X, 485–86. Grignon and Crawford both were traders sympathetic to the British cause.

77. McArthur to Monroe, September 26, 1814, in Carter, *Territorial Papers*, X, 485–86; McArthur to Monroe, October 10, 1814, Potawatomi File, Great Lakes Indian Archives; Whistler to Cass, October 26, 1814, Michigan Superintendency of Indian Affairs, Letters Received and Sent by the Superintendent, Microfilm M1, Roll 2, 23–24, National Archives.

78. "Minutes of a Council, January 29, 1815," *Michigan Historical Collections*, XXIII, 469–71; McDonall to Andre Bulger, February 18, 1815, *ibid.*, 476. Captain Bulger was a British officer serving in Wisconsin. Also see Stickney to Charles Larned, January 21, 1815, M1, Roll 2, 32–34, National Archives; Cass to the secretary of war, February 18, 1815, M1, Roll 2, 40–48, National Archives. Larned was a secretary in the Indian Department.

79. Posey to Monroe, November 28, 1815, Potawatomi File, Great Lakes Indian Archives; Whistler to Larned, January 15, 1815, M1, Roll 2, 30–31, National Archives; Cass to Woodbridge, February 14, 1815, Woodbridge Papers, Burton Collection; Woodbridge to Julie Woodbridge, February 18, 1815, *ibid.* Julie Woodbridge was William Woodbridge's wife.

80. Bulger to McDonald, November 14, 1814, *Wisconsin Historical Collections*, XIII, 21–22; statement by John Askin enclosed in McDonall to Bulger, February 18, 1815, *ibid.*, 82–83; Forsyth to Howard, July 6, 1814, in Carter, *Territorial Papers*, XVI, 446–47; Forsyth to the secretary of war, November 15, 1814, Berthrong Collection, University of Oklahoma. Askin was a merchant from Detroit.

81. James B. Moore to William Russell, November 19, 1814, Draper's notes, Draper Manuscripts, 26S194–96; Russell to Monroe, December 4, 1814, Berthrong Collection, University of Oklahoma; Secretary of war to Clark and Edwards, January 13, 1815, in Carter, *Territorial Papers*, XVIII, 116–17; Black Partridge and Petacho to Clark, March 4, 1815, Potawatomi File, Great Lakes Indian Archives. Moore commanded the rangers that attacked the Potawatomis.

82. Edwards to the secretary of war, March 8, 1815, in Carter, *Territorial Papers*, XVII, 145; "Speech to the Indians upon Ratification of Peace," *Michigan Historical Collections*, XXV, 620–21; Whistler to Cass, April 22, 1815, M1, Roll 2, 54–55, National Archives; Chandonnai to John Mason, April 25, 1815, *ibid.*, 49–51; Whistler to McArthur, May 12, 1815, Potawatomi File, Great Lakes Indian Archives. Mason was the superintendent of Indian trade.

83. McDonall to Bulger, May 2, 1815, *Wisconsin Historical Collections*, XIII, 144–45; Whistler to McArthur, May 1, 1815, *Michigan Historical Collections*, XVI, 87; McArthur to the secretary of war, May 5, 1815, *ibid.*, 101; "Niscaunma's (Mad Sturgeon's) Talk to Whistler," May 22, 1815, Potawatomi File, Great Lakes Indian Archives.

84. Forsyth to the secretary of war, April 13, 1815, *Wisconsin Historical Collections*, XI, 336–38; Forsyth to commissioners appointed to treat with the Indian Nations, May 30, 1815, *ibid.*, 338–41; "A Treaty of Peace and Friendship" Kappler, *Indian Treaties*, II, 110–11.

85. Whistler to Cass, July 2, 1815, M1, Roll 2, 77, National Archives; Whistler to Cass, July 20, 1815, *ibid.*, 96; Whistler to the secretary of war, July 6, 1815, Potawatomi File, Great Lakes Indian Archives.

86. Secretary of war to Harrison, McArthur, and Graham, June 9, 1815, M15, Roll 3, 208–13, National Archives; Harrison and Graham to William Crawford, September 9, 1815, *American State Papers: Indian Affairs*, II, 16–17; "Journal of the Proceedings of the Commissioners Appointed to Treat with the Northwest Indians at Detroit," *ibid.*, 17–25; "A Treaty Between the United States and the Indians, September 8, 1815," in Kappler, *Indian Treaties*, II, 117–19.

87. Forsyth to Edwards, March 31, 1816, *Wisconsin Historical Collections*, XI, 345–56; Blair, *Indian Tribes of the Upper Mississippi*, II, 278, fn. 103.

CHAPTER NINE

1. "Copy of a Memorandum of Exports and Imports to Certain Parts of the Indian Country . . . October 15, 1816," Forsyth Papers, Draper Manuscripts, 2T63. Also see Sheridan Warrick, "The American Indian Policy in the Upper Old Northwest Following the War of 1812," *Ethnohistory*, III (Spring, 1956), 109–11, and Bert Anson, "The Fur Traders in Northern Indiana, 1795–1850" (Ph. D. diss., Indiana University, 1953), 62, 72.

2. George Graham to Cass, April 19, 1816, M15, Roll 3, 331–32, National Archives; secretary of war to Indian agents, October 4, 1816, *ibid.*, 433; Thomas McKenney to Cass, June 21, 1816, M1, Roll 2, 250–51, National Archives. Also see Donald F. Carmony and Francis Paul Prucha (eds.), "A Memorandum of Lewis Cass Concerning a System for the Regulation of Indian Affairs," *Wisconsin Magazine of History*, LII (Autumn, 1968), 40–46. Graham was acting secretary of war. McKenney was a clerk in the War Department. He later became the first commissioner of Indian affairs.

3. William Claus to Caldwell, April 11, 1816, William Claus File, Chicago Historical Society; "Proceedings of a Council Held at Amherstburg, June 19, 1816," *Michigan Historical Collections*, XVI, 471–73; statement by Gabriel Godfroy, October 8, 1819, M1, Roll 4, 128–34, National Archives; Stickney to Cass, June 13, 1816, M1, Roll 2, 252–58, National Archives; speech by Metea, July, 1822, Potawatomi File, Great Lakes Indian Archives.

4. Benjamin Parke to the secretary of war, March 27, 1816, Potawatomi File, Great Lakes Indian Archives; E. Shipp to Lt. Col. William Lawrence, June 26, 1816, *ibid.* Parke was a judge in Indiana. Both Shipp and Lawrence served under Brigadier General Thomas A. Smith at Fort Armstrong, Rock Island. Also see Clark to Major William Puthuff, June 20, 1817, William Clark Papers, Kansas State Historical Society (microfilm). Pothuff was the Indian agent at Mackinac.

5. A. J. Dallas to Madison, June 19, 1815, M15, Roll 3, 223–24, National Archives; Dallas to Madison, June 27, 1815, *ibid.*, Roll 1, 909–11, National Archives; Dallas to Madison, July 7, 1815, *ibid.*, Roll 3, 241–43, National Archives. Dallas was acting secretary of war. Also see Prucha, *Sword of the Republic*, 124–28.

6. Thomas G. Conway, "Potawatomi Politics," *Journal of the Illinois State Historical Society*, LXV (Winter, 1972), 395–418. Conway argues that the tribal fragmentation facilitated government control over the Potawatomis.

7. Stickney to Graham, June 1, 1816, Potawatomi File, Great Lakes Indian Archives; Jouett to Cass, December 3, 1816, M1, Roll 2, 395–96, National Archives; Jouett to Cass, July 21, 1817, *ibid.*, 141–47; Cass to William Turner, May 26, 1819, *ibid.*, Roll 4, 77–78, National Archives. Turner was appointed Indian agent at Fort Wayne in 1818.

8. "Petition of the Citizens of Indiana to the President," 1815, Records of the Secretary of War Relating to Indian Affairs, Letters Received, Microfilm M271, Roll 1, 897–99, National Archives; secretary of war to Parke, September 6, 1816, M15, Roll 3, 414, National Archives; Graham to Edwards, February 20, 1817, *ibid.*, Roll 4, 8, National Archives; Graham to Cass, May 19, 1817, *ibid.*, 42–43.

9. Black Partridge to the president, September 1, 1815, in Carter, *Territorial Papers*, XVII, 227–28; Forsyth to Edwards, December 8, 1815, *ibid.*, 259–260; George Graham to General Thomas Smith, November 6, 1815, M15, Roll 3, 273–74, National Archives; Graham to Edwards, November 16, *ibid.*, 273.

10. Graham to Edwards, November 6, 1815, Potawatomi File, Great Lakes Indian Archives; "A Treaty of Peace, Friendship, and Limits . . . August 24, 1816," Kappler, *Indian Treaties*, II, 132–33.

11. The political structure of the Potawatomis caused much debate before the Indian Claims Commission. The majority opinion was that the tribe remained unified during the postwar period and that no major land cessions were made without the approval of the entire tribe. A minority opinion argued that the Potawatomis were divided into a several well-defined "bands," and that these bands autonomously sold different parts of the Potawatomi homeland. I agree that certain groups of Potawatomis periodically sold different parts of their territory, but I would disagree that any well-defined band structure existed. See Indian Claims Commission, *Indians of Ohio, Indiana, Illinois, Southern Michigan, and Southern Wisconsin*, II.

12. Cass to Johnston, July 15, 1817, M1, Roll 3, 137–40, National Archives; Jouett to Cass, September 15, 1817, *ibid.*, 177–78; "Articles of a Treaty Made and Concluded at the Foot of the Rapids of the Miami of the Lake," September 29, 1817, Kappler, *Indian Treaties*, II, 145–55.

13. Turner to Cass, March 17, 1818, M1, Roll 3, 298–99, National Archives; "Estimate of Expenses," enclosed in Johnston to Cass, April 30, 1818, *ibid.*, 364–69; Cass to McArthur, May 24, 1818, *ibid.*, 417–22; receipt of John Johnston, November 2, 1818, T58, Roll 1, 366, National Archives.

14. "Articles of a Treaty Made and Concluded at St. Mary's," October 2, 1818, Kappler, *Indian Treaties*, II, 168–69.

15. Calhoun to Cass and Sibley, June 1, 1820, M15, Roll 4, 437–38; Wolcott to Cass, January 1, 1821, M1, Roll 8, 5–6; Wolcott to Cass, March 31, 1821, *ibid.*, 244–46; Wolcott to Cass, June 23, 1821, *ibid.*, 292–94.

16. Henry Rowe Schoolcraft, *Travels in the Central Portions of the Mississippi Valley: Comprising Observations on its Mineral Geography, Internal Resources, and Aboriginal Population*, 337; "Proceedings of the Treaty at Chicago, August, 1821," Potawatomi File, Great Lakes Indian Archives.

17. "Proceedings of the Treaty at Chicago, August, 1821," Potawatomi File, Great Lakes Indian Archives.

17. "Proceedings of the Treaty at Chicago, August, 1821," Potawatomi File, Great Lakes Indian Archives.

18. Schoolcraft, *Travels in the Mississippi Valley*, 347–48 fn.

19. *Ibid.*, 387–88; Quaife, *Chicago and the Old Northwest*, 346.

20. "Articles of a Treaty Made and Concluded at Chicago . . . on August 29, 1821," Kappler, *Indian Treaties*, II, 198–201; Quaife, *Chicago and the Old Northwest*, 345–47.

21. Paré, "The St. Joseph Mission," 50–51, 54; Gilbert J. Garraghan, *The Jesuits of the Middle United States*, I, 423; Cunningham, *Land of Four Flags*, 68.

22. By far the best discussion of the Protestant missionary effort is Robert F. Berkhofer's prize-winning *Salvation and the Savage: An Analysis of Protestant Missions and American Indian Response*.

23. McCoy to William Staughton, May 19, 1820, Isaac McCoy Papers, Kansas State Historical Society; McCoy to Staughton, October 21, 1820, *ibid.* Staughton was the corresponding secretary of the Board of Foreign Missions. Also see Thomas Teas Scattergood, "Journal of a Tour to Fort Wayne and the Adjacent Country in the Year 1821," in *Indiana As Seen by Early Travelers*, ed. by Harlow Lindley, 250, and Nellie A. Robertson, "John Hays and the Fort Wayne Indian Agency," *Indiana Magazine of History*, XXXIX (September, 1943), 226. Hays served as Indian agent at Fort Wayne from 1820 till 1823.

24. McCoy to Luther Rice, April 17, 1821, McCoy Papers, Kansas State Historical Society; Isaac McCoy, *History of Baptist Indian Missions: Embracing Remarks on the Former and Present Condition of Aboriginal Tribes, Their Former Settlements within the Indian Territory and Their Future Prospects*, 95–96; George A. Schultz, *An Indian Canaan: Isaac McCoy and the Vision of an Indian State*, 50–53. Rice served as general agent of the Board of Missions.

25. McCoy, *History of Baptist Indian Missions*, 100–10; McCoy to Martha Galloway, July 27, 1821, McCoy Papers, Kansas State Historical Society; Quaife, *Chicago and the Old Northwest*, 345; "Articles of a Treaty Made and Concluded at Chicago . . . on August 29, 1821," Kappler, *Indian Treaties*, II, 198–201. Mrs. Galloway was a member of a local missionary society in Kentucky.

26. Charles Trowbridge to Cass, August 28, 1822, Potawatomi File, Great Lakes Indian Archives; Calhoun to Cass, June 12, 1822, M15, Roll 5, 278–79, National Archives; McCoy to Cass, November 14, 1822, McCoy Papers, Kansas State Historical Society; Cunningham, *Land of Four Flags*, 126–27. Trowbridge was Cass's secretary.

27. McKenney to Calhoun, July 16, 1824, Records of the Office of Indian Affairs, Letters Sent, Microfilm M21, Roll 1, 137, National Archives; statement on the condition of Indian schools, 1825, *ibid.*, Roll 2, 266, National Archives; Schultz, *Indian Canaan*, 59–60, 76. Also see William H. Keating, *Narrative of an Expedition to the Source of St. Peters River*, I, 148–55.

28. Johnston Lykins to McCoy, February 4, 1824, McCoy Papers, Kansas State Historical Society; Robert Simmerwell, "Chatechisms and Hymns Translated into the Potawatomi Language, Preceeded by Alphabet and a Few Notes on Phonetics," Ayer Collection, Newberry Library; report by John L. Leib, November 20, 1824, Records of the Office of Indian Affairs, Letters Received, Microfilm M234, Roll 419, 127–45, National Archives. Lykins was a teacher at Carey. Leib inspected the mission for Cass.

29. McCoy to James Lorry, March 1, 1825, McCoy Papers, Kansas State Historical Society; McCoy to Francis Wayland, May 23, 1825, *ibid.*; "Circular to the Baptist State Conventions," June 6, 1825, *ibid.*; McCoy, *History of Baptist Indian Missions*, 234–35, 262–63. Both Lorry and Wayland were Baptist ministers.

30. McCoy to Cass, July 1, 1823, Potawatomi File, Great Lakes Indian Archives; McCoy to Staughton, July 11, 1825, McCoy Papers, Kansas State Historical Society; letter of introduction for Medard Beaubien, January, 1826, *ibid.*; McKenney to John Tipton, January 27, 1827, M21, Roll 3, 341–42, National Archives; McCoy to Cass, June 30, 1827, M234, Roll 419, 984–85, National Archives. Tipton was the Indian agent at Fort Wayne. Beaubien was a student at Carey Mission.

31. McKenney to McCoy, October 13, 1826, M21, Roll 3, 188, National Archives; McCoy to William Hendrick, December 23, 1826, McCoy Papers, Kansas State Historical Society; McCoy to William McLean, December 25, 1826, *ibid.*; Schultz, *Indian Canaan*, 91–92, 121–22; Francis Paul Prucha, *American Indian Policy in the Formative Years: The Indian Trade and Intercourse Acts, 1790–1834*, 33. Prucha's volume contains the best discussion of federal Indian policy in this period.

32. Graham to Clark, August 31, 1817, Richard Graham Papers, Missouri Historical

Society; Schoolcraft to Calhoun, September 18, 1821, Potawatomi File, Great Lakes Indian Archives; McCoy to John Tipton, March 23, 1825, Nellie Armstrong Robertson and Dorothy Riker (eds.), *The John Tipton Papers*, I, 449–50; McCoy, *History of Baptist Indian Missions*, 280–81, 286.

33. Cass to Calhoun, February 13, 1827, M234, Roll 419, 669–71, National Archives; Simmerwell to McCoy, March 27, 1826, McCoy Papers, Kansas State Historical Society.

34. Forsyth to Clark, December 13, 1818, Forsyth Papers, Missouri Historical Society; Cass to Calhoun, July 17, 1822, M271, Roll 4, 41–42, National Archives; "A Report of the Horses, Hogs, Etc., Stolen and Killed within the Indian Agency for the State of Illinois Made by Richard Graham," June 1, 1821, Potawatomi File, Great Lakes Indian Archives; "Petition of the Citizens of Illinois," June 18, 1821, *ibid.*; McKenney to Clark, April 20, 1824, M21, Roll 1, 27, National Archives.

35. Calhoun to Clark, November 10, 1823, M15, Roll 6, 7–8, National Archives; Forsyth to Clark, April 9, 1824, Forsyth Papers, Missouri Historical Society; Forsyth to Clark, April 25, 1824, Potawatomi File, Great Lakes Indian Archives. For a description of the liquor traffic at Peoria, see James W. Covington, "The Indian Liquor Trade at Peoria," *Journal of the Illinois State Historical Society*, LXVI (Summer, 1953), 142–50.

36. Deposition by Joseph Ojia, April 19, 1824, Potawatomi File, Great Lakes Indian Archives; Forsyth to Clark, April 25, 1824, *ibid.* Ojia was an interpreter at Peoria. For a discussion of the government's inability to suppress the liquor traffic, see Prucha, *American Indian Policy*, 102–38.

37. "List of Goods at Chicago and Green Bay Factories, 1823," T58, Roll 1, 449–454, National Archives; "Merchandise Paid the Ottaways, Chipaways, and Poutewatimies for Their Annuity for 1828," Pierre Menard Collection, Business Papers, Illinois State Historical Society, Springfield; Jesse W. Weik, "An Unpublished Chapter in the Early History of Chicago," *Journal of the Illinois State Historical Society*, VII (January, 1915), 327–28. For a good description, including illustrations, of Potawatomi dress during this period, see Winter, *Journals and Paintings of George Winter*.

38. Stickney to Crawford, November 8, 1816, Potawatomi File, Great Lakes Indian Archives; Simmerwell to McCoy, October 7, 1829, McCoy Papers, Kansas State Historical Society; "Antoine Le Clair's Statement," *Wisconsin Historical Collections*, XI, 240–41.

39. Cass to Calhoun, M1, Roll 4, 278–82, National Archives.

40. "Abstract of Licenses Issued to Persons to Trade in the Indian Country," 1821–22, M271, Roll 4, 44–45, National Archives; "Abstract of Licenses Issued Within the Superintendency of Lewis Cass," 1824–25, M1, Roll 419, 93–96, National Archives; Ernest E. East, "The Inhabitants of Chicago, 1825–1831," *Journal of the Illinois State Historical Society*, 131–63; Keating, *Narrative of an Expedition*, I, 75.

41. Anson, "Fur Traders in Northern Indiana," 19–29; Keating, *Narrative of an Expedition*, I, 75–81; statement by Thomas Forsyth, Forsyth Papers, Draper Manuscripts, 2T58.

42. Ernest E. East, "Contributions to Chicago History from Peoria County Records," *Journal of the Illinois State Historical Society*, XXXI (April, 1938), 341–42; E. Reed to Cass, July 25, 1828, Potawatomi File, Great Lakes Indian Archives; Gurdon S. Hubbard, *The Autobiography of Gurdon Saltonstall Hubbard*, 146–47. Hubbard was a trader active on the Vermillion River in Illinois. He was married to a Potawatomi woman.

43. List of persons employed in the Indian Department, September 30, 1825, M21, Roll 2, 228, National Archives; East, "Contributions to Chicago History from Peoria," 341; Hickling, *Caldwell and Shabonee*, 31.

44. Tipton to Cass, May 10, 1827, Robertson and Riker, *John Tipton Papers*, I, 711–12; speech by Senachewine, November 23, 1829, M234, Roll 749, 801–805, National Archives; Conway, "Potawatomi Politics," 395–418. For an interesting discussion of factionalism and changing patterns of Indian leadership, see Berkhofer, *Salvation and the Savage*, 125–51, and Robert F. Berkhofer, "The Political Context of a New Indian History," *Pacific Historical Review*, XL (August, 1971), 357–82.

45. Secretary of war to Cass, Ray, and Tipton, May 24, 1826, M21, Roll 3, 93; "Articles of a Treaty Made and Concluded near the Mouth of the Mississinewa, on the Wabash . . . October 16, 1826," Kappler, *Indian Treaties*, II, 273–77; "The Wish of the Pottawatomie Nation as to the Disposition of the Education Fund," October 16, 1826, Robertson and Riker, *John Tipton Papers*, I, 596.

46. "Proceedings of the Treaty Commissioners," September 20–October 23, 1826, Documents Relating to the Negotiations of Ratified and Unratified Treaties with Various Indian Tribes, Microfilm T494, Roll 1, 874–906, National Archives; Cass, Ray, and Tipton to James Barbour, October 23, 1826, *American State Papers: Indian Affairs*, II, 683–85; "Articles of a Treaty Made and Concluded near the Mouth of the Mississinewa, on the Wabash . . . October 16, 1826," Kappler, *Indian Treaties*, II, 273–77.

47. "A Treaty Between the United States and the Pottawatamie Tribe of Indians . . . September 19, 1827," Kappler, *Indian Treaties*, II, 283–84; "Articles of a Treaty Between the United States and the Pottawatamie Indians," September 20, 1828, *ibid.*, 294–97.

48. E. Reed to Cass, July 25, 1828, M1, Roll 23, 141–43, National Archives; Reed to Cass, July 31, 1828, Cunningham, *Letter Book of Burnett*, 223–25; "Journal of the Proceedings Held on the St. Joseph's of Lake Michigan, September, 1828," M668, Roll 6, 192–96, National Archives; Cass to McKenney, September 22, 1828, *Michigan Historical Collections*, XXXVI, 565–66.

49. "Treaty Between the Indian Tribes," August 19, 1825, Kappler, *Indian Treaties*, II, 250–55; "Journal of the Proceedings of the Treaty of Prairie du Chien, August, 1825," Clark Papers, Kansas State Historical Society.

50. Cass to Barbour, August 17, 1827, M234, Roll 419, 777–81; Roger L. Nicholls, *General Henry Atkinson: A Western Military Career*, 119–36.

51. "List of Potawatomi Chiefs to Whom Annuities Were Paid," 1827, Alexander Wolcott File, Chicago Historical Society; Wolcott to Barbour, July 25, 1827, M234, Roll 132, 28–33, National Archives; Kinzie to Cass, August 3, 1827, *ibid.*, Roll 419, 789–92, National Archives; Hubbard, *Autobiography*, 168.

52. Kinzie to Cass, August 3, 1827, M234, Roll 419, 789–92, National Archives.

53. *Ibid.* Also see Hubbard, *Autobiography*, 171–73, and Quaife, *Chicago and the Old Northwest*, 315.

54. Unknown to McKenney, June 25, 1827, M234, Roll 315, 51, National Archives; "Talk of the Potawatomi Chiefs," August 8, 1827, *ibid.*, Roll 748, 212–13, National Archives; Pierre Menard, Jr., to Edwards, August 6, 1827, Executive Documents, Illinois State Archives, Springfield; talk by Senachewine, August 7, 1827, *ibid.*

55. Edwards to the secretary of war, September 4, 1827, Washburne, *Edwards Papers*, 309–10; Clark to Edwards, August 18, 1827, Executive Documents, Illinois State Archives; Clark to Menard, November 2, 1827, Governor's Correspondence, *ibid.*

56. Deposition by Samuel Mallory, May 17, 1828, Governor's Correspondence, Illinois State Archives; Tom McNeale to Edwards, May 18, 1828, *ibid.*; Menard to Clark, June 5, 1828, Menard Papers, Illinois State Historical Society; Myron Phelps to Edwards, June 30, 1828, M234, Roll 748, 593–94, National Archives. Mallory, McNeale, and Phelps were settlers living near the Spoon River.

57. Treaty at Green Bay, August 25, 1828, Kappler, *Indian Treaties*, II, 292–93; "Journal of the Treaty Proceedings," August, 1828, T494, Roll 2, 128–47, National Archives; commissioners to the Potawatomis, Ottawas, and Chippewas, June 25, 1829, *ibid.*, 166; Kinzie to Cass, June 28, 1829, M1, Roll 24, 331–33.

58. Menard to treaty commissioners, July 2, 1829, T494, Roll 2, 159–60, National Archives; "Proceedings of the Treaty Commissioners, 1829," *ibid.*, 187; "Articles of a Treaty Made and Concluded at Prairie du Chien," 1829, Kappler, *Indian Treaties*, II, 297–300. McNeil and Atwater were commissioners at the treaty.

59. Speech by Senachewine, November 23, 1829, M234, Roll 749, 801–805, National Archives; "Report of a Council Held with General William Clark and a Deputation of Pottowatamie Indians," August 1830, Potawatomi File, Great Lakes Indian Archives; Clark to the secretary of war, September 12, 1830, Clark Papers, Kansas State Historical Society; Menard to Clark, November 12, 1830, *ibid.*

60. John Bryant to Lyman Draper, December 16, 1878, Tecumseh Papers, Draper Manuscripts, 9YY28; speech by Shabbona, 1831, M234, Roll 642, 22–23, National Archives; speech by Nauntay, 1831, *ibid.*, 28–30; Clark to the secretary of war, August 11, 1831, Clark Papers, Kansas State Historical Society.

61. John Reynolds to the president, August 2, 1831, *Illinois Historical Collections*, IV, 178–79; Samuel Hamilton to Clark, September 1, 1831, M21, Roll 7, 362, National Archives; Clark to Cass, December 12, 1831, M234, Roll 642, 31–33, National Archives. Reynolds was governor of Illinois. Hamilton was an official in the Indian Office.

62. Cass to Calhoun, December 27, 1821, *Wisconsin Historical Collections*, XX, 237–38; John Tanner, *A Narrative of the Captivity and Adventures of John Tanner during Thirty Years' Residence Among the Indians in the Interior of North America*, ed. by Edwin James, 256. For a good description of Potawatomi villages in Indiana and southern Michigan, see the footnotes in Robertson and Riker, *John Tipton Papers*, Vols. I and II.

63. "Extract from a Statement Showing the Names and Numbers of the Diffferent Tribes of Indians . . . January 10, 1825," Potawatomi File, Great Lakes Indian Archives; "List of Potawatomi Chiefs to Whom Annuities Were Paid at Chicago, July 18, 1817," Wolcott File, Chicago Historical Society; "Pay Roll of the Wabash and Elk-heart Potawatamies for the Year 1828," Potawatomi File, Great Lakes Indian Archives; Menard to Clark, November 12, 1830, Clark Papers, Kansas State Historical Society.

64. "Minutes of a Treaty at Greenville," June 16–August 10, 1795, *American State Papers: Indian Affairs*, I, 564–82; Wolcott to Cass, March 3, 1820, M1, Roll 7, 93–96, National Archives. Also see David Baerris, "The Band Affiliation of Potawatomi Treaty Signatories" (multilithed), Great Lakes Indian Archives.

65. Baerris, "Band Affiliation of Potawatomi Treaty Signatories," 1–3; Indian Claims Commission, *Indians of Ohio, Indiana, Illinois.*

66. "Abstract of Provisions Issued to Indians by Thomas Forsyth, 1822–1823," Potawatomi File, Great Lakes Indian Archives; "Report on a Council Between Clark and the Potawatomis," August 26, 1830, M234, Roll 749, 1047–51, National Archives.

67. Conway, "Potawatomi Politics," 399; Wolcott to Cass, December 23, 1828, M1, Roll 23, 531–35, National Archives. Also see Hodge, *Handbook of American Indians*, II, 290.

68. Proclamation by John Reynolds, April 16, 1832, in Frank E. Stevens, *The Black Hawk War*, 113. For a good account of the Black Hawk War, see William T. Hagan, *The Sac and Fox Indians.*

69. "Memorandum of a Council Held at Malden, July 25, 1827," Woodbridge

Papers, Burton Collection; Forsyth to Clark, May 22, 1829, Governor's Letter Book, Illinois State Archives; Joseph Street to Clark, July 6, 1831, Clark Papers, Kansas State Historical Society; Clark to Cass, December 12, 1831, M234, Roll 642, 31–33, National Archives.

70. Isaiah Stillman to Reynolds, January 4, 1832, Governor's Correspondence, Illinois State Archives; Clark to Reynolds, January 28, 1832, *ibid.*; Jackson, *Black Hawk*, 119–21.

71. Owen to Reynolds, May 12, 1832, *Illinois Historical Collections*, XXXVI, 365–66; Owen to Herring, May 12, 1932, M234, Roll 132, 180–82, National Archives.

72. Jackson, *Black Hawk*, 122–25; Hagan, *Sac and Fox Indians* 158–61. Also see Stevens, *Black Hawk War*, 132–38.

73. A. C. Clybourne to Henry Clybourne, May 18, 1832, Letters Received by the Secretary of War, Main Series, Microfilm M221, Roll 112, 9981, National Archives; Atkinson to Dodge, May 17, 1832, *Illinois Historical Collections*, XXXVI, 377–78; Matson, *Memories of Shaubena*, 121–24. Also see the Shabbona File, Chicago Historical Society. A. C. Clybourne was a citizen of Chicago.

74. Owen to the superintendent of Indian affairs, May 24, 1832, M234, Roll 421, 233–34, National Archives; Stevens, *Black Hawk War*, 149–58; excerpt from *Missouri Intelligencer*, July 10, 1834, in Indian Papers, Missouri Historical Society.

75. "Ransom of Rachel and Sylvia Hall," Black Hawk War Research Notes, Whitney Collection, Illinois State Historical Society; Owen to Atkinson, June 11, 1832, *Illinois Historical Collections*, XXXVI, 574–75; Clark to Cass, June 30, 1832, Clark Papers, Kansas State Historical Society; Stevens, *Black Hawk War*, 157–58.

76. A. Edwards to Major General John R. Williams, June 1, 1832, *Michigan Historical Collections*, XXXI, 402–403; statement by citizens of Vincennes, May 29, 1832, Lasselle Papers, Indiana State Library; John Reynolds to Lewis Cass, May 22, 1832, Berthrong Collection, University of Oklahoma; John Hogan to Cass, May 25, 1832, M234, Roll 132, 148, National Archives. Edwards was an Indian agent in Michigan. Hogan was a captain in the Illinois militia.

77. Owen to Hogan and Almanzan Huston, May 24, 1832, *Illinois Historical Collections*, XXXVI, 431–32; Chicago residents to James Stewart, May 29, 1832, *ibid.*, 476; Owen to Atkinson, June 3, 1832, *ibid.*, 505–506. Huston was a colonel in the Michigan militia. Stewart was a subagent at Chicago.

78. Atkinson to Owen, May 31, 1832, *ibid.*, 491–92; "Potawatomi Indians in United States Service," *ibid.*, XXXV, 560–61; Owen to Herring, June 21, 1832, M234, Roll 132, 188–89; "Travel Journal of Lemuel Bryant from Ashfield Massachusetts to Chicago, 1832," Chicago Historical Society.

79. See "Interrogation of Indian Prisoners, August, 1832," in Letters Received by the Secretary of War, Unregistered Series Microfilm M222, Roll 31, 2280–2300, National Archives; Scott to Cass, August 19, 1832, *ibid.*, 2280. Also see Owen to Porter, August 27, 1832, M1, Roll 31, 215–16, National Archives, and Owen to Elias Kane, June 6, 1832, Kane Papers, Chicago Historical Society. Kane was a citizen of Kaskaskia.

CHAPTER TEN

1. The best discussion of the emergence of the removal policy can be found in Prucha, *American Indian Policy*, 224–49, and in Ronald D. Satz, *American Indian Policy in the Jacksonian Era*. Also see report by McKenny, March 22, 1830, in U.S. Congress, Senate, 21st Cong., 1st sess., *Sen. Doc. 110*, 2–3.

2. Francis Paul Prucha, "Andrew Jackson's Indian Policy: A Reassessment," *Journal*

of American History, LVI, (December, 1969) , 527–39; John Reynolds to the president, August 2, 1831, *Illinois Historical Collections*, IV, 178–79.

3. McCoy, *History of the Baptist Indian Missions*, 321; Schultz, *Indian Canaan*, 91–100.

4. E. Reed to Cass, July 12, 1828, M1, Roll 3, 203, National Archives; McCoy to Lykins, August 18, 1828, McCoy Papers, Kansas State Historical Society; McCoy to Clark, October 7, 1828, *ibid.*; Schultz, *Indian Canaan*, 101–10. McCoy's journal on this trip can be found in Lela Barnes (ed.) , "Journal of Isaac McCoy for the Exploring Expedition of 1828," *Kansas Historical Quarterly*, V (August, 1936) , 227–77.

5. Cass to Jennings, Davis, and Crume, July 11, 1832, M21, Roll 9, 44–47, National Archives; Owen to Porter, September 3, 1832, M1, Roll 31, 279–80, National Archives; Simmerwell to Lykins, November 5, 1832, McCoy Papers, Kansas State Historical Society.

6. Forsyth to Clark, November 5, 1819, Forsyth Papers, Missouri Historical Society; Forsyth to Clark, November 2, 1820, M271, Roll 3, 890–93, National Archives; Clark to the secretary of war, February 20, 1821, *ibid.*, 886–89.

7. Report of the commissioners, October, 1832, T494, Roll 2, 526–531, National Archives. The treaties can be found in Kappler, *Indian Treaties*, II, 353–55, 367–75.

8. *Ibid.*

9. *Ibid.*

10. Deposition by J. H. Kintree, July 1, 1834, M234, Roll 354, 874, National Archives; deposition by James Avaline, July 7, 1834, *ibid.*, 865–66; N. D. Grover to Marshall, January 18, 1833, Drusilla L. Cravens Papers, Indiana State Library. Also see Bert Anson, "Lathrop M. Taylor, Hanna and Taylor Partnership," *Indiana Magazine of History*, XLV (June, 1949) , 152–57. Kintree was a former employee of Grover, an Indian trader and federal official in Indiana. Avaline was a citizen of Allen County, Indiana.

11. Cass to Jennings, Davis, and Crume, July 11, 1832, M21, Roll 9, 44–47, National Archives; "Articles of a Treaty Made and Concluded on Tippecanoe River," October 26, 1832, Kappler, *Indian Treaties*, II, 367–70; "Articles of a Treaty Made and Concluded at Camp Tippecanoe," October 20, 1832, *ibid.*, 353–55.

12. Owen to Porter, December 29, 1832, M1, Roll 31, 801, National Archives; Edwards to Elias Kane and I. M. Robinson, June 5, 1832, in Edwards, *History of Illinois*, 369–72; Atkinson to Owen, November 16, 1832, M234, Roll 132, 241, National Archives; Nicolas Bolivin to Cass, January 10, 1833, *ibid.*, 268–69.

13. Reynolds to James Henry, Samuel Whitesides, Thomas Reynolds, and William Moore, November 15, 1832, Governor's Correspondence, Illinois State Archives; Atkinson to Owen, November 16, 1832, M234, Roll 642, 43, National Archives; Whitesides, Curry, Moore, and Reynolds to the governor, December 13, 1832, *ibid.*, Roll 132, 237–39; Reynolds to Dodge, December 13, 1832, *Illinois Historical Collections*, IV, 221.

14. Caldwell and Robinson to Owen, January 18, 1833, M234, Roll 132, 292–93, National Archives; Atkinson to Elbert Herring, March 17, 1833, *ibid.*, 260–61. Herring was appointed commissioner of Indian affairs late in 1832.

15. Cass to Marshall, June 19, 1832, M21, Roll 8, 463–65, National Archives; Marshall to Porter, February 25, 1833, M234, Roll 354, 698–700, National Archives; Clark to Reynolds, October 31, 1832, Executive Documents, Illinois State Archives. For a discussion of Kannekuk, see R. David Edmunds, "A History of the Kickapoo Indians in Illinois from 1750 to 1834" (M.A. thesis, Illinois State University, 1966) , 134–35, 143–46.

16. Cass to Pepper, March 6, 1833, M21, Roll 10, 96–99, National Archives. For an

extended discussion of the removal of Quiquito's people, see R. David Edmunds, "The Prairie Potawatomi Removal of 1833," *Indiana Magazine of History*, LXVIII (September, 1972), 240–53.

17. Pepper to General George Gibson, commissary general of subsistence, April 11, 1833. Berthrong Collection, University of Oklahoma; Cass to Lewis Sands, March 8, 1833, M21, Roll 10, 105, National Archives; Cass to Rudolphus Schoonover, March 8, 1833, *ibid.*, 105–106.

18. Montgomery to Gibson, June 20, 1833, U.S. Congress, Senate, *Correspondence on the Subject of the Emigration of Indians Between the 30th November, 1831, and the 27th December, 1833*, 23rd Cong., 1st sess., *Sen. Doc. 512*, I, 774–75; Pepper to Gibson, May 7, 1833, Letters Received, Commissary General of Subsistence, Potawatomi Emigration, Record Group 75, National Archives.

19. Kinzie to Porter, March 15, 1833, M1, Roll 32, 259–61, National Archives; Owen to Pepper, June 20, 1833, Letters Received, Commissary General of Subsistence, Potawatomi Emigration, RG 75, National Archives; Pepper to Gibson, August 12, 1833, Berthrong Collection, University of Oklahoma.

20. Lewis Sands, "Journal of Occurrences in the Pottawatomie Removal Under the Direction of Lewis H. Sands, Asst. Agt.," Berthrong Collection, University of Oklahoma.

21. *Ibid.*; William R. Montgomery, "Lieut. W. R. Montgomery's Journal During the Emigration of Pottawatomies in the Summer of 1833," *ibid.*; Montgomery to Gibson, August 15, 1833, Letters Received, Commissary General of Subsistence, Potawatomi Emigration, RG75, National Archives; Edmunds, "Prairie Potawatomi Removal of 1833," 252.

22. Edmunds, "Prairie Potawatomi Removal of 1833," 253.

23. Cass to Porter, Owen, and Weatherford, April 8, 1833, M21, Roll 10, 210–14, National Archives; "Journal of the Proceedings of a Treaty Between the United States and the United Tribe of Pottawottamies, Chipeways, and Ottawas," T494, Roll 3, 61–87, National Archives. For a lengthy discussion of this treaty, see Anselm J. Gerwing, "The Chicago Indian Treaty of 1833," *Journal of the Illinois State Historical Society*, LVII (Summer, 1964), 117–42.

24. "Journal of the Proceedings," T494, Roll 3, 61–87, National Archives.

25. "Articles of a Treaty made at Chicago," September 26, 1833, Kappler, *Indian Treaties*, II, 402–15.

26. Charles I. Latrobe, *The Rambler in North America*, II, 203–12; "Narrative of Peter J. Vieau," *Wisconsin Historical Collections*, XV, 460–63.

27. Latrobe, *Rambler in North America*, II, 206–12; Henry Van der Bogart to William Van der Bogart, September 15, 1833, Van der Bogart Papers, Chicago Historical Society. Henry Van der Bogart was a white observer at the treaty. William Van der Bogart was his father.

28. Van der Bogart to David Demarest, October 7, 1833, Van der Bogart Papers, Chicago Historical Society; Van der Bogart to Walter Montaith, October 14, 1833, *ibid.*; Gerwing, "Chicago Indian Treaty," 135.

29. Charges against George B. Porter, December 12, 1833, Kinzie Family Papers, Chicago Historical Society; Porter to Andrew Jackson, December 15, 1833, in Milo M. Quaife (ed.), "Documents: The Chicago Treaty of 1833," *Wisconsin Magazine of History*, I (March, 1918), 291–303; Benjamin Kercheval, Robert Forsyth, John Kinzie, and R. A. Kinzie to the U.S. Senate, January 10, 1834, M234, Roll 421, 652–56, National Archives.

30. John Schermerhorn to Herring, January 28, 1834, M234, Roll 132, 496–98,

National Archives. For a detailed discussion of the problem of the Platte Country in Potawatomi removal, see R. David Edmunds, "Potawatomis in the Platte Country: An Indian Removal Incomplete," *Missouri Historical Review*, LXVIII (July, 1974), 375–92.

31. Potawatomi chiefs to Owen, October 1, 1834, M234, Roll 132, 448–49, National Archives; Owen to Cass, October 3, 1834, *ibid.*; 446–47.

32. "List or Roll of Individuals Composing the Exploring Party," M234, Roll 134, 20–21, National Archives; "William Gordon's Journal of a Potawatomi Exploration West of the Mississippi, July 30–September 12, 1835," Indian Papers, Missouri Historical Society; Luther Rice to Tipton, April 23, 1836, *Indiana Historical Collections*, XXVI, 265–66; Quiquito to the president of the United States, November 20, 1835, M234, Roll 642, 84–85, National Archives.

33. Russell to Cass, January 19, 1836, M234, Roll 133, 420–21, National Archives; Anthony Davis to Tipton, January 19, 1836, *Indiana Historical Collections*, XXVI, 207–209. Davis was an "emigrating agent" to the Potawatomis at Fort Leavenworth.

34. Russell's Journal, September 21–December 2, 1835, Letters Received, Commissary General of Subsistence, Potawatomi Emigration, RG75, National Archives; Rice to Tipton, April 23, 1836, *Indiana Historical Collections*, XXVI, 265–66; Russell to Cass, January 19, 1836, M234, Roll 133, 420–21, National Archives.

35. Russell to Herring, January 19, 1836, M234, Roll 133, 425, National Archives; Potawatomis to Jackson, December, 1835, *ibid.*, 422–23; Cass to W. L. Ewing, February 20, 1836, M21, Roll 18, 91, National Archives; Herring to Clark, April 6, 1836, *ibid.*, 271. Ewing was a senator from Illinois.

36. Clark to Herring, April 8, 1835, M234, Roll 300, 696, National Archives; Henry Dodge to Clark, February 15, 1836, *ibid.*, Roll 751, 78; petition of Benton, Linn, and Harrison, February 8, 1836, *ibid.*, Roll 642, 835–39. Additional correspondence regarding Missouri's attempt to acquire the Platte Country can be found in U.S. Congress, Senate, 24th Cong., 1st sess., *Sen. Docs. 206* and *251*. Colonel Henry Dodge was in command at Fort Leavenworth.

37. Kercheval's journal, September 12–November 11, 1836, M234, Roll 134, 265–72, National Archives; Kercheval to Gibson, October 22, 1836, *ibid.*, 56–57; Kercheval to Gibson, November 6, 1836, *ibid.*, 260; Kercheval to Gibson, November 15, 1836, *ibid.*, 259.

38. John Dougherty to Clark, June 9, 1836, M234, Roll 215, 3, National Archives; Dougherty to Clark, July 14, 1836, *ibid.*, Roll 751, 107–108; Andrew S. Hughes to Clark, July 14, 1836, *ibid.*, 106; Bert Anson, "Variations of the Indian Conflict: The Effect of the Emigrant Indian Removal Policy, 1830–1854," *Missouri Historical Review*, LIX (October, 1964), 81–82. Dougherty was the Indian agent for the Upper Missouri Agency. Hughes was subagent for the Iowas.

39. Harris to Butler, January 9, 1837, M21, Roll 20, 402–16, National Archives; Harris to Davis, April 24, 1837, *ibid.*, Roll 21, 315; "Articles of a Treaty Concluded at Washington," February 11, 1837, Kappler, *Indian Treaties*, II, 488–89.

40. Harris to Clark, April 28, 1837, Territorial Papers of the United States, Wisconsin, Microfilm M236, Roll 43, 344–45, National Archives; Davis to Harris, May 13, 1837, M234, Roll 134, 138–39, National Archives; Jacob Van der Zee, "Episodes in the Early History of the Western Iowa Country," *Iowa Journal of History and Politics*, XI (July, 1913), 342–43.

41. Harris to Clark, November 3, 1836, M21, Roll 20, 88, National Archives; Davis to Clark, June 30, 1837, M234, Roll 134, 150, National Archives; Macomb to Atkinson, June 20, 1837, *ibid.*, Roll 360, 790–91.

42. Gaines to Harris, July 26, 1837, M234, Roll 134, 208–209, National Archives; E. A. Hitchcock to Harris, August 2, 1837, *ibid.*, 237–39; Gaines to the citizens of Missouri, July 20, 1837, *Niles' Register*, September 16, 1837; Gaines to Pointsett, August 22, 1837, M221, Roll 118, 2737–2742, National Archives. Lieutenant Hitchcock was a military disbursing agent at Jefferson Barracks.

43. Atkinson to Macomb, August 6, 1837, M234, Roll 134, 101–103, National Archives; James to George McGuire, August 16, 1837, *ibid.*, 161–62; James to Clark, December 14, 1837, *ibid.*, 446–48; "Extracts from the Diary of Rev. Moses Merrill, A Missionary to the Otoe Indians from 1832 to 1840," *Transactions and Reports of the Nebraska State Historical Society*, IV, 28. McGuire was chief clerk at the St. Louis superintendency.

44. McGuire to Harris, July 31, 1837, M234, Roll 361, 46, National Archives; "Muster Roll of Putawatamie Indians," *ibid.*, Roll 642, 138–42; Louis Barry (comp.), *The Beginnings of the West*, 330–31; U.S. Congress, House, *Report of the Commissioner of Indian Affairs*, 26th Cong., 2d sess., *House Doc.* 3, 253–54.

45. Harris to Tipton, July 17, 1837, McCoy Papers, Kansas State Historical Society; Harris to Atkinson, July 21, 1837, *ibid.*; Pointsett to Gaines, July 28, 1837, M21, Roll 22, 169, National Archives; Harris to Sands, September 12, 1837, *ibid.*, 316.

46. Unknown to Gibson, April 24, 1834, Letters Received, Commissary General of Subsistence, Potawatomi Emigration, RG75, National Archives.

47. Marshall to Herring, May 10, 1834, M234, Roll 361, 11–12, National Archives; Herring to Marshall, May 30, 1834, Letters Received, Commissary General of Subsistence, Potawatomi Emigration, RG75, National Archives.

48. Marshall to Herring, June 30, 1834, Letters Received, Commissary General of Subsistence, Potawatomi Emigration, RG75, National Archives; "Abstracts of Disbursements by William Gordon for the Removal and Subsistence of Indians, July 11–September 2, 1834," *ibid.*

49. Owen to Cass, November 17, 1834, M234, Roll 132, 464–65, National Archives; Pepper to Gibson, September 25, 1834, Letters Received, Commissary General of Subsistence, Potawatomi Emigration, RG75, National Archives; Pepper to Gibson, October 21, 1834, *ibid.*

50. Cass to J. B. Chapman, David Hillis, and John Parker, May 11, 1835, M21, Roll 16, 79–80, National Archives; Herring to Chapman, July 27, 1835, *ibid.*, 304–305; citizens to Congress, 1836, M234, Roll 355, 385–86, National Archives. For a general discussion of the loss of individual reservations by the Potawatomis and other tribes, see Paul Gates, "Indian Allotments Preceding the Dawes Act," in John G. Clark (ed.), *The Frontier Challenge: Responses to the Trans-Mississippi West*, 141–70. Chapman, Hillis, and Parker were appointed to locate the Potawatomi reservations.

51. Citizens of Indiana to Andrew Jackson, August 7, 1835, M234, Roll 355, 59–60, National Archives. Extensive correspondence containing charges of fraud and bribery in the selection of the reservations can be found in M234, Roll 355, and M21, Rolls 17–18, National Archives.

52. Cass to Marshall, July 12, 1834, M21, Roll 13, 172–74, National Archives; Herring to Marshall, September 12, 1834, *ibid.*, 382.

53. Marshall to Herring, December 23, 1834, M234, Roll 355, 186–87; Marshall to Cass, January 1, 1835, *ibid.*, 203–205. The treaties can be found in Kappler, *Indian Treaties*, II, 428–31.

54. Cass to Pepper, January 25, 1836, M21, Roll 17, 458–61; Pepper to Cass, April 27, 1836, T494, Roll 3, 350–51, National Archives; Pepper to Carey A. Harris, July 8, 1836, *ibid.*, 355–57. Harris succeeded Herring as commissioner of Indian affairs

during June, 1836. The treaties can be found in Kappler, *Indian Treaties*, II, 450–63.

55. John W. Edmonds to Harris, in John Edmonds, *Report on the Claims of Creditors of the Potawatomie Indians of the Wabash in 1836 and 1837*, 4.

56. John W. Edmonds, *Report on the Disturbance at the Potawatomie Payment, September, 1836*, 8. The treaties can be found in Kappler, *Indian Treaties*, II, 470–72.

57. Pepper to Cass, October, 1836, M234, Roll 355, 678–86, National Archives; Edmonds, *Report on the Disturbance*, 4–5.

58. Edmonds, *Report on the Disturbance*, 5.

59. *Ibid.*, 5–8; Coquillard to Edmonds, June 22, 1837, M234, Roll 355, 1041–47, National Archives; Potawatomi chiefs to Andrew Jackson, October 18, 1836, *ibid.*, 691–706.

60. Pepper to Cass, October, 1836, M234, Roll 355, 678–86, National Archives; Ward, Polke, Berthelet, and Stevenson to the secretary of war, October 27, 1836, *ibid.*, 784–85, Edmonds, *Report on the Disturbance*, 11–13.

61. Edmonds, *Report on the Claims*; George Winter, "Journal Written at Logansport," Winter Papers, Indiana State Library.

62. Potawatomi chiefs to Jackson, October 18, 1836, M234, Roll 355, 691–706, National Archives; Ewing to Butler, February 12, 1837, *ibid.*, 824–28; "Articles of a Treaty Concluded at Washington," February 11, 1837, Kappler, *Indian Treaties*, II, 488–89.

63. Henry Schoolcraft to Harris, January 6, 1837, M234, Roll 422, 558–59, National Archives; Russell to Harris, January 12, 1837, *ibid.*, Roll 134, 284–85; Schoolcraft to Harris, February 17, 1837, *ibid.*, Roll 422, 628; Harris to John Garland, April 15, 1837, M21, Roll 21, 261, National Archives. Schoolcraft was superintendent of Indian affairs in Michigan. Major Garland was a military disbursing agent supervising all Indian removals from the Old Northwest.

64. Harris to Kercheval, May 29, 1837, M21, Roll 21, 457–58, National Archives; Kercheval to Harris, June 17, 1837, M234, Roll 134, 247–48, National Archives; Harris to acting secretary of war, July 1, 1837, *ibid.*, 427.

65. Harris to Sands, July 14, 1837, M21, Roll 22, 103–104, National Archives; "Quarterly Statement of Agents and Others Employed in the Removal and Subsistence of the Pottawatamie Indians," M234, Roll 422, 511, National Archives; Schoolcraft to Harris, July 10, 1837, *ibid.*, Roll 133, 512–13; Schoolcraft to Harris, September 15, 1837, *ibid.*, Roll 134, 311–12. Also see James A. Clifton, *A Place of Refuge for All Time: Migration of the American Potawatomi into Upper Canada, 1830–1850.*

66. "Minutes of a Council Held with the Potawatomis,' September 3–4, 1837, M234, Roll 134, 237–41, National Archives.

67. *Ibid.*; Sands to Harris, September 9, 1837, *ibid.*, 336–37.

68. Sands to Harris, September 26, 1837, M234, Roll 134, 365, National Archives; Sands to Harris, October 13, 1837, *ibid.*, 385–86.

69. Entries for October 25–28, 1837, John Duret's diary, Duret Family Papers, Indiana Historical Society Library; Sands to Harris, October 28, 1834, M234, Roll 134, 398, National Archives; Barry, *Beginnings of the West*, 337–38. Duret was an assistant removal agent.

70. Entries for October 9–25 and November 20–21, 1837, Duret's diary, Duret Papers, Indiana Historical Society Library; deposition by Asa Stafford, January 4, 1838, M234, Roll 134, 572–74, National Archives; Isaac Bing to Harris, November 28, 1837, *ibid.*, 133–36; Lieutenant J. T. Sprague to Harris, November 19, 1837, *ibid.*, 422–25; Topinbee and others to the president, October 28, 1837, *ibid.*, 438–40. Stafford was a freighter employed by Sands. Bing was the enrolling agent for the removal. Sprague was the military disbursing agent on the trip.

71. Edwin James to Clark, November 14, 1837, M234, Roll 134, 444, National Archives; Harris to Clark, January 25, 1838, M21, Roll 23, 234–35, National Archives.

72. "Minutes of a Council Between the Potawatomis and the Government Agents," July–August, 1837, M234, Roll 361, 116–38, 150–60, National Archives; "Journal of a Visit to Lake Kee-wau-nay and Crooked Creek, 1837," in Winter, *Journal and Paintings of George Winter*, 98–147.

73. Pepper to Harris, August 12, 1837, M234, Roll 361, 166–67, National Archives; Indian agents to Harris, August 13, 1837, *ibid.*, Roll 361, 83–84.

74. Pepper to Harris, August 20, 1837, M234, Roll 361, 173–74, National Archives. George Proffit, "Journal of the Pottawattamie Emigration." This journal can be found interspersed between correspondence in M234, Roll 361, 108–206, National Archives. Also see Barry, *Beginnings of the West*, 331.

75. Thomas Timothy McAvoy, "The Indian Missions of Marshall County" (unpublished manuscript), McAvoy Papers, Indiana State Library; John G. Shea, *History of the Catholic Missions Among the Indian Tribes of the United States*, 393–96. Also see Irving McKee, *The Trail of Death: Letters of Benjamin Marie Petit*, 13–17.

76. McKee, *Trail of Death*, 18–19.

77. Lieutenant J. P. Simonton to Gibson, June 15, 1835, Letters Received, Commissary General of Subsistence, Potawatomi Emigration, RG75, National Archives; Pepper to Deseille, August 7, 1835, *ibid.*; Deseille to Pepper, October 10, 1835, *ibid.*; Deseille to Pepper, March 21, 1836, T494, Roll 3, 353, National Archives; Potawatomi chiefs to Herring, April 16, 1836, M234, Roll 355, 688, National Archives; Pepper to Deseille, April 18, 1836, *ibid.*, Roll 361, 85. Simonton was a military disbursing agent.

78. Cass to Pepper, January 25, 1836, M21, Roll 17, 458–61, National Archives; Cass to Potawatomi chiefs, February 9, 1836, *ibid.*, 384–85; McKee, *Trail of Death*, 21–22.

79. Potawatomi chiefs to Tipton, November 4, 1836, *Indiana Historical Collections*, XXVI, 312–13; Potawatomi chiefs to the president, April 6, 1837, M234, Roll 355, 1250–51, National Archives; Pepper to the secretary of war, October, 1836, *ibid.*, Roll 355, 678–86.

80. Pepper to Harris, May 13, 1837, M234, Roll 361, 79, National Archives; Pepper to Deseille, May 16, 1837, in "Documents: Correspondence on Indian Removal, Indiana, 1835–1838," *Mid-America*, XV (January, 1933), 185–86; McKee, *Trail of Death*, 25.

81. Harris to Pepper, March 29, 1838, M21, Roll 23, 519, National Archives; Harris to Pepper, June 11, 1838, *ibid.*, Roll 24, 331–32; Harris to Pepper, June 29, 1838, *ibid.*, 433–34.

82. Harris to Pepper, February 26, 1838, M21, Roll 23, 375–79.

83. Speech by Menominee, August 6, 1838, quoted in Irving McKee, "The Centennial of the Trail of Death," *Indiana Magazine of History*, XXXV (March, 1939), 36; Tipton to David Wallace, September 18, 1838, *Indiana Historical Collections*, XXVI, 713–18. Wallace was governor of Indiana.

84. Tipton to Wallace, August 31, 1838, *Indiana Historical Collections*, XXVI, 682; "Journal of an Emigrating Party of Pottawattomie Indians, 1838," *Indiana Magazine of History*, XXI (December 1925), 316–17; Daniel McDonald, *Removal of the Pottawattomie Indians from Northern Indiana*, 42–45.

85. Petit to his family, September 14, 1838, in McKee, *Trail of Death*, 90–93; "Journal of an Emigrating Party," 317–34. Also see Polke to Harris, September 19, 1838, in Dwight L. Smith (ed.), "A Continuation of the Journal of an Emigrating Party of Potawatomi Indians, 1838, and Ten William Polke Manuscripts," *Indiana Magazine of History*, XLIV (December, 1948), 403–404; Dwight Smith, "Jacob Hull's Detachment of the Potawatomi Emigration of 1838," *Indiana Magazine of History*,

XLV (September, 1949), 285–88. Hull conducted the smaller party of Potawatomis who had fallen behind the first removal.

86. "Journal of an Emigrating Party," 317–34; Hull to Polke, October 30, 1838, in Smith, "A Continuation of the Journal," 407.

87. "A Roll of Ottawa, Chipaway and Potawatamie Emigrated Indians . . . under the Direction of Isaac L. Berry," M234, Roll 752, 189, National Archives.

88. Samuel Milroy to T. Hartley Crawford, June 8, 1839, M234, Roll 356, 906–909, National Archives; citizens to the secretary of war, May 3, 1839, *ibid.*, Roll 423, 246. Ketchum to Crawford, September 28, 1839, *ibid.*, Roll 427, 306–307; "At a Council Held at Notawassippi," July 29, 1839, *Michigan Historical Collections*, X, 170–72. Milroy succeeded Pepper as the removal agent for Indiana. Crawford was commissioner of Indian affairs.

89. Pepper to Crawford, February 8, 1839, M234, Roll 361, 313, National Archives; Milroy to Polke, September 21, 1839, in Dwight Smith (ed.), "The Attempted Potawatomi Emigration of 1839," *Indiana Magazine of History*, XLV (March, 1949), 59; entry for October 7, 1839, in Polke's journal in *ibid.*, 72.

90. Milroy to Polke, October 23, 1839, in Smith, "Attempted Potawatomi Emigration," 65–66; Polke to Milroy, October 28, 1839, *ibid.*, 68; Milroy to Crawford, November 8, 1839, *ibid.*, 74–76.

91. J. E. Crary and John Norvell to Pointsett, January 1, 1840, M234, Roll 134, 667–68, National Archives; Milroy to Crawford, March 17, 1840, *ibid.*, Roll 357, 166–67; Polke to Milroy, January 14, 1840, in Smith, "Attempted Potawatomi Emigration of 1839," 76–77. Caray and Norvell were settlers from Coldwater.

92. Pointsett to Brady, February 26, 1840, U.S. Congress, House, 27th Cong., 2d. sess., *House Doc. 143*, 34; Brady to Crawford, June 13, 1840, M234, Roll 134, 649–51, National Archives; Brady to Crawford, August 24, 1840, *ibid.*, Roll 361, 369–71; "Muster Roll of a Band of Pottawatomy Indians Delivered at the Osage River Agency, October 6, 1840," *ibid.*, Roll 642, 234–36.

93. Brady to Crawford, August 24, 1840, M234, Roll 361, 369–71, National Archives; Ketchum to Crawford, March 25, 1840, *ibid.*, 407–12; Woodbridge to Ebsen G. Fuller, June 25, 1840, William Woodbridge Papers, Burton Historical Collections. Fuller was the prosecuting attorney in Branch County, Michigan. Also see Cecelia Bain Buechner, *The Pokagons.*

94. Brady to Crawford, August 24, 1840, M234, Roll 361, 369–71, National Archives; Grant Foreman, *The Last Trek of the Indians*, 118–19.

95. Crawford to Joshua Pilcher, October 17, 1840, M21, Roll 29, 323, National Archives; "Muster Roll of a Band of Putawatomie Indians Delivered at the Osage River . . . November 25, 1840," M234, Roll 642, 232–33, National Archives; Brady to Crawford, November 5, 1840, *ibid.*, Roll 427, 406–407.

EPILOGUE

1. Clifton, *A Place of Refuge for All Time.*

2. J. D. Doty to the secretary of war, October 6, 1841, M234, Roll 949, 19, National Archives; "Enumeration of Indians Within the Green Bay Subagency," October, 1842, *ibid.*, Roll 318, 777; Allen Hamilton to Crawford, May 13, 1844, *ibid.*, Roll 360, 135; William Medill to Henry Dodge, January 21, 1848, M21, Roll 40, 263, National Archives. Doty was governor of Wisconsin. Hamilton was an Indian agent in Indiana. Medill served as commissioner of Indian affairs from 1845 until 1849.

3. Ewing to Charles E. Mix, July 15, 1851, M234, Roll 678, 30–32, National Archives;

Mix to Elias Murray, August 2, 1851, M21, Roll 45, 35–36, National Archives; Mix to David Mitchell, August 18, 1851, *ibid.*, 74; Barry, *Beginnings of the West*, 1039–40. Mix was acting commissioner of Indian affairs. Mitchell was in charge of the St. Louis superintendency.

4. Publius V. Lawson, "The Potawatomi," *Wisconsin Archaeologist*, XIX (April, 1920), 41–116; Kenneth E. Tiedke, *A Study of the Hannahville Indian Community*, 5–15; Alexander Morstad, *The Reverend Erik Olsen Morstad: His Work Among the Wisconsin Pottawatomie Indians.*

5. Everett Claspy, *The Potawatomi Indians of Southwestern Michigan*, 15–43; Otho Winger, *The Potawatomi Indians*, 141–58.

6. L. B. Holcomb to Robert Stuart, June 4, 1843, M1, Roll 54, 638, National Archives; Stuart to Charles G. Hammond, July 5, 1844, *ibid.*, Roll 39, 470; "A Survey of Indian Groups in the State of Michigan," Potawatomi File, Great Lakes Indian Archives; George Quimby, "Some Notes on Kinship and Kinship Terminology Among the Potawatomi of the Huron," *Papers of the Michigan Academy of Science, Arts and Letters*, XXVIII, 537–42. Holcomb and Stuart were Indian agents in Michigan. Hammond was a politician in Michigan.

7. The treaties establishing new reservations can be found in Kappler, *Indian Treaties*, II, 557–59, 824–28, and 970–74. Also see Joseph Francis Murphy, "Potawatomi Indians of the West: Origins of the Citizens Band" (Ph.D. diss., University of Oklahoma, 1961).

Selected Bibliography

MANUSCRIPT MATERIALS

Ann Arbor, Michigan. University of Michigan. William L. Clements Library.
Jeffrey Amherst Papers.
Thomas Gage Papers.
Jehu Hay. "Diary of a Siege of Detroit."
Josiah Harmar Papers.
Anthony Wayne Papers.
Bloomington, Indiana. University of Indiana. Glenn A. Black Laboratory of Archaeology. Great Lakes–Ohio Valley Indian Archives Project. Potawatomi File.
Boston, Massachusetts. Massachusetts Historical Society. Winthrop Sargent Papers. Microfilm.
Chicago, Illinois. Chicago Historical Society.
Perry Armstrong File.
Billy Caldwell File.
William Claus File.
Christian Bowman Dolson File.
Ninian Edwards Papers.
Gurdon Saltonstall Hubbard Papers.
Indian Documents.
Elias Kent Kane Papers.
Kinzie Family File.
Lawe Papers.
John Mills File.
Shabbona File.
"Travel Journal of Lemuel Bryant from Ashfield, Massachusetts, to Chicago, 1832."
Henry Van der Bogart Papers.
Alexander Wolcott File.
Chicago, Illinois. The Newberry Library. Edward E. Ayer Manuscripts.
Detroit, Michigan. Detroit Public Library. Burton Historical Collection.
Hugh Brady Correspondence.
William Burnett Papers.
Lewis Cass Papers.
Diary of Thomas Gist.
Frederic Haldimand Papers.

John F. Hamtramck Papers.
Jacob Kingsbury Papers.
Labadie Family Papers.
Duncan McArthur Papers.
Translation of Pierre Margry, *Memoires et Documents, 1614–1754.* Microfilm.
Robert Navarre, Jr., Papers.
John Porteus Papers.
Simon Pokagon Papers.
Gabriel Richard Papers.
Solomon Sibley Papers.
Harold E. Stoll Papers.
C. C. Trowbridge Papers.
Jacob Varnum Papers.
William Woodbridge Papers.
Harrisburg, Pennsylvania. Pennsylvania State Archives. Baynton, Wharton, and Morgan Papers. Microfilm.
Indianapolis, Indiana. Indiana Historical Society Library.
Duret Family Papers. Microfilm.
William Henry Harrison Papers.
Samuel Milroy Papers. Microfilm.
Northwest Territory Papers.
Indianapolis, Indiana. Indiana State Library.
Joseph Bailly Papers.
Drusilla L. Cravens Papers.
Ewing Family Papers.
Hyacinth Lasselle Papers.
Thomas Timothy McAvoy Papers.
George M. Profitt Papers.
R. B. Whitsett Collection.
Otho Winger Papers.
George Winter Papers.
Madison, Wisconsin. State Historical Society of Wisconsin. Draper Manuscripts.
Draper's Notes. Microfilm.
Thomas Forsyth Papers. Microfilm.
Josiah Harmar Papers. Microfilm.
Tecumseh Papers. Microfilm.
Norman, Oklahoma. University of Oklahoma. Bizzell Memorial Library. Donald J. Berthrong Collection.
St. Louis, Missouri. Missouri Historical Society.
William Clark Papers.
John Dougherty Papers.
Thomas Forsyth Papers.
Richard Graham Papers.
Indian Papers.
Springfield, Illinois. Illinois State Archives.
Executive Documents and Governor's Letter Books, 1790–34.
Governor's Correspondence, 1814–40.
Springfield, Illinois. Illinois State Historical Society.
Pierre Menard Papers.
Business Papers.

Personal Papers. Microfilm.
Whitney Collection. Black Hawk War Research Notes.
Potawatomi Chiefs.
Potawatomi Chronology.
Ransom of Rachel and Sylvia Hall.
Springfield, Illinois State Museum. Photograph File.
Topeka, Kansas. Kansas State Historical Society.
William Clark Papers. Microfilm.
Isaac McCoy Papers. Microfilm.
Jotham Meeker Papers. Microfilm.
Valparaiso, Indiana. Historical Society of Porter County, Indiana. Joseph Bailly's Journal, 1799–1802.
Washington, D.C. National Archives.
General Records of the U.S. Government (Record Group 11) .
Ratified Indian Treaties (M668) . Microfilm. 1772–1848.
Records of the Bureau of Indian Affairs (Record Group 75) .
Documents Relating to the Negotiations of Treaties (T494) . Microfilm. 1801–53.
Letters Received by the Office of Indian Affairs (M234) . Microfilm.
Chicago Agency, 1824–27.
Council Bluffs Agency, 1836–51.
Fort Leavenworth Agency, 1824–51.
Fort Wayne Agency, 1824–30.
Great Nemaha Agency, 1837–51.
Green Bay Agency, 1824–50.
Indiana Agency, 1824–50.
Iowa Agency, 1825–37.
Iowa Superintendency, 1838–49.
Michigan Superintendency, 1824–51.
Ohio Agency, 1831–43.
Osage River Agency, 1824–54.
Potawatomi Agency, 1851–52.
St. Louis Superintendency, 1824–51.
Wisconsin Superintendency, 1836–48.
Letters Sent by the Office of Indian Affairs (M21) . Microfilm. 1824–51.
Records of the Commissary General of Subsistence. Potawatomi Emigration. Microfilm.
Records of the Michigan Superintendency (M1) . Microfilm. 1814–50.
Records of the Secretary of War Relating to Indian Affairs. Microfilm.
Letters Received (271) . 1800–23.
Letters Sent (M15) . 1800–24.
Records of the Superintendent of Indian Trade. Microfilm.
Letters Received (T58). 1806–24.
Letters Sent (M16) . 1807–23.
Records of the Office of the Secretary of War (Record Group 107) .
Letters Received by the Secretary, Main Series (M221) . Microfilm. 1832–40.
Letters Received by the Secretary, Unregistered Series. (M222). Microfilm. 1832–40.
Territorial Papers of the United States.
Wisconsin: 1836–48 (M236) . Microfilm. Rolls 38–46.

PRIMARY SOURCES

Congressional Documents

U.S. Congress, House. 27 Cong., 2 sess., 1842, *House Doc. 143.*

——, ——. *Report of the Commissioner of Indian Affairs,* 26 Cong., 2 sess., 1840, *House Doc. 3.*

——, Senate. 21 Cong., 1 sess., 1830, *Sen. Doc. 110.*

——, ——. 24 Cong., 1 sess., 1836, *Sen. Doc. 206.*

——, ——. 24 Cong., 1 sess., 1836, *Sen. Doc. 251.*

——, ——. *Correspondence on the Subject of the Emigration of Indians Between the 30th November, 1831, and the 27th December, 1833,* 23 Cong., 1 sess., 1834, *Sen. Doc. 512.*

Articles

Barnes, Lela, ed. "Journal of Isaac McCoy for the Exploring Expedition of 1828," *Kansas Historical Quarterly,* Vol. V, (August, 1936), 227–77.

Bushnell, David I., ed. "Journal of Samuel Montgomery," *Mississippi Valley Historical Review,* Vol. II (September, 1915), 261–73.

Carmony, Donald F., and Francis Paul Prucha, eds. "A Memorandum of Lewis Cass Concerning a System for the Regulation of Indian Affairs," *Wisconsin Magazine of History,* Vol. LII (Autumn, 1968), 35–50.

Denny, Ebenezer. "Military Journal of Major Ebenezer Denny," *Memoirs of the Historical Society of Pennsylvania,* Vol. VII, 237–409.

"Documents: Correspondence on Indian Removal, Indiana, 1835–1838," *Mid-America,* Vol. XV (January, 1933), 177–92.

"Extracts from the Diary of Rev. Moses Merrill, a Missionary to the Otoe Indians from 1832 to 1840," *Transactions and Reports of the Nebraska State Historical Society,* Vol. IV, 160–94.

Jordan, John, ed. "Narrative of John Heckewelder's Journey to the Wabash in 1792," *Pennsylvania Magazine of History and Biography,* Vol. XII, No. 2 (1888), 164–84.

"Journal of an Emigrating Party of Pottawattomie Indians, 1838," *Indiana Magazine of History,* Vol. XXI (December, 1925), 315–36.

Knopf, Richard C., ed. "A Precise Journal of General Wayne's Last Campaign," *Proceedings of the American Antiquarian Society,* Vol. LXIV (October, 1954), 273–302.

——. "A Surgeon's Mate at Fort Defiance: The Journal of Joseph Gardener Andrews for the Year 1795," *Ohio Historical Quarterly,* Vol. LXVI (January, April, July, 1957), 57–86, 159–88, 238–68.

——. "Two Journals of the Kentucky Volunteers, 1793 and 1794," *Filson Club History Quarterly,* Vol. XXVII (July, 1953), 247–81.

Lambing, A. A., ed. "Celoron's Journal," *Ohio Archaeological and Historical Publications,* Vol. XXIX, 335–96.

Pare, George, and Milo Milton Quaife, eds. "The St. Joseph Baptismal Register," *Mississippi Valley Historical Review,* Vol. XIII (September, 1926), 201–13.

Peckham, Howard H., ed. "Recent Documentary Acquisitions to the Indiana Historical Library Relating to Fort Wayne," *Indiana Magazine of History,* Vol. XLIV (December, 1948), 409–18.

Quaife, Milo Milton, ed. "A Diary of the War of 1812," *Mississippi Valley Historical Review,* Vol. I (September, 1914), 272–78.

———. "Documents: The Chicago Treaty of 1833," *Wisconsin Magazine of History*, Vol. I (March, 1918) , 287–303.

———. "General James Wilkinson's Narrative of the Fallen Timber Campaign," *Mississippi Valley Historical Review*, Vol. XVI (June, 1929) , 81–90.

———. "Henry Hay's Journal from Detroit to the Miami River," *Proceedings of the State Historical Society of Wisconsin at its Sixty-Second Annual Meeting*, 1915, 208–61.

———. "A Picture of the First United States Army: The Journal of Captain Samuel Newman," *Wisconsin Magazine of History*, Vol. II (September, 1918) , 40–73.

"Reports and Correspondence from Canadian Archives," *Historical Society of North West Ohio Quarterly Bulletin*, Vol. II (October, 1930) , 1–15.

Riddell, William R., ed. "French Report on the Western Front," *Journal of the Illinois State Historical Society*, Vol. XXIV (October, 1931) , 578–84.

Smith, Dwight, ed. "The Attempted Potawatomi Emigration of 1839," *Indiana Magazine of History*, Vol. XLV (March, 1949) , 51–80.

———. "A Continuation of the Journal of an Emigrating Party of Potawatomi Indians, and Ten William Polke Manuscripts," *Indiana Magazine of History*, Vol. XLIV (December, 1948) , 392–408.

———. "Jacob Hull's Detachment of the Potawatomi Emigration of 1838," *Indiana Magazine of History*, Vol. XLV (September, 1949) , 285–88.

———. "Notes on the Wabash River in 1795." *Indiana Magazine of History*, LVI (September, 1954) , 277–290.

———. "William Wells and the Indian Council of 1793." *Indiana Magazine of History*, LVI (September, 1960) , 217–226.

Wainwright, Nicholas, ed. "George Croghan's Journal, 1759–1763," *Pennsylvania Magazine of History*, Vol. LXXI (October, 1947) , 305–444.

Whickar, J. Wesley, ed. "Shabonee's Account of Tippecanoe," *Indiana Magazine of History*, Vol. XVII (December, 1921) , 353–63.

"William Clark's Journal of General Wayne's Last Campaign," *Mississippi Valley Historical Review*, Vol. I (December, 1914) , 418–44.

Williams, Mentor L., ed. "John Kinzie's Narrative of the Fort Dearborn Massacre," *Journal of the Illinois State Historical Society*, Vol. XLVI (Winter, 1953) , 342–62.

"Winthrop Sargent's Diary While with General Arthur St. Clair's Expedition Against the Indians," *Ohio Archaeological and Historical Quarterly*, Vol. XXXIII (July, 1924) , 327–72.

Books

American State Papers, Indian Affairs. 2 vols. Washington, Gales and Seaton, 1832–34.

American State Papers, Military Affairs. 7 vols. Washington, Gales and Seaton, 1832–61.

Barnhart, John D., ed. *Henry Hamilton and George Rogers Clark in the American Revolution*. Crawfordsville, Ind., R. E. Banta, 1951.

Blair, Emma H., ed. *The Indian Tribes of the Upper Mississippi Valley and the Region of the Great Lakes*. 2 vols. Cleveland, Arthur H. Clark Company, 1911.

Bond, Beverly W., ed. *The Correspondence of John Cleve Symmes*. New York, Macmillan Company, 1903.

A Brief Account of the Proceedings of the Committee Appointed by the Yearly Meeting of Friends, Held in Baltimore for Promoting the Improvement and Civilization of the Indian Natives. London, Phillips and Fardon, 1806.

Buell, Rowena, ed. *The Memoirs of Rufus Putnam*. Boston, Houghton, Mifflin and Company, 1903.

Carter, Clarence E., ed. *The Correspondence of General Thomas Gage with the Secretaries of State, 1763–1775*. 2 vols. New Haven, Yale University Press, 1931.

——. *The Territorial Papers of the United States*. 27 vols. Washington, D.C., Government Printing Office, 1934–.

Casselman, Alexander C. *Richardson's War of 1812*. Toronto, Historical Publishing Company, 1902.

Collections of the Illinois State Historical Library. 34 vols. Springfield, Illinois State Historical Library, 1903–.

Collections of the Massachusetts Historical Society. Third Series. 10 vols. Boston, Published by the Society, 1825–49.

Collections of the Michigan Pioneer and Historical Society. 40 vols. Lansing, Thorp and Godfrey and others, 1874–1929.

The Collections of the State Historical Society of Wisconsin. 25 vols. Madison, Published by the Society, 1854–.

Cruikshank, Ernest A., ed. *The Correspondence of Lieutenant Governor John Graves Simcoe*. 5 vols. Toronto, Ontario Historical Society, 1923–31.

——. *Documents Relating to the Invasion of Canada and the Surrender of Detroit, 1812*. Ottawa, Government Printing Bureau, 1912.

Cunningham, Wilbur M., ed. *Letter Book of William Burnett*. Fort Miami Heritage Society of Michigan, 1967.

Darnell, Elias. *A Journal Containing an Accurate and Interesting Account of the Hardships, Sufferings, Battles, Defeat and Captivity of those Heroic Kentucky Volunteers and Regulars, Commanded by General Winchester, in the Years 1812–1813*. Philadelphia, Lippincott, Gambo and Company, 1854.

De Peyster, Arent Schyler. *Miscellanies by an Officer, 1774–1813*. 2 vols. New York, A. E. Chasmor Company, and others, 1888.

Dunn, Caroline, and Eleanor Dunn, trans. and eds. *Indiana's First War: An Account Made by Bienville of His Expedition Against the Chickasaws*. Indianapolis, Indiana Historical Society, 1924.

Dunn, Jacob Piatt, ed. *Documents Relating to the French Settlements on the Wabash*. Indianapolis, Indiana Historical Society, 1894.

——. *The Mission to the Oubache*. Indianapolis, Indiana Historical Society, 1902.

Edmonds, John W. *Report on the Claims of Creditors of the Potawatomi Indians on the Wabash in 1836 and 1837*. New York, Scathcherd and Adams, 1837.

——. *Report on the Disturbance at the Potawatomie Payment, September, 1836*. New York, Scathcherd and Adams, 1837.

Edwards, Ninian W. *History of Illinois from 1778 to 1833*. Springfield, Illinois State Journal, 1870.

Esarey, Logan, ed. *Messages and Letters of William Henry Harrison*. 2 vols. Indianapolis, Indiana Historical Commission, 1922.

Fitzpatrick, John C., ed. *The Writings of George Washington*. 39 vols. Washington, D.C., Government Printing Office, 1931–44.

Flick, Alexander, ed. *The Papers of Sir William Johnson*. 13 vols. Albany, University of the State of New York, 1921–62.

Gipson, Lawrence Harvey, ed. *The Moravian Indian Mission on White River*. Indianapolis, Indian Historical Bureau, 1938.

Goodman, Alfred T., ed. *Journal of Captain William Trent*. Cincinnati, Robert Clarke Company, 1871.

Griswold, Bert J., ed. *Fort Wayne, Gateway of the West, 1802–1813*. Indianapolis, Indiana Historical Bureau, 1927.

Hamilton, Edward P., trans. and ed. *Adventure in the Wilderness: The American Journals of Louis Antoine de Bougainville, 1756–1760*. Norman, University of Oklahoma Press, 1964.

Hopkins, Gerrard. *A Mission to the Indians from the Indian Committee of Baltimore to Fort Wayne in 1804*. Philadelphia, T. Elwood Zell, 1862.

Houck, Louise, ed. *The Spanish Regime in Missouri*. 2 vols. R. R. Donnelly and Sons, 1909.

Hubbard, Gurdon S. *The Autobiography of Gurdon Saltonstall Hubbard*. Chicago, Lakeside Press, 1911.

Hughes, Thomas. *A Journal of Thomas Hughes*. Cambridge, The University Press, 1947.

Hunt, Gailland, ed. *Journals of the Continental Congress, 1774–1789*. 34 vols. Washington, D.C., Government Printing Office, 1902–37.

Jackson, Donald, ed. *Black Hawk: An Autobiography*. Urbana, University of Illinois Press, 1964.

———. *The Journals of Zebulon Montgomery Pike*. 2 vols. Norman, University of Oklahoma Press, 1966.

Kappler, Charles, ed. *Indian Treaties, 1778–1883*. 2 vols. New York, Interland Publishing Company, 1972.

Keating, William H. *Narrative of an Expedition to the Source of St. Peters River*. 2 vols. London, George B. Whittaker, 1825.

Kellogg, Louise Phelps. *Early Narratives of the Northwest, 1634–1699*. New York, Charles Scribner's Sons, 1917.

Kinniard, Lawrence, ed. *Spain in the Mississippi Valley, 1765–1794, Annual Report of the American Historical Association for 1945*. 3 vols. Washington, American Historical Association, 1949.

Knopf, Richard C., ed. *Anthony Wayne, A Name in Arms: The Wayne-Knox-Pickering-McHenry Correspondence*. Pittsburgh, University of Pittsburgh Press, 1960.

———. *Letters to the Secretary of War, 1812, Relating to the War of 1812 in the Northwest. Vol. IV in Document Transcriptions of the War of 1812 in the Northwest*. Columbus, Ohio Historical Society, 1959.

———. *The National Intelligencer Reports the War of 1812 in the Northwest. Vol. II in Document Transcriptions of the War of 1812 in the Northwest*. Columbus, Ohio Historical Society, 1957.

Krauskopf, Frances, trans. and ed. *Ouiatanon Documents*. Indianapolis, Indiana Historical Society, 1955.

Lajeunesse, Ernest J., ed. *The Windsor Border Region*. Toronto, University of Toronto Press, 1960.

Latrobe, Charles I. *The Rambler in North America*. 2 vols. London, R. B. Seeley and W. Burnside, 1835.

Lindley, Harlow, ed. *Indiana as Seen by Early Travellers*. Indianapolis, Indiana Historical Commission, 1916.

McKee, Irving. *The Trail of Death: Letters of Benjamin Marie Petit*. Indianapolis, Indiana Historical Society, 1941.

Minutes of the Provincial Council of Pennsylvania. 16 vols. Harrisburg, Theodore Fenn Company, 1852–53.

Nasatir, A. P., ed. *Before Lewis and Clark: Documents Illustrating the History of the Missouri, 1785–1804*. 2 vols. St. Louis, Historical Documents Foundation, 1952.

O'Callaghan, Edward B., *Documents Relative to the Colonial History of the State of New York*. 15 vols. Albany, Weed, Parsons, and Company, 1853–87.

Parish, John, ed. *The Robert Lucas Journal of the War of 1812 During the Campaign Under General William Hull*. Iowa City, State Historical Society of Iowa, 1906.

Peckham, Howard H., ed. *George Croghan's Journal of His Trip to Detroit in 1767*. Ann Arbor, University of Michigan Press, 1939.

Pennsylvania Archives: First Series. 12 vols. Philadelphia, Joseph Severins and Company, 1852–56.

Pennsylvania Colonial Records. 17 vols. Harrisburg, Theodore Fenn Company, 1838–53.

Pouchot, Francois, *Memoir Upon the Late War in North America Between the French and English*. 2 vols. Roxbury, Mass. W. Elliott Woodward, 1866.

Quaife, Milo Milton, ed. *The Siege of Detroit in 1763*. Chicago, Lakeside Press, 1958.

———. *War on the Detroit: The Chronicles of Thomas Vercheres de Boucherville and the Capitulation by an Ohio Volunteer*. Chicago, Lakeside Press, 1940.

———. *The Western Country in the 17th Century: The Memoirs of Antoine Lamothe Cadillac and Pierre Liette*. New York, Citadel Press, 1962.

Robertson, Nellie Armstrong, and Dorothy Riker, eds. 3 vols. *The John Tipton Papers*. Indianapolis, Indiana Historical Bureau, 1942.

Rowland, Dunbar, and A. G. Sanders, eds. *Mississippi Provincial Archives: French Dominion, 1729–1740: French Dominion*. 3 vols. Jackson, Press of the Mississippi Department of Archives and History, 1927–32.

Schoolcraft, Henry Rowe. *Historical and Statistical Information Respecting the History, Condition, and Prospects of the Indian Tribes of the United States*. 6 vols. Philadelphia, Lippincott, Grambo, and Company, 1851.

———. *Travels in the Central Portions of the Mississippi Valley: Compromising Observations on its Mineral Geography, Internal Resources, and Aboriginal Population*. New York, Collins and Hannay, 1825.

Smith, Dwight L., ed. *From Greenville to Fallen Timbers: A Journal of the Wayne Campaign*. Indianapolis, Indiana Historical Society, 1952.

Smith, James. *An Account of the Remarkable Occurrences in the Life and Travels of Colonel James Smith*. Lexington, K., John Bradford, 1799.

Smith, William Henry, ed. *The St. Clair Papers*. 2 vols. Cincinnati, Robert Clarke and Co., 1882.

Stevens, Sylvester, and Donald Kent, eds. *The Papers of Colonel Henry Bouquet*. 19 vols. Harrisburg, Pennsylvania Historical Commission, 1940.

Tanner, John. *A Narrative of the Captivity and Adventures of John Tanner During Thirty Years Residence Among the Indians in the Interior of North America*. Minneapolis, Ross and Haines, 1956.

Thornbrough, Gayle, ed. *The Correspondence of John Badollet and Albert Gallatin, 1804–1836*. Indianapolis, Indiana Historical Society, 1963.

———. *Letter Book of the Indian Agency at Fort Wayne, 1809–1815*. Indianapolis, Indiana Historical Society, 1961.

———. *Outpost on the Wabash, 1787–1791*. Indianapolis, Indiana Historical Society, 1957.

Thwaites, Reuben G., ed. *Early Western Travels, 1748–1846*. 32 vols. Cleveland, Arthur H. Clark Company, 1904–1907.

———. *The Jesuit Relations and Allied Documents*. 73 vols. Cleveland, Burrows Brothers, 1896–1901.

Walker, William P., ed. *Calendar of the Virginia State Papers and Other Manu-*

scripts. 11 vols. Richmond, R. F. Walker and others, 1875–93.

Washburne, E. B., ed. *The Edwards Papers.* Chicago, Fergus Printing Company, 1884.

Washington, H. A., ed. *The Collected Writings of Thomas Jefferson.* 9 vols. New York, Taylor and Maury, 1853–54.

Winter, George. *The Journals and Indian Paintings of George Winter, 1837–1839.* Indianapolis, Indiana Historical Society, 1948.

Newspapers

Niles Register. September 16, 1837.

SECONDARY SOURCES

Unpublished Materials

Baerris, David. "The Band Affiliation of Potawatomi Treaty Signatories." This multilithed report can be found in the Great Lakes–Ohio Valley Indian Archives Project, Glenn A. Black Laboratory of Archaeology, Indiana University.

Wheeler-Voegelin, Erminie. "Before the Claims Commission: An Ethnohistorical Report on the Indian Use and Occupancy of Royce Area 66 ceded by the "Ottoway, Chippeway, Wyandotts and Pottawatamie nations of Indians" to the United States pursuant to the Treaty made at Detroit on November, 17, 1807." This multilithed report can be found in the Great Lakes–Ohio Valley Indian Archives Project, Glenn A. Black Laboratory of Archaeology, Indiana University.

Theses and Dissertations

Anson, Bert. "The Fur Traders in Northern Indiana." Ph.D. diss., Indiana University, 1953.

Edmunds, R. David. "A History of the Kickapoo Indians in Illinois from 1750–1834." M.A. thesis, Illinois State University, 1966.

Krauskopf, Frances. "The French in Indiana, 1700–1760." Ph.D. diss., Indiana University, 1953.

Murphy, Joseph Francis. "Potawatomi Indians of the West: Origins of the Citizens Band." Ph.D. diss., University of Oklahoma, 1961.

Articles

Allison, May. "The Government of Illinois," *Transactions of the Illinois State Historical Society for the Year 1907,* 277–92.

Alvord, Clarence W. "The Conquest of St. Joseph Michigan, by the Spaniards in 1781," *Missouri Historical Review,* Vol. II (July, 1908), 195–210.

Anson, Bert. "The Early Years of Lathrop M. Taylor, the Fur Trader," *Indiana Magazine of History,* Vol. XLIV (December, 1948), 367–83.

———. "Variations of the Indian Conflict: The Effect of the Emigrant Removal Policy, 1830–1854," *Missouri Historical Review,* Vol. LIX (October, 1964), 64–89.

Baerris, David. "Chieftainship among the Potawatomi," *Wisconsin Archaeologist,* Vol. LIV (September, 1973), 114–34.

Barnhart, John D. "Lieutenant Governor Henry Hamilton's Apologia," *Indiana Magazine of History,* Vol. LII (December, 1956), 383–96.

Bauxar, J. Joe. "The Historic Period," *Illinois Archaeology: Bulletin No. 1 of the*

Illinois Archaeological Survey, 40–58.

Berkhofer, Robert F., Jr. "The Political Context of a New Indian History," *Pacific Historical Review*, Vol. XL (August, 1971) , 357–82.

Blasingham, Emily. "The Depopulation of the Illinois Indians," *Ethnohistory*, Vol. III (Summer, Fall, 1956) , 193–224, 361–412.

———. "The Miami Prior to the French and Indian War," *Ethnohistory*, Vol. II (Winter, 1955) , 1–6.

Burnham, John. "Mysterious Battle Grounds in McLean County, Illinois," *Transactions of the Illinois State Historical Society for the Year 1908*, 184–91.

Caldwell, Norman. "Fort Massac: "The American Frontier Post," *Journal of the Illinois State Historical Society*, Vol. XLII (Winter, 1950) , 265–87.

Case, Thomas. "The Battle of Fallen Timbers," *Northwest Ohio Quarterly*, Vol. XXXV (Spring, 1963) , 54–68.

Chapman, Carl. "The Indomitable Osage in the Spanish Illinois (Upper Louisiana) , 1763–1804," in *The Spanish in the Mississippi Valley, 1762–1804*, ed. John Francis McDermott. Urbana, University of Illinois Press, 1974, pp. 286–313.

"Chicago Indian Chiefs," *Bulletin of the Chicago Historical Society*, Vol. I (August, 1935) , 105–18.

Clifton, James A. "Potawatomi Leadership Roles: On *Okama* and Other Influential Personages," *Proceedings of the 1974 Algonquian Conference, Mercury Series*, 1974, 1–55.

Conway, Thomas G. "Potawatomi Politics," *Journal of the Illinois State Historical Society*, Vol. LXV (Winter, 1972) , 395–418.

Covington, James W. "The Indian Liquor Trade at Peoria," *Journal of the Illinois State Historical Society*, Vol. XLVI (Summer, 1953) , 142–50.

Deale, Valentine. "The History of the Potawatomis Before 1722," *Ethnohistory*, Vol. V (Fall, 1958) , 305–60.

East, Ernest E. "Contributions to Chicago History from Peoria County Records," *Journal of the Illinois State Historical Society*, Vol. XXXI (April, 1938) , 323–43.

———. "The Inhabitants of Chicago, 1825–1831," *Journal of the Illinois State Historical Society*, Vol. XLII (March, 1949) , 40–56.

Edmunds, R. David. "The Illinois River Potawatomis in the War of 1812," *Journal of the Illinois State Historical Society*, Vol. LXIII (January, 1970) , 341–62.

———. "Pickawillany: French Military Power versus British Economics," *Western Pennsylvania Magazine of History*, Vol. LVIII (April, 1975) , 169–84.

———. "Potawatomis in the Platte Country: An Indian Removal Incomplete," *Missouri Historical Review*, Vol. LXVIII (July, 1974) , 375–92.

———. "The Prairie Potawatomi Removal of 1833," *Indiana Magazine of History*, Vol. LXVIII (September, 1972) , 240–53.

———. "Wea Participation in the Northwest Indian Wars, 1790–1795," *Filson Club History Quarterly*, Vol. XLVI (July, 1972) , 241–54.

Faye, Stanley. "The Fox's Fort—1730," *Journal of the Illinois State Historical Society*, Vol. XXVIII (October, 1935) , 123–63.

Fitting, James E., and Charles Cleland. "Late Prehistoric Settlement Patterns in the Upper Great Lakes," *Ethnohistory*, Vol. XVI (Fall, 1969) , 289–302.

Gates, Paul. "Indian Allotments Preceeding the Dawes Act," in *The Frontier Challenge: Responses to the Trans-Mississippi West*, ed. John G. Clark. Lawrence, University of Kansas Press, 1971, pp. 141–70.

Gerwing, Anselm J. "The Chicago Indian Treaty of 1833," *Journal of the Illinois State Historical Society*, Vol. LVII (Summer, 1964) , 117–42.

Hockett, Charles F. "The Position of Potawatomi in Central Algonkian," *Papers of the Michigan Academy of Science, Arts and Letters,* Vol. XXVIII, 537–43.

Holand, Hjalmar R. "The Sign of the Cross," *Wisconsin Magazine of History,* Vol. XVII (December, 1933) , 155–67.

Horsman, Reginald. "The British Indian Department and the Abortive Treaty of Lower Sandusky, 1793," *Ohio Historical Quarterly,* Vol. LXX (July, 1961) , 189–213.

———. "The British Indian Department and the Resistance to General Anthony Wayne," *Mississippi Valley Historical Review,* Vol. XLIV (September, 1962) , 269–90.

———. "Wisconsin and the War of 1812," *Wisconsin Magazine of History,* Vol. XLVI (Autumn, 1962) , 3–15.

Hunter, William A. "Refuge Fox Settlements among the Senecas," *Ethnohistory,* Vol. III (Winter, 1956) , 11–20.

Jacobs, Wilbur. "Presents to the Indians along the French Frontiers in the Old Northwest, 1748–1763," *Indiana Magazine of History,* Vol. XLIV (September, 1948) , 245–56.

———. "Was the Pontiac Uprising a Conspiracy?" *Ohio State Archaeological and Historical Quarterly,* Vol. LIX (January, 1950) , 26–37.

James, James A. "The Significance of the Attack on St. Louis, 1780," in *Proceedings of the Mississippi Valley Historical Association,* Vol. II, 206–17.

Jenks, A. E. "The Wild Rice Gatherers of the Upper Lakes," in *Nineteenth Annual Report of the Bureau of American Ethnology.* (1904) , 1056–74.

Kellogg, Louise Phelps. "The Fox Indians Under the French Regime," *Proceedings of the State Historical Society of Wisconsin at its Fifty-fifth Meeting,* 142–88.

———. "A Wisconsin Anabasis," *Wisconsin Magazine of History,* Vol. VII (March, 1924) , 322–39.

Kinniard, Lawrence. "The Spanish Expedition Against Fort St. Joseph in 1781, A New Interpretation," *Mississippi Valley Historical Review,* Vol. XIX (September, 1932) , 173–91.

Krenkel, John. "British Conquest of the Old Northwest," *Wisconsin Magazine of History,* Vol. XXXV (Autumn, 1951) , 49–61.

Lawson, Publius. "The Potawatomi," *Wisconsin Archaeologist,* Vol. XIX (April, 1920) , 41–116.

Love, William. "A Quaker Pilgrimage," *Maryland Historical Magazine,* Vol. IV (March, 1909) , 1–24.

McKee, Irving. "The Centennial of the Trail of Death," *Indiana Magazine of History,* Vol. XXXV (March, 1939) , 27–41.

Meek, Basil. "General Harmar's Expedition," *Ohio Archaeological and Historical Quarterly,* Vol. XX (January, 1911) , 74–108.

Nasatir, A. P. "The Anglo-Spanish Frontier in the Illinois Country During the American Revolution, 1779–1783," *Journal of the Illinois State Historical Society,* Vol. XXI (October, 1928) , 291–358.

Pare, George. "The St. Joseph Mission," *Mississippi Valley Historical Review,* Vol. XVII (June, 1930) , 24–54.

Pargellis, Stanley. "Braddock's Defeat," *American Historical Review,* Vol. XLI (January, 1936) , 253–69.

Parsons, Joseph A. "Civilizing the Indians of the Old Northwest, 1800–1810," *Indiana Magazine of History,* Vol. LVI (September, 1960) , 195–216.

Pease, Theodore Calvin. "The Revolution at Crisis in the West," *Journal of the Illinois State Historical Society,* Vol. XXIII (January, 1931) , 664–82.

Prucha, Francis Paul. "Andrew Jackson's Indian Policy: A Reassessment," *Journal of American History*, Vol. LVI (December, 1969) , 527–39.

———. "Indian Removal and the Great American Desert," *Indiana Magazine of History*, Vol. LIV (December, 1963) , 299–322.

Quimby, George. "Some Notes on Kinship and Kinship Terminology among the Potawatomi of the Huron," *Papers of the Michigan Academy of Science, Arts and Letters*, Vol. XXVIII, 537–42.

Rea, Robert R. "Henry Hamilton and West Florida," *Indiana Magazine of History*, Vol. LIV (March, 1958) , 49–56.

Robertson, Nellie. "John Hays and the Fort Wayne Indian Agency," *Indiana Magazine of History*, Vol. XXXIX (September, 1943) , 221–36.

Schoolcraft, Henry R. "Discourse Delivered Before the Historical Society of Michigan," in *Historical and Scientific Sketches of Michigan*. Detroit, S. Wells and G. L. Whitney, 1834, 103–13.

Smith, Dwight. "Wayne's Peace with the Indians of the Old Northwest, 1775," *Ohio Archaeological and Historical Quarterly*, Vol. LIX (July, 1950) , 239–55.

Spooner, Harry L. "The Historic Indian Villages of the Peoria Lake Area," *Journal of the Illinois State Archaeological Society*, Vol. I (January, 1944) , 15–18.

Stanley, George. "The Indians in the War of 1812," *Canadian Historical Review*, Vol. XXXI (June, 1950) , 145–65.

Taggert, Frederick J. "The Capture of St. Joseph, Michigan, by the Spaniards in 1781," *Missouri Historical Review*, Vol. V (July, 1911) , 214–28.

Tohill, Louis. "Robert Dickson, British Fur Trader on the Upper Mississippi," *North Dakota Historical Quarterly*, Vol. III (October, 1928; January, April, 1929) , 5–49, 83–128, 182–203.

Van der Zee, Jacob. "Episodes in the Early History of the Western Iowa Country," *Iowa Journal of History and Politics*, Vol. XI (July, 1913) , 323–63.

VanStone, James. "Canadian Trade Silver from Indian Graves in Northern Illinois," *The Wisconsin Archaeologist*, Vol. LI (March, 1970) , 21–30.

Walters, Alta. "Shabonee," *Journal of the Illinois State Historical Society*, Vol. XVII (October, 1924) , 381–97.

Warren, William. "History of the Objibways," *Collections of the Minnesota Historical Society*, Vol. V, 21–394.

Warrick, W. Sheridan. "The American Indian Policy in the Upper Old Northwest Following the War of 1812," *Ethnohistory*, Vol. III (Spring, 1956) , 109–25.

Weik, Jesse. "An Unpublished Chapter in the Early History of Chicago," *Journal of the Illinois State Historical Society*, Vol. VII (January, 1915) , 329–48.

Whickar, John Wesley, "Pierre Moran, or Chief Parish of the Pottawatomie Indians," *Indiana Magazine of History*, Vol. XXIII (June, 1927) , 229–36.

Wilson, Frazer. "St. Clair's Defeat," *Ohio Archaeological and Historical Quarterly*, Vol. XI (July, 1902) , 30–43.

Books

Alvord, Clarence W. *The Illinois Country, 1673–1818*. Chicago, A. C. McClurg and Company, 1922.

Anson, Bert. *The Miami Indians*. Norman, University of Oklahoma Press, 1970.

Baerris, David, Erminie Wheeler-Voegelin, and Remedios Wycoco-Moore. *Indians of Northeastern Illinois*. New York, Garland Publishing Company, 1974.

Bald, Clever. *Detroit's First American Decade*. Ann Arbor, University of Michigan Press, 1948.

Barry, Louise, comp. *The Beginnings of the West: Annals of the Kansas Gateway to the American West*. Topeka, Kansas State Historical Society, 1972.

Berkhofer, Robert F., Jr. *Salvation and the Savage: An Analysis of Protestant Missions and American Indian Response, 1787–1862*. New York, Atheneum Books, 1972.

Berthrong, Donald J. *Indians of Northern Illinois and Southwestern Michigan*. New York, Garland Publishing Company, 1974.

Boggess, Arthur C. *The Settlement of Illinois, 1778–1830*. Chicago, Chicago Historical Society, 1908.

Bond, Beverly W., Jr. *The Foundations of Ohio*. Columbus, Ohio State Archaeological and History Society, 1941.

Brice, Wallace. *History of Fort Wayne*. Fort Wayne, Ind., D. W. Jones and Son, 1868.

Buechner, Cecilia Bain. *The Pokagons*. Indianapolis, Indiana Historical Society, 1933.

Burnet, Jacob. *Notes on the Settlement of the Northwestern Territory*. Cincinnati, Derby, Bradley, and Company, 1847.

Bushnell, David. *Tribal Migrations East of the Mississippi*. Smithsonian Miscellaneous Collections, Vol. LXXXIX, No. 12. Washington, Smithsonian Institution, 1862–.

Butterfield, Consul Wilshire. *History of the Girtys*. Cincinnati, Robert Clarke Company, 1890.

Callendar, Charles. *Social Organization of the Central Algonkian Indians*. Milwaukee Public Museum Publication in Anthropology No. 7. Milwaukee, Board of Trustees, 1962.

Carter, Clarence E. *Great Britain and the Illinois Country, 1763–1774*. Washington, American Historical Association, 1910.

Charlevoix, Pierre Francois Xavier. *History and General Description of New France*. Trans. and ed. by John Gilmary Shea. 6 vols. London, Francis Edwards, 1902.

Claspy, Everett. *The Potawatomi Indians of Southwestern Michigan*. Dowagiac, Mich., Everett Claspy, 1966.

Clifton, James. *A Place of Refuge for All Time: Migration of the American Potawatomi into Upper Canada, 1830–1850*. Ottawa, National Museum of Canada, in press.

Colden, Cadwallader. *The History of the Five Indian Nations Depending on the Province of New York in America*. Ithaca, Cornell University Press, 1958.

Cunningham, Wilbur. *Land of Four Flags*. Grand Rapids, William B. Erdman's Company, 1961.

Downes, Randolph C. *Council Fires on the Upper Ohio*. Pittsburgh, University of Pittsburgh Press, 1969.

Eccles, William J. *The Canadian Frontier*. New York, Holt, Rinehart, and Winston, 1969.

English, William Hayden. *Conquest of the Country Northwest of the Ohio, 1778–1783, and Life of General George Rogers Clark*. 2 vols. Indianapolis, Bowen-Merril Company, 1896.

Foreman, Grant. *The Last Trek of the Indians*. New York, Russell and Russell, 1972.

Garraghan, Gilbert J. *The Jesuits of the Middle United States*. 3 vols. New York, American Press, 1938.

Gibson, A. M. *The Chickasaws*. Norman, University of Oklahoma Press, 1971.

———. *The Kickapoos: Lords of the Middle Border*. Norman, University of Oklahoma Press, 1963.

Gilpin, Alec R. *The War of 1812 in the Old Northwest*. East Lansing, Michigan State University Press, 1958.

Gipson, Lawrence Henry. *The British Empire Before the American Revolution*. 15

vols. New York, Alfred A. Knopf, 1939–1970.

Goldstein, Robert A. *French-Iroquois Diplomatic and Military Relations, 1609–1701.* The Hague, Mouton and Company, 1969.

Griswold, Bert. *The Pictorial History of Fort Wayne, Indiana.* Chicago: Robert O. Law Company, 1917.

Hagan, William T. *The Sac and Fox Indians.* Norman, University of Oklahoma Press, 1958.

Hanna, Charles A. *The Wilderness Trail.* 2 vols. New York, G. P. Putnam's Sons, 1911.

Havighurst, Walter. *Wilderness for Sale: The Story of the First Western Land Rush.* New York, Hastings House, 1956.

Hickling, William. *Caldwell and Shabonee.* Chicago, Fergus Printing Company, 1877.

Hodge, Frederick W., ed. *Handbook of American Indians North of Mexico.* Bulletin 30 of the Bureau of American Ethnology. 2 vols. New York, Rowan and Littlefield, 1971.

Horsman, Reginald. *Expansion and American Indian Policy, 1783–1812.* East Lansing, Michigan State University Press, 1967.

––––––. *Matthew Elliott, British Indian Agent.* Detroit, Wayne State University Press, 1964.

Houck, Louise. *A History of Missouri.* 3 vols. Chicago, R. R. Donnelly and Sons, 1908.

Hunt, George T. *The Wars of the Iroquois: A Study in Intertribal Trade Relations.* Madison, University of Wisconsin Press, 1967.

Hunter, William A. *Forts on the Pennsylvania Frontier, 1753–1758.* Harrisburg, Pennsylvania Historical and Museum Commission, 1960.

Indian Claims Commission. *Indians of Ohio, Indiana, Illinois, Southern Michigan, and Southern Wisconsin.* 3 vols. New York, Garland Press, 1974.

Jacobs, Wilbur. *Wilderness Politics and Indian Gifts: The Northern Colonial Frontier, 1748–1763.* Lincoln, University of Nebraska Press, 1950.

James, James A. *The Life of George Rogers Clark.* Chicago, University of Chicago Press, 1928.

Kellogg, Louise Phelps. *The British Regime in Wisconsin and the Old Northwest.* Madison, State Historical Society of Wisconsin, 1935.

––––––. *The French Regime in Wisconsin and the Old Northwest.* Madison, State Historical Society of Wisconsin, 1925.

Kinietz, W. Vernon. *The Indian of the Western Great Lakes, 1615–1750.* Ann Arbor, University of Michigan Press, 1965.

Kinzie, Juliette. *Wau-Bun, the Early Day in the Northwest.* Chicago, Lakeside Press, 1932.

Landes, Ruth. *The Prairie Potawatomi: Tradition and Ritual in the Twentieth Century.* Madison, University of Wisconsin Press, 1970.

McAfee, Robert B. *History of the Late War in the Western Country.* Lexington, Ky., Worsley and Smith, 1816.

McCollough, Almeda, ed. *The Battle of Tippecanoe: Conflict of Cultures.* Lafayette, Tippecanoe County Historical Association, 1973.

McCoy, Isaac. *History of Baptist Indian Missions: Embracing Remarks on the Former and Present Condition of Aboriginal Tribes: Their Former Settlements within the Indian Territory and their Future Prospects.* Washington, Isaac McCoy, 1840.

McDonald, Daniel. *Removal of the Pottawattomie Indians from Northern Indiana.* Plymouth, Ind., D. McDonald and Company, 1899.

Mason, Edward G. *Early Chicago and Illinois.* Chicago, Fergus Printing Company, 1890.

Mathews, John Joseph. *The Osages: Children of the Middle Waters*. Norman, University of Oklahoma Press, 1961.

Matson, Nehemiah. *Memories of Shaubena*. Chicago, D. B. Cooke and Company, 1878.

Morstad, Alexander. *The Reverend Erik Olsen Morstad: His Work Among the Wisconsin Pottawatomie Indians*. Clearwater, Fl., The Eldnar Press, 1971.

Nichols, Roger L. *General Henry Atkinson: A Western Military Career*. Norman, University of Oklahoma Press, 1965.

Parkman, Francis. *The Conspiracy of Pontiac*. New York, Collier Books, 1962.

———. *The Jesuits in North America*. Boston, Little, Brown and Company, 1963.

———. *La Salle and the Discovery of the Great West*. New York, The New American Library, 1963.

———. *Montcalm and Wolfe*. 3 vols. Boston, Little, Brown and Company, 1899.

Peckham, Howard H. *The Colonial Wars, 1682–1762*. Chicago, University of Chicago Press, 1964.

———. *Pontiac and the Indian Uprising*. Princeton, Princeton University Press, 1947.

Prucha, Francis Paul. *American Indian Policy in the Formative Years: The Indian Trade and Intercourse Acts, 1790–1834*. Lincoln, University of Nebraska Press, 1970.

———. *The Sword of the Republic: The United States Army on the Frontier, 1783–1846*. New York, Macmillan Company, 1969.

Quaife, Milo Milton. *Chicago and the Old Northwest, 1673–1835*. Chicago, University of Chicago Press, 1913.

Quimby, George Irving. *Indian Culture and European Trade Goods: The Archaeology of the Historic Period in the Western Great Lakes Region*. Madison, University of Wisconsin Press, 1966.

Reynolds, John. *My Own Times, Embracing also the History of My Life*. Chicago, Fergus Printing Company, 1887.

———. *Pioneer History of Illinois*. Chicago: Fergus Printing Company, 1887.

Ritzenthaler, Robert. *The Potawatomi Indians of Wisconsin*. Bulletin of the Public Museum of Milwaukee, Vol. XIX. Milwaukee, Board of Trustees, 1953.

———, and Pat Ritzenthaler. *The Woodland Indians of the Western Great Lakes*. Garden City, N.Y., Natural History Press, 1970.

Satz, Ronald D. *American Indian Policy in the Jacksonian Era*. Lincoln, University of Nebraska Press, 1975.

Scanlan, Charles. *Indian Creek Massacre and Captivity of the Hall Girls*. Milwaukee, Reic Publishing Company, 1915.

Schultz, George A. *An Indian Canaan: Isaac McCoy and the Vision of an Indian State*. Norman, University of Oklahoma Press, 1972.

Shea, John G. *History of the Catholic Missions among the Indian Tribes of the United States*. New York, P. J. Kennedy, 1883.

Sheehan, Bernard. *Seeds of Extinction: Jeffersonian Philanthropy and the American Indian*. Chapel Hill, University of North Carolina Press, 1973.

Skinner, Alanson. *The Mascoutens or Prairie Potawatomi Indians*. Bulletin of the Public Museum of the City of Milwaukee, Vol. VI. Milwaukee, Board of Trustees, 1924.

Slick, Sewell Elias. *William Trent and the West*. Harrisburg, Archives Publishing Company of Pennsylvania, 1947.

Slocum, Charles E. *History of the Maumee River Basin from the Earliest Account to its Organization into Counties*. Defiance, Ohio, Charles E. Slocum, 1905.

Smith, Huron H. *Ethnobotany of the Forest Potawatomi Indians*. Bulletin of the

Public Museum of the City of Milwaukee, Vol. VII. Milwaukee, Board of Trustees, 1933.

Sosin, Jack. *The Revolutionary Frontier, 1763–1783*. New York, Holt, Rinehart and Winston, 1967.

Steck, Francis Borgia. *The Joliet-Marquette Expedition, 1673*. Quincy, Ill., The Franciscan Fathers, 1928.

Stevens, Frank E. *The Black Hawk War*. Chicago, Frank E. Stevens, 1903.

Temple, Wayne C. *Indian Villages of the Illinois Country*. Illinois State Museum Scientific Papers, Vol. II. Springfield, State of Illinois, 1958.

Tiedke, Kenneth E. *A Study of the Hannahville Indian Community*. East Lansing, Michigan State University Department of Sociology and Anthropology, 1951.

Tucker, Glenn. *Tecumseh: Vision of Glory*. New York, Bobbs Merrill Company, 1956.

Vogel, Virgil J. *Indian Place Names in Illinois*. Springfield, Illinois State Historical Society, 1963.

Volwiler, Albert T. *George Croghan and the Westward Movement, 1741–1782*. Cleveland, Arthur H. Clark Company, 1926.

Wainwright, Nicholas B. *George Croghan, Wilderness Diplomat*. Chapel Hill, University of North Carolina Press, 1959.

Wallace, Anthony F. C. *The Death and Rebirth of the Seneca*. New York, Alfred A. Knopf, 1970.

Wheeler-Voegelin, Erminie, and David Stout. *Indians of Illinois and Northwestern Indiana*. New York, Garland Publishing Company, 1974.

———, and Helen Hornbeck Tanner. *Indians of Northern Ohio and Southeastern Michigan*. New York, Garland Publishing Company, 1974.

———, and ———. *Indians of Ohio and Indiana Prior to 1795*. 2 vols. New York, Garland Publishing Company, 1974.

———, and J. A. Jones. *Indians of Western Illinois and Southern Wisconsin*. New York, Garland Publishing Company, 1974.

Winger, Otho. *The Potawatomi Indians*. Elgin, Ill., The Elgin Press, 1939.

Woehrman, Paul. *At the Headwaters of the Maumee: A History of the Forts of Fort Wayne*. Indianapolis, Indiana Historical Society, 1971.

Index

Abnaki Indians: 55
Abraham, Chapman: 88
Acculturation: 22–23, 38, 102, 163, 223–24, 226–28, 240, 264–65
Achonenave (Huron chief) : 57
Algonkians: 46
Allouez, Claude: 6, 8
Amherstburg, Ontario: 158, 166–67
Amherst, Sir Jeffrey: 75–77
André, Louis: 9
Aptakisic (Half Day) : 247
Armstrong, John (Secretary of War) : 202
Ashkibee (Potawatomi chief) : 104–105
Ashkum (More and More) : 148, 258–60
Atkinson, Henry: 238, 253–54
Aubbeenaubbee (Potawatomi chief) : 229

Badin, Stephen T. (missionary among St. Joseph Potawatomis): 264
Bailly, Joseph: 201
Balfour, Henry: 77–78
Barron, Joseph: 259
Bathelet, S. B.: 260
Baudry, Toussaint: 6
Beauharnois, Charles de la Boische: 35, 38

Beaujeu, Daniel de: 50
Bellestre, Marie François Picote, Sieur de: 46
Bennet, Thomas: 106–107
Benton, Thomas Hart: 249, 251
Berry, Isaac S.: 266, 268
Bertrand, Joseph: 156, 229
Bienville, Jean Baptiste le Moyne de: 40–41
Big Ears: 85–87, 90
Big Foot (Mawgehset): 230–31, 250, 261–63
Blackbird (son of Siggenauk): 185–87
Black Hawk: 235–39
Black Partridge: see Mucktypoke
Bloody Bridge, Battle of: 89
Blue Licks, Battle of: 114
Bondie, Antoine: 189–90
Boone, Daniel: 114
Boonesborough, Ky.: 100
Bougainville, Antoine de: 53
Bouquet, Henry: 76, 91–92
Braddock, Edward: 50–51, 70
Bradstreet, John: 56, 91
Brady, Hugh: 269–70
Brady, S. P.: 270
Brady, Thomas: 111
Brant, Joseph: 118, 127–28
Brisay, Jacques (Marquis Denonville): 12
Brouillette, Michael: 170

Brownstown, Ill.: 183–84, 188
Bryant's Station: 113
Burgoyne, John: 100–101
Burnett, Abraham: 222–23, 228
Burnett, William: 156, 188, 222,
    228

Cadillac, Antoine de la Mothe: 14,
    15, 27, 28
Cahokia, Ill.: 35, 101, 104, 110, 134,
    157, captured by Clark, 101;
    conference at, 181
Cahokia Indians: 49; *see also* Illi-
    nois Confederacy
Caldwell, Billy (Sauganash): 216,
    271; described, 172; at Battle of
    Brownstown, 188; at Battle of
    Thames, 198; educated, 222; fur
    trader, 228; elected to office, 228;
    at Big Foot's village, 231; at
    Treaty of Prairie du Chien, 232;
    opposes Black Hawk, 236–239;
    awarded land at Tippecanoe
    treaties, 242; at Chicago Treaty
    (1833), 247–48; explores lands in
    west, 250; removes to Platte
    Country, 251
Caldwell, William: 113, 172
Calhoun, John C.: 220
Callieres, Louis Hector, Count de:
    24–25
Campbell, Donald: 57, 58, 76–79
Campbell, John: 92, 97
Campbell, William: 132
Canoku (Fat Woman): 73
Carey Mission: 223–24, 225, 240
Cashkoa (Fast Walker): 133
Cass, Lewis: 228, 229, 232, 241, 255,
    257; at Chicago Treaty (1821),
    220–21; at Chicago Treaty
    (1833), 247–49
Celoron, Pierre Joseph: 40, 44–46
Champlain, Samuel de: 3
Chandonnai, Charles: 201

Chandonnai, Jean Baptiste: 188,
    202, 241
Chasgieds: 20–21; *see also* Potawa-
    tomi Indian shamans
Chebass (Little Duck): 202, 204,
    216, 228; makes peace with
    Americans, 206; at Treaty of St.
    Mary's, 220
Checawkose (Little Crane): 258–
    59, 269
Cherokee Indians: 41, 156
Chevalier, Louis: trades at the St.
    Joseph's, 78; in Pontiac's revolt,
    83, 289, fn. 22; assists British,
    102–105, 108; removed from St.
    Joseph's, 110
Chibiabos (mythological figure):
    20
Chicago, Ill.: 12, 58, 110, 135, 147,
    156, 157, 158, 164, 191, 200, 215,
    216, 217, 242, 243, 244, 250, 261,
    266; Potawatomi villages at, 34,
    48, 90, 233–34, 238; in War of
    1812, 184–88; agency reestab-
    lished at, 216; treaties at, 220–
    22, 247–49
Chickasaw Indians: 39–41, 97, 146,
    241
Chippewa Indians: 3, 35, 41, 42,
    48, 53, 56, 76, 91, 102, 107, 109,
    111, 114, 116, 118, 122, 128, 129,
    130, 131, 153, 158, 163, 164, 168,
    170, 179, 220, 268; raid Picka-
    willany, 47; in Pontiac's Rebel-
    lion, 80–90; at Mississinewa
    conference, 181–82; at Fort
    Meigs, 196; sign armistice, 199;
    at Treaty of Spring Wells, 206;
    at Treaty of Fort Meigs, 219
Choctaw Academy: 224, 228
Choctaw Indians: 39, 241
Chouteau, Auguste: 218
Cicott, E. V.: 260
Clark, George Rogers: 66, 67, 107;

meets with Siggenauk, 101–102;
captures Vincennes, 105
Clark, William: 71, 172–73, 201,
218, 233, 256
Clay, Green: 196
Coe-coosh (The Hog): 61
Comee (Potawatomi warrior):
237–38
Congee (Bear Paws): 221
Contrecoeur, Charles Pierre
Pecaudy, Sieur de: 50
Coquillard, Alexis: 151, 230, 266,
274; at 1836 annuity payment,
259–60; as removal agent, 269–
70, 274
Council Bluffs Subagency: 253,
254, 268, 270, 274
Courtemanche, Augustin le Gar-
deur de Repentigny: 24
Cox, Rebecca: 174
Craig, Thomas: 194
Crawford, Hugh: 88
Crawford, William: 113
Creek Indians: 39, 241
Creole influence: 22, 32, 38, 58, 78,
96, 99, 101, 110, 154, 156, 194,
226–27
Croghan, George (American mili-
tary officer): 202
Croghan, George (British trader):
42, 45, 75, 79, 93; meets with
Potawatomis, 57, 77, 97–98; cap-
tured by Kickapoos, 94
Crow Prairie: 174
Crume, Marks: 241–42
Cruzat, Francisco: 111
Cuyler, Abraham: 84–85

Dablon, Claude: 8–9
Dalyell, James: 88–89
Daumont, Francis, Sieur de Saint
Lusson: 9
Davis, Anthony: 253
Davis, John: 241–42
Davis, William: 237

Dearborn, Henry (Secretary of
War): 160
Delaware Indians: 45, 76, 79, 116,
118, 127, 130, 195; attack Fort
Pitt, 83; meet with St. Joseph
Potawatomis, 90; attacked by
British, 91, 92; killed at
Gnaddenhutten, 112–13; cede
lands, 163–69; at Mississinewa
conference, 181–82; at Treaty of
Spring Wells, 206; at Treaty of
Fort Meigs, 219
Delaware Prophet: 79, 80
Dennis, Alexander: 155
Dennis, Phillip: 162
Denny, James: 188
De Peyster, Arent: 102, 104, 105,
106, 107, 109, 110, 111, 112, 114
Deseille, Louis: 264–66
Detroit, Mich.: 31, 46, 47, 56, 94,
95, 102, 104, 108, 109, 112, 114,
117, 156, 158, 160, 164, 170, 174,
179, 183, 191, 194, 198–99, 217,
220, 273; besieged by Foxes, 28–
29; Potawatomis settle at, 29–30;
tribes resettled at, 29–30; Huron
revolt at, 41–43; occupied by
British, 57–58; shortage of trade
goods at, 75–79; in Pontiac's
Rebellion, 80–90; raided by
Potawatomis, 90–92, 97; Pota-
watomis disperse from, 98–99;
Americans occupy, 153; British
capture, 189; British evacuate,
197
Dickson, Robert: 184, 197, 199–
200, 201, 203
D'Mouch-Kee-Kee-Awh: 62
Dorchester, Guy Carleton, Lord:
123, 129
Douglass, Ephriam: 114–15
Dubuisson, Charles Regnault,
Sieur: 28–29
Dudley, William: 196
Dumaw Creek culture: 4

Dunlap's Station: 122
Duquesne, Ange, Marquis: 49
Du Quindre, Dagneaux: 109
Du Sable, Baptiste Point: 156

Edmonds, John W.: 260
Edwards, Ninian: 138, 173, 178,
    218, 231; mobilizes militia
    against Potawatomis, 173–74;
    evacuates family, 193; attacks
    Potawatomi villages, 193–94
Elkhart River: 120; Potawatomis
    on, 158; Five Medals' village on,
    159; American expedition to,
    191, 197
Ellicott, George: 162
Elliott, Alexander: 192
Elliott, Matthew: 127, 133, 192
Eustis, William (Secretary of War):
    169
Ewing, George W.: 152, 259–261

Fallen Timbers, Battle of: 69,
    130–32
Five Medals: 133, 136, 158, 161,
    163, 164, 169, 181, 196, 216;
    interest in agriculture, 159, 162;
    visits Washington, 159–60; ad-
    dicted to whiskey, 165; opposes
    Shawnee Prophet, 165, 166, 170,
    171; influence declining, 167,
    170, 178, 182; at Mississinewa
    conference, 182; at siege of Fort
    Wayne, 189; village destroyed,
    191–92; signs armistice, 199; at-
    tends peace conference, 202; at
    Treaty of St. Mary's, 220
Fleurimont, Nicolas Joseph des
    Noyelles, Sieur de: 36
Forsyth, Robert: 201, 271
Forsyth, Thomas: 182, 226; ran-
    soms Helm, 188; captured by
    Craig, 194; threatened by Dick-
    son, 201
Fort Assumption: 40

Fort Carillon: 52, 53
Fort Chartres: 36; Pontiac at, 93;
    British occupy, 96; Potawatomis
    raid near, 97, 98
Fort Clark: 201, 203, 216
Fort Crevecoeur: 11
Fort Dearborn: 155, 183, 184, 185,
    186–87, 216
Fort Defiance: 130, 132
Fort Duquesne: 49–50, 56
Fort Edward: 53, 55
Fort Edward Augustus: 83
Fort Frontenac: 56
Fort Greenville: 129, 133, 134, 182;
    established, 128; treaty at, 135
Fort Harrison: 202; established,
    176; attacked by Kickapoos and
    Potawatomis, 193
Fort Leavenworth: 244, 247, 253,
    254, 255
Fort Massac: 101, 156
Fort Miami: 129, 132
Fort Miamis: 42, 45, 81
Fort Meigs: 195, 196–97, 219
Fort Necessity: 49
Fort Niagara: 50, 56
Fort Pitt: 76, 83
Fort Recovery: 128, 130
Fort Sandusky: 83
Fort St. Joseph: 32, 58, 78, 81–83,
    110, 111–12
Fort Stephenson: 197
Fort William Henry: 52, 53, 58
Fort Washington: 120
Fort Wayne: 158, 160, 161, 162,
    163, 164, 167, 169, 173, 182, 193,
    197, 203, 204, 205, 217; estab-
    lished, 133, 153; Main Poc at,
    167; besieged by Potawatomis,
    189–91; McCoy's school at, 222;
    creoles at, 227
Fox Indians: 5, 7, 12; want Iro-
    quois alliance, 13, 24; disrupt
    fur trade, 27, 35; attack Detroit,
    28; oppose Louivigny, 30; make

peace with French, 30, 38; attack Illinois Confederacy, 34–35; flee toward Iroquois, 35–37, 283n. 43; flee to Iowa, 37; join with Sacs, 37–38; *see also* Sacs

Fraser, Alexander: 93

Frontenac, Louis de Baude, Comte de: 12, 13, 14, 15, 24

Fur trade: 155–56; Potawatomis enter, 5–8; revoked by French, 14; Potawatomi dependence upon, 17, 23, 226–28; shortage of French goods, 26, 31, 41–43, 75; disrupted by Foxes, 27, 35; British attempt to control, 31, 38, 39, 41–46; shortage of British goods, 75–76, 78; Louisiana creole traders in, 96, 99, 110, 115, 153–54

Gage, Thomas: 97, 98

Gaines, Edmunds P.: 253

Galissonniere, Michel Rolland Barin, Comte de la: 43, 44

Gameline, Antoine: 85

Gautier, Charles: 104

Gayachiouton (Seneca chief): 76

Gladwin, Henry: 77, 80, 85–90

Gnaddenhutten Massacre: 112

Godfroy, Gabriel: 228

Gomo or Masemo (Resting Fish): 126, 127; meets with Tecumseh, 172; meets with Clark, 173; conference with Levering, 175; conference with Edwards, 179–81; hostility toward Americans, 183, 194; refuses Dickson's invitation, 200; town burned, 201; makes peace with Americans, 201; supplies food to Fort Clark, 203; dies, 204

Gordon, William: 255

Graham, Richard: 216, 217, 218, 225

Green Bay, Wis.: 5, 15, 24, 77

Griffon (ship): sinks in storm, 10–11

Groseillers, Medart Chouart de: 5

Guignas, Michel: 35

Hall, Rachel and Sylvia: 237–38

Hamelin, Jean Baptiste: 110–11

Hamilton, Henry: 102; meets with Potawatomis at Detroit, 99, 100; captures Vincennes, 104; surrenders to Clark, 105

Hamilton, James: 44

Hamtramck, John: 120, 122, 125

Hardin, John: 121

Harmar, Josiah: 120–21

Harris, Carey: 254, 261

Harrison, Albert G.: 251

Harrison, William Henry: 71, 155, 160, 164, 168, 170, 178, 192, 195; conference with Potawatomis, 161, 181; signs treaties with several tribes, 163; at Treaty of Fort Wayne, 169; meets with Tecumseh, 171; at Battle of Tippecanoe, 176–77; relieves Fort Wayne, 191; at siege of Fort Meigs, 196; invades Canada, 198; at Treaty of Spring Wells, 206

Harrodsburgh, Ky.: 100

Heald, Nathan: 185, 186, 188

Hebert, Edward: 179

Helm, Leonard: 101

Helm, Linai: 188

Helm, Margaret: 188

Henry, Patrick: 101

Herring, Elbert: 251

Hesse, Emmanuel: 108–109

Hopkins, Gerard: 162

Hopkins, Samuel: 193

Howard, Benjamin: 200–201

Hubbard, Gurdon S.: 254

Hull, William: meets with Potawatomis, 164, 168, 174; at Brownstown Conference, 183–

84; orders Fort Dearborn evacuated, 184; surrenders Detroit,
189
Hunt, Abner: 122
Huron Indians: 3, 12, 14, 26, 28, 30,
31, 35, 37, 57, 76, 91, 99, 114, 117;
attacked by Iroquois, 5; revolt
against French, 41–43; in Pontiac's Rebellion, 80–90; *see also*
Petuns *and* Wyandots
Hutchins, Thomas: 79

Illinois Confederacy: 7, 10, 28, 93,
134; attack Winnebagos, 5;
raided by Iroquois, 11–12; attacked by Foxes, 34–35; defeat
Foxes, 36; attacked by Potawatomis, 48–49, 157; *see also*
Cahokias, Kaskaskias, *and*
Peorias
Iowa (Wabash Potawatomi
leader): 150, 260, 271; sells lands,
259; bribed by Pepper, 266
Iowa Indians: 170
Iroquois Indians: 4, 7, 23, 26, 35,
44, 45, 56, 98, 100, 115, 116, 128,
129; attack Hurons and Petuns,
5; raid western tribes, 11–12; attacked by Potawatomis and
allies, 13–14; make peace with
French, 24–25; expand British
trade into west, 31, 42; urge
conciliation, 126; *see also*
Mohawks, Onandagas, *and*
Senecas
Irwin, Matthew: 184

Jackson, Andrew: 240, 250
James, Edwin: 253
Jefferson, Thomas: 155, 160–61,
163, 168
Jennings, Jonathan: 241–42
Jesuits: 4, 8–9, 10, 11, 14, 25
Johnson, Richard M.: 197

Johnson, William: 56, 77, 98
Johnston, John: 171, 174, 178
Johnston, Stephen: 189
Jonquiere, Pierre Jacques de
Taffnel, Marquis de: 45
Jouett, Charles: 157, 216, 217

Kakima (daughter of Nanaquiba):
156
Kankakee River: 175; Potawatomi
villages on, 48, 96, 98, 125, 154,
157, 244, 269; Burnett warehouse on, 156; liquor trade on,
225
Kannekuk (Kickapoo Prophet):
244
Kaskaskia, Ill.: 101, 107, 108, 134,
155
Kaskaskia (Indians): 156–57; *see
also* Illinois Confederacy
Keesass (The Sun): 134, 160, 161,
166, 169, 170
Keewaunay (Prairie Chicken): 149,
208–209, 259
Kegangizi (evil spirit): 20
Kentucky: 100–101, 112–14, 119–
20
Kercheval, Benjamin: 249
Kercheval, Gholson: 251–52, 261
Ketchum, Isaac: 268
Kickapoo Indians: 5, 7, 12, 24, 26,
28, 29, 34, 35, 36, 83, 92, 116, 118–
19, 120–22, 134, 154, 155, 161,
163, 170, 172, 173, 185–87, 195,
200, 238, 241; capture George
Croghan, 94; at Prophetstown,
177; raid Missouri, 179; at
Mississinewa conference, 181–
82; villages destroyed, 193
Kinkash (Potawatomi chief): 258
Kinzie, John: 156, 186, 188, 249
Kirk, William: 162–63
Kiouqua (Returning Bear): 91
Knox, Henry (Secretary of War):
117–18, 125

La Balme, Augustin de: 111
La Barbue (the Bearded One): 157
Lacelle, Jacques: 86
Lachine, Quebec: 13
La Demoiselle: *see* Old Briton
Lafromboise, Alexander: 156, 248
La Gesse (The Quail): 111, 125, 126, 127, 135
La Grue (The Crane): 48
Lancaster, Pa. treaty: 44
Langlade, Charles: 48–49, 104–107, 108
La Salle, Robert Cavalier de: 10–11, 64
Latham, James: 226
Latrobe, Charles: 248–49
Le Claire, Antoine: 156, 228, 242
Le Grand Couete (The Big Tail): 119
Le Gris (Miami chief): 44
Le Petit Bled (Little Corn, New Corn): 106–107, 108, 109, 112; defeats Hamelin, 110–11; at Treaty of Greenville, 135
Levering, Samuel: 175
Lincoln, Benjamin: 127–28
Linctot, Maurice Godfroy: 106, 107
Linn, Lewis: 249, 251
Liquor trade: 160, 162, 164–65, 168, 224–25; at Peoria, 226; at Chicago, 248
Little Turtle: 71, 121, 162; goes to Washington, 159–60; opposes treaty, 161; village destroyed, 191
Logan (Shawnee chief): 192
Logan, Benjamin: 117
Logansport, Ind.: 244–47, 261
Longueuil, Paul Joseph le Moyne, Chevalier de: 42–43
Louis XIV: 14
Louivigny, Louis de la Porte de: 30

Machiouquisse (Little Bad Man):

99; urges peace with the British, 90, 92, 95; at Oswego conference, 94
Mackahtahmoah (Black Wolf): 170, 265
Mackisabe (The Eagle): 28–29
Macomb, Alexander: 253
Madouche (Potawatomi chief): 36–37
Mad Sturgeon: *see* Nuscotomeg
Magaago (Potawatomi chief): 161
Main Poc (Crippled Hand): 154, 156, 167, 179, 182, 183, 184, 185, 198; attacks Osages, 157, 158, 173; description of, 166; visits Shawnee Prophet, 166; visits Washington, 168; visits Prophetstown, 170; wounded by Osages, 173; establishes village at Crow Prairie, 174; goes to Amherstburg, 175; wounded on Canard River, 188; at Battle of Monguaga, 188; signs armistice, 199; returns to Illinois, 199; camp on Yellow River, 202; visits Mackinac, 204; dies, 206
Manamol (Potawatomi chief): 157
Manitowoc, Wis.: 15
Marquette, Louis: 9
Marshall, William: 145; feeds Potawatomis, 244; visits Washington, 255; buys Potawatomi lands, 257
Mascoutens: 5, 7, 12, 13, 27, 28, 34, 35, 36, 48, 83, 94, 277n. 5
Maumee River: 42, 45, 47, 83, 104, 129, 153, 191, 192, 195, 196; Miamis move to, 25; Pontiac flees to, 90; as center for Indian resistance, 117, 118, 120–21, 123, 124, 126, 127; Wayne marches to, 130–32
Maxinkuckee, Lake, Ind.: 257
McArthur, Duncan: 198, 202–203, 206

McCoy, Isaac: 142; establishes mission among Potawatomis, 222–24; urges removal, 240; leads exploring party west (1828), 241
McKee, Alexander: 113, 115, 123
McKee, Thomas: 166
McKenney, Thomas: 240
Mechingan (Potawatomi village at Green Bay, Wis.): 5
Meigs, Return J.: 189
Menard, Pierre, Jr.: 232
Menominee (Potawatomi chief): 260, 261; visits McCoy, 222–23; fights removal, 265–67; removed to west, 267–68
Menominee Indians: 9, 12, 24, 38, 48, 49, 53, 156, 172, 174, 200, 273
Menoquet (Potawatomi chief): 210
Metea (The Sulker): 140, 229; at siege of Fort Wayne, 189–91; attends peace conference, 202; at Treaty of Spring Wells, 206; receives British pension, 216; at Treaty of Fort Meigs, 219; at Treaty of St. Mary's, 220; at Treaty of Chicago (1821), 220–21; dies, 228
Miami Indians: 7, 10, 12, 14, 24, 25, 28, 79, 92, 116, 117, 118, 119, 120–21, 125, 127, 158, 160, 161, 163, 169; dispute with Ottawas, 26–27; promote British trade, 31, 35, 44–47; attack Fort Miamis, 42, 83; at Mississinewa conference, 181–82; at Fort Dearborn, 185–87; at Treaty of Spring Wells, 206
Michicaba (Snapping Turtle): 255
Michigameas: 49; *see also* Illinois Confederacy
Michigan (British sloop): 87
Michilimackinac (Mackinac): 3, 11, 12, 13, 24, 26, 30, 47, 76, 90, 104, 105, 106, 107, 108, 273; occupied by British, 77; in Pontiac's Rebellion, 83; in War of 1812, 184, 202
Millouisillyny (Potawatomi chief): 54
Milroy, Samuel: 268–69
Milwaukee, Wis.: 15, 90, 102, 107, 134, 233
Mingo Indians: 113
Mohawk Indians: 5, 11, 12, 118; *see also* Iroquois
Monguaga, Battle of: 188
Monroe, James: 169
Montcalm, Marquis de: 65; captures Oswego, 52; campaigns in New York, 54–55
Montgomery, William R.: 246–47
Montreal, Quebec: 5, 12, 30, 42, 43, 55; visited by the Potawatomis, 6, 7, 8, 13, 27, 32, 38, 52; peace conference at, 24–25
Moran, Pierre, or Perish (The Stutterer): 202, 204; urges attack upon Fort Wayne, 189; receives British pension, 216; at Treaty of St. Mary's, 220
Moravians: 162
Morris, Thomas: 91–92
Mota: sells lands, 257
Muccose (Young Bear): 224; 257
Mucktypoke (Black Partridge): 201, 203, 218; at Fort Dearborn attack, 186–187; rescues prisoners, 188; village destroyed, 194; at Portage des Sioux Treaty, 204
Muir, Adam: 191–92
Munro, George: 54

Naakewoin (Wind Striker): 111
Nagauwatuk (Noise Maker): 241
Nanaquiba (Water Moccasin): 90, 94, 96, 156; leads Potawatomis against Fort William Henry, 54; meets with Bradstreet, 91; ransoms prisoners, 97; accompanies Hamilton to Vincennes, 102–104

Naswakay (The Counselor): 264
Natchez Indians: 39
Nauntay (son of Chief Senache-
wine): 233
Net, The: 270
Neutral Indians: 3, 4, 5
Nicolas (Orontony): 42–43
Ninivois: 77, 81, 85, 90, 91, 99;
leads Potawatomis against Fort
William Henry, 54; greets
British at Detroit, 57; attends
British conference at Oswego,
94–95
Nipissing Indians: 46
Nokaming (Burrowing Wolf): 85,
86
Notawkah (Rattlesnake): 207, 265
Nottawasippi, Mich.: 268, 269,
270–71
Nuscotomeg (Mad Sturgeon): 202;
at Fort Dearborn attack, 185–87;
at Battle of Thames, 198; makes
peace with Americans, 204; at
Treaty of Spring Wells, 206; at
Treaty of St. Mary's, 220

Ogee, Joseph: 228
Okia (The Bay): 133–34, 136
Old Briton (La Demoiselle): 44–
45, 46, 47
Onandaga Indians: 12; *see also*
Iroquois
Onanghisse (Shimmering Light):
22, 25; assists La Salle at Green
Bay, 10; visits Montreal, 10, 13,
14, 15; warns French, 14–15
Onanghisse (late eighteenth-cen-
tury chief): 92
Opewa Indians: 57
Orontony: *see* Nicolas
Osage River subagency: 253, 254,
260, 268, 271, 274
Osage Indians: 49, 93, 98, 156, 168,
169, 200; Spanish incite Pota-
watomis toward, 154; Potawato-

mis raid, 154, 155, 157, 173; ask
U.S. for protection, 157; intercept Potawatomis, 158; wound
Main Poc, 173
Otchik (Potawatomi chief): 32
Ottawa Indians: 3, 5, 7, 13, 14, 28,
30, 31, 35, 37, 38, 41, 42, 46, 52,
53, 54, 56, 57, 76, 91, 102, 107,
109, 111, 114, 116, 118, 122, 128,
129, 130, 131, 153, 158, 163, 164,
168, 170, 184, 195, 202, 218, 270;
establish trade monopoly, 6;
dispute with Miamis, 26–27; raid
Pickawillany, 47; in Pontiac's
Rebellion, 80–90; at Prophetstown, 177, 179; at Mississinewa
conference, 181; sign armistice,
199; at Treaty of Spring Wells,
206; at Treaty of Fort Meigs,
219; at Chicago treaty (1821),
220–21; accompany McCoy west,
241
Ouakousy (The Fox): 54
Ouiatanon: 81
Ouilmette: 156
Oushala (Fox chief): 34
Oybischagme (Potawatomi chief):
54
Owen, Thomas: 236, 238–39, 247–
49

Pamtipee (Potawatomi chief): 270
Pashpoho (Potawatomi chief): 213,
259, 269
Pasteur, Thomas: 134
Patogoshuk (Lead in a Heap): 263
Payne, John: 191
Pemoussa (Fox chief at Detroit):
29
Peoria, Ill.: 49, 106, 111, 172, 173,
179, 181, 183, 188; Potawatomis
form villages at, 125, 182; Potawatomis kill livestock at, 178; Edwards' expedition to, 193–94;
evacuated by Craig, 194;

Howard's expedition to, 200–201; sub-agency established at, 216; liquor trade at, 225–26

Peoria Indians: 48–49

Pepinawah (Potawatomi chief): 259, 265

Pepper (Potawatomi chief): 181, 203

Pepper, Abel C.: 141, 261; appointed removal agent, 244; failure of exploring party, 246; leads exploring party west, 255–56; buys Potawatomi reservations, 257–59; at 1836 annuity payments, 259–60; warns Deseille, 265; buys Menominee's reservation, 265; bribes Iowa, 266; resigns, 268

Perrot, Nicolas: 6–8, 12, 13

Perry, Oliver: 197

Peshibon (Potawatomi chief): 92

Petit, Benjamin Marie: 266

Petit Coeur de Cerf: 96

Petun Indians: 5; *see also* Hurons *and* Wyandots

Piankashaw Indians: 36, 116, 156; at Pickawillany, 45; ambush Potawatomis, 109; sue for peace, 125; at Vincennes conference, 161; at Treaty of Fort Wayne, 163

Pickawillany (Miami village): 43–47

Pickering, Thomas: 127–28

Piqua, Ohio: 183

Platte Country, Mo.: 249–54, 271

Point Pelee: 84

Pointsett, Joel: 269

Pokagon, Leopold: 214, 229; seeks priests, 264; remains in Michigan, 266, 274

Polke, William: 260, 269

Pontiac: 94, 97, 288n. 14; besieges Detroit, 80–90; abandons siege, 90; in Illinois, 92–93

Porter, George B.: 247–49

Potawatomis: split from Ottawa-Chippewas, 4; flee to Wisconsin, 4; trade with Ottawas, 6; assist La Salle, 10–11; attack Iroquois, 11–14; move back to Michigan, 15; aid French against Foxes, 28–29, 30, 36–37; establish village at Detroit, 29–30; help Foxes to make peace with French, 38; assist French against Chickasaws, 39–41; participate in King George's War, 42–43; migrate into Illinois, 48; at Braddock's Defeat, 50–51; in French and Indian War, 52–58; epidemics among, 47, 55, 132, 252, 264, 268; in Pontiac's Rebellion, 80–90; raid Kentucky, 112, 119–20; argue over land policy, 118; at Harmar's Defeat, 121; at St. Clair's Defeat, 124; attack Fort Recovery, 130; at Treaty of Greenville, 135–36; at Brownstown and Monguaga, 188; besiege Fort Wayne, 188–99; at River Raisin, 195; at Fort Meigs, 196; at Battle of the Thames, 198; at Treaty of Spring Wells, 206; in Black Hawk War, 236–39; flee to Canada, 273; return to Wisconsin, 273; remain in Wisconsin and Michigan, 274–75; *see also* bands *listed below*

——: band nomenclature, 234–35

——: clothing, 17, 226

——: farming, 15–16, 159, 162–63, 227

——: fishing, 16, 59

——: housing, 16–17, 60

——: kinship, 18–19, 22

——: life cycle, 18–19

——: medicine bundles, 19

——: mixed blood, influence of,

38, 223, 224, 228–30, 242
——: political structure, 21–22, 48, 96, 98, 99, 105, 153, 165–66, 169–70, 216–20, 228–30, 234–35, 316n. 11
——: population, 233–34
——: shamans, 20–21
——: supernatural, belief in, 20, 23
——: vision quest, 19
——: warfare, 23
—: Citizens Band, 275
—: Detroit Potawatomis, 29–30, 37, 38, 43, 46, 53, 54, 56, 57, 79, 91, 98; suffer epidemic, 47; assist Pontiac, 80–88; form new villages, 99; raid New York, 99–100; support Hamilton, 102–105; repudiate land cessions, 117; support Shawnees, 129; retreat from Ohio, 130; refrain from Osage war, 159; loyalty uncertain, 167
—: Huron Potawatomis, sign treaty in 1809, 168; meet with Hull, 174; village destroyed, 203; annuity payments, 217, 219, 220; at Treaty of Fort Meigs, 219; at Treaty of St. Mary's, 220; removal of, 270–71; remain in Michigan, 274
—: Illinois River Potawatomis, 30, 48, 90, 96, 98, 125–26, 134; attack Osages, 154–58, 168, 173; visited by Tecumseh, 172; raid southern Illinois, 174, 183, 193, 200, 201, 204; at Prophetstown, 176; at Tippecanoe, 182; at Ft. Dearborn attack, 184–88; make peace with Americans, 203; annuity payments, 217, 233; repudiate Sac and Fox treaty, 217–18; Treaty at St. Louis (1816), 218; at Chicago treaty (1821), 221; split over Prairie du Chien Treaty,

232–33; withdraw to Rock River, 233
—: Prairie Potawatomis, 275; at Tippecanoe treaties, 241–43; flee to Indiana, 244; removed to Kansas (1833), 246–47; removed to west (1835), 251; (1834), 255; (1837), 261–63; (1838), 268
—: St. Joseph's Potawatomis, 15, 32, 37, 38, 43, 44, 45, 47, 53, 54, 58, 79, 98; attack Illinois Confederacy, 48–49; capture Fort St. Joseph's, 81–83; attack Detroit, 85–89, 90, 92; form new villages in Wisconsin and Illinois, 90, 96; ambushed by Piankashaws, 109; becoming pro-British, 110; urge compromise with Americans, 129; at Fallen Timbers, 132; at Malden, 200; remain hostile to U.S., 202; make peace with Americans, 206; annuity payments, 217, 220, 262; at Treaty of Fort Meigs, 219; at Treaty of St. Mary's, 220; at Chicago Treaty (1821), 221; send exploring party west, 241; at Osage River Subagency, 254; in 1837 removal, 262–63; in 1840 removals, 270–71; remain in Michigan, 266, 274
—: Wabash Potawatomis, 244, 275; friendly to the U.S., 164; attacked in Ohio, 182; at Malden, 195; at Treaty of Fort Meigs, 219; at Treaty of St. Mary's, 220; annuity payments, 217, 220; at Chicago Treaty (1821), 221; at Osage River subagency, 254; reservations held by, 256–59; heavily indebted, 258; at 1836

annuity payment, 259–60; want removal, 260; remove west (1837), 264; (1838), 267–68
—: Woods Potawatomis, 248
Pouchot, Francis: 56
Poure, Eugene: 111–12
Prairie du Chien, Wis.: 108, 216, 232–33
Presque Isle, Mich.: 56, 76, 84
Prideaux, John: 56
Proffit, George: 264
Putnam, Rufus: 125–26
Procter, Henry: 195–98

Quakers: 159, 162–63
Quapaw Indians: 93
Quiquito (Moving Sun): 244, 246–47, 250

Radisson, Pierre-Espirit: 5
Randolph, Beverly: 127–28
Ray, James B.: 228
Raymond, Charles de: 45
Red Bird: 230
Reynolds, John: 235, 238, 239, 243
Reze, Frederick: 264
Rhea, James: 189–91
Rice, Luther (Naoquet): 228
River Raisin Massacre: 195
Roche de Bout on the Maumee River: 130
Robinson, Alexander or Chechepinquay (The Squinter): 137, 216, 217, 271; friendly to whites at Chicago, 185, 188; rescues Healds, 188; fur trader and interpreter, 228; at Big Foot's village, 231; at Treaty of Prairie du Chien, 232; opposes Black Hawk, 236–39; awarded lands at Tippecanoe treaties, 242; at Chicago treaty (1833), 247–48; explores lands in west, 250; goes to Washington, 251; denounces

1837 annuity payment, 262
Rogers, Robert: 57
Ross, John: 93
Russell, John B. F.: 250–51

Sabrevois, Jacques: 31–32
Sac Indians: 7, 9, 14, 26, 34, 35, 36, 49, 90, 118, 154, 169, 173; flee Michigan, 5; join with Foxes, 37–38; capture Mackinac, 83; surrender Osage prisoners, 157; cede lands at Vincennes, 163, 235; Main Poc among, 166; at Prophetstown, 170; Tecumseh among, 172; at Ft. Dearborn attack, 185–87; join Dickson, 200; in Black Hawk War, 235–39
St. Ange, Jean: 36
St. Ange, Louis: 93
St. Asaphs, Ky.: 100
St. Clair, Arthur: 68, 118, 119, 120, 135; expedition against Indians, 123–24
St. Francis Xavier mission among Potawatomis: 8–9
St. Joseph River: Potawatomis move to, 15, 24–25; mission established at, 25; French build fort at, 32; Potawatomi villages along, 48, 96; traders on, 155–56; Potawatomis remain on, 274
St. Leger, Barry: 100
St. Louis, Mo.: 111, 134, 179, 194, 200, 201, 219, 253, 264; British attack, 108; Potawatomis attend conferences at, 157, 172, 173; treaty at, 218
St. Mary's, Ohio: treaty at, 219–20
Sands, Lewis: 271; supervises 1833 Prairie Potawatomi removal, 244–46; supervises 1837 removal, 261–63; fired, 263
Sandusky, Ohio: 42
Sangamon River: 193, 194, 200, 215

Sault Ste. Marie, Mich.: 4, 8, 9

Schlosser, Francis: 78, 81–83, 85, 86

Schoolcraft, Henry: 221

Schoonover, Rudolphus: 244

Scott, Charles: 122

Senachewine or Petacho (Swift Water): 201, 216, 217, 228, 231; at Portage des Sioux treaty, 204; opposes Treaty of Prairie du Chien, 232–33; dies, 233

Seneca Indians: 2, 24, 42, 79, 98, 118, 205, 219; raid Wisconsin, 11; attacked by western Indians, 12; urge revolt against British, 76; in Pontiac's Rebellion, 83–84

Shabbona (Burly Shoulders): 72, 188, 216; description of, 172; at Prophetstown, 177; at Battle of Thames, 198; at Big Foot's village, 231; rewarded by Americans, 232; warns whites in Black Hawk War, 237; removes to west, 252

Shabbona's Grove, annuity payment at: 262

Shawmagaw (The Soldier): 231

Shawanikuk (Southern Thunder): 241

Shawnee Prophet, or Tenskwatawa (The Open Door): 171, 173, 174, 178; doctrines, 165; meets with Main Poc, 166; moves to Prophetstown, 167; at Battle of Tippecanoe, 176–77

Shawnee Indians: 45, 76, 79, 83, 92, 116, 118, 119, 127, 128, 130, 154, 158, 168; Bouquet attacks, 91; Logan destroys villages, 117; at Harmar's Defeat, 120–21; missionaries among, 163; at Prophetstown, 170; at Battle of Tippecanoe, 177; at Mississinewa conference, 181–82; at Treaty of Spring Wells, 206; at

Treaty of Fort Meigs, 219

Shequenebec: 178–79

Shickshack (Nine): 231

Shirley, William: 50

Sibley, Solomon: 220

Siggenauk or Le Tourneau (Blackbird): meets with Clark, 101–102; opposes Langlade, 107; assists Americans, 109; attacks Fort St. Joseph, 110–12; ransoms captives, 134; at Treaty of Greenville, 135

Simcoe, John: 127, 133

Simmerwell, Robert (missionary among Potawatomis): 223

Simonton, I. P.: 259–60

Sioux Indians: 8, 13, 26, 27, 49, 169, 250; Potawatomis attack, 9; Foxes make peace with, 34

Sprague, James T.: 262

Stevenson, R. B.: 260

Stickney, Benjamin: 206, 216; meets with Potawatomis, 181–83; at siege of Fort Wayne, 189–91

Stillman, Isaiah: 237

Stockbridge Indians: 126

Sunaget (Hard Times): 211

Taber, Cyrus: 259

Takay (Huron chief): 80

Talon, Jean: 6

Teaatoriance (Seneca chief): 76

Terre Coupe on the Saint Joseph River: 96, 109

Tecumseh (Shawnee chief): at Vincennes, 171; recruits tribes, 172; visits southern tribes, 176; at conference on Mississinewa, 181–82; on the Tippecanoe, 182; at Malden, 182, 184; saves prisoners at Ft. Meigs, 196; denounces Procter, 197; killed, 198

Thompson, Squire (trader in Michigan): 225

Tippecanoe, Battle of: 74, 176–77
Tippecanoe River: 44, 105, 122,
    129, 160, 161, 163, 182, 189, 192,
    223, 228, 229, 255; Potawatomi
    villages on, 104, 134, 135, 153,
    154, 233, 234; Prophetstown es-
    tablished on, 167; treaties ne-
    gotiated at, 241–43, 256, 257,
    271; claims payment at, 258–60
Tipton, John: 212, 228; encourages
    Potawatomi indebtedness, 258;
    forces removal of Menominee,
    267
Todd, John: 114
Tonty, Alphonse de: 31, 32, 34
Tonty, Henry: 11
Topinbee (He Who Sits Quietly):
    143, 158, 160, 161, 163, 165, 216,
    217, 222, 225; warns of attack
    upon Ft. Dearborn, 186; signs
    armistice, 199; attends peace
    conference, 202; at Treaty of
    Spring Wells, 206; at Treaty of
    St. Mary's, 220; at Treaty of
    Chicago (1821), 221; dies, 228
Topinbee (The Younger): 263
Toquamee (Autumn): 237–38
Treaties: Carey Mission (1828),
    229; Chicago (1821), 220–22;
    Chicago (1833), 247–50; Fort
    Finney (1786), 116, 118; Fort
    Harmar (1789), 118–19, 127;
    Fort Industry (1805), 163; Fort
    McIntosh (1785), 118–19; Fort
    Stanwix (1784), 116, 118; Fort
    Wayne (1803), 161–62; Fort
    Wayne (1809), 169–70; Ghent
    (1815), 204; Greenville (1795),
    71, 134–36, 154, 155, 160;
    Grouseland (1805), 169; Mis-
    sissinewa, (1826), 228–29; Port-
    age des Sioux (1815), 204–205;
    Prairie du Chien (1829), 146,
    232; St. Louis (1805), 157; St.
    Louis (1816), 218; St. Mary's

(1818), 219–20; Tippecanoe
    (1832), 241–43, 256, 257, 271;
    Vincennes (1792), 126
Trigg, Stephen: 114
Trimble, Allen: 193
Turkey Foot (Potawatomi chief):
    154, 155, 157

Vanmeter, John: 155
Vaudreuil, Pierre Rigaud de (Gov-
    ernor of New France): 52
Vaudreuil, Philippe Rigaud de:
    27, 31–32, 35
Villiers, Louis Coulon de: 45–46
Villiers, Nicolas Coulon de: 36
Vincennes, Ind.: 102, 120, 122, 176,
    177, 179, 235; captured by Helm,
    101; captured by Hamilton, 104;
    captured by Clark, 105; Pota-
    watomis sign treaty at, 125–27;
    Potawatomis attend conference
    at, 160–61; Tecumseh at, 176–77
Viveau, Jacques (merchant at Mil-
    waukee): 156

Wabanim (nineteenth-century
    Potawatomi chief): 254–55
Wabanum (White Dog): 57
Wabash River: Miami villages on,
    28; Potawatomi villages on, 134,
    156, 233; liquor trade on, 160;
    missions on, 162; Indiana wants
    white settlement on, 219
Wabeme (White Pigeon): 179, 183,
    193, 203
Wabeno: 20–21
Wabokieshiek (White Cloud)
    (Winnebago Prophet): 236
Wallace, David: 267
Wapakoneta (Shawnee village):
    165
Wapawee (White Hair): 176;
    meets with Edwards, 179–81;
    village attacked, 194; at Portage
    des Sioux treaty, 204

Ward, Ebenezer (payment claims commissioner): 260

Washee (The Swan): 85, 90, 91, 94; captures Ft. St. Joseph, 81–83; jealous of Pontiac, 86; abandons siege of Detroit, 89

Washington, George: 159

Wasson (Chippewa chief): 91

Waubansee (He Causes Paleness): 139, 231, 237; attacks boat on Wabash, 176; at Battle of Tippecanoe, 177; rescues prisoners at Ft. Dearborn, 188; agrees to amended Chicago treaty, 250; removes to west, 252

Waweachsetoh (Potawatomi chief): 126

Wayne, Anthony: 71, 134; rebuilds army, 128; constructs forts, 129; at Fallen Timbers, 130–32; signs armistice with Potawatomis, 133; at Treaty of Greenville, 135–36

Wea Indians: 36, 45, 116, 120, 121, 122, 156, 161; ask for peace with Americans, 125; cede lands, 163; at Potawatomi removal camp, 244

Weatherford, William (treaty commissioner): 247

Wells, Samuel: 191

Wells, William: 71, 162, 163, 164; opposes Shawnee Prophet, 165; meets with Main Poc, 167; at Ft. Dearborn, 185–87; killed, 187

Weesionas (Potawatomi chief): 258

Wewesah (Potawatomi chief): 259

Whistler, John: 216

White Crow (Winnebago): 238

Wilkinson, James: attacks Weas and Kickapoos, 122; meets with Osages, 157

Winchester, James: 192; defeated by Indians, 194–95

Windigo (Man Eater): accompanies Hamilton against Vincennes, 104–105; signs Treaty of Ft. Harmar, 119; makes peace with Americans, 133

Winamac (The Catfish) (early eighteenth-century Potawatomi chief): 25, 32; establishes village near Detroit, 29; son captured by Foxes, 34; makes peace between French and Foxes, 38

Winamac (Potawatomi chief, friendly to U.S.): 181, 183; asks government for agricultural aid, 163; at Treaty of Ft. Wayne, 169; assists Harrison, 170; denounced by Tecumseh, 171, 181; visits Prophetstown, 176; threatened by settlers, 179; at Ft. Dearborn, 185; at Treaty of Ft. Meigs, 219; dies, 307n. 66

Winamac (Potawatomi chief, hostile to U.S.): 173; at Prophetstown, 177; attacks Ft. Wayne, 189–91; killed, 192

Winnebago Indians: 4, 8, 9, 24, 34, 38, 49, 156, 179, 200, 273; attacked by Illinois Confederacy, 5; leave Fox alliance, 35; Main Poc among, 166; at Prophetstown, 170; Tecumseh among, 172; at Battle of Tippecanoe, 177; blamed for raids at Peoria, 181; at Mississinewa conference, 181–82; join Dickson, 184; raid near Chicago, 184; at Ft. Dearborn attack, 185–87; at Malden, 195; fail to kill Forsyth, 201; in Red Bird Uprising, 230–31; at Treaty of Prairie du Chien, 232–33

Wiske (mythological figure): 20

Wolcott, Alexander: 144, 216, 220

Wyandot Indians: 116, 168, 195; oppose U.S. land claims in Ohio, 118; kill American messengers, 125; at Prophetstown, 170; at Mississinewa conference, 181; at Brownstown conference, 183– 84; sign armistice, 199; at Treaty of Spring Wells, 206; at Treaty of Ft. Meigs, 219

Yellow River, Potawatomi villages on: 202, 223, 257, 264, 266

The Civilization of the American Indian Series

1. Forgotten Frontiers: A Study of the Spanish Indian Policy of Don Juan Bautista de Anza, Governor of New Mexico, 1777–1787. Alfred Barnaby Thomas.
2. Indian Removal: The Emigration of the Five Civilized Tribes of Indians. Grant Foreman.
3. Wah'Kon-Tah: The Osage and the White Man's Road. John Joseph Mathews.
4. Advancing the Frontier, 1830–1860. Grant Foreman.
6. The Rise and Fall of the Choctaw Republic. Angie Debo.
8. The Five Civilized Tribes. Grant Foreman.
9. After Coronado: Spanish Exploration Northeast of New Mexico, 1696–1727. Alfred Barnaby Thomas.
10. Naskapi: The Savage Hunters of the Labrador Peninsula. Frank G. Speck.
12. Cherokee Messenger. (A Life of Samuel Austin Worcester). Althea Bass.
14. Indians and Pioneers: The Story of the American Southwest Before 1830. Grant Foreman.
15. Red Cloud's Folk: A History of the Oglala Sioux Indians. George E. Hyde.
16. Sequoyah. Grant Foreman. (Cherokee).
17. A Political History of the Cherokee Nation, 1838–1907. Morris L. Wardell.
19. Cherokee Cavaliers: Forty Years of Cherokee History as Told in the Correspondence of the Ridge-Watie-Boudinot Family. Edward Everett Dale and Gaston Litton.
21. The Cheyenne Way: Conflict and Case Law in Primitive Jurisprudence. Karl W. Llewellyn and E. Adamson Hoebel.
25. The Navajo and Pueblo Silversmiths. John Adair.
26. The Ten Grandmothers. Alice Marriott. (Kiowa).
27. María: The Potter of San Ildefonso. Alice Marriott. (Pueblo).

28. The Indians of the Southwest: A Century of Development Under the United States. Edward Everett Dale.
29. Popol Vuh: The Sacred Book of the Ancient Quiché Maya. Adrián Recinos.
30. Sun in the Sky: The Hopi Indians of the Arizona Mesa Lands. Walter Collins O'Kane. (Hopi).
32. Red Men Calling on the Great White Father. Katharine C. Turner.
33. A Guide to the Indian Tribes of Oklahoma. Muriel H. Wright.
34. The Comanches: Lords of the South Plains. Ernest Wallace and E. Adamson Hoebel.
35. The Hopis: Portrait of a Desert People. Walter Collins O'Kane.
36. The Sacred Pipe: Black Elk's Account of the Seven Rites of the Oglala Sioux. Joseph Epes Brown.
37. The Annals of the Cakchiquels, with Title of the Lords of Totonicapán. Adrián Recinos.
38. The Southern Indians: The Story of the Civilized Tribes Before Removal. R. S. Cotterill.
39. The Rise and Fall of Maya Civilization. J. Eric S. Thompson.
40. The Last War Trail: The Utes and the Settlement of Colorado. Robert Emmitt.
41. The Indian and the Horse. Frank Gilbert Roe.
42. The Nez Percés. Tribesmen of the Columbia Plateau. Francis Haines.
43. The Navajos. Ruth M. Underhill.
44. The Fighting Cheyennes. George Bird Grinnell.
46. Sitting Bull, Champion of the Sioux: A Biography. Stanley Vestal.
47. The Seminoles. Edwin C. McReynolds.
49. The Blackfeet: Raiders on the Northwestern Plains. John C. Ewers.
50. The Aztecs: People of the Sun. Alfonso Caso.
51. The Mescalero Apaches. C. L. Sonnichsen.
52. The Modocs and Their War. Keith A. Murray.
53. The Incas of Pedro de Cieza de León. Pedro de Cieza de León.
54. Indians of the High Plains: From the Prehistoric Period to the Coming of Europeans. George E. Hyde.
56. Maya Hieroglyphic Writing: An Introduction. J. Eric S. Thompson.
57. Spotted Tail's Folk. A History of the Brulé Sioux. George E. Hyde.
59. Five Indian Tribes of the Upper Missouri: Sioux, Arickaras, Assiniboines, Crees, Crows. Edwin Thompson Denig.
60. The Osages: Children of the Middle Waters. John Joseph Mathews.
61. Redskins, Ruffleshirts, and Rednecks: Indian Allotments in Alabama and Mississippi, 1830–1860. Mary Elizabeth Young.
62. A Catalog of Maya Hieroglyphs. J. Eric S. Thompson.
63. The Kiowas. Mildred P. Mayhall.

64. Indians of the Woodlands: From Prehistoric Times to 1725. George E. Hyde.
65. The Cherokees. Grace Steele Woodward.
66. The Southern Cheyennes. Donald J. Berthrong.
67. Aztec Thought and Culture: A Study of the Ancient Nahuatl Mind. Miguel León-Portilla.
69. Empire of the Inca. Burr Cartwright Brundage.
70. The Kickapoos: Lords of the Middle Border. A. M. Gibson.
71. Pueblo Gods and Myths. Hamilton A. Tyler.
72. The Sioux: Life and Customs of a Warrior Society. Royal B. Hassrick.
73. Hosteen Klah: Navaho Medicine Man and Sand Painter. Franc Johnson Newcomb.
74. The Shoshonis: Sentinels of the Rockies. Virginia Cole Trenholm and Maurine Carley.
76. Warriors of the Colorado: The Yumas of the Quechan Nation and Their Neighbors. Jack D. Forbes.
77. Ritual of the Bacabs. Ralph L. Roys.
79. Indian Crafts of Guatemala and El Salvador. Lilly de Jongh Osborne.
80. Half-Sun on the Columbia: A Biography of Chief Moses. Robert H. Ruby and John A. Brown.
81. The Shadow of Sequoyah: Social Documents of the Cherokees. Jack Frederick and Anna Gritts Kilpatrick.
82. Indian Legends from the Northern Rockies. Ella E. Clark.
83. The Indian: America's Unfinished Business. William A. Brophy and Sophie D. Aberle, M.D.
85. The Mixtec Kings and Their People. Ronald Spores.
86. The Creek Frontier, 1540–1783. David H. Corkran.
87. The Book of Chilam Balam of Chumayel. Ralph L. Roys.
89. Indian Life on the Upper Missouri. John C. Ewers.
90. The Apache Frontier: Jacobo Ugarte and Spanish-Indian Relations in Northern New Spain, 1769–1791. Max L. Moorhead.
91. The Maya Chontal Indians of Acalan-Tixchel. France V. Scholes and Ralph L. Roys.
92. Pre-Columbian Literatures of Mexico. Miguel Léon-Portilla.
93. Pocahontas. Grace Steele Woodward.
94. Indian Skin Paintings from the American Southwest. Gottfried Hotz.
95. American Indian Medicine. Virgil J. Vogel.
97. Fraud, Politics, and the Dispossession of the Indians. Georgiana C. Nammack.
98. The Chronicles of Michoacán, tr and ed by Eugene R. Craine and Reginald C. Reindorp.

99. Maya History and Religion. J. Eric S. Thompson.
101. Plains Indian Art from Fort Marion. Karen Daniels Petersen.
102. Book of the Gods and Rites and The Ancient Calendar. Fray Diego Duran.
103. The Miami Indians. Bert Anson.
105. The Arapahoes, Our People. Virginia Cole Trenholm.
106. A History of the Indians of the United States. Angie Debo.
108. Requiem for a People. Stephen Dow Beckham.
109. The Chickasaws. Arrell M. Gibson.
110. Indian Oratory: A Collection of Famous Speeches by Noted Indian Chieftains. W. C. Vanderwerth.
111. The Sioux of the Rosebud: A History in Pictures. Henry W. and Jean Tyree Hamilton.
112. Mission Among the Blackfeet. Howard L. Harrod.
113. Chief Bowles and the Texas Cherokees. Mary Whatley Clarke.
114. The Kansa Indians: A History of the Wind People. William E. Unrau.
115. Apache, Navaho, and Spaniard. Jack D. Forbes.
116. Peter Pitchlynn: Chief of the Choctaws. W. David Baird.
117. Life and Death in Milpa Alta: A Nahuatl Chronicle of Díaz and Zapata. Fernando Horcasitas.
119. Cry of the Thunderbird: The American Indian's Own Story. Charles Hamilton.
120. The Cayuse Indians. Robert H. Ruby and John A. Brown.
121. An Indian Canaan: Isaac McCoy and the Vision of an Indian State. George A. Schultz.
122. Crowfoot. Hugh A. Dempsey.
123. The Dawes Act and the Allotment of Indian Land. D. S. Otis.
124. Picture Writing from Ancient Southern Mexico: Mixtec Place Signs and Maps. Mary Elizabeth Smith.
125. Victorio and the Mimbres Apaches. Dan L. Thrapp.
126. Red World and White: Memories of a Chippewa Boyhood. John Rogers (Chief Snow Cloud).
127. Why Gone Those Times? Blackfoot Tales by James Willard Schultz.
128. The Pawnee Indians. George E. Hyde.
129. On the Trail of the Arawaks. Fred Olsen.
130. The Flathead Indians. John Fahey.
131. Maya Cities: Placemaking and Urbanization. George F. Andrews.
132. Indian Rawhide: An American Folk Art. Mable Morrow.
133. Fire and the Spirits: Cherokee Law from Clan to Court. Rennard Strickland.
134. Pueblo Animals and Myths. Hamilton A. Tyler.
135. The Hill-Caves of Yucatan. Henry Mercer.

136. The Cheyenne and Arapaho Ordeal: Reservation and Agency Life in Indian Territory, 1875–1907. Donald J. Berthrong.
137. Olmec Reliigon: A Key to Middle America and Beyond. Karl W. Luckert.
138. The Chinook Indians: Traders of the Lower Columbia River. Robert H. Ruby and John A. Brown.
139. Las Monjas: A Major Pre-Mexican Architectural Complex at Chichén Itzá. John S. Bolles.
140. Dress Clothing of the Plains Indians. Ronald P. Koch.
141. Indian Dances of North America. Reginald and Gladys Laubin.
142. Geronimo: The Man, His Time, His Place. Angie Debo.
143. The Zapotecs: Princes, Priests, and Peasants. Joseph W. Whitecotton.
144. The Toltecs: Until the Fall of Tula. Nigel Davies.
145. The Potawatomis. R. David Edmunds.
146. The Menominees. Patricia Ourada.
147. Pueblo Birds and Myths. Hamilton A. Tyler.
148. The Chippewas. Edmund Jefferson Danziger, Jr.